Song and Garden

Garden

BIRDS

of North America

327 species portrayed in color
and fully described

Song and Garden
BIRDS
of North America

By ALEXANDER WETMORE

Research Associate and former Secretary of the Smithsonian Institution
past President of the American Ornithologists' Union
Trustee of the National Geographic Society

AND OTHER EMINENT ORNITHOLOGISTS

A volume in the Natural Science Library prepared by
NATIONAL GEOGRAPHIC BOOK SERVICE
Merle Severy, Chief

Foreword by
MELVILLE BELL GROSVENOR
Editor-in-Chief and Board Chairman,
National Geographic Society

NATIONAL GEOGRAPHIC SOCIETY, WASHINGTON, D.C.

Eastern Meadowlark, Frederick Kent Truslow

554 illustrations, 508 in full color

Photographs by **ELIOT PORTER, ARTHUR A. ALLEN, FREDERICK KENT TRUSLOW, ALLAN D. CRUICKSHANK,** and others. Paintings by **ALLAN BROOKS, WALTER A. WEBER**

Chapters by

John W. Aldrich
Research Staff Specialist, U. S. Fish and Wildlife Service

Arthur A. Allen
Founder, Laboratory of Ornithology, Cornell University

E. Thomas Gilliard
Former Curator, Department of Ornithology
American Museum of Natural History

Crawford H. Greenewalt
Research Associate, American Museum of Natural History

Philip S. Humphrey
Chairman, Department of Vertebrate Zoology
U. S. National Museum

George H. Lowery, Jr.
Director, Museum of Natural Science, Louisiana State University; past President, American Ornithologists' Union

Robert M. McClung
Former Curator of Mammals and Birds
New York Zoological Society

Alden H. Miller
Former Director, Museum of Vertebrate Zoology, University of California; past President, American Ornithologists' Union

Roger Tory Peterson
Ornithologist, author of A Field Guide to the Birds

Olin Sewall Pettingill, Jr.
Director, Laboratory of Ornithology, Cornell University

Austin L. Rand
Chief Curator of Zoology, Chicago Natural History Museum past President, American Ornithologists' Union

Robert W. Storer
Curator of Birds, Museum of Zoology, University of Michigan

George Miksch Sutton
Research Professor of Zoology, University of Oklahoma

This book was prepared under the editorial guidance of **MELVILLE BELL GROSVENOR** and **FREDERICK G. VOSBURGH** by the following staff:

MERLE SEVERY, *Editor and Art Director*
PATRICIA COYLE NICHOLSON, *Designer*
ANNE DIRKES KOBOR, *Picture Editor*

SEYMOUR FISHBEIN, EDWARDS PARK, WAYNE BARRETT, *Assistant Editors;* **MARY SWAIN HOOVER, ROSS BENNETT,** *Editorial Staff*

Biographies written by **GOODE P. DAVIS, JR., EDWARD C. SHEPHERD, ROBERT M. McCLUNG, JOSEPH A. CALLANAN,** *and others*

"THERE HE IS!" *Bird watchers thrill at the*

JOHN M. LAVERY, CHARLES R. MILLER, *Production;* **WILLIAM W. SMITH, JOE M. BARLETT,** *Engravings and printing*

BARBARA V. KETCHUM, JOYCE A. McKEAN, CONSTANCE CALLAWAY, MARY ANNA RICE, *Assistants;* **DOROTHY M. CORSON,** *Index*

Composed by National Geographic's Phototypographic Division
Printed and bound by R. R. Donnelley and Sons Co., Chicago

First three printings 500,000 copies
Revised printing (1975) 250,000 copies
Fifth printing (1976) 125,000 copies

LIBRARY OF CONGRESS
CATALOG CARD NUMBER 64-23367
STANDARD BOOK NUMBER 87044-006-3

sight of wings flashing above a Massachusetts meadow where Thoreau once roamed.

Foreword

I'LL NEVER FORGET THE THRILL of first seeing and hearing the birds at Wild Acres, the Maryland farm my family moved to from Washington, D. C., when I was 11. My father, Gilbert H. Grosvenor, would take us children on bird walks. We'd stand silently in the woods and listen to a song cascading from the treetops, then move about until he could spot the singer with binoculars. He'd show the bird to us and describe its habits, and we'd try to remember the song.

We were eager to have birds nest near the house, so we put out nesting material and fresh water. That first summer we had many species but no flickers, though a pair nested in an old apple tree on a neighbor's property. Then a winter storm blew the tree down, and I got permission to saw it up. I hung up the part with the nest hole in a dying cherry tree a few yards from our house. Next spring we had flickers.

Wren houses were easy to make from shingles, and my father offered 25 cents for each family they attracted. I put them up everywhere. Then I noticed that our martin apartment house lured martins by the dozen. If I could make one like that for wrens, I'd be rich! So I built one to accommodate 18 families—four dollars and fifty cents' worth. The trouble was, only one family moved in. That was how I learned the difference between colonial nesters like martins and privacy-loving wrens.

In two years we had attracted so many birds that the U. S. Biological Survey suggested a bird census of Wild Acres. I helped point out the nests to Dr. Wells Cooke during that exciting week in June, 1915—flickers, bluebirds, yellow warblers, orchard orioles, catbirds, song sparrows, chipping sparrows, phoebes, house wrens, robins, kingbirds, and martins. On a single acre adjoining the house there were 59 nesting pairs—a record that ornithologists consider remarkable to this day!

And to this day birds delight me. With my family I watch them bring springtime to the sanctuary of our garden. They thrive on the insects, so I spare the insecticides. Besides, poisons might be absorbed by earthworms and thus kill our robins.

Bird habits fascinate us—the peck order, the rites of courtship. One mockingbird called our holly tree home and fought like fury to defend it. One winter an intruding mocker had him down on the snow and was pecking him when I rescued him and took him to another tree. Soon I heard another shrill outburst. Our mocker had fluttered back into the fray. Three times I saved that bird, marveling that he'd rather die than give up his territory with its storehouse of red berries.

Such dramas open our eyes to nature, a realm of knowledge your Society has explored in many *National Geographic* articles and in the two-volume *Book of Birds,* edited by my father in the 1930's and now a collector's item.

Song and Garden Birds of North America continues that great tradition. In this book you can look up any of 327 species—nearly all that breed north of Mexico—study its picture, and learn its life history, breeding and winter ranges, and characteristics. (A companion volume presents water, prey, and game birds.)

We were fortunate in having Alexander Wetmore, dean of American ornithologists, as chief author and consultant. He checked each page of text for accuracy, every illustration for fidelity of color. He and Book Service Editor Merle Severy asked other ornithologists to introduce bird families and recheck species biographies. Dr. Wetmore's Smithsonian colleague, Philip S. Humphrey, and naturalist Robert M. McClung read proofs. My long-time associate, Frederick G. Vosburgh, a meticulous editor and bird enthusiast, reviewed every word.

From thousands of color photographs, as well as the famous bird portraits for *National Geographic* by Allan Brooks and Walter A. Weber, we selected 554 illustrations that show each bird to best advantage for identification. Where the female's plumage differs significantly from the male's, both sexes are portrayed.

I also wanted you to hear the birds' melodies. So we made this a "singing book." Tucked in back are recordings of the songs of 70 species. Designer Patricia Coyle Nicholson came up with a unique system for quickly finding the song you want. And the symbol ♪ next to a bird's name in the book tells you its song is in the album.

We have followed the fifth edition of the *Check-list of North American Birds,* published by the American Ornithologists' Union, for species names, ranges, and generally for order of presentation. Lengths given cover both male and female.

Helping produce *Song and Garden Birds of North America* has heightened my pleasure in the world of birds. As you turn these pages, may you share my enjoyment.

Melville Bell Grosvenor

6

Contents

Blackburnian warbler

Steller's jay

Summer tanager

Kiskadee flycatcher

Belted kingfisher

American goldfinch

Robin

Walter A. Weber
National Geographic staff artist

Painted bunting

Cardinal

9

SECRETS OF NATURE'S FEATHERED CREATURES

The Way of a Bird

By ALEXANDER WETMORE

"THERE BE THREE THINGS which are too wonderful for me," says Agur, son of Jakeh, in the Bible's Book of Proverbs. "Yea, four which I know not: The way of an eagle in the air; the way of a serpent upon a rock; the way of a ship in the midst of the sea; and the way of a man with a maid." Like Agur, untold numbers of men and women have marveled at "the way of an eagle in the air"—or, for that matter, the way of a sparrow in the garden.

Active, abundant, often brightly colored and gaily vocal, birds are certainly among the most noticeable of man's fellow inhabitants on earth.

ON RUSHING WINGS *a flock of red-winged blackbirds explodes from a thicket, wheels, and heads north. With joy and wonder we watch them pass in eager answer to the call of spring.*

Ornithologist Frank M. Chapman called them "the most eloquent expression of Nature's beauty, joy, and freedom."

Like so many before me, I have watched birds and learned about them for as long as I can remember. It was Chapman's *Handbook of Birds of Eastern North America* that taught me how to make study skins of various species for the collection I started as a boy in Wisconsin. After all these years I am well aware of the fascination of these creatures. I also know the difficulty of trying to explain many of their ways—for example, the way of an eagle in the air.

What flight secrets enable the eagle to soar effortlessly on outstretched wings? How does a hummingbird hover—and even fly backward? Why do many birds migrate, and how do they find their way? How can the body feathers of a male scarlet tanager be red in spring and green after the post-breeding molt? Why do birds sing, and how? And while we are about it, what *is* a bird? How does it differ from other animals?

B**IRDS HAVE** internal skeletons like those of their fellow vertebrates, the mammals, reptiles, amphibians, and fish. Birds are warm-blooded—able to maintain a fairly constant body temperature regardless of their surroundings. Of the other animals, only mammals share this trait. Birds have beaks and feet modified in many ways to facilitate the gathering of special foods.

BLOSSOMS QUIVER, *a brown thrasher*

Like the mammals, birds evolved from reptiles. The earliest bird we know, the fossil *Archaeopteryx* ("ancient bird"), had a reptilian head and a tail somewhat like a lizard's. Its jaws were armed with teeth. In the 150 million years since this pigeon-sized creature lived, birds have lost their teeth and improved their looks. But they retain so many ancient features that Thomas Huxley, the famous 19th century anatomist, claimed they are merely "greatly modified reptiles." Among the modifications is the protective coat of feathers. Birds alone wear that.

What a wondrous thing a feather is! So beautiful are feathers in color and pattern that man since antiquity has used them for adornment. Though soft and "light as a feather," they are incredibly strong and resilient, bending gracefully to the wind. Seemingly quite simple in form, they are a marvel of intricate design and efficiency.

Arthur A. Allen (also page 11)

lands. Faster than the eye is the instant grace of air-curved feather and lifted wing.

Like the hair of a mammal or the scales of a reptile, feathers are horny outgrowths of the skin. Sprouting from a follicle, a tiny pit in the bird's skin, the feather pushes outward enclosed in a sheath of keratin, the same substance that forms the bird's beak and claws — as well as your fingernails. Blood carries oxygen and food to the feather through the opening at the base of its tapering shaft.

Growth is fast — often a quarter-inch or more a day. The budding primary flight feathers of a sparrow, for example, may reach full size in just 12 days.

When a feather is full grown, the opening at the base of its shaft closes and the feather dies. If it is lost, another immediately starts to grow in its place. In addition, a follicle may regenerate a feather during each molt — that time when a bird sheds his old coat and replaces it with fresh plumage.

13

SUMMER TANAGER'S BRILLIANCE *flecks the deep forest, a display too often veiled by leaves, too seldom seen. To glimpse this secret star you must stalk and scan.*

In temperate regions most birds molt at least once a year, normally at the close of the nesting season. Some species have a second complete or partial molt through which they assume their breeding plumage in early spring. The molt is gradual, a few feathers falling at a time, so that a bird is never naked. Most species lose and renew their flight feathers in sequence so they can still fly. But some waterfowl shed these important feathers all at once and are "grounded" until new ones are grown.

Feathers grow only in well-defined tracts on a bird's body. The number of feathers varies with the size of the bird—about 940 for a ruby-throated hummingbird, something like 25,000 for a whistling swan. And the count varies with the season, as I learned years ago when I set myself the task—a tedious one, I must admit—of counting the body-covering contour feathers on several species. One goldfinch taken in late winter had 2,368 feathers. Another late in June totaled only 1,439.

IN SPRING the male of many species, like the scarlet tanager and the American goldfinch, wears bright plumage quite different from his winter garb. How does he change color? His chemistry and hormonal activity change with the rhythm of the seasons, and it is this internal clockwork that triggers growth of those feathers needed to bring him into breeding colors. The female, mainly responsible for incubating the eggs and caring for the young, generally wears duller, more protective colors than the male. A male indigo bunting in breeding season is brilliant blue; his mate is drab brown—she looks like a different species.

The red of the cardinal, the orange of the Baltimore oriole, the yellow of the evening grosbeak all are pigmental colors. They result from deposits of chemical compounds called carotenoids in the growing feathers.

The blue of a bluebird's feather, on the other hand, comes from its cell structure. The basal pigment is dark. But a colorless layer of cells above scatters the light until only blue reaches the eye. If you hammer a bluebird's feather, destroying this cell pattern, it turns dull and dark.

Iridescent feathers have tiny ridges and platelets, so they reflect colors according to the angle of light. This is why the gorget of the ruby-throated hummingbird flashes now orange-red, now gleaming crimson or black. It also explains the rippling green, purple, and bronze of the grackle in breeding livery.

The plumage of some birds changes

Eastern bluebird, Thase Daniel

THE BLUEBIRD: *In such small living things nature finds its fairest expression— as though the summertimes of youth were fragmented into bright, pulsing gems that dip from tree to flower stalk, and perch, and sing.*

These bits of warmth and gaiety you love, and when you are a child, you tell them so.

Pigeons in New York's Central Park; Bates Littlehales, National Geographic photographer

without any molt taking place. Snow buntings, streaked with brown and black in winter, become black and white in summer. The brown feather tips break off and expose the different colors beneath. In similar fashion, throat feathers of the male house sparrow wear away, revealing a jaunty black bib in spring.

Fussy as girls fixing their hair, birds preen tirelessly, arranging and rearranging, then drawing plumes through their beaks to smooth them. Most birds have an oil gland above the base of the tail. They massage this with their bills, then rub the oil through their feathers to dress and waterproof them. Finally they stretch each wing, give themselves a last luxurious scratch, and settle down contentedly. In warm sunshine they often spread their wings and bask.

Birds bathe frequently. I like to watch sparrows dip and sport in puddles, ruffling their plumage and making the water fly. Birds also take energetic dust baths to

LOOK UP? LOOK DOWN AS WELL! *On the very ground you tread, some creatures of flight— the painted redstart for one—hide their flashing colors in earth's protective cloak.*

condition their feathers, perhaps to rid themselves of mites. In one instance, where they could not find dust, sparrows were seen to bathe in a bowl of sugar.

Hidden beneath the contour feathers that give the body a smooth, streamlined form are fluffy down feathers, which act as insulation. Herons wear a type called powder downs. These grow continuously but never molt—instead their tips break off in bits as fine as talcum. When the heron fluffs its feathers, the powder dusts through the plumage and helps keep it in good condition.

I once reared a nestling great blue heron. Each evening it would come to rest on my knee, clucking and touching my face in friendly fashion. It was still young, so had no oil gland. But it would nibble the powder-down tracts on its breast, then draw the big feathers through its bill to preen them with powder.

If you were to take one of those feathers, you would see that a series of parallel filaments called barbs extends diagonally from either side of the shaft. Through a microscope, however, you would discover that the sleek vane is made up of literally millions of smaller side branches, overlaid in a herringbone pattern and meshed with hooks at the tips of the smallest branches.

If you draw the barbs apart, then smooth them, they rejoin neatly as though a zipper had closed. That is what a preening bird does when it pulls its feathers through its beak.

Eliot Porter

AT REST, a bird's wing folds into a Z shape, with elbow and hand pointing to the rear. Extended, the wing displays the arrangement of its flight feathers.

The big primaries, usually ten, are attached to the hand section. Forearm and upper arm bear a greater number of smaller feathers—the secondaries and tertials. All overlap one another like shingles.

As the wing beats forward and downward on the downstroke, upward and backward on the upstroke, the primaries twist back and forth in a figure-eight pattern like sculling oars. Pushing against the air, they propel the bird forward. The feathered forearm and upper arm form an airfoil—the same kind of wing surface that gives a plane lift.

The great marvel is that the bird can instantly change the area, pitch, shape, and directional movement of the whole wing—even of individual
(Continued on page 20)

Sometimes, if you give heed, a small cry,
a riffle of wings may give them quite away.

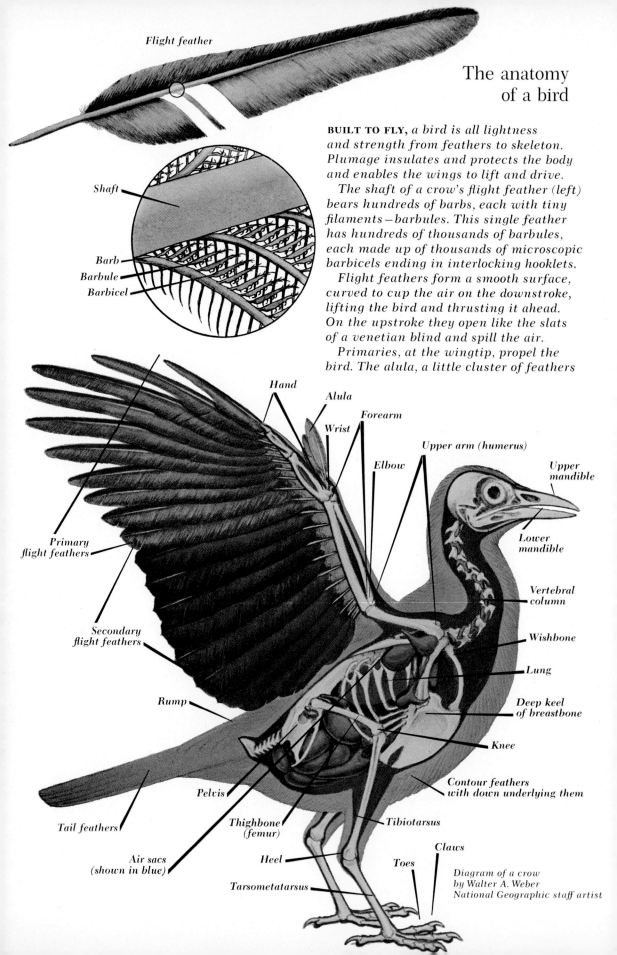

Flight feather

The anatomy of a bird

BUILT TO FLY, *a bird is all lightness and strength from feathers to skeleton. Plumage insulates and protects the body and enables the wings to lift and drive.*

The shaft of a crow's flight feather (left) bears hundreds of barbs, each with tiny filaments—barbules. This single feather has hundreds of thousands of barbules, each made up of thousands of microscopic barbicels ending in interlocking hooklets.

Flight feathers form a smooth surface, curved to cup the air on the downstroke, lifting the bird and thrusting it ahead. On the upstroke they open like the slats of a venetian blind and spill the air.

Primaries, at the wingtip, propel the bird. The alula, a little cluster of feathers

Shaft

Barb
Barbule
Barbicel

Hand
Alula
Wrist
Forearm
Elbow
Upper arm (humerus)
Upper mandible
Lower mandible
Vertebral column
Wishbone
Lung
Deep keel of breastbone
Knee
Contour feathers with down underlying them
Tibiotarsus
Claws
Toes
Heel
Tarsometatarsus
Thighbone (femur)
Pelvis
Air sacs (shown in blue)
Tail feathers
Rump
Secondary flight feathers
Primary flight feathers

Diagram of a crow by Walter A. Weber National Geographic staff artist

jutting from the wing's thumb, acts like slots on a plane, smoothing the airflow to get every bit of lift.

Secondary feathers, along the forearm and upper arm of the wing, help smooth and shape its lifting surface. With big tail feathers the bird controls its flight. Contour feathers streamline the body, and the underlying layer of tiny, fluffy feathers — the down — conserves its heat and wards off dampness from the skin.

Powerful pectoral muscles keep the wings beating — no small task on migratory flights. They bulge across the chest and are anchored to the deep keel of the breastbone. Their weight lowers the center of gravity and helps ballast the wing-borne body.

Feeding such muscles calls for a tremendous combustion of fuel, so the metabolism is fast. The heart pounds furiously, the blood circulates rapidly, and the lungs utilize every bit of oxygen they take in. A reserve air supply fills the sacs which cram the niches between other organs. These air sacs also help dissipate internal heat and are linked to porous bones which are hollow like a plane's tubular struts.

A bird grips its perch and scratches for food with toes and claws. And to do what other animals do with forepaws, birds use their bills, adapted to serve as tools.

The crossbill's twisted mandibles pry open scales of evergreen cones so his tongue can reach the seeds beneath. The flicker digs his sturdy beak into soil or wood to uncover ants for his sticky tongue. With long, slender bill the hummingbird probes for nectar, then sucks it through his tubular tongue. The shrike wields his beak as a weapon to kill and rip apart prey.

Above: Red crossbill, David G. Allen

Red-shafted flicker, H. A. Thornhill, National Audubon Society

Loggerhead shrike, Frederick Kent Truslow

Rivoli's hummingbird
Robert J. Niedrach and Walker Van Riper

19

THE MARVEL OF FLIGHT CAPTURED ON FILM: *Raising his wings, a bluebird takes off on*

feathers—and so masters the air. In flight he shifts his big tail feathers, usually 12 or 14 in number, up or down or from side to side to climb, descend, or change direction. When he comes in for a landing, he lowers and fans them out to slow down—like wing flaps on a plane.

Some birds have unusual forms of feathers. Flycatchers and redstarts have bristly feathers at the base of their bills, forming a net to help catch insects on the fly. The flight feathers of an owl have fringed edges which make the beat of the wings silent as the bird swoops down on nocturnal prey. The tail feathers of a woodpecker are stiff; they serve as props for the bird as it climbs a tree. And in many birds certain feathers form special features—the "ears" of an owl, the "horns" of a horned lark, the crest of a cardinal or a waxwing, the ruff of a ruffed grouse.

T HE SHAPE AND STRUCTURE of a bird enable it to fly as effortlessly as a fish swims. The condor sails on motionless wings; the swallow banks and swoops in ballet-like movements; the goldfinch undulates like a roller coaster. The gull is a master aerial acrobat, looping, snap rolling, and performing other maneuvers that a plane cannot begin to attempt. I remember, one crisp fall day on the Blue Ridge in Virginia, watching ravens sport over the slopes on swift currents of air. Suddenly as one sailed past me he flipped over on his back, apparently stunting for the sheer joy of it. "Look what I can do!" he seemed to gloat as he swept by upside down.

The shape of a bird's wings affects its style of flight. Sparrows have short, round-

Approaching another perch, he lets down legs; tail fans out as a brake. Body rears for

Electronic flash lasting only 1/5000 of a second freezes wing action of two bluebirds lured by tidbits into making a series of studio flights; Bernard Corby and Hance Roy Ivor

the downbeat, legs trailing, tail up. He dips his tail to level off and tucks in his legs.

tipped wings and flutter from branch to branch, from bush to lawn – a few feet at a time. Swallows and falcons have longer, pointed wings and fly very fast with precise, darting maneuvers. Condors and vultures have great broad wings with long primaries sticking out like fingers. Air flows past these surfaces with so little turbulence that the slightest forward motion of the wings gives them lifting power. And so these big birds can soar and wheel effortlessly high in the sky.

The long, narrow wings of an albatross, too, provide a great deal of lift. On ocean voyages I have watched these birds sail over the waves for hours, hardly ever flapping, using every vagrant current of air, alternately gliding and soaring up to where the fresher breeze adds lift.

Most perching birds – members of that huge, complex order which includes the true songbirds – flap their wings fairly constantly to keep flying. The crow beats about three times a second, the chickadee strokes ten times as fast. The ruby-throated hummingbird ordinarily moves its wings about 50 times a second, but in rapid flight may increase the beat to 200 times a second.

A hovering hummingbird beats its wings parallel to the ground. They perform like the blades of a helicopter, except that they sweep back and forth instead of rotating. Their thrust enables the little bird to fly straight up or down and to hover, motionless except for the blurred beat of its wings. Since the bird can rotate the arm of each wing and thus change the pitch, it is able to dart off forward or backward.

Most songbirds fly slower than you would think to watch them – they average no

balance. Feathers pivot to let air through wings. Springy legs absorb landing shock.

more than 20 to 30 miles an hour in easy flight. Many waterfowl and shore birds fly twice that fast, and the peregrine falcon, or duck hawk, diving after its prey, has been clocked at nearly 180 miles an hour.

In their everyday search for sustenance most songbirds fly at an altitude of less than 150 feet. Hawks and vultures, on the other hand, may soar a mile high to scan wide areas for food. When migrating, most birds fly below 3,000 feet, but ducks and even small perching birds have been seen above 20,000 feet.

FOR THOUSANDS OF YEARS men have marveled that birds disappear every fall, then reappear in the spring. "Yea, the stork in the heaven knoweth her appointed times," noted the prophet Jeremiah, "and the turtle [dove] and the crane and the swallow observe the time of their coming." Many thought, as Aristotle did, that swallows hibernated by submerging in swamps. Olaus Magnus, a medieval Swedish scholar, reported that fishermen found clusters of the birds in the mud.

Peasants in southern Europe believed that small birds hitched rides across the Mediterranean on the backs of big birds. I ran across this ancient superstition in Argentina, where country folk recently from Europe assured me that in winter many small birds travel thus to Africa.

Even this theory of migration is tame compared to that published in England in 1703 by " a Person of Learning and Piety." He maintained that the birds passed the winter by journeying to the moon—taking 60 days for the trip!

Only in recent years have the facts of bird migration been discovered, through birdbanding, radar observations, and other studies. We know of the remarkable journeys made by sea birds such as the Arctic tern, whose annual round-trip flight between north and south polar regions may total 22,000 miles! We are also learning more about the amazing flights of smaller birds such as the ruby-throated hummingbird. Weighing little more than a tenth of an ounce, this mite braves 500 miles of open water on its migration across the Gulf of Mexico.

I was astounded recently by a report of the white-crowned sparrow's ability to find its way home across North America, starting from a strange territory and flying a totally unfamiliar route. Normally the western races of this species stay on their side of the continent. In an experiment 574 whitecrowns were caught in California, banded, brought to Maryland, and released. Although most of them haven't been accounted for, eight were found back in their California winter home a year later. How these birds navigated over the continent remains a mystery.

There is no mystery, however, about the enormous amount of energy a bird uses on migratory flights—even on its daily rounds. Its rate of metabolism is high. The huge, four-chambered heart—a hummingbird's is one-fifth its body weight—pumps blood quickly, beating as fast as ten times a second. Temperature is higher than that of most mammals. Sparrows average above 108° F., and in wood pewees I have recorded normal temperatures up to 112°. This would be a fatal fever for humans.

Birds have no sweat glands, but their air sacs serve to cool their bodies. They also lose heat by opening their beaks and vibrating the walls of their throats.

To stoke their internal engines, birds need large amounts of fuel. Young starlings sometimes devour their own weight of insects and berries in a day; kingfishers have been known to eat *twice* their weight in fish. After one meal a flicker's stomach was found to contain 5,040 ants; a bobwhite's held 10,000 pigweed seeds. Whoever coined the phrase "eat like a bird" didn't know what he was talking about!

When food is hard to get, some birds can adapt by slowing down their body processes. Thus, if bad weather prevents European swifts from finding food for their

FLAPPING AND PECKING, *male American goldfinches display pale winter plumage as they fight over food beneath Spanish moss. Few stay north when snow flies.*

nestlings, the young become torpid. Their temperatures drop; they remain motionless for as long as ten days. When food is again available, they recover quickly. This saving of a bird's energy in lean times is a sort of hibernation on a small scale.

The theory that certain birds really do hibernate had long been considered superstition. Then in 1946, Dr. E. C. Jaeger found a poor-will lying torpid in a rock crevice in the Chuckwalla Mountains of California. He checked the bird during a period of 85 days. Its respiration was drastically slowed. It ate no food, though a poor-will ordinarily eats hundreds of insects a day, and its temperature never rose above 67°, though 106° is normal. In spring it aroused and flew away. Later observations verified that these birds hibernate. An Indian name for them, in fact, means "sleeper."

Flashing colors of birds in courtship finery gladden our hearts in spring, and so do the songs they sing. The cheery caroling of the robin on the lawn, the exuberant torrent of sound from the house-hunting wren are as much a part of the season as daffodils, apple blossoms, roller skates, and baseball. We listen with pleasure to the flood of song from the mockingbird and the merry notes of the bobolink. And at dusk we may hear the lonesome cry of the whip-poor-will or the eerie call of the screech owl. How, we wonder, do birds make such a variety of sound?

In man, the center of speech is the larynx, in the upper part of the throat. But in a bird, the voice box is in the syrinx — an organ at the lower end of the windpipe where it branches into each lung. Air expelled from the lungs passes over delicate membranes in the chamber of the syrinx, causing them to vibrate and produce sound. Muscles controlling the membranes change the pitch. The structure of the syrinx varies with the species and determines whether the characteristic song will be a whistle, a croak, or a rippling torrent of sounds.

When garden birds sing during their courtship season, the song alone identifies the bird to experienced bird watchers — and to other birds of the same species. The male sings to warn rivals away from his territory and to advertise his presence to prospective mates. Soon he courts and wins a female, and the pair build their nest.

Birds are among the world's most skillful nest builders. Few other creatures exhibit such a variety of architecture or materials. Many birds place their nests inside shelters. Kingfishers, for example, burrow in riverbanks; woodpeckers drill cavities in trees; other birds use natural tree hollows or birdhouses. But most construct nests in the open — on the ground or among the branches of trees and bushes.

The nest can be a tiny, exquisite bowl which hummingbirds fashion from lichens and plant down fastened with spider silk. It can be a communal tree house as big as a haystack which colonies of African weavers build. Baltimore orioles

MASTER BUILDER, *the Baltimore oriole (opposite) suspends her finely woven nest in a tree. The cliff swallow (below), a cliff dweller in the West, plasters its mud nest under barn eaves in the East. The sociable bird lives in colonies.*
Arthur A. Allen. Opposite: Frederick Kent Truslow

Black-capped chickadee

Chipping sparrow

Brown thrasher

Cedar waxwing

White-breasted nuthatch

Western kingbird

Yellow-shafted flicker

Common crow

Eastern meadowlark

Loggerhead shrike

Red-winged blackbird

Robin

weave bags that swing from the tips of elm branches. Cliff swallows make neat bottle-shaped homes of mud plastered against walls. Some birds of prey construct stick nests eight or ten feet wide and deep.

I recall visiting an islet off the north coast of Panama in search of Audubon's shearwaters, which nest in burrows. Their musky smell greeted me as I landed, and I soon found a hole and plunged my hand in. I was elbow-deep when I suddenly wondered about snakes. Just then something bit me savagely. What a relief it was to feel feathers and to drag out an irritated bird!

Whatever its size and shape, the nest serves as the bird's home, the receptacle for the clutch of eggs. Bird eggs vary considerably in size. Largest is that of the ostrich—about seven inches long by nearly six inches wide, big enough to make an omelet for a dozen people. Hummingbirds lay the smallest; those of the vervain hummer of Jamaica and Hispaniola are about the size of peas.

Most eggs are oval or slightly pointed at one end. But owls lay almost round eggs, and swifts produce long, elliptical ones. Auks lay eggs on rock ledges or bare shelves where you would think they might easily tumble off. But because they are decidedly pointed at one end, they roll in tight circles.

The female often bears the brunt of incubation, but in many species the parents share the task of sitting on the eggs. The smooth-billed ani of the American tropics usually makes it a group effort, perhaps a dozen birds setting up a cooperative nursery. The females lay their eggs in a single bulky nest in a tree. Then they and

Red-eyed vireo

Ruby-throated
hummingbird

Long-billed marsh wren

Starling

Dickcissel

Barn swallow

Belted kingfisher

Scrub jay

House wren

Blue-gray
gnatcatcher

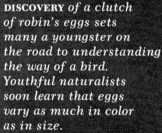
Summer tanager

House sparrow

Yellowthroat

Rowland Scherman

DISCOVERY *of a clutch
of robin's eggs sets
many a youngster on
the road to understanding
the way of a bird.
Youthful naturalists
soon learn that eggs
vary as much in color
as in size.*

*Generally those eggs
laid in concealing burrows
are white, while those
deposited in open nests
or on the bare ground
are colored and often
streaked or spotted.*

*Scientists believe that
all birds once laid
white eggs, as their
reptilian ancestors did.
Color and markings
gradually evolved as
protective camouflage.*

Eggs from the Smithsonian
Institution collection
photographed by Robert S. Oakes
National Geographic staff

their mates take turns incubating the communal clutch that may contain 20 or more eggs. But the sociable birds keep bringing leaves and twigs to the nest and eventually some of the eggs are covered. Not warmed or turned regularly, these never hatch.

For the male emperor penguin incubation is a lone ordeal. Through the black Antarctic winter, when temperatures plunge to 70° below zero, he nestles the single egg on his feet beneath a belly flap. For two months he never leaves the egg to feed, but lives off his body fat. If he moved away, the egg would instantly freeze.

When the young of waterfowl and game birds hatch, they are covered with down. They are strong, active infants, able to follow their mother wherever she goes. On the other hand, newly hatched hummingbirds, kingfishers, and woodpeckers, as well as newborn songbirds, arrive in the world blind, naked or nearly so, and helpless. Parent birds face a full-time task in caring for such utterly dependent young.

SUPERB EYESIGHT aids in the search for food. Birds have the keenest vision of all living things—far sharper than man's. A soaring eagle can spot its prey a mile below, and a chickadee, watchful of the distant hawk, can instantly focus on the tiniest insect before its bill.

A bird's eyes are protected by three lids—upper, lower, and a third called the nictitating membrane which winks across the eyeball like a shade. The eyes are large and usually placed well to the sides of the head, giving a wide field of vision. The eyes of owls, however, face forward, providing the binocular vision and depth perception needed for striking at rapid prey. The eyes move little, but the flexible neck enables the owl to peer in any direction.

Acute hearing also helps birds in their search for food. Woodpeckers are believed to be able to tell when insect larvae move deep in the wood of a tree. Robins are thought to hear the rustling of earthworms underground. Barn owls certainly locate and capture mice in total darkness by hearing alone.

A bird's sense of touch also is well developed, but its sense of smell and taste are poor—though vultures find carrion through its odor.

Some birds dine chiefly on insects and thus help man battle these pests. Swifts, swallows, and flycatchers dart after flies and mosquitoes; warblers glean caterpillars from leaves and branches; titmice and brown creepers dig tiny larvae from bark crevices. Woodpeckers drill into tree trunks for wood borers. Ground-dwelling birds hunt ants and beetles in the grass, or scratch and probe for them in the earth.

Other birds feed on seeds. Buds, tender shoots, berries, nuts, and nectar augment bird diets. Gulls and vultures scavenge. Ducks and wading birds take a heavy toll of water insects. Birds of prey help check prolific rodents.

Lacking teeth, a bird attacks food with its beak, crushing it or breaking it into bite-size chunks which can be swallowed whole. Many species have a crop—a compartment in the gullet where food is stored. Strong enzymes in the front of the stomach start the digestive process; the muscular gizzard crushes and grinds the food, preparing it for rapid absorption. Food passes through the bird's body in minutes.

Many birds exhibit special behavior when gathering food. Nuthatches, jays, and woodpeckers, for example, store nuts and seeds for future use. Shrikes skewer their prey on thorns and twigs as a butcher hangs sides of beef from hooks. A few species use "tools." One of the finches of the Galapagos Islands grasps a thorn in its bill to probe for insects hidden in crannies. Gulls carry clams high in the air and drop them on rocks to break the shells and get at the meat. According to Pliny, the Greek

WORKING MOTHER: *A wood thrush brings home an insect meal for her hungry young. Landing, she joggles the nest; the infants react by gaping. Their bright gullets stimulate the parents to gather food tirelessly.*

Frederick Kent Truslow

poet Aeschylus was killed in 456 B.C. when a bearded vulture dropped a large turtle on him—evidently mistaking his bald head for a stone!

Yet in brain development and intelligence birds rank well behind mammals—hence our expression "bird-brained." Crows are among the smarter birds. I have watched them seemingly play tricks on animals just for the fun of it.

Edward Howe Forbush, the famed New England ornithologist, tells of a pet crow which accompanied its owner when he went ice fishing out on a lake. The crow

TOP-HEAVY TODDLERS, *fresh from their burrow, face the outside world. Big heads and strong bills will soon serve these young belted kingfishers when catching finny food.*

David G. Allen

watched the man bait hooks and lower them through holes in the ice, running each line through a device that at a tweak would trigger a signal flag. As soon as the man turned his back, the crow sprang each flag, one after the other, then made a sound which only could be described as laughter!

But crows are an exception. Most bird behavior is mechanical—the response to instincts. Birds are able to learn from experience, however, and can store memories. Parrots and mynas, as everyone knows, may learn to imitate human words.

Though limited in reasoning power, the bird's brain is highly specialized in one respect: It transmits nerve responses quickly and efficiently. It must. The bird's survival depends on its split-second reactions to danger.

Dodging its enemies and guarding against other perils, the bird fulfills its obligations to nature by mating, hatching its young, and feeding them. Day after day, from dawn to dusk, it hunts for food to plunge into those gaping little mouths.

The helpless infants develop rapidly. Body weight increases as much as 20 to 50 percent daily; feathers soon sprout and grow, and every day the young become more venturesome. Finally the crucial time comes when they leave the sheltering nest and make their first faltering flights. Like millions of generations of their kind before them, they instinctively know that the way of a bird is in the air.

Birds in Your Garden

By ALEXANDER WETMORE

SPARROWS fluttered about the yard, pecking bits of bread and mixed seed scattered on the ground. A nuthatch plucked suet from a mesh basket fastened to a tree trunk. Two blue jays squabbled over a sunflower seed in a hopper. A robin dipped its bill in the birdbath. From the patio my wife and I idly watched the birds on this warm afternoon. Then it happened.

A sparrow swooped low over our lily pool. A bullfrog leaped from his sunning place. Splash! With sticky tongue and forelegs the lord of our pond snared the bird in midair, then plunged to devour it.

I had seen unwary birds by our pond's edge fall victim to a frog's wide-ranging appetite. But this was the first time I had witnessed an ordinary garden-variety

BIRDS WHO COME TO DINNER wade in at a Georgia feeder. Goldfinches in winter garb join myrtle warblers at right. A cardinal drops in for a snack.
Arthur A. Allen

Maryland bullfrog bring down a bird flying full tilt a foot or so above the water. It was one of many surprises that have come to me in my long years of studying birds.

My earliest boyhood memories are associated with birds. I recall a "butcher bird" that seized a sparrow before my astonished eyes and bore it off; also a red-eyed bird with greenish back that ate the puckery berries of a prickly ash near our house. Years later I learned that the sparrow-killer was a northern shrike, the berry eater a red-eyed vireo.

One winter day I watched a woodpecker sidle down a tree to peck at a bone abandoned by my dog. Intrigued, I tied some suet to the tree trunk. To my delight the woodpecker sampled it. Then my cat climbed up and stole the fat.

After some thought I tied another piece of suet to a stick and fastened it at the center of a wire

BREAKFAST IN THE ROSE GARDEN: *With a thrust of its bill, a chipping sparrow feeds its streaked young. This familiar dooryard dweller with the rufous cap is often seen hopping about in search of caterpillars.*

DINNER AT THE POOL: *Low-flying sparrow falls prey to high-jumping bullfrog. In his Maryland garden the author saw the amphibian burst from the water, seize the bird with tongue and forelimbs, then fall back to swallow it. Frogs in turn often make meals for owls, grackles, and crows.*

Walter A. Weber
National Geographic staff artist

strung between two trees. This stratagem frustrated the cat, and I had the pleasure of watching many woodpeckers come to the bait. Some were large, some small, but all were black and white. Each size included individuals with spots of bright red on their crowns. At times they were joined by a "sapsucker"—a smaller, gray bird that often hung head down. Several years later my first bird book taught me that this bird was actually a white-breasted nuthatch, and that the woodpeckers were the hairy and the downy species, the males sporting the red crowns.

Encouraged by this first venture in bird feeding, I harvested a lot of sunflower heads and other seed-bearing plants and hung them in a storeroom to dry. But mice got to them and ate everything except several bunches of box-elder seeds. When cold weather came I hung these out and saw my only evening grosbeak of the winter.

Birds have their special tastes. Thrushes, mockingbirds, and thrashers enjoy berries and other fruit. Woodpeckers like suet. Sparrows and finches eat seeds of various kinds. The blue jay, in addition, loves peanuts. I find it amusing to watch a greedy jay pick up a peanut—which is a beakful—try vainly to seize another, discard the first in favor of the second, and continue this frantic exchange until finally it gives up and carries away a single one. Occasionally a resourceful jay crams a small-sized peanut in its mouth, then manages to grasp another with its bill.

When I started to feed birds seriously I found that house sparrows crowded my feeding shelves. To remedy that I broadcast seed on the lawn, for these birds are primarily ground foragers. I find them interesting to watch.

I spread food out — some in feeders, some in suet holders, and some on the ground — so aggressive birds will not get it all. Some species are intolerant of others. At the suet holder the starling dominates the downy woodpecker. At the feeders the nuthatch shoulders aside the chickadee, and the white-throated sparrow lords it over the junco. Birds of the same kind usually establish a "peck order." Number one bird rates first place at the table, number two takes second place, and so on. Low bird on the totem pole risks being left out entirely.

The mockingbird guards its feeding territory throughout the winter. A newly arrived mocker took over our garden one September. Other birds and chipmunks gave way to its bluster. But presently a box turtle plodded across the grass. The mocker made its usual rush, then stopped a foot away. After a careful inspection it backed off, choosing to ignore the strange creature. Later a frog flopped out of the pool. The mocker advanced several times, waving its wings. Suddenly the frog splashed back. That did it. The startled bird quit the premises.

B IRDS DISPLAY a variety of eating habits. Seedeaters, for example, attack sunflower seeds in several ways to secure the nourishing meat. The mourning dove merely swallows them whole, for its muscular stomach, with the aid of fine gravel, will crush and grind them. The tufted titmouse goes at it much harder. I remember a family of three that sat in a row on the rod supporting a feeder, each bird holding a

BLUE JAY *deftly fields a peanut tossed at handout time. Bright flight feathers fan out as he flaps off with his prize. Jays raid other birds' nests in spring and gobble eggs and young, thus earning their reputation as rascals. But the author enjoys their company and has made friends with those that visit his yard.*

EVENING GROSBEAKS *(below) revel in sunflower seeds at a feeding station in central New York. These thick-billed seedeaters of the northern woodlands generally shun civilization in summer. But when people supplement the sparse winter diet with offerings such as this, the yellow males and dusky females accept the invitation. Suddenly they flock to the feast, calling softly as they pitch in.*

F. Richard Baxter, National Geographic staff. Below: David G. Allen

sunflower seed under its toes. Working in unison, the titmice cracked the hulls with expert blows of their bills. The constant *tack tack tack* suggested a telegrapher's key pounding out Morse code. They hammered so rapidly that I feared for their toes. When a meaty center slipped and fell, they swooped down and seized it in midair.

Blackbirds and sparrows simply break the hulls in their nutcracker bills and extract the meat. The grackle appears to do the same thing, but from the roof of its mouth projects a vertical plate with a sharp edge—a built-in sheller against which it rotates seeds or nuts until the hull is shucked.

Like a child with a dish of candy, a nuthatch tries several seeds, finally selects one, and flies off with it. The bird wedges its prize in the bark of a tree where—living up to its older name "nuthack"—it hacks the hull with its bill. Hunger satisfied, the little "upside-down bird" then may store seeds in crevices for future meals.

At least it works that way in the wild. In our yard the thieving jays, sparrows, and gray squirrels have learned to seek out the stores for themselves.

BIRDHOUSES, *properly built and placed (opposite), should lure winged tenants. Wrens adopt any style of house from rustic to early mailbox if it's 6 to 10 feet from the ground. A red-breasted nuthatch finds a home in the wren house above, but to bar house sparrows the entrance should be only 1 to 1¼ inches wide. Raise the bluebird house 8 to 12 feet in an open area; cut a 1½-inch hole. Purple martins prefer to nest higher, from 15 to 20 feet; their apartments have 2½-inch entryways. A treelike home, 6 to 20 feet up, delights the flicker; make it 16 to 18 inches tall with a 2½-inch hole. And for the chickadee a rustic lean-to, 6 to 15 feet high with a 1⅛-inch door, is a palace indeed.*

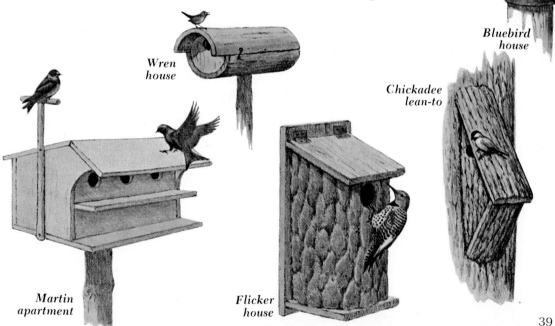

Bluebird house

Wren house

Chickadee lean-to

Martin apartment

Flicker house

Blue jay

Purple
finches

Tufted
titmice

Evening
grosbeak

EASTERN BIRDS *gather for a welcome banquet
of suet, grain, and sunflower seeds.
All these species, some foraging afar, might be
seen in a Maryland garden on a January day.*

Walter A. Weber, National Geographic staff artist

Carolina
chickadee

White-breasted
nuthatch

Carolina
chickadee

Downy
woodpecker

Song
sparrow

Cardinal

Blue jay

White-throated
sparrow

Slate-colored juncos

41

F. Richard Baxter, National Geographic staff

Squirrels at first seem interesting additions to a garden. They approach feeding stations timidly, eat daintily, and give the birds their turn. But having gained confidence, they take over and leave nothing for the birds. I have known them to knock the lids off seed cans, even to chew through latticework to reach such supplies.

Placing a feeder out of reach of squirrels is easier said than done. Impudent and fearless, they surmount ordinary barriers with ease. Sometimes it helps to suspend a feeder from a wire—but be sure it is away from overhanging branches, otherwise the bushy-tailed acrobats merely jump to the feeder from a perch above it. The best way I know to discourage squirrels is to elevate the feeder at least five feet on a pipe, then attach a concave metal disc just below the shelf. Such baffles should be at least two feet across and fastened loosely so they will tilt.

Other furred animals visit our bird feeders. At night wood mice and flying squirrels clean up leftovers. Raccoons, after investigating the garbage can, may nose about to see if any meat or fruit is available. A poky opossum has been a regular night visitor in our yard, for we put out table scraps for him. After eating his fill, he meticulously licks his long fingers clean, then wanders on.

A<small>LMOST ANY SUPERMARKET</small> sells wild-bird food in winter—various seeds and mixtures. Many people also attract birds to their feeders with chicken scratch, livestock grain, apple peelings, and suet from the Sunday roast. Others concoct combinations such as peanut butter mixed with kitchen fats and seeds.

Some friends once wrote that they had fed a ton and a half of sunflower seed in one winter to a flock of purple finches. And a Potsdam, New York, enthusiast puts out 60 pounds of birdseed every day during the winter. For dessert he serves shelled walnuts and peanuts, suet, and peanut butter and bread. Little wonder that evening grosbeaks in his vicinity are said to be the fattest in the state!

Special feeders lure hummingbirds. These glass or plastic tubes have one or two openings through which the birds sip a sweetened fluid. Formulas vary from three to six parts water to one of sugar or honey. Feeding hummingbirds is a simple matter in the United States, for it usually involves a small number of birds. Not so in the American tropics. One friend in Venezuela fed 300 to 400 hummingbirds in his garden daily, mixing more than two gallons of sugared water. A hummingbird specialist in Brazil has kept more than 100 species in his aviaries. Hundreds of other hummingbirds range about his country home. He told me that he uses about 40 pounds of sugar daily to prepare the formula for this horde!

Hummingbirds supplement their diet of flower nectar or sweetened water with protein in the form of thrips, other tiny insects, and spiders. Certain tropical species hover in early morning amid clouds of gnats which they pick off, one by one. I have examined hummingbird stomachs that were filled with the hard remains of solid food. As digestion proceeds, this forms into tiny compact pellets which are regurgitated to make room for another meal.

In summer ruby-throated hummingbirds daily visit the bergamot and salvia blossoms in our garden. They appear suddenly, backs shining in the sun as they poise and turn, probing the flowers on humming wings. Quick as they come they flash away. Red attracts them, as I saw

CAUGHT IN THE ACT, *a bushy-tailed robber feigns innocence as he sits before the sunflower seed husks that mark his stolen dinner. To gray squirrels, feeders are fair game. Prodded by greed, they get past antisquirrel devices with the ingenuity of safecrackers. They even tightrope to a hanging feeder, drop to its sloping roof, scrabble to hook a claw on the tray, then claim the hoard.*

The female cardinal (opposite) ranges far in search of grain and cares little whether the feeder has been raided as long as she finds morsels amid the litter.

Arthur A. Allen

CEDAR WAXWING *and robins (upper), wintering in a Georgia garden, feast on
fire-thorn berries. Evergreen shrubs like this pyracantha attract birds.*

Plantings make a colorful bird haven of your garden

SHELTERING SHRUBS *and trees must grow in your garden before birds will settle in it. With proper plantings even a city lot can become a sanctuary. New York's bird watchers flock to Central Park, their green oasis amid skyscraper canyons. Its varied trees and bushes offer food and cover to migrants winging above the city.*

Fruit-bearing vines, bushes, and trees lure many birds. People are not alone in enjoying raspberries and blackberries. So do more than 140 of our familiar birds. Wild grapes and cherries delight 80 or more species. The scarlet or purple fruit of elders stains the bills of some 120 birds. Dogwoods provide pickings for nearly 100. Arrowwood, black haw, holly, and rose appeal to many species.

For nesting, birds seek foliage thick enough to shield them from predators and severe weather, yet not too dense to fly through. A close-set belt of evergreen shrubs does the job nicely. Thickets of hemlock or red cedar tangled with honeysuckle, Virginia creeper, and catbrier help bar marauding cats.

one pleasant September morning in Chicago. At a lakefront park dozens of rubythroats in southward migration were feeding constantly from the red cannas, but paused only casually at the yellow blossoms that alternated in the flower beds.

Water also lures hummingbirds. They like to fly through the spray of a lawn sprinkler and take a quick shower bath.

Shrubs and trees attract birds, offering food as well as shelter. Evergreens make effective shields against enemies and weather, and some serve as year-round roosts. For two years a jay with an injured wing lived in a holly tree in our backyard. Unable to fly, he hopped up the branches as though mounting a ladder and so was safe from cats. He would come with a hop, skip, and a jump when I scattered food for him out on the lawn.

The bold blue jay with vivid colors and pointed crest often hides its fledglings in shrubbery until they can fend for themselves. Their soft voices and baby ways compensate for the raucous thievery and destructive habits of the parents. By fall the young jays have learned the alarm note that scatters nearby birds with a rush of wings. Then they have yard and feeders to themselves.

Cardinals are all-year residents of sheltered shrubbery. Both parents feed the young. Indeed, the male is so solicitous he sometimes brings food to his mate as well as the hatchlings. One male, flying to the edge of a backyard pond, even brought food to goldfish. The fish, quick to learn how to get a handout, would surface and the bird would jam the food down their gaping mouths (page 324). His reaction probably was

WESTERN BIRDS on a winter morn crowd a California garden. A titmouse and a chickadee pluck cotoneaster berries; others partake of the feeder's bounty.

Plain titmouse

Brown towhee

Steller's jay

House finches

Chestnut-backed
chickadee

Chestnut-backed
chickadee

Scrub jay

White-crowned
sparrow

Plain titmouse

Oregon
juncos

Golden-crowned
sparrow

Fox sparrow

47

From Library of Congress

Allan D. Cruickshank and (above) Thase Daniel, both National Audubon Society

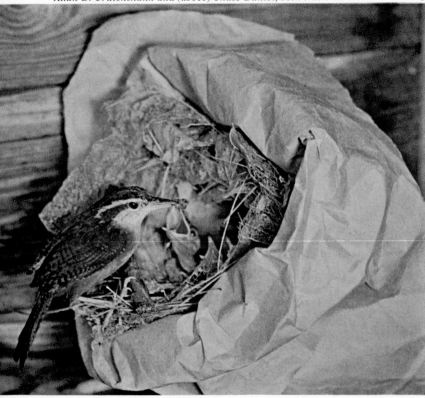

WRENS NEST ANYWHERE, *as Audubon indicated by painting house wrens in an old hat. Bewick's wren (top) raises a brood courtesy of rural free delivery.*

Carolina wren (left) built a nest in a bag of nails. The kindly carpenter bought more nails to avoid disturbing this family.

Another pair of Carolina wrens made their home in a basket— atop some dynamite!

triggered by the brightly colored fish mouths, somewhat like those of his young.

Some birds will nest anywhere. One spring a robin built her home on the ledge of our bathroom window. She became so tame that when we tossed earthworms beside her, she accepted them without ruffling a feather.

Birdhouses lure hole-nesting species such as bluebirds and wrens. But if boxes are not available, house wrens will make do with practically any shelter: an upturned flowerpot, a mailbox, a discarded shoe, a tin can, even the pocket of a scarecrow's coat. One adventurous pair reportedly built a nest on the rear axle of an automobile. When the car was driven the wrens went along for the ride. In spite of this vagabond existence they successfully raised a family.

Any bird box spells home to purple martins. Do-it-yourself carpenters can indulge their wildest fancies in building elaborate Victorian mansions with gingerbread cupolas or modern dwellings in the Frank Lloyd Wright style. It's all the same to the martins. Once they start nesting in a certain place they keep coming back.

THE KISS OF THE SUN FOR PARDON
THE SONG OF THE BIRDS FOR MIRTH
ONE IS NEARER GODS HEART
IN A GARDEN
THAN ANYWHERE ELSE ON EARTH

David G. Allen. Overleaf: Arthur A. Allen

A BIRDBATH *draws birds to a garden. Fill it no more than 2½ inches deep.*

SOON A WINGED VISITOR *like this gay eastern bluebird will send spray flying.* ▶

They have a remarkable homing instinct. One martin fancier took his birdhouse down during the winter for cleaning and painting. In the spring, before the house was back in place, a small flock of martins circled the spot where it had been. Even while the owner was hastily installing it, many of the twittering birds entered it.

Feeding baby birds is a full-time job, as human foster parents soon learn, so don't undertake to care for strays unless you are certain it is necessary. The young of most songbirds will take bread crumbs mixed with the yolk of hard-boiled eggs and moistened with a few drops of water or cod-liver oil. Canned dog food makes a handy ration. In addition, most fledglings will eat bits of cut-up fruit, carefully pushed down their gullets with blunt tweezers. Young birds generally require food every hour or even oftener, from early in the morning until nightfall.

Birds of prey occasionally menace our regular garden visitors—but after all, the predators have to eat too. One enterprising sparrow hawk took to flying close in below the ledge of my office window at the Smithsonian Institution in Washington, D. C., then zooming up out of this concealment to seize one of the fat house sparrows pecking at the seed I had put out. This seemed a little unfair to the sparrows, so I discontinued feeding them at that spot.

I once saw a Cooper's hawk trap a sparrow so skillfully that his actions seemed almost human in their foresight. The sparrows were eating seeds out of a feeder, roofed over but open at either end. The hawk swooped toward one entrance to startle the birds. As they fled frantically through the other, he looped over the roof and snatched one of them.

Frederick Kent Truslow

YELLOW WARBLER, *sitting in her nest on a warm June day, opens her bill to cool off by panting.*

Predators help keep burgeoning numbers of birds in check. But failing that, nature has other ways of controlling populations. We see a small example of this right in our garden. For as summer wanes, our sparrows, having increased through two or three broods, may number 75 or more. Then a disease, apparently not affecting other species, takes heavy toll. By the time cold weather comes half the band has died. Perhaps only a dozen sparrows survive the winter.

Migrant warblers may appear briefly in the fall, passing through on their way south. Starlings gather in huge flocks. Purple martins by the hundreds fly overhead, and if either they or the starlings have their fall roosts near your home, their incessant chattering can make life almost unbearable.

In winter birds may have difficulty finding food and shelter. In Kansas I have seen horned larks and Lapland longspurs unable to fly because a freezing rain had formed ice balls on their wing tips. But the coldest weather holds no terror for the resident mocker. On bleak mornings he rests on the edge of the chimney, warmed by heated bricks and currents of air. Fire thorn, holly, and other berries fill his winter larder. A mockingbird that stayed with us one winter relished dried currants and raisins, soon learned to expect them on a window ledge, and scolded loudly when none were there. During the day he often perched on the ledge and waved his wings.

He soon became bold enough to hop inside the open window and eat from a box of currants while we watched only a few feet away.

The mockingbird easily ranks as the most conspicuous resident of our yard in spring. With widely varied repertory he sings throughout the day. Frequently he somersaults in the air, showing off the white markings of tail and wings. In full moonlight he may sing all night long.

He is a gifted mimic. One warm morning, with my office window at the Smithsonian open, I wondered why the police officer directing traffic at the distant corner was having so much trouble. Then I saw that a mockingbird was "assisting" the policeman, giving whistle for whistle—with a few extra thrown in.

At home the soft but insistent call of the blue jay often wakes me in the morning. "Get up!" he seems to

John E. Fletcher, National Geographic photographer

THE AUTHOR *welcomes birds to his Maryland garden. Baffle keeps squirrels from the feeder.*

say. "Get up and give me my breakfast." I dress and go out to fill the feeders with mixed seed, to scatter bread and seed on the ground, and to put fresh suet in a mesh basket. I toss a few peanuts to the jay. Then I fill the two birdbaths and start for the house. Hungry birds are down and eating before I get there.

From the living room window the view of the back lawn, with feeders, baths, and pool against a background of shrubs and trees, presents an endless attraction. Birds are always in view, the source of much of our pleasure and relaxation.

JEWELED LILLIPUTIANS
ON SLENDER WINGS

The Hummingbirds
Family Trochilidae

By CRAWFORD H. GREENEWALT

WHAT IS A HUMMINGBIRD? When first I became interested I put the question to my ornithological friends. Here is a sample of what they supplied:

"Schizognathous anisodactyle Apodiformes with 8 pairs of ribs; bill long and slender, gape not deeply cleft; tibial bridge absent; nostrils lateral, broadly operculate; tongue extensile ... no Sterno-tracheal muscles ... no gall bladder; no adult down...."

Even though "gape not deeply cleft" has a fine Shakespearean swing, I must say that I had to search elsewhere.

To Audubon the hummingbird was a "glittering fragment of the rainbow ... [a] lovely little creature moving on humming winglets through the air, suspended as if by magic in it, flitting from one flower to another."

The common name of the family varies with different language areas. In French it's *oiseau-mouche*, or fly-sized bird; in Spanish, *picaflor*, peck the flower; and in Portuguese, *beija-flor*, kiss the flower. In some of the Lesser Antilles you hear *murmures*, the murmurers; and in Cuba, the phonetic *zum-zum*.

The Indians of Central and South America do better with their common names—*ourissa, huitzitzil, guanumbia, quinde*, signifying "rays of the sun," "tresses of the daystar," and the like. Even in scientific nomenclature the sun, the stars, and precious stones appear frequently. The name *Topaza pyra*, for example, means the "fiery topaz"; *Stellula*, the "little star"; *Chrysolampis*, the "golden torch."

All this begs the question: "What is a hummingbird?" As a layman I would say that if you see a very small bird hovering, body motionless, before a flower—then you have seen a hum-

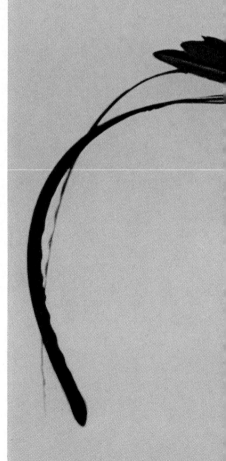

HUNGRY HUMMINGBIRD *hovers*
before a nectar-laden hibiscus.
Pennant-tailed Trochilus polytmus,
which lives only on Jamaica,
is one of some 320 species,
all native to the western hemisphere.

3/10 larger than life-size; Crawford H. Greenewalt
© American Museum of Natural History

mingbird, whether you are in Saskatchewan, Ecuador, or Tierra del Fuego. Wherever flowers bloom in the western hemisphere, expect the ubiquitous and adaptable hummingbird. It is found in the forest, the garden, the mountains, the desert, on the plains, and most profusely in equatorial jungles. Of the more than 300 species only the rubythroat nests in the eastern United States. The West boasts 13 nesting species, but several of these barely get north across the Mexican border.

Generally hummingbirds do not migrate far; however, the rubythroat and the rufous – a West Coast species – travel at least 2,000 miles from breeding site to winter quarters. The rubythroat even crosses the Gulf of Mexico, a remarkable accomplishment for a creature scarcely three inches in length.

The family includes the smallest bird known to man, the 2¼-inch-long Cuban "bee." The largest hummingbird, an inhabitant of the Andes, measures 8½ inches.

For its size a hummingbird outperforms any warm-blooded animal. While hovering, it has an energy output per unit of weight about ten times that of a man running nine miles an hour. If a 170-pound man led the equivalent of a hummingbird's life, he would burn up 155,000 calories a day and evaporate about 100 pounds of perspiration an hour. If his water supply ran out, his skin temperature would soar above the melting point of lead, and he would probably ignite. There is much to be said for our relatively sedentary existence.

A hummingbird's power plant must be refueled every 10 to 15 minutes. The daily intake of sugars, the principal food, may amount to half the bird's weight. Dining 50 or 60 times a day calls for special equipment, and the hummingbird has it – a tubular tongue that works much like a suction pump. Highly extensible, it dips deeply into a flower and sucks up the nectar.

After all this, it might be asked what the hummingbird does at night. Normally, it sleeps. But it may pass into a state of suspended animation or torpor, during which the body temperature drops and the energy output sinks to only one-twentieth that of normal sleep. I believe that if it has not fed well during the day it will enter the torpid state in order to stretch out its energy reserves. Arousal from torpor is almost instantaneous.

The hummingbird depends almost wholly upon its wings to move from one place to another; in fact, its legs are so underdeveloped that it cannot walk in the ordinary sense. I have seen a hummingbird sidle along on a perch, but even for the shortest distances it is more apt to use wings than feet. Wing muscles account for 25 to 30 percent of its weight.

Hummingbird flight differs from that of any other bird. Only the hummingbird can hover with body mo-

Arthur A. Allen. Opposite: Frederick Kent Truslow

BEGGING FOR FOOD, *rubythroat nestlings jab tiny bills at mother as she alights at their walnut-sized cradle in New York (opposite). When they open wide she plunges deep to pump in nourishment.*

BACKING *from a feeder, a female broadtail draws in her hollow tongue. All hummingbirds have such a "soda straw" for sipping nectar.*

MAKING A FAST GETAWAY, *a female rubythroat leaves her hovering position (upper left) by reversing her wings to fly backward. A twist of the body puts her virtually on her back while she changes direction 180°. Right side up again (upper right), she darts off at full speed. The entire sequence takes about two-tenths of a second.*

A rubythroat hovers with its wings beating about 50 times a second. To count these strokes, the author records the sound of flight on tape running at 15 inches a second. Then he plays it back at quarter-speed on an instrument that transcribes the sound on graph paper.

Drawings by Dale Astle from high-speed motion pictures taken by the author; © American Museum of Natural History

tionless, use "reverse gear" to fly backward, and get propulsion and lift on both the downbeat and upbeat of its wings. Actually, its wing plane functions in much the same way as a helicopter's rotor.

Studying the flight characteristics of hummingbirds led me to evolve – with much kindly assistance – a camera dubbed "Mark I." It is neither elegant nor compact, but it does start instantly, permit film speeds up to 2,500 frames per second, and can be triggered by interrupting a beam of light shining on a photocell. The birds in effect become their own photographers.

Inducing the birds to fly at various controlled forward velocities presented a stumbling block, but inspiration finally came: an aerial treadmill. We built a wind tunnel about 18 inches in diameter with a powerful fan at one end. The fan's output could be varied to any required velocity. We placed a feeder at the exit end of the tunnel, its spout centered in the airstream.

A bird coming in to feed, confronted with a head wind of any given velocity, would perform precisely as if it were flying at a similar speed, although its position with respect to feeder and camera would remain stationary.

My children, lacking their father's thirst for scientific knowledge, speedily christened the setup "Daddy's Torture Chamber." I hasten to plead not guilty to torture, for the birds seemed actually to enjoy the challenge. With the noisy fan going at full blast, the buzz of the camera affected them scarcely at all, and at high wind velocities they seemed almost to make a game of it.

It was amusing to note the difference between the wisdom of maturity and the brashness of youth. The adult females soon learned to line up with the feeder about eight to ten feet downwind from the tunnel exit. They would then work their way in fits and starts until they eventually achieved the goal. At first the impatient

IN HIS OUTDOOR STUDIO, *the author photographs the wonder of hummingbirds in flight. When Crawford H. Greenewalt, former Chairman of the Board of E.I. du Pont de Nemours & Company and a Trustee of the National Geographic Society, ranges the hemisphere for hummingbird pictures, he pays two plane fares — one for 250 pounds of camera gear. He stations himself and his unique equipment — nothing like it is commercially available — near a hummingbird's nest or lures the iridescent males into camera range with a sugar-water feeder. The birds take their own pictures when they fly through a beam of light shining on a photocell. This triggers an electrical impulse which trips shutter and flash. It all happens in a fortieth of a second.*

"If I tried to trip the shutter manually," he explains, "my slower reaction time — more than a tenth of a second — would result in a view of departing tail feathers or no bird at all."

John E. Fletcher, National Geographic photographer

young birds would fly diagonally up into the wind stream, only to be blown head over heels when they met the full blast. But under their mother's tutelage they finally learned how to reach the feeder.

After two years of experimentation and several hundred high-speed sequences, it became clear that hummingbirds can attain a top speed of just under 30 miles an hour. When the wind tunnel was boosted to that speed, the birds would enter the slipstream well downwind and fly to within a tantalizingly short distance of the feeder, only to find themselves unable to make the grade.

I did not investigate backward flight by reversing the fan so that it produced suction. The thought of one of these birds being drawn into the blades was much too horrible to contemplate. After all, I certainly did not want to risk making "Daddy's Torture Chamber" a reality.

In their day-to-day living hummingbirds are fearless, pugnacious, curious, and seemingly fully aware of their aerial capabilities. We see this in their almost complete disregard for humans. Even in the wilderness hummingbirds will approach within five to ten feet of a man. In urban communities they will feed from the hand; indeed, I have seen them perch on a finger. This is not at all because they have love and affection for humanity. It is only a reflection of confidence in their ability to make a fast getaway should anything untoward happen.

Hummingbirds are said to be attracted by anything red. My own experience supports this view. I have seen them on many occasions explore the red plastic knobs of my camera tripod. Once they prodded at my red tie, doubtless to see whether it contained anything good to eat. Again, when I was photographing caged birds in Ecuador, someone hung a thermometer filled with red alcohol on the cage, and each of the hummingbirds tested it for nutritional value.

Like most other birds, hummingbirds establish territories which they defend vigorously. Their belligerence, however, goes far beyond the simple needs of defense; I suspect that hummingbirds engage in aerial jousts mostly for the fun of it.

WHEN IT COMES TO COURTSHIP AND MATING, I am afraid I can tell no tales of marital fidelity and "growing old together." Each male is a feathered Don Juan with interests limited to food, fighting, and courtship. His courtship display is a veritable aerial circus as he power-dives in front of his dazzled mate-to-be so that she can see the light reflected from his iridescent feathers.

The female who has been courted and won leaves the male to his philandering and begins building her nest immediately. The egg quota is almost invariably two, and incubation lasts 12 to 16 days. I have had camera, flash lamps, and myself within four feet of a nest under construction, and the fearless lady went on building—paying not the slightest attention to me.

The feeding process is a fearsome sight. As the young stretch out their gaping mouths, the mother inserts her bill to a depth that makes one certain that it will come through on the other side, and literally pumps in the nourishment. The longer the bill, the more terrifying the act. The method seems to work, however, for there is no record of a mother impaling a baby bird.

The young in most cases resemble the adult female, who is generally duller than her consort. The male does not acquire his resplendent iridescence until after the first molt, about a year after hatch.

Few other birds are so brilliant. The iridescent colors are structural, like a rainbow or a drop of oil on wet pavement; not pigmentary, like a red tie or a blue dress. They are also highly directional. For one to see the iridescence, the bird must receive direct lighting from a source behind the observer. Then the colors flash with astonishing intensity. If the bird turns its head a few degrees, they disappear.

My work with the electron microscope and the spectrophotometer has shown for the first time the precise nature of the structure in hummingbird feathers that is responsible for these brilliant colors. The colored portions of the feather are a mosaic of tiny elliptical platelets. Each platelet is somewhat like a pancake liberally filled with air bubbles. It is this structure that produces the almost pure spectral hues one sees in the flash of a hummingbird gorget.

Hummingbird watchers in the United States see largely reds and purples. Farther south the spectrum spans the whole range from brilliant red to brilliant blue with all the intervening hues. However, iridescence is not always a reliable trademark; many species of hummingbirds have none at all.

I photographed my first hummingbird one sultry summer afternoon in 1953. It was a male rubythroat, come to Delaware for courtship after a bachelor's winter in Mexico. Since then I have traveled some 100,000 miles photographing various species in Brazil, Ecuador, Venezuela, Cuba, Jamaica, Panama, Arizona, California, and Colorado. I wouldn't have missed a mile, or an hour, anywhere along the way.

Male rubythroat, length 3-3¾"; Crawford H. Greenewalt © American Museum of Natural History (also opposite)

Ruby-throated Hummingbird
Archilochus colubris

"THE HUMBIRD," noted New England colonist William Wood in 1634, "is one of the wonders of the Countrey...no bigger than a Hornet...as glorious as the Raine-bow." And a contemporary, Gov. Nicolas Denys of the French territory of Acadia, added that the throat of this creature glowed "brighter than the ruby."

The rubythroat—best known hummingbird in the United States and the only one that nests east of the Mississippi—still excites wonder. A subdued hum, perhaps accompanied by an angry-sounding squeal or a fretful chattering, announces the presence of this sprite. Darting through woodlands and across fields, it beats its wings so rapidly that it seems to be moving between two wisps of mist.

This species sips the nectar from thistles, jewelweed, trumpet vines, and other blossoms—preferring the bright blossoms that match its throat. A large part of the bird's diet consists of small spiders and insects. Like other members of its family, the rubythroat must feed abundantly and regularly to keep up its energy supply.

It can be attracted to yards and gardens with artificial feeders—small bottles of syrupy sugar water. Experiments have shown that a hummingbird will consume a teaspoonful of sugar daily. When the sap is running, this bird sometimes dines at holes drilled by sapsuckers.

Most North American hummingbirds do not wander far from their breeding grounds. The rubythroat is an exception. To provide sufficient fuel for its annual migratory flight across the Gulf of Mexico, this tiny traveler may add 50 percent to its normal weight in the days before departure. Migration has other hazards. Sometimes late frosts take a heavy toll of northing birds.

In courtship the male, his gorgeous bib ablaze in the sunlight with deep, glowing orange or red, performs a series of great pendulum arcs directly in front of the female. These sweeps are so precise they give the impression that the bird is upheld by a swinging wire.

The female—who differs from the male in having white-tipped outer tail feathers and a whitish throat—builds the nest, incubates the eggs, and feeds the young with no help from her indifferent mate. Using plant down and lichens, she makes an inch-deep cup, and with spider webs anchors it to a branch, usually 10 to 30 feet above the floor of an open woodland. In this tiny home she lays two pea-size eggs, pure white and without gloss.

The mother feeds her young by regurgitation, usually standing on the edge of the nest with her tail braced against its side and thrusting her beak repeatedly into the wide-open, upraised bills. In plumage the young resemble mother.

After about two weeks the fledglings try their wings. From the outset they are expert fliers—hovering, backing, and darting about.

True to the aggressive nature of its family, the rubythroat is quick to fight. Almost any aerial intruder into this bird's established territory risks attack, regardless of size.

Range: central Alberta to Nova Scotia, south to central Texas and S. Florida; winters to Panama. *Characteristics:* green crown and back. Male has red throat, whitish breast, notched tail. Female (page 56) has whitish throat and white-tipped outer tail feathers.

ale and (lower) female blackchins
ngth 3⅓-3¾"

Male (lower) and female lucifers, length 3¾"; Allan Brooks

Black-chinned Hummingbird
Archilochus alexandri

WERE ITS GORGET FLAME-COLORED instead of black and violet, this hummingbird would be taken for a rubythroat of the west. Indeed, the females of the two species, lacking the distinctive colors of the males, are often confused in Texas where their ranges overlap.

The blackchin frequents semiarid country—chaparral canyons and foothills where flowers provide food. Most vocal of all hummingbirds, it sings a high-pitched song similar to the sound made by whistling through the teeth. Its chase note resembles a staccato smacking of the lips.

After an aerial courtship in which the male flies a series of figure 8's, the female builds a walnut-size nest of plant down bound with spider webs, often on a drooping limb. She lays two dull white eggs.

Range: S. British Columbia to N. W. Mexico and central Texas; winters to S. Mexico. *Characteristics:* green head and back. Male has black chin, blue-violet throat, white collar.

Lucifer Hummingbird
Calothorax lucifer

A RESIDENT OF MEXICO, this hummingbird barely crosses the border, confining its summer visits largely to the Chisos Mountains of Big Bend National Park in Texas.

A forked tail and a dazzling gorget that changes from violet-purple to reddish purple or blue in different lights mark the male lucifer. His plumage was used in gorgeous feather mantles by the Aztecs of Montezuma's day. The female lacks the bright gorget.

The lucifer feeds on nectar from the flowering spikes of the agave and robs spider webs of their insect booty. In its pilfering the bird moves circumspectly through the sticky net, darting to safety whenever the larger spiders run out to defend their prey.

In a family noted for aggressiveness, the lucifer has established itself as more pugnacious than most, showing its mettle during prolonged aerial combats between males in courtship.

In a shrub the female builds a nest of down, bud scales, blossoms, and spider webs for her two white eggs. The young resemble the female.

Range: Mexico and (casually) W. Texas. *Characteristics:* green crown, curved bill. Male has purple throat, grayish breast, rusty sides, forked tail. Female has buff underparts.

Two male Anna's, length 3½-4"; Crawford H. Greenewalt © American Museum of Natural History

Anna's Hummingbird
Calypte anna

ONE OF THE HUMMINGBIRDS in the collection of an early 19th century Duke of Rivoli was named Rivoli's for the Duke (page 67). Another was named Anna's, in honor of the Duchess. The Duke was the son of the French marshal Massena, victor at the battle of Rivoli in Italy in 1797.

Despite the echoes of nobility in its name, the Anna's is not at all cosmopolitan. In fact it is the only hummingbird that breeds generally within a single state – California – and winters mainly within the United States. It takes its favorite nectars from the eucalyptus and flowering tree tobacco and searches foliage for small insects. Occasionally it poaches on sapsucker borings.

Most familiar west of the Sierra Nevada, in thickly populated as well as in wild regions, the male Anna's presents a changing panoply. At one turn of the head the rose-red crown and throat cast a purplish hue as the sides glow with fires of green and copper. At another turn the bright colors fade into a velvety black. The female may display a red patch on her spotted throat.

Courtship opens with a distinctive series of nuptial flights by the male. After a long climb he power-dives in a perfect circle, coming within inches of the female's balcony branch. At the bottom of the circuit he utters a "bark" like that of the California ground squirrel; on the up-swing, a squeaky song.

The nest site – a wooded canyon, a citrus grove, or a utility pole – is usually near water. Often the female lays two white eggs while the nest of soft down is still a platform, adding the walls later. She usually broods twice a year.

Range: California and Baja California; winters to S. Arizona and N. W. Mexico. *Characteristics:* green back, grayish underparts. Male has red throat and crown; female has green crown, spotted throat.

Male Costa's, length 3-3½"
Lyman K. Stuart
Left: female, Allan Brooks

Male broadtail, length 4-4½"
Crawford H. Greenewalt
© *American Museum of*
Natural History
Right: female, Allan Brooks

Costa's Hummingbird
Calypte costae

COSTA'S HUMMINGBIRD frequents the sage, greasewood shrubs, and eucalyptus groves of the warmer southwestern areas, moving quietly from one flower clump to another to dine on nectar, as well as a variety of small insects and spiders.

The quiet habits of this bird give way to more active behavior at the approach of the nesting season. The courting male, his amethyst gorget feathers projecting like an oversize bow tie, ascends a hundred feet or more, then swoops down. He passes close to his plainer-hued mate to rise to his former level on the opposite side.

His diving speed is so great that often the only indication of his presence is a whirring or shrill whistle. Ornithologist W. L. Dawson described it as "fairly terrifying in its intensity...like the shriek of a glancing bullet."

The female builds her nest—a thimble of sage leaves, shredded bark, and lichens—in cactus, sagebrush, a date palm, or on a dead yucca stalk. The young hatched from the two white eggs soon resemble the adult female.

The species was named in 1839 for the French collector of hummingbirds, Louis Marie Pantaléon de Costa, Marquis de Beau-Regard.

Range: central California and S. W. Utah to N. W. Mexico. *Characteristics:* green back. Male has purple crown and throat, projecting gorget feathers, green sides and belly. Female has green crown, whitish underparts.

Broad-tailed Hummingbird
Selasphorus platycercus

IN 1867 THE DUKE OF ARGYLL wrote in *The Reign of Law* that no bird could fly backwards. In 1947 Dr. Harold E. Edgerton, pioneer in high-speed photography, proved what ornithologists had maintained all along—that the Duke was wrong. The evidence, a multiple exposure taken with a flash lasting 1/5000 of a second, appeared in *National Geographic* and showed a broad-tailed hummingbird *backing* from a feeder.

Dr. Edgerton's photographs also revealed the source of the male broadtail's strange trilling, unique among North American hummingbirds. The bird's first two primary feathers narrow at the tips, forming slots. In courtship dives air rushes through the slots to produce a whistle. The female's primaries are normally shaped.

This species feeds on flowers in town gardens and follows the seasonal blooming from the foothills into the higher mountain meadows. It nests on a low branch of a willow or alder and raises two broods of two each in a season.

Range: central California to N. Wyoming, south to Guatemala. *Characteristics:* green crown and back. Male has red throat, white breast; female has buff-tinged sides, some rufous in tail.

Male rufous, length 3³/₁₀-3⁹/₁₀"

Male Allen's, length 3¹/₃"; Allan Brooks

Rufous Hummingbird
Selasphorus rufus

GLOWING IN THE SUN like live coals, tiny birds swarm over columbines, painted cups, and flowering madroño trees. Vibrant with energy, they flash across their feeding grounds – green-backed females overshadowed by spectacular males with flaming throats and the reddish-brown backs that give the species its name. The rufous hummingbirds dash at rivals, competing for red flowers and favored perches, chattering, seemingly in constant turmoil.

Champion traveler in the family, the rufous ranges into Alaska – farther north than any of its relatives. Some of its other names indicate the extent of its travels. Captain Cook discovered the species off Vancouver Island in 1778 and naturalists labeled it the Nootka Sound hummingbird. The Taos Indians of New Mexico saw the male's brilliant colors and called it "sunbird."

From winter quarters in Mexico the rufous follows a low-level route north. Southbound, it follows the crests of the Rockies and the Sierra Nevada. In summer alpine meadows come alive with the sound of its whirring wings.

The male dazzles his mate with a courtship flight in which he swings down from high in the air like a feathered fireball to pause fleetingly an inch away; then he rises for another dive.

In a bush, tree, or shrub the rufous builds a nest of moss and shreds of bark, lined with down. In it the female lays two white eggs, incubates them, and rears the young. Ornithologist William Finley watched her at work:

"After she had spread her tail like a flicker to brace herself, she craned her neck and drew her dagger-like bill straight up above the nest. She plunged it down the youngster's throat to the hilt and started a series of gestures that seemed to puncture him to the toes. Then she stabbed the other twin till it made me shudder. She was only giving them dinner after the usual hummingbird method of regurgitation, but it looked to me like the murder of the infants."

Range: S. Alaska to N. California and W. Montana; winters to S. Mexico. *Characteristics:* Male has red throat, rufous back, tail, and belly. Female has green back, rufous sides.

Allen's Hummingbird
Selasphorus sasin

NOISY REVELER of California's coastal mountain meadows and brushy canyons, this scrappy hummingbird stands ready to defend his feeding grounds against all comers. He has even been known to put large hawks to rout.

Only a green upper back distinguishes the fiery-throated male Allen's from the rufous. The females cannot be told apart in the field. In hand, the rufous shows her smaller size and narrower tail feathers.

Allen's hummingbirds feed on the nectars of brightly colored flowers and tiny insects and spiders about the blooms. The patches of pollen seen on the birds' heads testify to their service in cross-fertilization of plants.

A metallic buzzing and mouselike squeaks accompany the male's courtship flights. After a series of pendulum flights in a shallow arc, he pulls up in a steep, wavering climb to a hundred feet for a swift, noisy dive to the female.

On a drooping vine or a tree limb the female fashions a tiny cup of moss, lichens, and down for her two white eggs. After nesting, Allen's hummingbirds scatter widely until the fall, when they swing down through southern California and Arizona to their winter quarters.

Range: S. Oregon to S. California; winters to N. W. Mexico. *Characteristics:* green crown and back, rufous sides and tail. Male has red throat.

Calliope Hummingbird
Stellula calliope

AVERAGING THREE INCHES in length and one-tenth of an ounce in weight, this is the smallest bird in the United States. Its generic name *Stellula*, little star, fits especially well, for when the male becomes excited his metallic purple-red gorget feathers rise and spread above his snow-white chest. Except for a lightly spotted throat and sides washed with brown, the female closely resembles the male.

This hardy mite sweeps up from Mexico to summer in the western mountains. Among the canyons and forest glades it sips nectar and hunts insects on the wing.

The male objects vigorously when others encroach on his foraging and nesting territory, and he pursues interlopers with rapid flight and squeaky call notes. Less spectacular in courtship than some of his relatives, the male calliope flies vertical semicircles past his mate, making a loud metallic sound on the downward sweep.

On a limb under a canopy of foliage the female places a nest atop or near a pine cone or mistletoe knot. The nest so closely resembles them that it is usually discovered only when the bird flies near. The calliope lays two white eggs.

Range: Central British Columbia to N. Baja California, east to W. Colorado; winters to S. Mexico. *Characteristics:* green crown and back. Male has purple-red throat feathers; female has dusky throat, brownish sides.

Rivoli's Hummingbird
Eugenes fulgens

ONE OF THE LARGEST hummingbirds in North America, this bird averages nearly five inches overall. In size only the bluethroat challenges the Rivoli's, named for a duke (page 64).

Handsomely plumaged in glossy black, bright bronzy greens, and rich purple, the male Rivoli's displays a different color with every change in position. At a distance it looks all black. Lacking the black belly and purple crown, the female is more uniformly greenish above and dusky below.

Mainly a resident of Central America, this bird barely crosses the border into the United States. Ranging up to 10,000 feet in the mountains of the Southwest, it feeds on mescal and other flowers and a wide variety of insects.

The Rivoli's sometimes sails on set wings much like a swift. The wingbeats are slower than those of smaller hummingbirds, and they produce a soft sound unlike the sharp buzzing of other members of the family.

High in an alder or maple tree on a small, well-hidden limb, sometimes overhanging a mountain stream, the Rivoli's saddles a nest of down covered with lichens and anchored with spider webs. In it she lays two white eggs.

Range: mountains of S. Arizona and S. New Mexico, south to Nicaragua. *Characteristics:* green back. Male has emerald-green throat, purple crown, black belly. Female has spotted throat, dusky underparts.

Male Rivoli's, length 4½-5"
Crawford H. Greenewalt
© *American Museum of Natural History*
(also left and opposite, left)

Male calliope, length 2⅘-3½"

Blue-throated Hummingbird
Lampornis clemenciae

A LIGHT BLUE GORGET, white streaks around the eyes, and prominent white patches on its big tail serve to identify this unusually large hummingbird. The bluethroat is the only hummingbird normally found in the United States in which the male has white tail spots.

Like the other giant among North American hummingbirds, the Rivoli's, the bluethroat frequents the wooded streams of southwestern canyons and smaller mountain ranges. Across the border in Mexico it resorts to higher elevations, up to 12,000 feet.

The bluethroat exhibits the family's characteristic fighting instincts. In 1950 a National Geographic Society party photographing hummingbirds in Arizona's Huachuca Mountains observed a male bluethroat guarding two man-made feeding stations. When the party set up a third feeder, the bird discovered it and began to guard all three. The additional work appeared to upset and excite him, and he hit a male Rivoli's with such force he knocked the intruder out.

On another occasion a young bluethroat jumped into the fray when a Cooper's hawk at-tacked a guinea hen. The youngster valiantly dive-bombed to the attack, hitting the raider from above and behind. Finally the hawk gave up. Uttering the squeaky *peep, peep* characteristic of excited bluethroats, the bird returned to his perch to ruffle and preen his feathers.

In addition to the sharp, squeaking call, the male has a simple song of three or four notes, repeated at short intervals while he perches with head elevated. But the bluethroat is quieter than some of the smaller hummingbirds.

Swift on the wing, he takes long rest periods on low, open perches. Foraging amid the lush streamside growth of mountain gorges, he gathers nectar and insects — particularly plant lice — from honeysuckle, gilia, agave, and other flowers.

The males present a vigorous courtship display, though perhaps not as spectacular as that of others in this flamboyant family. Two male courting bluethroats may stage a prolonged aerial contest through the treetops before one triumphs to mate with the observing female.

The bluethroat's specific name *clemenciae* — meaning in one sense "kind" or "gentle" — honors a Frenchwoman. By a happy coincidence the word also means "tame" or "domesticated." It is an apt name, for the bluethroat likes to make its home close to the dwellings of man.

Early records report that the birds build nests in ferns and other low plants along canyon streams, but in recent years nests have also been found under bridges and water towers, in barns and house eaves. One was placed in the crook of a

suspended lard pail handle; another on a loop of wire. The female fashions the cradle of down and mosses, secured with cobwebs. Sometimes the bluethroat's home is made almost entirely of spider silk. Ornithologist Herbert Brandt examined one nest and estimated it contained "some 15,000 miles of spider and insect thread, and therefore probably the longest amount of material of any nest on record."

When first built the nest averages three inches in height. But bluethroats may use the same nest over and over, building it higher each time. One found in Arizona had been used five times. The female usually lays two sets of two white eggs each season.

Range: mountains of S. Arizona and S.W. Texas, south to S. Mexico. *Characteristics:* green crown and back, gray underparts, white streaks around eye; large blue-black tail with prominent white patches. Throat is blue in male, solid gray in female.

Male bluethroat, length 4½-5¼"; Crawford H. Greenewalt
© *American Museum of Natural History (also opposite, upper)*

Female Rieffer's, length 4"

Rieffer's Hummingbird
Amazilia tzacatl

ABUNDANT in the warmer areas of the Americas, this glittering green hummingbird with a bright chestnut tail rarely straggles far enough north to cross the Texas border.

A bird of the forest edge, the Rieffer's seems at home in cultivated areas and about houses. Inquisitive and active, it darts among bright blossoms seeking nectar and tiny insects.

The male forgoes the more dynamic courtship displays performed by many of his relatives. Instead he sits on a favorite perch in the sun and, with tail spread and wings fluttering, pours forth a chirping, twittering courting song.

The nest is placed in a tree or shrub and may be decorated with growing moss. The female, a paler version of the male, lays two white eggs. She incubates alone and between sittings goes off to get new down, sometimes pilfering from her neighbors, even though the nest may be well lined already. Like other hummingbirds, she feeds her young by regurgitation.

Range: E. Mexico to N. South America; accidental in Texas. *Characteristics:* green head, back, and throat; chestnut tail. Female is duller.

Male buffbelly, length 4-4½"
Walter A. Weber
National Geographic staff artist

Buff-bellied Hummingbird
Amazilia yucatanensis

SPRING LURES this green-throated visitor across the Rio Grande into Texas. A shrill twitter advertises its presence as it darts easily among the tangled thickets, pasture bushes, open gardens, and citrus groves of the delta country. George Miksch Sutton heard the low roar of its flight and was reminded of a "tiny electric fan turned on, then quickly off."

Although it apparently does not migrate over most of its range, this noisy hummingbird generally leaves Texas at the beginning of fall for winter quarters in Mexico.

The buffbelly is one of the larger and plainer hummingbirds, and the sexes look alike. Both exhibit fawn underparts, a reddish-brown tail, and a brilliant green throat.

Energetic, chivvying birds, buffbellies will interrupt their probing for nectar to squeak defiance at each other or at larger birds who dare invade the feeding preserve.

In the Rio Grande Valley these birds make their homes in open woodland and along the borders of chaparral thickets, though much of their original habitat has been cleared to make room for orchards and vegetable farms.

Look for the nest in the saddle of a small, drooping limb or in the fork of a horizontal twig three to eight feet from the ground. The tiny home is neatly built of vegetable fiber, covered with lichens and bits of dried flowers and bark and lined with thistledown. The two white eggs seem rather small for the size of the parents, who may raise two broods in a season.

Range: S. Texas to British Honduras. *Characteristics:* green upperparts, throat; buff belly, red or pink bill, rufous tail.

Male Xántus', length 3¼"; Allan Brooks

Xántus' Hummingbird
Hylocharis xantusii

NAMED FOR NATURALIST John Xántus de Vesey, who discovered it in 1859, this bird ranges through southern Baja California. Its center of abundance is the region near La Paz, where as many as 200 have been seen in an hour, frolicking and feeding among red-blooming shrubs.

The Xántus' is curious and noticeably unafraid of man. Naturalist Ira L. Wiggins got a memorable going-over from one black-crowned male: "For the space of a trifle over three minutes he flew around my head, down to my feet, between my legs, up one side of my body and down the other, zig-zagged in front of my face, hovered and circled. On four occasions as it made the circuits around my head the bird ... touched the lenses of my glasses with the tip of its beak."

The female hangs a nest of leaves and seed husks from small twigs, or saddles it on the branch of a fig or cottonwood tree. Ravens often destroy the two white eggs or the nestlings.

Range: S. Baja California. *Characteristics:* green back, chestnut tail. Male has black face, green throat and breast, black-tipped reddish bill, white eye stripe. Female has brownish crown and underparts. Young resemble the female.

White-eared Hummingbird
Hylocharis leucotis

A BOLD WHITE ARC behind the eye immediately identifies this little hummingbird of the highlands among its many companions.

Toughness distinguishes him too. At the slightest sign of an invasion of his favored flower beds, a white-ear quickly whirls to the attack. These birds have been spotted volplaning down at the Rivoli's and bluethroats, driving the much larger hummingbirds into headlong flight.

Though they appear regularly in the hummingbird communities of Arizona, the white-ears are more abundant in the clearings and bushy mountainsides of Mexico and Central America. Here

Male and (lower) female white-ears, length 3½"; Allan Brooks

the typical bell-like *tink, tink, tink* announces the "singing assemblies" of males seeking mates. Perched 60 to 100 feet apart, they call vigorously to the unseen females.

The female builds the nest of woolly insect galls and oak leaf hairs loosened by leaf-mining larvae. Spiders furnish the webs for binding. The cup holds two white eggs.

Range: S. Arizona to Nicaragua. *Characteristics:* white ear stripe, black-tipped red bill, green back and underparts. Male has blue-and-green throat, purple crown.

Violet-crowned Hummingbird
Amazilia verticalis

FOR YEARS SCIENTISTS wondered about the violet-crowned hummingbird: Did it reside in the United States, or was it only a casual visitor? The answer lay hidden somewhere in Guadalupe Canyon, a gorge straddling the border between Arizona and New Mexico.

There several of these red-billed birds with dark caps and gleaming white underparts had been sighted, chattering around the towering agave—but not nesting. And without a nest sighting there was no proof of residence. That honor, naturalist Herbert Brandt wrote in 1951, "is one of the prizes for the student of the future."

In 1957 ornithologist Seymour Levy visited the canyon and saw a violetcrown feeding regularly at a blooming agave. The bird was a female,

Male broadbill, length 3¼-4"

Male violetcrown, length 3¾-4¼"; Eliot Porter

and observing her carefully, Levy saw signs of a recent brood patch. But a violent rainstorm, the worst in years, prevented a search for the nest he suspected was there.

Two years later Levy and Prof. Dale Zimmerman found in the canyon's sycamores four lichen-thatched cups, two on the New Mexico side, two in Arizona. The nests were out of reach, but the men saw the builders. And protruding above the rim of one violetcrown home was something that looked like a tiny beak.

Range: S. Arizona and New Mexico to S. Mexico. *Characteristics:* black-tipped red bill, green back, white underparts. Crown in male is violet, greenish blue in female and young.

Broad-billed Hummingbird
Cynanthus latirostris

A BROAD, BRIGHT RED BILL with a dusky tip, easily spotted at a distance, is the telltale mark of this handsome green bird.

A blue throat lends another touch of color to the male broadbill. His lighter-hued mate looks like other female hummingbirds, except that her gray underparts are unspotted.

Broadbills live in the foothills of the southwestern border ranges—in arroyos and canyons and along stream banks. At rest they perch on dead twigs in the cool morning sun or in shade as the day's heat grows. Sucking nectar and gleaning insects, they flit from flower to flower in a jerky, irregular pattern—a distinctive trait. Other hummingbirds dart directly from one sweet bloom to another.

The broadbill also seems to be a quieter and less active bird. "Frequently, after aggressive flight," reported Alexander Wetmore, "I have seen two combatants perch four or five inches apart for a few seconds, while with raised wings they gave a low, chattering call."

A subdued humming accompanies ordinary flight. But the male's courtship dives, as he swings back and forth before the female, produce a much higher tone, like the *zing* of a bullet.

The female molds her nest on a shrub or low limb, combining fine shreds of bark and plant fibers, bits of lichens, and spider silk. In it she lays two white eggs.

Range: S. Arizona to S. W. Texas, south to S. Mexico. *Characteristics:* broad black-tipped red bill, green back. Male has blue throat, green breast, blue-black tail. Female has unmarked gray throat and underparts.

71

The Kingfishers

Family Alcedinidae

BEAK AGAPE, he swoops low over the clear stream and abruptly knifes in. He seizes his prey, a small, spiny sculpin which made the mistake of swimming too near the surface. Adroitly, the belted kingfisher (*Megaceryle alcyon*) noses up and breaks into the air, wings thrashing, heavy bill clamped on his gleaming prize.

Now he flies up to a branch in a tall, dead tree. He stuns the fish by cracking its head against the bough, then flips it into the air

Photomontage from a high-speed sequence by G. Ronald Austing

73

and catches it head first. With a gulp he polishes off breakfast and settles down to wait for his mid-morning snack. He will sit quietly for a long time watching for the flicker of a fin above the stream bed.

This kingfisher, one of a world-ranging family, owes its name *alcyon* to classical mythology. Alcyone, daughter of Aeolus, grieved so deeply when her husband perished in a shipwreck that she threw herself into the sea. The pitying gods transformed both lovers into kingfishers who roamed the water side by side. During the periods when they nested on the open sea, the waves calmed and the weather held fine. And these are still called halcyon days.

Six of the 87 kingfisher species inhabit the western hemisphere. Only two of these, the belted and the green kingfisher, breed north of the Rio Grande. The belted kingfisher is a common and unmistakable sight with his blue-gray back and chest band and white belly. He appears throughout North America wherever the water is clear enough to reveal fish. Powerful beak and massive head give him a top-heavy look. His bushy crest, when damp, reminds one of the crew cut of a college athlete just come from a shower.

The belted kingfisher jealously guards his fishing rights, patrolling his stretch of stream or shoreline and advertising its boundaries with his harsh, grating call. The penetrating, high-pitched sound is similar to the clicking of a fisherman's reel, and one who has heard it racketing over a crystal-clear fishing stream will always associate it with the riffle of fast water, the fragrance of the wilderness. His courtship call has been described as a mewing.

The bird flies gracefully but with a changing tempo of wingbeats—first an easy stroke as he scuds so low that his wingtips brush the water, then a quickening beat as he climbs suddenly and hovers above a likely target. He fishes in brackish water as well as fresh. Though he sometimes catches the young trout in a hatchery, he is hardly a threat to the angler's sport. In fact, the bird seems to prefer chub and sculpin, both of which are destructive to trout fry.

The kingfisher usually selects fingerlings to dive on, since each makes a handy beakful. But he may snag a fish as long as he is, perhaps a sucker or pickerel. He

BELTED KINGFISHER, *hovering over water, may dive 50 feet for a fish dinner. His heavy head and neck absorb the shock. Where fish are scarce the birds make do with crustaceans, reptiles, even insects.*

Male belted kingfisher, length 11-14½"; G. Ronald Austing (also opposite)

swallows it anyway, and an inch or two of tail is left sticking out from his bill while quick-acting digestive juices are taking care of the rest.

The kingfisher is a solitary bird, seldom seen in groups except during courtship. After mating, the male and female usually make their home in tunnels driven into steep walls of clay or sand. The banks of creeks and ponds are natural locations, but the birds may choose the side of a railroad cut, far from water, or even the cliff formed by an excavation.

Digging with their heavy bills and shoving the loose earth to the entrance with their feet, the mated birds take turns at their tunnel. They burrow from about 3 to 15 feet, usually near the top of the bank. The corridor may be straight or crooked, but the round, domed nesting cavity at its end is always slightly higher than the entrance to provide drainage. Swallows occasionally share the same tunnel entrance with kingfishers, apparently nesting in divergent burrows.

The female belted kingfisher, distinguished by a rusty band across her breast, lays six to eight pure white eggs on a bed of sand or regurgitated fish bones. The parents share in incubating them, a 23- or 24-day task. At first the blind, naked babies cling together in a living ball, warming each other more efficiently than could their mother, who is too short-legged to stand over them. By two weeks their pin feathers have grown; by about four weeks, when able to fly, they leave home.

When the young appear outside, they try their wings in short, erratic flights. For a while they remain in the family party as their parents continue to care for them. Finally the adults refuse to feed them, forcing the youngsters to fish for themselves. Soon the family breaks up, and young and old go their separate ways.

Female (left) and male green kingfishers, length 7-8½"; Allan Brooks

THE GREEN, or Texas, kingfisher (*Chloroceryle americana*) is a much smaller member of the family. He is no larger than a bluebird, except for his pickax bill. In the Southwest, wherever a stream is clear and free of the usual silt, this little green-backed bird may be seen skimming just above the surface. To catch a minnow he makes short, skillful dives, often from a rock that rises only a foot or so above the water.

The green kingfisher, like the belted, closely guards his fishing rights. His stretch of stream seems to have definite limits; observers approaching him have noted that he moves ahead of them for a time, then doubles back to his territory. Where he and the belted are found together, the larger kingfisher frequently harries him off the feeding ground. The green's call is shriller than the belted's. He alternates it with a sharp *tick tick tick*, accented with a twitch of his tail.

At nesting time the bird digs a tunnel, seldom more than a yard long. Its entrance is often concealed. In the nest cavity three to six white eggs are laid and incubated, the parents spelling each other at warming the clutch. Since the tunnel is usually only a few feet above the water, flash floods are always a threat to the brood. Sometimes fire ants kill and eat the nestlings.

As with belted kingfishers, a rusty breastband differentiates the sexes. But there is a switch. The male green kingfisher wears it, not the female. She has one or two dark green bands instead. The young resemble her.

Belted kingfisher—*Range:* N. W. Alaska to central Labrador, south to Panama and West Indies; migratory in the north. *Characteristics:* ragged crest, blue-gray back and breastband, white underparts. Female has a second (rusty) breastband.

Green kingfisher—*Range:* S. Arizona and S. Texas south to central South America. *Characteristics:* dark, glossy green back, white underparts and wing spots, dark green spots on sides. Male has rusty breastband. Female has one or two green bands. Young resemble the female.

Coppery-tailed Trogon

Family Trogonidae

Male coppery-tailed trogon, length 11-12"
Arthur A. Allen. Below: female, Thase Daniel

Apache warriors of Cochise and Geronimo once hid in the forested mountains of southeastern Arizona while dusty cavalrymen hunted them. Now peace reigns over these wild hills beside the Mexican border. The sun bakes their ridges of jumbled rock, and, deep in their gorges where the air is still, wilted leaves and pine needles droop listlessly.

A low, coarse cry breaks the brooding silence: *kowm kowm kowm kowm kowm kowm*, like the call of a hen turkey. Something moves high in the branches of a canyon sycamore — a breathtakingly brilliant bird with glossy-green head and neck, white-banded breast, geranium-red belly, and highly burnished tail. This is the coppery-tailed trogon, big and beautiful, which lives like a hermit in the Huachucas, Santa Ritas, and perhaps other ranges north of the border. Of the 34 species that make up the family Trogonidae, only this one *(Trogon elegans)* breeds in the United States.

Among its 19 New World cousins is the magnificent quetzal, clad in metallic green, its 14-inch body bearing 24-inch tail plumes. Ancient Aztecs and Mayas worshiped the quetzal as a god. Modern Guatemalans honor it as their national bird.

The female coppery-tailed trogon is less gaudy than her mate. Her head and back are brown, her underparts pinkish. She wears a white spot on each cheek. Both birds have the same richly hued tail and the eye rings that give them a bespectacled, earnest look.

They grip their perches as parrots do with yoke-toed feet — two toes facing forward, two back. They sit erect and quiet for long periods. Then a large insect, a moth perhaps, comes close, and one bird may rise on fluttering wings, long tail moving to keep balance, and pick off a midair meal with a clop of the thick yellow bill. They supplement their diet with small fruits.

Trogons usually nest high in such tree cavities as old flicker holes. On the floor of rotted wood the female lays three or four dull white eggs. The male helps incubate them. Juvenile birds look much like their mother until their first autumn.

Range: S. Arizona south to N. W. Costa Rica; casually in S. Texas. *Characteristics:* stout bill, eye rings, square-tipped copper tails. Male has deep green head and back, red belly. Female has brown head and back, pinkish underparts, white cheek marks. Young resemble female.

JACKHAMMERS OF THE FOREST

The Woodpeckers
Family Picidae

By GEORGE H. LOWERY, JR.

James T. Tanner, National Audubon Society

O UTSIDE MY WINDOW in Baton Rouge, Louisiana, a red-bellied woodpecker has just alighted on the side of a pecan tree. Its stiff tail feathers brace against the trunk. Its strong, yoked toes—two in front and two behind on each foot—firmly grasp the bark. Thus anchored vertically, it rears its head and delivers a series of trip-hammer strokes with its chisel-like beak.

Anyone watching such a performance might wonder why the bird's brain is not jarred loose. Having skinned many a woodpecker for museum collections, I myself am not surprised at this ability to withstand shock. The bones of the skull are thick and heavily ossified—almost as hard as concrete.

Further examination reveals another startling structural feature. The bony roots of the tongue do not attach to the bottom of the skull, as they do in most other birds. Instead they wrap around the cranium and anchor at the base of the bill. In a sense a woodpecker has part of its tongue on top of its head!

Why? Although I cannot actually see what is happening, the woodpecker outside my window is about to provide the answer. Its beak chisels deeper and deeper below the surface. Now the tip of its bill finds the tunnel of a wood borer. But the insect larva still remains out of reach. Like a dart the tongue, made extensible by its peculiar structural arrangement, shoots out more than twice the length of the bird's head. With backward projecting barbs near the pointed tip and sticky mucous from large salivary glands, it rakes out the morsel.

Neat rows of punctures in a live oak in my yard remind me that not all woodpeckers use their stretchable tongues in the same way. The yellow-bellied sapsucker, after drilling to the cambium layer, laps up the oozing sap, then returns to eat insects attracted to the holes. Its tongue, instead of being barbed, is bristled at the tip—like a bottle brush. A flicker's tongue, on the other hand, is ideal for gathering ants and their larvae. It is longer, has few barbs, and is liberally coated with a gluey secretion. The flicker spends much of its time feeding on the ground.

Down in the swamp not far away, my red-bellied friend, with the help of its mate, has excavated a nest cavity in a dead tupelo gum tree. The red-cockaded woodpecker of southern pine forests goes its relative one better: It chisels out a home in a living tree. The power tools that enable woodpeckers to drill in the trunks of trees —and, alas, sometimes in telephone poles—benefit not only themselves but other

DOWNY WOODPECKER *grasps birch bark with strong toes and braces with his tail as he feeds his young at a nest hole in Maine. Juvenile ivorybill (above) drew blood from his captor's hand just after banding, then perched on his cap. Rare 1938 Louisiana photograph is one of the last of this vanishing species.* 79

Eliot Porter

birds ranging in size from chickadees to wood ducks. These, and even small mammals such as flying squirrels, take up residence in abandoned woodpecker holes. Starlings don't even wait for the builder to vacate but oust him. As a result, redheaded woodpeckers are disappearing where starlings abound.

Woodpeckers advertise territorial claims by a staccato drumming. In fact, percussive sound is their major contribution to the orchestration of bird chorus. During courtship the cadence of their tattoos seems to have coded significance, taking the place of song. I have often called up a woodpecker, imitating its drumming by rapping on a hollow tree with my jackknife.

ALL THE FEATURES that make a woodpecker a woodpecker give it special opportunities for success wherever trees grow. In consequence, the Picidae have spread to most wooded areas of the globe, 22 of the 175 species breeding in the United States and Canada. Near my home I can see seven kinds in a single morning.

The competition for food and living space led to individual specializations that account for the many differences within the family. The rigor of competition perhaps induced some woodpeckers to take up residence in the desert Southwest and adjacent parts of Mexico. There six species thrive among "forests" of yucca and cactus. The gilded flicker and the Gila woodpecker apparently evolved in that area, for they occur nowhere else.

The emperor among woodpeckers, the ivorybill, became too specialized for its own good. It needed vast stretches of virgin forest to find the favorite item in its diet, the succulent grubs of "betsy bugs"—beetles that burrow in the rotting wood of dead trees. The clearing of primeval forests eliminated this food source and started the decline of the ivorybill. It simply could not adapt almost overnight to such radical change in its environment.

I first saw living ivorybills on Christmas morning in 1933. A chilling rain drizzled through the giant trees of the virgin hardwood bottomland swamp near Tallulah, Louisiana. My father and I and two companions had walked four hours since daybreak and had covered nearly five miles. At every turn white-tailed deer bounded into fog-shrouded patches of canebrake. Mallards and wood ducks sprang up from the acorns that covered the flats along the way. And once eight wild turkeys came within 30 feet of us when we imitated their calls. But we had begun to despair of finding the rarest of all North American birds.

Then suddenly we heard a sound we had never heard before—a tin-horn, nasal *yaamp yaamp*. We tensed and moved toward an opening where a great dead tree had fallen. On the rotting snag that had been its base sat four ivory-billed woodpeckers—immense birds, fitting companions to the immense trees in this primeval forest.

I also cherish the memory of an April day in 1935 when I watched a pair of these birds share duties at a nest in a live red maple. On that same day I stood beneath a huge Nuttall oak and caught a chip of wood which a flame-crested male flung down from his perch. I believe I am the only man alive who has a piece of wood personally autographed by an ivory-billed woodpecker.

To me the apparent passing of the ivorybill leaves a void in the world of birds which nothing else can quite fill. But day in and day out its small relatives remind me of their presence. I hear the rapid *wick wick wick* of the yellow-shafted flicker, the eruptive *kuk-kuk-kukkuk-kuk* of the pileated woodpecker, the rolling *chur-r-r-r-r* of the redbelly, the sharp *pleek* of the hairy, and the modest *peek* of the downy.

BARBED TONGUE AND CHISEL BEAK *equip the red-bellied woodpecker to hunt tree-boring grubs. Fledgling yellow-shafted flickers (inset) will forage on the ground, lapping up ants with "flypaper" tongues.*

Frederick Kent Truslow and (inset) Arthur A. Allen

Red-shafted Flicker
Colaptes cafer

AT REST, this western woodpecker hides his brilliance beneath folded wings. Then he flies up from some mountain meadow, and salmon-red wing linings wink against the somber, wooded slopes—a sudden gladdening sight. No wonder California Indians prized the plumage of the red-shafted flicker for their headdresses.

Ranging from the Great Plains to the Pacific, the redshaft frequents low, hot valleys, forages on sagebrush flats, penetrates coniferous forests, even ventures up the shoulders of the Rockies to timberline. Farms and cutover woods suit him best, but his white rump often flashes across lawns of a college campus or city park.

Alighting crosswise on a limb, the redshaft bows vigorously to right and left and utters an explosive *claip*. The brown-capped head is gray on cheeks and throat. The breast is spotted and dark bars cross the brown back and wings. The red shafts of wing and tail feathers gave this flicker its name.

Courting birds face each other with heads tilted back, necks outstretched, and bills pointed skyward. Their bodies sway from side to side and their heads are in constant motion—the bills wave like an orchestra conductor's baton.

The male flicker, distinguished by his red moustache, claims his breeding territory with a rousing tattoo. He drums on a hollow trunk, a dead branch, a television antenna, a galvanized iron roof—anything that will serve as a sounding board. The drumming echoes far, both to warn off rivals and to inform his mate that he has found a nest site and seeks her approval.

Often the pair settles upon the stub of a lightning-shattered cottonwood or sycamore along a canyon floor. On mountain slopes it may be a pine. In treeless country flickers simply chip out a nest in a gatepost or telegraph pole; some burrow into the bank of a creek. On a farm in the Nevada desert country one pair fashioned a hole in a haystack. The birds frequently bore through the walls of houses and barns and lay their eggs on beams, piling enough chips around to keep the eggs from rolling off.

Flickers sometimes accept a bird box, enlarging the door if necessary. If chips do not carpet the floor, the birds will chisel into the box to accumulate them.

The male flicker starts home building by making a few preliminary stabs with his bill at the chosen site. Both birds share the task of drilling, with time out for removing chips and debris. Their cooperation continues after the 5 to 12 lustrous white eggs arrive; the male helps incubate them, taking the night shift.

After the young hatch, in about 12 days, the parents join in pumping predigested food down infant gullets. In three weeks the young graduate to pulped insects. A week later they leave the nest, following their parents about and gradually learning to forage.

The red-shafted flicker lacks the chisel-sharp bill of most forest woodpeckers, and its tongue is only slightly barbed. So instead of drilling into trees for the larvae of wood-boring beetles, the redshaft seeks morsels requiring less labor. It probes for ants, snatches grasshoppers, and seizes insects in midair, twisting and turning skillfully to follow their erratic flight. Berries and other fruits in season add to the menu, and acorns provide a winter staple.

The redshaft is one of many birds that eat the fruit of poison oak and sumac. Apparently only the waxlike covering of the berries provides nourishment; the seeds are regurgitated or pass through the bird's intestine without damage—even without losing the power to germinate. And so, unwittingly, the birds sow fresh crops of these poisonous plants.

Range: S. E. Alaska to central North Dakota, south to N. Nicaragua. *Characteristics:* brown crown, gray cheeks and throat, black chest band, barred brown back, white rump, spotted underparts; salmon-red under wings and tail. Male has red moustache.

RED-SHAFTED FLICKER *feeds her nestling regurgitated food. Male (above) sports red moustache.*
Length 12½-14"; Allan Brooks and (opposite) D. E. Williams

Male yellowshaft, length 12-14"; Walter A. Weber, National Geographic staff artist
Inset: female, Allan Brooks

Yellow-shafted Flicker
Colaptes auratus

THE BIRD flashes overhead in undulating flight, white rump bobbing, and darts through a shaft of early sunlight. Instantly it takes on a golden hue. Bright yellow undersides of wings and tail trap the sun's rays and toss them back with a breathtaking glow.

The bird soars to perch in a tall tree and a moment later a loud *wicker wicker wicker* rings across the March countryside. "Wake up, wake up, wake up!" calls the yellow-shafted flicker, signaling the beginning of spring.

This woodpecker ranges the breadth of the continent in the Far North. In the United States it dwells east of the Rockies, although it may winter as far west as California.

The yellowshaft has the same plumage pattern as its western cousin the redshaft, but the colors differ. The easterner's wing and tail feathers have yellow shafts instead of red. Its head is gray, cheeks and throat are brown—the reverse of the redshaft's coloring. The male has a black moustache, not red. And both sexes wear a red crescent on the nape which the redshaft lacks.

On the Great Plains the two flickers meet and interbreed. Resulting hybrids show varying de-

grees of blending. Many individuals are "orange-shafted" or have a moustache colored red on one side and black on the other.

The yellowshafts return to their breeding grounds in time for the first flush of spring. Ardent suitors drum courting messages on resonant limbs, roofs, or antennas to the annoyance of people who are trying to sleep. Birds posture and dance before one another—two males often vying for a female, or two females performing for a single male (page 182). Mated birds join in digging their nest chamber, generally in the dead trunk or branch of a deciduous tree.

A prolific bird, the flicker usually lays six to eight white eggs. One mother incubated 19 in a single nest. Another endured experimental nest robbing to lay 71 eggs in 73 days!

Both parents feed the babies by regurgitation, and mealtime battles rage among the young for priority at the entrance hole. After a month the brood takes flight. Fledglings of both sexes (inset, page 81) wear the father's black moustache.

After a couple of weeks the day of weaning arrives. A fledgling clamors to be fed. The adult tolerates the begging awhile, then vigorously pecks the youngster until he sidles off.

Flickers thrive in lightly wooded regions near

open farmland. They occasionally visit deep deciduous woods and in the South are common in burned-over pine barrens. They venture into suburban gardens to share the lawns with robins. They hammer into colonies of ants and gather them on a sticky tongue that extends more than two inches beyond the bill. The stomach of one flicker yielded some 5,000 ants.

As autumn approaches, the birds feed largely on berries and begin foraging together in family groups. Soft notes replace the ringing springtime calls. Winter drives many of the northernmost residents south in migratory flocks. They often gather by the thousands beside a wide bay or estuary, working up courage to cross. Some hardy flickers stay all winter on sheltered New England beaches, feeding on bayberries and the torpid insects in drift seaweed.

Starlings compete aggressively for berries and often drive flickers from their nesting cavities. But with other birds this woodpecker seems to live in harmony. He has endeared himself to Americans from Florida to Alaska. They have given him 132 local names, such as "yarrup," "high-hole," and "golden-winged woodpecker." Alabama adopted him as the state bird; her soldiers marched off to the Civil War with feathers of the "yellowhammer" stuck in their hats.

Range: central Alaska to Newfoundland, south (east of the Rockies) to S. Texas, Florida, and Cuba; winters also in Arizona and California. *Characteristics:* gray crown, brown cheeks, red nape crescent, black neckband, barred brown back, white rump, spotted underparts; yellow under wings and tail. Male has black moustache.

Gilded Flicker
Colaptes chrysoïdes

COMBINE THE HEAD of a redshaft and the body of a yellowshaft and you have a gilded flicker. He lives in the southwestern deserts where the giant saguaros stand tall with upcurved arms. These cacti offer the flickers nesting and roosting sites and retreats from violent spring rainstorms. And they provide the birds with a diet of ants, other insects, and cactus fruit.

The gilded flicker repays his debt to the saguaro. He drills into the pulpy trunk for the caterpillars of a tiny moth. These larvae carry bacteria that infect the plants with pulp-destroying lesions. Feasting on the insects, the woodpecker cleans out the afflicted areas. As a result healthy tissue may regenerate.

Mated flickers usually chisel a two-foot-deep nest chamber in the trunk or arm of a saguaro. Like the Gila woodpeckers, the flickers must wait until the sap stops flowing and hardens before the nursery can be used. After the four white eggs hatch, one of the threats to the nestlings is the gopher snake, which can climb the spiky cactus plant.

All three species of flickers winter in southern Arizona. Of these only the gilded ventures regularly into the saguaros. This bird loses much of its shyness in late summer when nesting is over.

Range: S. E. California, S. Arizona, and N. W. Mexico. *Characteristics:* brown crown, gray cheeks, black neckband, barred brown back, spotted underparts; yellow under wings and tail. Male has red moustache.

Male gilded, length 10-12"; Eliot Porter

Pileated Woodpecker
Dryocopus pileatus

A BARRAGE of heavy blows shatters the early morning stillness of a New England forest. A blur of red, high in a dead tree, marks the source of the noise. It is the brightly crested head of a pileated woodpecker arcing back and forth to deliver battering strokes with his sharp black bill. When the powerful bird pauses, the echoes still ring and the last chips, some as large as a man's hand, thud to the ground.

Yankee woodsmen identify him quickly by the sudden distant thunder of his drilling. "Listen to the logcock," they whisper, using the bird's oldest common name. And they try to get a glimpse, for the size of this winged Paul Bunyan is as startling as the sound he makes—a thing to see and to describe to wives and children.

Often the bird is too shy to spot. Working in high foliage, he keeps limbs and trunks between himself and the observer. A screen of leaves usually veils his swift and silent flight.

But with luck the watcher may see him spread white-splashed black wings, 25 to 30 inches across, and sweep from one tree to another. A powerful flyer, he holds a straight course, beating steadily and purposefully, long neck held fairly straight, red crest lowered, black body bulking as big as a crow's. It's an unforgettable sight.

This master woodchopper leaves his mark on certain trees, sometimes honeycombing them with distinctive rectangular holes. Three to four inches across, these tunnel downward one to three feet. Chips carpet the ground below.

Colonies of black carpenter ants inspire this effort. They penetrate upward from the base of a tree and in time can kill it. Pileated woodpeckers unerringly locate contaminated trees and chop to the heart of each colony. In winter the birds banquet so extensively on these ants that stricken trees often recover.

Beetle larvae draw the huge bird to dead trees. The woodpecker combs a weathered snag with skill and energy, tearing off great sheets of bark and chiseling out every grub. By excavating erect but decayed trees, *pileatus* sometimes weakens them so that they crash to the ground, hastening the return of organic material to the soil.

It takes a large woodlot to support a pair of these "stump-breakers." The pileateds declined when pioneers cleared off mature hardwood forests—and sometimes shot the birds for sport and food. In the 19th century these birds were commonly offered for sale in city markets, but Audubon considered them tough and "extremely unpalatable." By the turn of the 20th century the species was rare in the East. Then second-growth forest cloaked abandoned farms and the big birds showed up again. Today they occasion-ally visit suburban feeding stations to snack on suet. And where conditions are favorable—as in the Okefenokee Swamp of Georgia—the pileated woodpecker may become nearly as common as the red-bellied woodpecker.

Still, the big, spectacular bird remains essentially a symbol of primeval wilderness. Seek him where venerable trees mask the banks of a southern stream, in storm-riven north woods where beaver dwell, in western evergreen forests. In the South he is somewhat smaller than his northern and western relatives.

In spring the woods resound to his flickerlike calls: *whucker whucker whucker*. The mated birds call in duets; later they maintain contact with sharp *kuks*. They greet the dawn with a "bugle call." At dusk they jerkily descend riverside trees for a drink, then drum a rolling tattoo before roosting.

A long drum roll on a resonant limb may echo in fall and winter as a male pileated makes the rounds of his territory. In spring the same tattooing ushers in his courtship. It reverberates through the forest, carrying as far as a mile. A favorite drumming limb may serve him for years.

F OR NESTING, these woodpeckers choose a tall, branchless stub in dense forest well within the leafy canopy of live trees. They return to the same vicinity, often to the same tree, year after year. But the couple makes a new apartment each year. Sometimes a favorite tree is riddled with their oval entrances. The mates jealously guard their wooded estate. They face trespassing pileateds with crests erect and wings stiffly spread. Sometimes rival birds grapple fiercely.

The three to five white eggs take 18 days to hatch. The adults share incubation duties; when one arrives to tend the eggs, the other raps an acknowledgment from within the cavity, then flies off. The male usually takes over at night.

After the youngsters leave the nest, aged about 26 days, the vacated home may be taken over by a wood duck, flying squirrel, or an owl. The pileateds may use the chamber themselves as a roosting hole, or they may excavate new sleeping quarters for the winter.

Pileated woodpeckers successfully avoid the attacks of small hawks like the Cooper's and the sharp-shinned by dodging adroitly around the tree trunks. But the peregrine falcon is an effective enemy. This falcon pursues the straight-flying woodpecker like a bullet and strikes him down with explosive force.

Range: N. W. Canada to Nova Scotia, south to central California and S. Florida. *Characteristics:* crow-sized, black body, red crest, white stripes on face and neck; white wing patches show in flight. Female has black forehead and lacks red whisker stripe.

PILEATED WOODPECKERS *rendezvous at their royal palm apartment in the Florida Everglades.*
Male (lower) and female, length 16-19½"; Walter A. Weber, National Geographic staff artist

Red-bellied Woodpecker
Centurus carolinus

THIS NOISEMAKER, nicknamed "chad" or "chack" for one of his calls, is also known as the guinea or zebra woodpecker. The only bar-backed woodpecker with the entire crown red, he haunts groves of deciduous trees east of the Rockies. In southern swamp timber he may outnumber all other woodpeckers. In settled areas he frequently visits backyards and orchards.

The red-bellied woodpecker is one of the few members of the family that eat more vegetable matter than insects. His fare includes berries, corn, and acorns which he stores for winter. In Florida he eats the pulp of oranges.

Pairs begin courtship by drumming side by side. The red-capped male continues the tattoo inside the nest hole after excavating it. His gray-crowned mate taps back from outside. Rival females sometimes try to steal both the cavity and its excavator.

The set of three to five, rarely eight, white eggs hatches in two weeks. If other birds intrude into the territory, the parents may battle the invaders for hours, crests bristling.

Range: S. E. Minnesota to W. New York and Delaware, south to S. Texas and Florida Keys. *Characteristics:* black-and-white barred back, gray-white underparts tinged with red. Crown is all red in male, gray with red nape in female, dusky, sometimes tinged with red, in juveniles.

Male (left) and female redbellies, length 9-10½"

Golden-fronted Woodpecker
Centurus aurifrons

WHEN THE TELEGRAPH came to the Texas plains late in the 19th century, golden-fronted woodpeckers attacked the soft pine poles. One Texan reported: "A line running out of San Antonio to a ranch nine miles distant was almost destroyed by these birds." To stop the damage, open season was declared on the woodpeckers. Shotguns were handed out to railroad section crews, hunters helped, and the golden-fronted woodpeckers radically decreased in number.

Normally, this noisy, conspicuous bird with barred back and orange nape excavates a nest in live mesquite and post oaks. Mated pairs use the same nursery for several years. In April they produce four to seven white eggs, which hatch after two weeks. They scour tree trunks and probe telephone poles for beetles and their larvae, borers, and ants. They also eat grasshoppers, acorns, berries, and other wild fruit.

The golden-fronted and red-bellied woodpeckers are found together in a limited area of central Texas. They are similar in general appearance and habits. The goldenfront's orange nape patch helps distinguish him at rest.

Range: Texas and S. W. Oklahoma to Nicaragua. *Characteristics:* black-and-white barred back, gray underparts tinged with yellow, white rump and wing patches, orange nape, yellow patch near bill. Male has red crown patch.

Male goldenfront (right), length 8½-10½"; Allan Brooks

Gila Woodpecker
Centurus uropygialis

THIS VIGOROUS little woodpecker forages beside the Gila River in the deserts of southern Arizona. His black-and-white striped back and white wing patches give him away as he explores riverside willows and cottonwoods and darts up adjacent canyons. His rolling *churr* call is heard most often among the giant cactus groves that are his favorite haunt.

The Gila woodpecker is the carpenter of the saguaros, and his efforts provide shelter for many desert creatures. Flycatchers, snakes, and mice often tenant abandoned woodpecker holes. Little owls may take over by force and drive the Gilas out. If the Gila digs a nest hole he must wait until the saguaro sap hardens the inside walls into a gourdlike lining. Instead, a pair may use one of the roosting cavities they excavated before the nesting season.

The male Gila, who wears a jaunty red cap, helps incubate the three to five white eggs. The parents catch insects on the wing and glean the cactus and the ground around it for ants to feed their young. They themselves eat mistletoe berries and cactus fruit or may loiter near a ranch house for corn or tidbits.

Range: S. E. California to S. W. New Mexico, south to central Mexico. *Characteristics:* barred back, white wing patches, gray-brown head and underparts. Male has round red cap.

Red-headed Woodpecker
Melanerpes erythrocephalus

WHO COULD MISTAKE this gaudy woodpecker? Other eastern species sport a red cap or crest; only this one is scarlet from the collar up. With white rump and wing patches and black shoulders, the redhead is a familiar sight in open country where there are scattered groves of trees.

Pairs chase each other noisily and dig nest holes in dead snags or utility poles. The female lays four or five, rarely seven, white eggs. Youngsters wear ash-brown plumage so different from their parents' that naturalists in colonial days thought them a separate species.

In winter the red-headed woodpecker lives on acorns from his own storehouse—a cavity or crevice in a tree trunk. He fills it in the fall and plugs the opening with bark and splinters.

Insects and fruit form most of summer's diet. Redheads hack legs and wing covers off grasshoppers on "meat block" stumps and eat the rest. Attracted by grasshoppers that have been killed by cars, redheads land on midwestern highways and in turn are often killed by the hundreds.

Range: S. Saskatchewan to S. New Hampshire, south to N. New Mexico and Florida; migratory in the north. *Characteristics:* red head, black back, white rump and wing patches. Young have dusky head and back.

Acorn woodpecker, length 8-9½"
H. A. Thornhill, National Audubon Society

Acorn Woodpecker

Melanerpes formicivorus

MASKED in red, white, and black, this far western woodpecker lives in little groups whose members work together to store acorns. Within a strictly defined territory eight or ten birds labor to tamp the nuts, point first, into holes they have bored in a tree trunk, usually pine or oak. One such tree in California was inlaid with some 50,000 acorns. Sometimes a bird hammers in pebbles as well as acorns. Squirrels, scrub jays, and other birds often raid the storehouses.

Home building, too, may be communal for the acorn woodpecker, also called the California woodpecker. Calling *ja-cob, ja-cob* in raucous voices, six or eight birds may join to excavate a cavity for a winter roost or for nesting. Females usually lay four or five white eggs. Larger numbers in nests possibly indicate home sharing. Parents feed their young bits of acorn.

Range: S. Oregon and California to W. Texas, south to Colombia. *Characteristics:* red crown, black-and-white face, whitish eyes, yellowish throat, black back, white rump and wing patches.

Lewis' Woodpecker

Asyndesmus lewis

TOILING through the Montana wilderness in 1805, Meriwether Lewis saw a big, dark woodpecker flying with the rowing wingbeat of a crow. He collected a specimen, which went to President Jefferson along with the Lewis and Clark Expedition's biological collection. Later, science named the species for the explorer.

In the western plateau country Lewis' woodpecker frequents open stands of pine and oak and scattered trees beside streams. A favorite haunt is the charred remnant of a burned-over forest. There, near the top of a blackened snag, seldom less than 80 feet high, a pair of birds digs a nest cavity for a clutch of five to nine white eggs. These hatch in about two weeks. Three weeks later the fledglings emerge to play noisy tag through the ghostly treetops.

From a high lookout station Lewis' woodpecker flies out to snap up insects. He sometimes joins the swallows on their low-level forays. And he feeds freely on the ground, eating ants, grasshoppers, crickets, and beetles. In tree fissures he stores acorns for his winter fare.

Range: S. British Columbia to N. W. Nebraska, south to S. California and S. New Mexico; winters to W. Texas and N. Mexico. *Characteristics:* red face, gray throat and collar, pink belly, greenish-black back and wings; crowlike flight.

Lewis', length 10½-11½"; Allan Brooks

Yellow-bellied Sapsucker
Sphyrapicus varius

A LONG, brush-tipped tongue enables this woodpecker to indulge his craving for sap. He drills rows of tiny wells through the inner bark of trees, eats some of the cambium, then uses his extensile tongue to lap up the fluid that fills the wells. The sticky seepage also attracts insects, hummingbirds, and squirrels. The woodpecker picks off ants and beetles from his wells and from foliage. He also eats berries.

The male yellow-bellied sapsucker returns to his breeding grounds undeterred by April snows. He fights other males for possession of nesting and sap trees: birches and maples in the east, aspens in the west.

Females arrive in a week; their suitors drum to lure them to the nest sites. Then each pair goes through a bobbing courtship dance. The birds drill their chamber in a dead tree or an outwardly sound tree with a decaying heart, often near water. They leave a few chips in the cavity as a bed for the eggs.

After brooding three to six, rarely seven, white eggs, the parents stuff their offspring with sap and with ants and other insects which they first soften by pounding on the bark or a "workshelf" of tree fungus.

The throat patch of the yellowbelly, red in the male, varies in the female. It is white in the eastern female, partly red in the western female. The red-breasted sapsucker, a subspecies in the northwest, has a solid red head and breast. Both forms have long white wing patches.

Range: S. E. Alaska to Newfoundland, south to S. California, S. South Dakota, and N. Georgia; winters to Panama. *Characteristics:* red crown and forehead, black-and-white face, barred back, white wing patches. Male has red throat; eastern female has white throat. Young are brown.

Williamson's Sapsucker
Sphyrapicus thyroideus

FOR YEARS ornithologists considered the black-robed male and the brown-headed, zebra-backed female as two distinct species. Then, in 1873, Henry W. Henshaw found these dissimilar birds sharing the same nests and knew they must be mated pairs of Williamson's sapsucker.

The birds bore for sap in western mountain trees, but mainly they eat the succulent inner bark and insects. Mated birds may return to the same nesting tree – usually a conifer – year after year. Their calls are weak, like the squeaking of rubber dolls. The female incubates four to six white eggs. When danger threatens, her mate taps a rapid-fire warning on a nearby limb. Campers often hear his signal.

Range: S. British Columbia to Colorado, south to S. California and N. New Mexico; winters to W. Texas and central Mexico. *Characteristics:* white rump, yellow belly. Male has black crown and back, striped face, red throat, white wing patches. Female has brown head, barred back.

Male and (inset) female Williamson's, length 9½"; Eliot Porter

*Male (upper) and female yellowbellies, length 8-9"
Allan Brooks*

Downy Woodpecker
Dendrocopos pubescens

OUR SMALLEST WOODPECKER is quiet in dress and manner but not at all shy. He visits the backyard; his cheerful *peek* and his long, rattling call resound from the bird feeder. Walk toward him as he pecks at a tree trunk and he will merely circle to the other side, then peer around the tree to see if the coast is clear.

The downy woodpecker may be found in most of the wooded areas north of Mexico. He often feeds with chickadees and nuthatches in open woodlots and city parks. He probes the bark of trees for larvae, drilling right around the trunk with his short awl of a bill. He also hunts for insects on the outer branches, dangling from twigs to pick them from the leaves.

In spring the female downy chooses a nursery site—usually in the soft wood of a decaying stub—and her mate joins her in carving out a bed for the three to six white eggs. He also helps incubate them. The young hatch in 12 days.

Like many birds, downies go through a brief amorous stage in autumn. Rivals of both sexes drum and dance in front of each other, bills waving, or grapple in flight. But with the onset of cold weather the little birds go their own ways. Each individual digs a roosting hole in his own territory, for these are year-round residents.

Range: woodlands of United States and Canada. *Characteristics:* small size, black-and-white wings and head, white back, spotted outer tail feathers. Male has red patch on back of head.

Hairy Woodpecker
Dendrocopos villosus

A LARGE REPLICA of the downy with a longer bill, the hairy woodpecker keeps more to the forest and less to the vicinity of houses than his diminutive cousin. When identification is doubtful, look for the spread tail. If the outer feathers are solid white, the bird is a hairy; the downy has black spots on the same feathers.

The hairy woodpecker helps guard our forests against destructive beetle grubs. He drills holes, then draws the larvae from their tunnels with his barb-tipped, extensile tongue. In eastern North America he prefers woodlands with rough-barked hardwoods such as oak, hickory, and maple. In the west he also inhabits coniferous forests. He flies strongly with deep undulations. His swift passage through tangled foliage is a miracle of split-second timing.

The female hairy chips a nest out under a limb; in the South she may choose a chinaberry tree in the suburbs. She lays three to five white eggs, and her mate helps care for the young.

Mated pairs drum back and forth to maintain

Upper: male and female downies, length 6-7"
Lower: male hairy, length 8½-10½"; Allan Brooks

Male ladderback, length 6-7½"; Eliot Porter

Male Nuttall's, length 7-7½"; Allan Brooks

year-round contact. In autumn each partner stakes out a separate territory. Then the female raps a loud "come hither." The male answers and finally comes to join her. Like downies, they put on an amorous display reminiscent of spring courtship, chasing each other in high, joyful loops. After a few days, the male returns to the solitude of his own grounds until spring.

Range: woodlands of North America. *Characteristics:* black-and-white wings and head, long bill, white back and outer tail feathers. Male has red patch on back of head.

Ladder-backed Woodpecker
Dendrocopos scalaris

Vast stretches of hot, treeless desert seem a curious habitat for a woodpecker. Yet to the ladderback such country is home. He forages amid creosote bushes and cholla cacti, often feeding on the ground. In less arid regions this woodpecker frequents post oaks, hackberries, and other trees, not far from water. With each hop up a trunk he sounds his thin *queep.* The call sometimes develops into a rolling *chirrup.*

The ladderback feeds on ants, caterpillars, and the larvae of wood-boring beetles as well as fallen cactus fruit.

Mated ladderbacks dig a nest hole in a Joshua

tree, dry agave stalk, utility pole, or fence post. Both adults share the 13-day incubation of the four or five white eggs resting on a bed of fine chips. Before they leave the nest the young of both sexes sport the red caps of their father. In adult plumage the females have black caps.

Range: S. E. California to S. Colorado and W. Oklahoma, south to Nicaragua. *Characteristics:* black-and-white striped face, barred back. Male and young have red cap.

Nuttall's Woodpecker
Dendrocopos nuttallii

To glimpse Nuttall's woodpecker, bird watchers in California follow any narrow canyon into the foothill country west of the Sierra Nevada. Where clumps of sycamore, alder, and bay trees screen a murmuring stream they halt and wait. Eventually a hoarse *prrip,* often lengthened to a high-pitched rattle, reveals a small black-and-white woodpecker gleaning insects from the bark or hanging upside down on a limb.

He also frequents the oaks and Digger pines that dot sunny slopes and varies his insect diet with poison oak and other berries. In typical woodpecker fashion he drums on resonant limbs during spring courtship. A mated pair then takes up housekeeping in a dead limb. The male helps excavate the nest and incubate the four or five pure white eggs, which hatch in about 14 days.

Range: California, west of the Sierras and the desert, to N. Baja California. *Characteristics:* black-and-white striped face, barred back. Male and young have red cap.

Arizona Woodpecker
Dendrocopos arizonae

"NEVER COMMON, never noisy, and never at rest." So ornithologist Frederick Fowler characterized the Arizona woodpecker, the only woodpecker in the United States with a solid brown back. Despite his name, the bird lives mainly in Mexico. A denizen of the live oaks, he roams the canyons and timbered slopes where Arizona and New Mexico join Sonora. In winter he descends to the foothills where oaks mix with ash, maple, and black walnut trees.

This species feeds singly or in small family groups, often accompanied by titmice and Mexican jays. Climbing in rapid spirals, the woodpeckers comb the undersides of limbs and even investigate foliage. Seldom drilling, they pick tiny insects out of pits and crannies in the bark. They also thrive on berries and acorns.

When alarmed, one member of a band gives a sharp warning *tseek* that puts the rest to flight. They dodge dexterously behind trunks and limbs or fly from tree to tree until out of sight.

With the advent of spring these woodpeckers disperse over the mountainsides, ranging up to 7,500 feet. Mated birds jointly excavate a cavity in the underside of a leaning stub.

The female lays three or four white eggs. Both parents exchange sharp greeting notes while relieving each other at the entrance during incubation. Young birds have the red nape patch of their father, but the females soon lose it. The juveniles are a darker brown than their parents, whose plumage fades in the strong desert sun.

Range: S. E. Arizona and S. W. New Mexico to central Mexico. *Characteristics:* brown back, spotted breast, striped face. Male has red nape.

Red-cockaded Woodpecker
Dendrocopos borealis

STRIDENT CALLS from pine tops in the South locate a small woodpecker with a showy white cheek patch. It is usually in a tight company of six to ten birds which chase each other restlessly and keep in continuous vocal touch. They climb trunks in rapid spirals and prefer to remain concealed in the very crown of the trees.

Only a closeup view reveals the male's thin red cockade which gives the species its name. Family groups comb limbs and terminal twigs for insects and pine seeds. Probing for beetle grubs, the birds back down trunks in jerky hops.

Ants, caterpillars, and wild grapes help satisfy their appetites. They also extract worms from ears of ripening corn.

Where a farmer has burned his woodlot to improve pasturage, red-cockaded woodpeckers thrive amid the hardy old surviving trees. They usually nest in an outwardly healthy pine which is dead at heart.

Mated birds drill their nest hole to the rotten core. Flowing pitch hardened around the opening marks the excavation. Often the eggs are sticky from it. Both adults share the two-week incubation of the three to five white eggs. After the young are grown, the family remains together throughout fall and early winter.

A pair produces one brood a season, using the same cavity until the dying tree stops exuding resin. Then bluebirds, white-breasted nuthatches, or flying squirrels appropriate the chamber.

Range: E. Oklahoma to S. Maryland, south to E. Texas and S. Florida. *Characteristics:* black cap, white cheeks, black-and-white barred back. Male has red cockade.

*Male Arizona
length 7-8"
Allan Brooks*

*Male red-cockaded
length 8½", Allan Brooks*

White-headed Woodpecker
Dendrocopos albolarvatus

A BRANCH STUB topped by snow breaks away from a tree trunk—and turns into a bird: the only woodpecker in the United States with a white pate. Head and wing patches contrast with his black body, yet this bird blends well with charred trunks in the Cascades and Sierra Nevada.

The white-headed woodpecker finds almost all his food among the giant conifers—the sequoias, pines, and Douglas firs. Searching for ants, spiders, and wood borers, he generally begins low down on the tree and works his way up to the very top before flying off. Varying his technique, he may alight on the underside of a limb and hop down the trunk. Thorough and diligent, he pokes his head into old crevices in the tree and twists from side to side.

To get at insects hidden between the rough bark layers, the whitehead uses his bill as a crowbar and pries off fragments of bark. From cones on the outer branches he collects pine seeds that form half his diet. As he passes from one tree to another he sounds a sharp *chick*.

He nests in dead standing pines that are hard outside, soft inside. In the cavity his mate lays three to five, sometimes seven, white eggs.

Range: S. British Columbia to S. California and W. Nevada. *Characteristics:* white head and wing patches, black body. Male has red nape.

Male whitehead, length 9″
Allan Brooks

Black-backed Three-toed Woodpecker
Picoïdes arcticus

FOREST FIRE sweeping through a wilderness in the Far North leaves charred stubs in desolate array. Wood borers start feeding on the fire-killed trees. After them comes *arcticus*, back blending perfectly with the blackened timber. His three toes serve as well as the usual four, anchoring him while he strips away bark and exposes the burrowing grubs.

Hopping up and down a burned tree with restless energy, he emits shrill cries which Audubon compared to "those of some small quadruped suffering great pain."

The bird ranges evergreen forests, nesting in stubs, poles, or living trees with rotted hearts. The female lays four or five white eggs.

Range: central Alaska to Newfoundland, south to central California, N.W. Wyoming, and N. New England. *Characteristics:* black back, white underparts, black-and-white barred sides. Male and young have yellow cap.

Male (left) and female black-backed three-toed woodpeckers length 9-10″, Allan Brooks

95

Male northern three-toed, length 8-9½″; Alfred M. Bailey

Northern Three-toed Woodpecker
Picoïdes tridactylus

ALASKAN INDIANS have a legend about this quiet dweller in the deep spruce forests. They say he devoured his mate in a time of famine and wiped his claws clean on the top of his head. Proof? Look at the yellow "mark of the fat" which remains to this day.

In both species of three-toed woodpeckers adult males and juveniles of both sexes wear golden crowns. The northern has white bars on his back to distinguish him from the black-backed variety. In burned-over areas he works near the bases of fire-blackened conifers, prying off great slabs of bark, relentlessly chiseling out the larvae of wood-boring beetles.

Mated pairs usually cut a nest hole in a dead stub for a set of four white eggs.

Range: northern tree line in Alaska and Canada, south to Oregon, Arizona, New Mexico, Minnesota, and N. New England. *Characteristics:* black-and-white barred back and sides. Male and young have yellow cap.

Ivory-billed Woodpecker
Campephilus principalis

THE LARGEST North American woodpecker is also the rarest—it may even be extinct. The ivorybill, on wings spanning up to 33 inches, ranged through stretches of virgin forest that once cloaked river bottoms in the Southeast.

Fortunate observers said he flew with the speed and endurance of a duck, ceaselessly searching for sweet gums and oaks that had recently been attacked by fire or damaged by storm. Such dying trees harbor large beetle larvae next to the sapwood. These grubs were the ivorybill's staff of life.

Alighting on a tree so stricken, this Samson among birds smashed his "ivory dagger" into the tight-fitting bark to get the grubs before they retreated into their tunnels. He also ate grapes, persimmons, and hackberries. The male ivorybill wore a red crest, the female wore black. Their folded wings showed big white areas, whereas the smaller pileated woodpecker looks mostly black when not flying. And at work the bigger bird did not gouge as deep.

In 1935 Arthur A. Allen waded through "gumbo" in the wild Singer Tract of northern Louisiana to search out nesting ivorybills. "The brilliant yellow eye, the enormous ivory-white bill, the glossy black plumage with the snowy white lines from the head meeting in the glistening white of the wings, are as vividly pictured in my mind as if I were still sitting on that narrow board in the treetop," he wrote in *National Geographic.* For eight days Allen's party studied the great birds and recorded their *yaps, kents,* and heavy *bam bam* drumming.

But other men have brought new sounds to the wild forests. The roar of bulldozers, the snarl of loggers' power saws echo through the ivorybill's strongholds, even in the Singer Tract. In 1963 ornithologists diligently searched this area and found no sign of the bird.

Never plentiful, the ivory-billed woodpecker has been shot relentlessly by hunters since colonial days. In the 18th century Mark Catesby noted: "The Bills of these Birds are much valued by the Canada Indians, who make Coronets of 'em for their Princes and great warriors, by fixing them round a Wreath, with their points outward. The Northern Indians having none of these Birds in their cold country, purchase them of the Southern People at the price of two, and sometimes three Buck-skins a Bill."

The species at one time fed in pine forests bordering the cypress swamps of Florida. Though no recent sightings have been confirmed from that state, the ivorybill may survive somewhere in the remnants of the trackless cypress swamps.

The mighty birds mated for life. They nested high in a live tree, often stripping away yards of bark below a cavity from 14 to 20 inches deep. Like a changing of the guard, parents relieved each other tending the two or three eggs, calling musically with bills pointed up.

Range: (formerly) Illinois to North Carolina, south to Texas and Florida. *Characteristics:* large size, ivory bill, black body, white wing patches. Male has red crest, female black.

IVORY-BILLED WOODPECKERS *search for grubs in a tangled Florida cypress swamp.*
Male (lower) and female, length 20″; Walter A. Weber, courtesy National Park Service

The Tyrant Flycatchers
Family Tyrannidae

By OLIN SEWALL PETTINGILL, JR.

WATCH A PHOEBE AT WORK when an insect comes into view. It darts from its streamside perch and with unfailing accuracy closes its mandibles over the tiny prey with a precise, audible snap. Should the bird capture a mayfly too large to be swallowed, the insect is borne back to the perch against which it can be beaten and softened, then devoured.

Nearly all flycatchers hawk insects. And nearly all, like the phoebe, are garbed in somber colors – grays and browns mostly. Of course there are exceptions, notably the scissor-tailed and vermilion flycatchers.

Few birds in the world can match the butterfly grace and beauty of the scissortail. In Oklahoma and Texas summer has not arrived until this lovely creature returns to the open country. One of the breathtaking incidents in my life was my first view of a scissortail in the air, intermittently revealing its salmon-pink underwings and flanks and, when changing course, spreading the black-and-white streamerlike feathers of its deeply forked tail. Between sallies for insects it sits trim and sedate on wires, fence posts, and low trees.

The vermilion flycatcher has to be seen in its native desert and mesquite country of the Southwest to be believed. No camera, no artist can capture the male bird's color, glowing in the sun like an ember suddenly cast from the fire. One would think that all the brilliance in the flycatcher tribe had been saved to make this one species the uncontested standard-bearer.

From Alaska to Tierra del Fuego there are 265 species of Tyrannidae. No other family has more look-alikes, to the dismay of beginning bird watchers. In fact, of the 30 species that regularly range north of Mexico, nine – belonging to the genus *Empidonax* – appear nearly identical in size and color. All flycatchers share certain peculiarities: upright posture, as though they were more alert than most birds; flattish, slightly hooked bills, usually fringed at the base with bristle-like feathers; and a belligerent nature. They rule supreme over their domains, as exemplified by the eastern kingbird, appropriately dubbed *Tyrannus tyrannus*.

At the University of Michigan Biological Station, where I teach ornithology in the summer, a pair of eastern kingbirds nested in a tree above a path. To most people passing below, the birds were indifferent. But not to one hatless man with a shining bald pate. Every time he walked under the tree, down swooped the male to deliver a painful nip before the victim – a botanist who never cared much for birds in the first place – could hustle away.

More commonplace are the kingbird's attacks on crows. The mere sight of one of these large black birds overhead sends the male tyrant into a paroxysm of fury. In an instant he takes pursuit, climbing on stiffly vibrating wings; then he lunges again and again, sometimes even plucking a feather from the crow's back.

I risk attack – and not always from the air – every time I investigate a tyrannid nest. In Mexico I marveled at the location of a kiskadee nest in a bull-horn acacia

SHARP-EYED *ash-throated flycatcher returns to his saguaro home to devour a cicada piecemeal. Small insects he swallows in flight.*

Eliot Porter

shrub swarming with ants. If I as much as touched a thorny branch, the ants were on my hand ready to sting; yet they never bothered the kiskadees. How could a nest be better protected than by thorns and an army of bellicose ants?

I have long since given up searching for a wood pewee's nest. Though usually saddled on an exposed limb, it looks like an ordinary knot or fungus growth. The trick is to watch a mated pair until one of the birds flies to the nest.

Phoebes select a site near a handy supply of mud, their principal building material. Occasionally they make a mistake. In Michigan I watched a pair of eastern phoebes trying to build on the underside of a bridge spanning a sandy stream bed. Day after day they attempted to start the nest with mouthfuls of wet sand. As fast as the sand dried, it fell onto a ledge below. After three futile weeks the birds gave up, leaving enough sand on the ledge to fill a pail.

On their breeding grounds flycatchers are vociferous if not musical, and several species sound pleasing, memorable phrases: the emphatic, almost happy *fee-be* of the eastern phoebe, recently returned to his home under a bridge arching over a spring freshet; the lackadaisical *pee-a-wee* of the eastern wood pewee, idling among the oaks on a lazy summer afternoon; the loud *hick, three-bee-er* of the olive-sided

A BIRD IN THE HAND — *a great crested flycatcher — lights up young faces at an Alexandria, Virginia, school. Trapped in fine netting (below), the bird is gingerly handled, banded, then released without harm.*

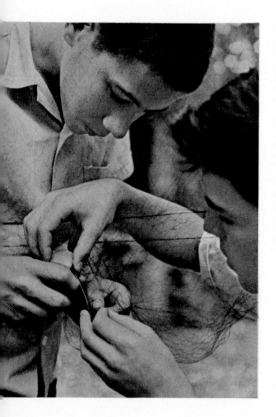

flycatcher, sending echoes across a mountain valley from a lofty spruce stub.

Flycatchers tend to be early risers, frequently beginning the morning chorus. Outside my cottage in Michigan during the summer, it is a sharp *chebec*, the total song of the least flycatcher, which reminds me that dawn is breaking and it will soon be time to be meeting my ornithology class. Just a few *chebecs* are delivered at first, as though the airwaves were being tested, but by the time I am dressed and leaving the cottage, they are coming at the rate of 60 per minute.

As winter approaches and insects become scarce, most North American tyrannids move southward to tropical America. The eastern phoebe merely migrates to the Gulf states, and several other species remain at home in the Southwest. In a class by himself is the vermilion flycatcher, notorious for wintering in unexpected places. One February I was astonished to see a brightly plumaged male in Everglades National Park, Florida—more than 1,000 miles east of his breeding grounds.

In the spring phoebes return north with the first tinges of green on the land and the first flights of emerging insects. Several weeks later less hardy species begin to appear. By summer all the tyrant flycatchers have arrived, and forest and countryside are the richer for their presence.

ON GOES BRACELET, *away goes bird. Where to? When? The U. S. Fish and Wildlife Service finds answers in recovered bands. First in America to band a bird probably was Audubon, when he tied a silver thread to a flycatcher, an eastern phoebe.*

Rowland Scherman

101

Scissortails, length 11-15"; Walter A. Weber
National Geographic staff artist

Scissor-tailed Flycatcher
Muscivora forficata

THE GRACE AND BEAUTY of the male scissortail as he wheels and dips and dives in his spring-time courting dance stand out as one of the spectacular sights in the world of birds.

He begins with a climb to about a hundred feet, plunges down a fourth of the way, zigs up, zags down again and again, all the while sounding a rolling cackle like rapid, high-pitched hand-clapping—an explosion of sound and color. Final-ly he shoots straight up; at the zenith he topples down in two or three incredible backward somer-saults, displaying to his mate his soft salmon-pink underwings. Through it all his long, flowing tail adds a graceful rhythm.

This fantastic sky ballet is repeated through the courting days and often until the eggs hatch.

For all the painstaking ardor of the courtship rites scissortails make little fuss about their nest. They may choose a small tree, a mesquite bush, the crossbar of a telegraph pole, or the framework of a bridge. Ornithologist Arthur C. Bent watched one trying to build a home on the wings of a windmill. When the vanes moved, the nest was destroyed, but the bird started a new one several times.

The nest is a compact cup of twigs, weeds, grass, cotton, and sometimes twine, lined with softer materials. In it the female lays one egg a day until the set of four to six is complete. The eggs are creamy white spotted boldly with brown and pale purple. The young, with short tails, re-semble the western kingbird.

At rest the scissortail presents a trim, slender outline. The white, black, soft gray, and salmon-pink combine in pleasing contrast. Texans call this beauty the "bird of paradise," and Oklaho-mans adopted it as their state bird.

The scissortail sits for hours on a fence post or on the limb of a lonely tree along a prairie road. When a grasshopper, cricket, or beetle comes in-to view, the bird flies out to seize the snack with a sharp click of the beak. Seeds and small fruits vary the menu, but insects form the largest part of this flycatcher's diet.

Cavorting through the trees in company, scis-sortails snap their long streamers open and shut and chatter in a shrill twitter or a harsh *keck* or *kew*. In defense of their homes these stream-lined birds rocket through the air to harass crows and hawks tirelessly until the invaders retire. One scissortail was seen hitching a ride on the back of a retreating bird.

Early in September old and young gather in flocks for the southward trek. They travel mainly at night, pausing by day to hunt insects.

Though their favorite breeding grounds are in the central and southwestern states, scissor-tails often wander far afield—as far as Hudson Bay, Massachusetts, and California.

A relative, the fork-tailed flycatcher (*Musci-vora tyrannus*) of Central and South America, has wandered as far north as New England. It resembles the scissortail in form and size but lacks the salmon-pink coloring.

Range: E. New Mexico, Nebraska, and W. Ar-kansas, south to S. Texas; winters S. Mexico to Panama, sparingly in Florida. *Characteristics:* long black-and-white forked tail, gray body, black wings, salmon-pink sides and wing linings, orange crown patch.

Eastern Kingbird
Tyrannus tyrannus

SPIRIT, DASH, AND COURAGE characterize this "tyrant of tyrants." Perched erect in his full-dress suit of black and white, his head thrown back, the eastern kingbird keeps a constant lookout for food and trouble.

Unlike most birds, which defend only the immediate vicinity of their nests, the kingbird doesn't wait for an enemy to come near. And size hardly matters to this little demon of the air. Let a crow, vulture, or large hawk pass by his chosen territory and he circles out at once. Slowly at first, then gaining speed with wings beating rapidly and the white tip of his fan-shaped tail standing out, he mounts higher. With a series of challenging shrieks, he darts down at the enemy in a savage attack, striking for his back. When the intruder has been driven off, *tyrannus* returns to his watchtower, announcing victory in a burst of stuttering notes.

In quieter mood this bird of the open country skims above the grass, wings only quivering. It seems to fly with the tips of its wings. Over water it plunges to the surface repeatedly to bathe, in the manner of swifts and swallows. At rest the

Eastern kingbirds, length 8-9"
Upper: Allan Brooks
Lower: Allan D. Cruickshank
National Audubon Society

kingbird perches on a high limb from which it can swoop down to capture the insects that comprise the bulk of its fare. In late summer it also feeds on small wild fruits.

Once men hunted the kingbird because of a mistaken belief that it consumed too many honeybees. Audubon deplored the wholesale slaughter. Today farmers favor *tyrannus* for harrying crows and hawks from chicken yards.

The eastern kingbird also enjoys protection as a songbird. In addition to the battle cry the repertory includes a chattering *tzi tzee* call and a true song, a rolling series of sharp notes with a sweet, phoebe-like ending.

Courtship begins with a series of short, quick dips fairly close to the ground. For nesting, eastern kingbirds pick a variety of open sites in a breeding range that covers most of the United States and southern Canada. Often they prefer stumps or snags on submerged land or a limb overhanging water. They also favor orchards and roadside trees. In areas of the West where trees are few, fence posts may serve.

Kingbirds rarely bother about natural cover to protect their homes; instead they rely upon their own vigilance and fighting skill. They build a bulky cradle, twiggy and unkempt on the outside, compact and comfortably lined on the inside with fine grass, roots, and hair.

The nest contains three or four, rarely five, white or creamy eggs heavily splotched with brown and bluish gray. These beautiful eggs hatch after 13 to 14 days.

Kingbirds remain mostly in family units until late August, when they gather in small flocks and sit, nearly silent, on wires, fences, and trees. Then they begin the long journey south.

Range: N. British Columbia to Nova Scotia, south to N. E. California, central Texas, the Gulf Coast, and S. Florida; winters in South America. *Characteristics:* black back, white underparts, white band along tip of tail; concealed red crown patch, rarely seen.

Western
length 8-9½″

Cassin's
length 8-9″

Tropical
length 8-9½″

Allan Brooks

Cassin's Kingbird
Tyrannus vociferans

FROM A WOODED HILLSIDE in the Southwest, just
before daybreak, comes a clamor of rattling cas-
tanet sounds as if an army of birds were engaged
in mortal combat. The first light clarifies the
scene: The yellow-bellied Cassin's kingbirds are
not even quarreling but simply sounding a vociferous welcome to the new day from the tops of
tall trees. These tyrants of the foothills seem to
be saying, "Come here, come here."

In courtship *vociferans* twitters rapidly as he
throws his breast upward and wheels about nearly upright in an erratic dance. In an oak, cottonwood, sycamore, or on a fence post the Cassin's
builds a bulky cup of twigs, weeds, and bark,
often decorated with feathers and blossoms. It
holds three to five spotted white eggs.

The Cassin's seems to be more vegetarian than

most flycatchers, adding a heavier proportion of
wild grapes and berries to its insect fare.

Range: central California to S. Montana and
S. W. Kansas, south to S. Mexico; winters to Guatemala. *Characteristics:* gray crown, olive-gray
back, orange-red crown patch, white chin, yellow
belly, blackish tail.

Western Kingbird
Tyrannus verticalis

AT FIRST GLANCE there's little to distinguish this
bird from the Cassin's and tropical kingbirds.
All three combine a yellow belly, gray head, and
red crown patch. A close look at the tail is the
best way to identify them. A white band borders
the western's black tail. The Cassin's lacks the
edging, and the tropical has a forked brown tail.

Where they meet in the great sycamore stands
of Arizona, *verticalis* and *vociferans* get on well

together, even as tenants of the same tree. Sometimes, however, they fight like furies. Naturalist Herbert Brandt watched one battle royal in which two bullying Cassin's, outnumbered ten to one, were "thoroughly punished."

Near the canyon floors the western kingbird is more numerous. Higher up the proportion reverses. The western seems more nervous and active, scrimmaging and screaming, darting and turning, dashing after crows, ravens, or hawks – any large bird that comes too close to its nest. Uttering a sharp *whit* or *whit-ker-whit*, the kingbird drives off the intruder with sharp pecks.

The western feeds on flying insects and earthbound beetles. A bird of open country, it nests in small groves, on posts, towers, and telephone poles, or in ranch buildings. The three to five white eggs spotted with brown and lavender are laid in a saucer of weed stems and twigs lined with softer fibers and feathers.

Over the past century the western, also known as the Arkansas kingbird, has steadily extended its range eastward. During the fall wandering it has straggled along the East Coast as far north as Nova Scotia. *Range:* S. British Columbia to S. Manitoba, south to N. W. Mexico and W. Texas; winters S. Mexico to Nicaragua, and in small numbers along S. E. United States coast. *Characteristics:* gray head and chest, olive-gray back, orange-red crown patch, yellow belly, white-edged black tail.

Tropical Kingbird
Tyrannus melancholicus

CALL IT tropical, olive-backed, or Couch's. They are all names for the fork-tailed kingbird of Latin America that ventures into the borderlands of Texas and Arizona.

The common kingbird of the lower Rio Grande Valley, it haunts the topmost branches of mesquite, ebony, retama, persimmon, madroño, and shittimwood. The chaparral fairly rings with its noisy, staccato *queer* or *chi-queer*, sounded in a series of ascending notes. It also frequents the scattered trees of open farmlands and stream borders, flying out from a commanding perch to pursue winged insects.

The tropical builds its nest on a horizontal limb, preparing a cup of small branches and twigs lined with soft rootlets and often the dark hairlike heart of Spanish moss. The three to five eggs have a delicate creamy pink or buff ground color, though the spottings are the brown and lavender typical of other kingbird eggs. *Range:* S. E. Arizona and S. Texas to Argentina; migrates in northern portions. *Characteristics:* gray head, orange-red crown patch, white throat, olive-gray back, yellow belly, slightly forked, dusky brown tail.

Gray Kingbird
Tyrannus dominicensis

THIS TRIM, GRAY SOUTHERNER thrives in wild mangrove swamps or busy streets. It doesn't seem to care as long as the ocean is nearby.

In mid-April, not long after winter vacationers return north, the noisy gray kingbirds arrive in Florida from the south. The long bill and ghostly pale plumage quickly identify them.

The new arrivals waste little time in getting down to domestic duties. They prefer a mangrove or an oak for nesting and build a home of coarse twigs and grass so flimsily that the contours of the eggs can often be seen from beneath. The eggs number three or four, rarely five, and are glossy pink blotched with shades of rich brown and lavender.

Normally tame and approachable, *dominicensis* fiercely defends its homestead, even against humans. Hawks, turkey vultures, and great white herons often feel its wrath.

The gray loves to sit on telephone wires – especially those alongside roads in the Florida Keys – and scan the air for insects. It also feeds on seeds and berries. In Jamaica this kingbird has been seen to capture hummingbirds and dash them to death against tree limbs before devouring them – an unusual habit.

Chattering almost incessantly, the gray kingbird repeats a shrill, rolling three-noted call that sounds like *pe-cheer-y*.

Range: coastal areas, South Carolina to Florida and West Indies; winters to N. South America. *Characteristics:* large bill, pale gray upper parts, whitish belly, square, notched tail.

Gray kingbird, length 9-9½"
Helen Cruickshank

Great crest
length 8-9"

Ashthroat
length 7½-8½"

Oliraceous
length 6½-7¼"

Sulphurbelly
length 7½-8½"

Allan Brooks

Great Crested Flycatcher
Myiarchus crinitus

ENTER ANY EASTERN WOODLAND or old orchard in summer, walk quietly, and listen. Suddenly the air fills with throaty whistles, a *wheep* or rolling *prreeet*. An "ungrateful brawling noise," Mark Catesby, the 18th century naturalist, called it. Look carefully. On a limb pointing skyward, half hidden by foliage, appears the noisemaker —the showy great crested flycatcher.

See the crest rise and the flash of yellow belly and reddish-brown wings and tail as the bird darts out after passing insects. This flycatcher seizes most of its prey on the wing, but it also seeks food on the ground and in bark crevices.

The great crest breeds in any tree hole large enough to hold its bulky nest. Hollow logs, drainpipes, or bird boxes may also serve. Once chosen, the cavity may be used for years.

The cradle is formed of leaves, bark, fur, and feathers. This bird's inherent trait of weaving

in snakeskin—once thought to be a means of scaring off invaders—has been changed by modern civilization. Today the bird is as likely to use bits of cellophane or aluminum foil. Apparently it likes something shiny in its nest. The four to six, rarely eight, creamy eggs, finely streaked and spotted with brown and lavender, are courageously defended by the great crest.

A similar species, Wied's crested flycatcher (*Myiarchus tyrannulus*), has duller underparts. It inhabits the Southwest and tropical America.

Range: S. E. Saskatchewan to New Brunswick, south to central Texas and S. Florida; winters to Colombia. *Characteristics:* olive head, gray chest, yellow belly, light wing bars, rufous tail.

Ash-throated Flycatcher
Myiarchus cinerascens

EXTREME HEAT holds no threat for this pale western copy of the great crested flycatcher. The ashthroat is as much at home below sea level in Death Valley as it is at 9,000 feet in the southern Sierra Nevada.

Ashthroats have been found incubating in iron pipes exposed to the desert sun. They have nested in eaves, bird boxes, mailboxes, and tin cans. One pair in California raised a family in the knotted leg of a pair of hanging overalls.

More often ashthroats lay a bed of hair and grass in a tree hole. The female, who looks like her mate, incubates the four or five creamy eggs streaked with brown or purple. These birds feed on wasps, flies, and beetles. They winter in the southern reaches of their breeding range.

Range: S. Oregon and E. Washington to W. Colorado and N. Texas, south to S. Mexico. *Characteristics:* brown head and back, white wing bars, whitish throat, yellow belly, rufous tail.

Olivaceous Flycatcher
Myiarchus tuberculifer

SMALL COUSIN of the ashthroat, the olivaceous flycatcher summers in the dense scrub-oak thickets of southern Arizona and New Mexico. Farther south it is a year-round resident.

A mournful, slurring whistle pierces the air as these birds fly about seeking insect food. They nest in tree cavities, laying three to five eggs streaked with brown and purple.

Range: S. E. Arizona and S. W. New Mexico to central South America. *Characteristics:* gray throat, yellow belly, light wing bars, rufous tail.

Sulphur-bellied Flycatcher
Myiodynastes luteiventris

FROM THE TOPMOST LIMBS of the magnificent sycamores in southern Arizona canyons comes a shrill call like the squeaking of a wagon wheel that needs greasing.

The calling bird has striking plumage to match his voice, but you might search his habitat for weeks without seeing him. For the sulphur-bellied flycatcher is extremely shy, and his streaked body blends with the lights and shadows of the surrounding foliage.

The sulphurbelly is a late arrival, reaching Arizona in late May. He feeds on berries and other wild fruit as well as insects and sometimes stains his beautiful feathers with berry juice. During the breeding season the petulant calls contrast with a soft dawn song.

Nesting birds usually form a cup of walnut leaf stems in a sycamore cavity. If the hole is too large they first fill it with rubbish from the ground. The three or four eggs are white or buff blotched with chestnut or lavender. The same nesting cavity may be used for years.

Range: S. E. Arizona to Costa Rica; winters in W. South America. *Characteristics:* yellow crown patch and underparts, streaked body, black stripe through eye, bright rufous tail.

Kiskadee Flycatcher
Pitangus sulphuratus

THIS GIANT, bullheaded flycatcher calls his name: *kis-ka-dee*. On the island of Trinidad people hear it as *Qu'est-ce qu'il dit? Qu'est-ce qu'il dit?* and say the bird is asking in French, "What's he saying? What's he saying?"

The Derby flycatcher, as the kiskadee is also known, sings melodiously and utters a variety of other calls.

Ranging through the Texas chaparral, this noisy insect hunter is active and quarrelsome, especially during the cooler hours of the day. At times he perches motionless over water. Then, like a kingfisher, he suddenly dives headlong to seize tiny fishes near the surface.

In mating display the kiskadee stands erect and bends his head to expose his flaring crest. He flutters his wings rapidly and snaps his bill, emitting loud, cracking sounds.

The kiskadees build a bulky, globular nest of moss, grass, weeds, and twigs, with the entrance at the side. The two to five eggs are creamy with dark brown spots.

Range: S. Texas to Trinidad and central South America. *Characteristics:* black-and-white face, yellow crown patch and underparts, rufous wings and tail. Young lack the crown patch.

Kiskadee, length 9-10½"
Allan Brooks

Eastern phoebe, length 6¼-7¼"; Allan D. Cruickshank, National Audubon Society

 Eastern Phoebe

Sayornis phoebe

As THE FIRST BUZZ of insect life spreads north across the land in early spring, a dull gray-brown bird follows closely after. Light on the wing, he twists and tumbles with the swiftness of a butterfly. He may fling himself skyward, clamp onto a flying insect with an audible snap of his bill, then float down to rest.

The graceful harbinger no sooner alights than his tail begins to twitch up and down. The moving tail and upright posture are sure signs of the eastern phoebe, but if there's any doubt left his clearly enunciated call in two syllables, the first strongly accented, will soon identify him: *fee-be, fee-be, fee-be.*

Around barnyards east of the Rockies it is a welcome sound. The gray tail-wagger is popular with farmers. He eats nothing of value and destroys great quantities of wasps, ants, beetles, and moths. In colder weather the phoebe eats small wild fruits and seeds.

It was Audubon who discovered, by banding several with a silver thread tied "loose enough so as not to hurt" the leg, that phoebes return year after year to the same nest site. Originally, phoebes nested mainly on rock cliffs in ravines and along streams, but they quickly adapted to man-made structures. Nowadays favorite sites are bridge girders and house eaves, farm sheds and unused machinery.

The female usually lays five white eggs on a nest of mud and moss lined with hair and grass. When they leave the nest the fledglings' wings are crossed by two brownish bars that fade in maturity; their backs are pale olive.

The phoebes come north early and stay until the killing frosts of late fall. A few remain as far north as New England through the winter.

Range: N. W. Canada to New Brunswick, south to E. New Mexico and W. South Carolina; winters from Southeast and Gulf Coast states to S. Mexico. *Characteristics:* gray-brown head and back, whitish underparts, black bill; habitually wags its tail. Young have wing bars and olive backs.

Black phoebe, length 6¼-7"
Allan D. Cruickshank, National Audubon Society

Say's phoebe, length 7-8"
George M. Bradt, National Audubon Society

Black Phoebe
Sayornis nigricans

IN THE GREEN VALLEYS and coastal plains of the Southwest this black-and-white phoebe is a bird for all seasons. It is one of the few flycatchers in the United States that do not migrate and the only one with a black breast.

Looking like a pencil sketch come to life, *nigricans* perches on a low limb or fence near a canyon stream, a well-watered lawn, or even near the man-made canyons of downtown Los Angeles. Tail swishing, he sounds a sharp *tsip* or sings his soft *fi-bee, fi-bee* as he watches the ground for insect prey. He dives down to snap at beetles, wasps, or flies. Larger insects are beaten against the perch and devoured.

The black phoebe is a peaceable flycatcher and keeps largely to itself except when breeding. In courtship the male rises on tremulous wings to a height of 40 or 50 feet and sings to the female. They nest near water and under a sheltering projection — a rock ledge, a bridge beam, or an eave. They form a cup of fibered mud pellets and line it with grass, animal hairs, and feathers. Sometimes phoebes get caught in a loop of hair woven into the mud and strangle themselves.

In the set of three to six white eggs, one or two are often marked with red dots. When the young are ready to fly, the male teaches them to catch food on the wing, while the female prepares the nest for a second brood.

Range: California to central Texas, south to Argentina. *Characteristics:* black upper parts and breast, white belly. Wags tail.

Say's Phoebe
Sayornis saya

EASILY RECOGNIZED by its pale rusty belly and dull black tail, the Say's, named in honor of the 19th century naturalist Thomas Say, replaces the eastern phoebe west of the hundredth meridian. Even more restless than its eastern counterpart, the westerner flits about in search of bees, wasps, dragonflies, and grasshoppers, darting back and forth from its perch with quick wing strokes in swift, usually zigzag flight.

This phoebe frequents ranches, sagebrush plains, rocky ravines, foothills, and desert borders. Unlike the black phoebe of the Southwest, it shows no special fondness for watercourses and forages widely over stunted vegetation.

The bird utters a soft, plaintive *pee-ur*, quite unlike the eastern phoebe's note, often twitching its tail and raising its crest as it sounds the call.

In the southern portions of their range many of these phoebes are year-round residents. Others set forth early in spring to seek breeding territories as far north as central Alaska.

They breed in cliff crevices, caves, old mine shafts, wells, under bridges, and against ranch buildings. The nest of vegetable fibers, hair, and spider-web binding holds four or five eggs. These are usually white, but one or two may be flecked with brown. Say's phoebes sometimes raise two broods in a season.

Range: central Alaska to W. Manitoba, south to central Mexico; winters to S. Mexico. *Characteristics:* grayish-brown back, pale rusty underparts. Wags black tail.

Upper: Traill's, length 4¼-6¾"; Bob and Elsie Boggs

Yellowbelly, length 5-5¾"; Eliot Porter

Yellow-bellied Flycatcher
Empidonax flaviventris

AMONG THE EASTERN members of the Empidonax flycatcher group the yellowbelly is the easiest to identify. It has the dark back, light eye rings, and two wing bars common to the genus, but the yellowish breast is distinctive.

Usually well out of sight in moss-carpeted evergreen forests, this shy bird betrays its presence with a simple *chu-wee* call. An imitation of a squeaking mouse may lure it into view.

The yellowbelly usually hides its nest in heavy moss on the ground or on a stump. The four or five white eggs are spotted with brown.

Range: N. British Columbia to Newfoundland, south to N. North Dakota and N. Pennsylvania; winters from S. Mexico to Panama. *Characteristics:* olive-green back, yellowish throat, breast, wing bars, and eye rings.

Traill's Flycatcher
Empidonax traillii

A SMALL, DARK OLIVE FIGURE darts out of a swamp thicket to snap up an insect. Traill's flycatcher may linger awhile on a topmost twig but he soon returns to cover. He has the whitest throat in the Empidonax group and looks browner than the almost identical Acadian and least flycatchers.

Arriving in the north when summer is at hand, the Traill's haunts alders and willows bordering eastern streams and swamps. In the Midwest he frequents shrubby upland pastures; in the far west, muskeg and mountain meadows. His call sounds like *fee-be-o* in the northerly regions; farther south it varies to *fitz-bew.*

The nest, a loose cup of grass, weed stems, and bark, is usually suspended fairly close to the ground in a clump of bushes. It holds three or four creamy or pinkish eggs spotted with brown.

Named by Audubon for his friend Dr. Thomas S. Traill of Liverpool, *traillii* is also known as the little flycatcher in the west, and the alder flycatcher in the east. Differences in voice and habitat have led to the suggestion that *traillii* be divided into two separate species.

Range: Alaska to Nova Scotia, south to Baja California and Virginia; winters from S. Mexico to Argentina. *Characteristics:* dark olive-brown back, white underparts, wing bars, eye rings.

Acadian, length 5½-6¾"; Eliot Porter

Hammond's Flycatcher
Empidonax hammondii

EVEN EXPERTS may despair of telling the Hammond's, dusky, and gray flycatchers apart. Habitats differ, but in migration these three western birds may leave their typical haunts.

Differences in plumage are minute. The Hammond's generally shows more olive in its back and more yellow in its underparts than the dusky (page 112). The gray's plumage shows very little, if any, olive or yellow.

One of the earlier spring migrants, the Hammond's often swings north through the lowlands in the company of warblers, kinglets, chickadees, and nuthatches. Once settled, it makes short forays for winged insects from the higher limbs of evergreens. Its thin song, often repeated, sounds like *se-lip twur treeip.*

In the southern reaches of its breeding range the Hammond's may nest as high up as 11,000 feet in the Sierra Nevada. Mated pairs saddle a cup of bark strips, grass, and fibers on a limb. The three or four white eggs are sometimes speckled. They hatch after about 12 days.

Range: S. Alaska to central Alberta, south to central California and N. New Mexico; winters from S. E. Arizona to Nicaragua. *Characteristics:* olive-gray back, whitish underparts tinged with yellow; white wing bars and eye rings.

Acadian Flycatcher
Empidonax virescens

IN THE CONFUSION over the look-alike flycatchers this denizen of the deep forests got stuck with the wrong common name. The species was named for a bird taken in Acadia, or Nova Scotia. Scientists later learned that the Acadian never reaches Nova Scotia and that the first bird identified as one must have been another species. But the established common name hung on.

The shy *virescens* has a greener back than other members of the Empidonax group and is the one that nests in most of the South. It hunts beetles, bees, and ants from low, shaded limbs in beech trees and swamp woodlands.

The female hangs a shallow basket of fine plant fibers between horizontal twigs. Threads of insect silk, used to secure the structure, stream down from the nest rim. The two to four white or buffy-white eggs are dotted with brown.

Around the nest the birds sound an abrupt *wicky-up* much like a hiccup. At other times they sing an explosive *spit-chee.*

Range: S. E. South Dakota to S. Connecticut, south to S. E. Texas and central Florida; winters from Costa Rica to N. South America. *Characteristics:* greenish-gray back, buffy wing bars, light eye rings; sides washed with yellow.

Allan D. Cruickshank, National Audubon Society

Upper: Hammond's, length 5-5½"

Least flycatcher, length 5-5¾"; C. G. Hampson

Least Flycatcher
Empidonax minimus

WITH A TWITCH of the tail and an upward jerk of the head, the least flycatcher vehemently sounds his call: *chebec.* So familiar is the sound in northern orchards and open woodlands that many people call him the chebec.

Bold and scrappy, *minimus* will pursue an insect so close to a man's head that the snapping bill can be heard. In the spring the orchards resound with the cries of males fighting over newly arrived females. Mated pairs place a nest of shredded bark, down, and grass in a tree fork. The cup holds four creamy eggs. Sometimes the birds raise a second brood on the same site.

Range: S. W. Yukon to Nova Scotia, south to N. Wyoming and N. Georgia; winters N. Mexico to Panama. *Characteristics:* gray-green back, whitish underparts, white wing bars, eye rings.

111

Dusky Flycatcher
Empidonax oberholseri

RANGING through the foothills and middle slopes of the western mountains – in the chaparral and among the willows, aspen, piñon, and juniper – the dusky flycatcher searches for insect rations and a summer home.

A pair may allow other birds to enter the chosen summer territory, but they scold vigorously at any intrusion near the nest. The breeding site is usually a crotch in a low sapling or bush. The male gathers grass and weed fibers, chews them until they are pliable, and packs them into place with feet and bill. The female shapes and weaves the soft shreds.

The male also performs a heavy share of nest tending during the 12- to 15-day incubation. He guards the nursery, sits on the three or four white eggs on occasion, and flits about gathering food. In some areas severe wind gusts and rainstorms wipe out entire broods by blowing the young out of the nests or drowning them.

Heard close by, the dusky's loud *tsee-wick* call closely resembles the *chebec* of the least flycatcher. The male dusky also sings a peculiar jerky song divided into couplets.

Range: S. Yukon to S. W. Saskatchewan, south to S. California and N. New Mexico; winters to S. Mexico. *Characteristics:* olive-gray back, whitish underparts washed with yellow, white wing bars and eye rings.

Gray Flycatcher
Empidonax wrightii

IN THE SAGEBRUSH PLAINS of the Great Basin, sage thrashers and Brewer's sparrows pore over the ground or the bushes for their food. But the gray flycatchers, which also inhabit the semi-arid country, perch atop the taller bushes and scan the air for their insect prey.

Grayest of the western Empidonax flycatchers, these birds are best distinguished by their habitat and song. They sound a vigorous *chiwip* and fainter *cheep* in a variety of combinations.

Gray flycatchers nest in sagebrush and piñon or juniper trees. They build a loose cup of grass, weeds, and bark shreds and line it with feathers. The three or four white or creamy eggs hatch in 14 days. In Arizona two birds were seen shading their nestlings from the desert sun.

Range: central Oregon to central Colorado, south to central California and W. New Mexico; winters to S. Mexico. *Characteristics:* gray back, whitish underparts, white wing bars, eye rings.

Western Flycatcher
Empidonax difficilis

SHADE AND WATER attract the western flycatcher. He dwells in quiet glens cut by trickling streams and hidden by tall trees. He sounds a sharp *pseet* and sometimes sings his dawn song – *pseet trip seet* – all day long.

As he forages in the openings between the trees, the bird displays the olive-brown back and yellow-tinged belly and throat that make him look so much like the yellow-bellied flycatcher of the east. The westerner seems to eat more ladybird beetles than any other flycatcher. He also preys on flies, bees, ants, and moths.

The western flycatcher may nest on a tree limb, but he often leaves the solitude of the forest to raise a family. One brood was reared in a fern basket on a porch in California. Other nests have been found in stream banks, in deserted woodcutters' huts, in outbuildings, under the roofs of water tanks, and in canyon walls.

When western flycatchers find a suitable beam

Dusky flycatchers, length 5¼-6"; Eliot Porter

Gray flycatcher, length 5½"
Walter A. Weber
National Geographic staff artist

Upper: western flycatcher, length 5½-6"; Eliot Porter

Buffbreast, length 4½-5"; Allan Brooks

The female, who wears the same buff-and-brown plumage as her mate, builds the cup of plant fibers, binds it to the branch with spider webs, lines it with fine grass, hair, and feathers, and decorates it with lichens. In it she lays three or four creamy eggs. Squirrels, jays, hawks, and lizards all try to rob the tiny flycatcher's nest.

Among the tall pines and small oaks of the hillsides that slope up from the canyons, the buffbreast lives on beetles, bugs, and ants.

Range: highlands of central Arizona and New Mexico south through W. Mexico to Honduras; winters from Mexico to Honduras. *Characteristics:* brownish head and back, buffy underparts, white eye rings and wing bars.

Coues', length 7-7¾"; Allan Brooks

in an unoccupied building, they may use it year after year until the beam is covered with a row of old nests. Often they build the nest with dark green moss. On a soft lining of shredded bark the female lays three or four white eggs spotted with reddish brown. Both parents help feed the nestlings, and they defend them with typical flycatcher devotion.

Range: S. E. Alaska to S. W. South Dakota, south in mountains to Honduras; winters from Mexico to Honduras. *Characteristics:* olive-brown head and back, throat and underparts washed with yellow; white eye rings, wing bars.

Buff-breasted Flycatcher
Empidonax fulvifrons

THIS SMALL TYRANT of the southwestern mountains defends his home with cunning as well as wrath. At the approach of a human intruder the male buffbreast, handsome underparts glowing in the sunlight, flies to a decoy tree. He sounds his *chicky-whew* call and scolds insistently as though guarding the nest. Actually the cradle is in another tree perhaps a hundred yards away.

If their newly built nest has been discovered, the pair may destroy it and move to a new site.

Coues' Flycatcher
Contopus pertinax

THE JAY, HAWK, OR SQUIRREL that invades the breeding territory of Coues' flycatcher has a fight on its hands. *Ho-say-ma-re-ah*, cries the enraged male Coues' as he swoops to the attack and drives off the marauder with snapping beak and whirring wings.

"José María," as he is known in the mountains of the Mexican borderlands, protects not only his own home but also the nearby nests of less aggressive small birds. The gray, bushy-headed Coues' breeds at altitudes up to 10,000 feet. The nest of grass and weeds, usually placed high in a conifer, holds three or four white eggs.

Range: central Arizona and W. New Mexico south to Nicaragua; winters to Guatemala. *Characteristics:* bushy crest, gray back and breast, buffy belly; lower mandible is yellow.

113

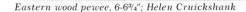

Western wood pewee, length 6-6½"
Allan D. Cruickshank, National Audubon Society

Eastern wood pewee, 6-6¾"; Helen Cruickshank

Eastern Wood Pewee
Contopus virens

AT THE HEIGHT of spring, when the countryside basks in full bloom and fresh green, the eastern wood pewee arrives to send his sweet, plaintive call through the woodlands. In the filtered light amid the large trees the peaceful gray-brown bird is often an unseen singer, a disembodied voice.

But the tranquil whistle—*pee-a-wee peea*—repeated over and over all day long tells us he is there. In the half light of early morning and at twilight the pewee varies his phrases to convert the slow soliloquy into a charming song.

The pewee looks like the eastern phoebe but has noticeable wing bars and does not twitch his tail. His wings, extending halfway down the tail, are longer than those of the phoebe or the Empidonax flycatchers, which the pewee also resembles.

From a high, shaded perch the pewee sallies over clearings, fields, and marshland to feed on flies, beetles, bees, and ants. He may take several in a single dash, returning to the perch with insect-filled beak.

The female usually builds the nest on a dead, lichen-covered limb in an orchard or woodland free of underbrush. She fashions a frame of weed stems and bark shreds, lines it with plant down, and fastens it with spider webs. She sheaths the whole in lichens to look like part of the limb. Her three creamy-white eggs are usually splotched with brown at the larger end. They hatch in about 12 days.

After 16 days the young leave the nest but sit huddled together waiting to be fed, uttering mouselike squeaks. Blue jays sometimes rob the unaggressive pewees of their eggs and young. *Range:* S. Manitoba to Nova Scotia, south to central Texas and central Florida; winters from Costa Rica to N. South America. *Characteristics:* gray-brown back, whitish breast and wing bars; lower mandible is yellow.

114

Western Wood Pewee
Contopus sordidulus

EXCEPT FOR ITS DARKER BREAST and underwing coverts, *sordidulus* matches its eastern counterpart in plumage. But their calls differ. Both sound melancholy, but the westerner's whistled *pee-er* is more nasal, comes out quicker, and lacks the cadence of the eastern wood pewee's longer song. Toward evening the westerner's call grows louder and more frequent, its mournful tones complementing the deepening shades.

Found alike in town and countryside, this wood pewee frequents fruit orchards and shade trees, woodlands bordering streams and lakes, and in the Southwest the more open canyons up to 6,000 feet. An industrious flycatcher, he operates for hours from a lookout perch on a dead branch, seizing enormous numbers of wasps, beetles, flies, and ants. One western pewee was seen making 18 captures in three minutes; the air was warm and many insects were on the wing.

The female builds the nest, often on a dead branch. She lays a bed of fine grass, hair, and, occasionally, bright feathers on a cup of plant fibers and stems. The cradle usually lacks the lichen sheath found around eastern pewee nests. Instead, western pewees camouflage their homes with dead leaves, bits of cocoon, and spider webs. The female incubates her three spotted white eggs for 12 days, while the male guards the territory against jays and other nest robbers.

Range: central Alaska to central Manitoba, south to Central America; winters to N. South America. *Characteristics:* gray-brown back, olive-gray breast and sides, whitish wing bars; lower mandible is yellow.

Oliveside, length 7-8"; Allan Brooks

Beardless Flycatcher
Camptostoma imberbe

THIS GRAY MITE of the Southwest lacks the bristles at the base of the bill which help other flycatchers to capture insects in flight.

Although it sometimes seizes food on the wing, the beardless more often searches the smaller twigs for larvae and scale insects. Sometimes it hops about actively like a warbler; at other times it works slowly like a vireo. It also feeds on berries. The beardless sings a loud, cheerful ditty which helps locate the bird.

In a mistletoe clump or a palmetto it builds a grassy globe with a side entrance. The nest holds two or three brown-speckled white eggs.

Range: S. Arizona and S. Texas, south to N. W. Costa Rica. *Characteristics:* small size, olive-gray back, whitish underparts, light brownish wing bars, indistinct eye ring, small bill.

Beardless, length 4¼"; Allan Brooks

Olive-sided Flycatcher
Nuttallornis borealis

IN THE COOL coniferous forests a loud, whistled *hick, three-bee-er* draws attention to a stout flycatcher surveying his domain from the tip of a tall tree. The large head, olive "vest," and white tufts flanking the lower back instantly identify him as the olive-sided flycatcher.

The solitary sentinel dashes out now and then to snatch a bee or winged ant. If an intruder approaches his nest he sounds a warning *pip pip pip*. His mate may leave the twiggy saucer to help him defend the three white or buff eggs marked with brown.

Range: N. Alaska to Newfoundland, south to Baja California and W. North Carolina; winters in South America. *Characteristics:* dark olive back and sides, whitish throat, yellowish belly, white tufts on sides of rump.

Vermilion Flycatcher
Pyrocephalus rubinus

THE MALE VERMILION, with his fiery crown and breast, is a breathtaking sight in the arid Southwest, rivaling even the brightest springtime flowers. Compared to most of his flycatcher relatives, he looks like a scarlet tanager among a flock of sparrows. *Brasita de fuego* – "little coal of fire" – he's called in Spanish.

His courtship flight before the plainer female is unforgettable. He shoots up from a weed stalk on vibrating wings, crest flaring, glowing breast puffed out. As he mounts in rising circles he sings a cheerful *ching-tink-a-le-tink*. At the apex of his flight – as high as 50 feet – he pours forth his song with redoubled effort. Then he slowly flutters down to claim the brownish-gray form hidden in a leafy bower.

Vermilions nest in sycamore, mesquite, oak, or hackberry – usually near an irrigation ditch or a stream. On a horizontal fork the female builds a flat cup of plant fibers and lines it with down, hair, fur, and feathers. She often decorates the exterior with lichens. The two or three white eggs are gems – creamy white and heavily wreathed at the larger end with brown and lavender. They hatch in about 12 days. Immature birds resemble the adult female.

The vermilion flits nervously from weed stalk to bush to low tree limb, making frequent sallies for flies, beetles, and bees on the wing. It may also alight on the ground to seize a grasshopper and return to the perch to beat the insect against a limb and devour it.

While foraging, vermilions seem indifferent to human intrusion. But near the nest the male upholds the reputation of the tyrant family.

Vermilions exhibit an unusual migration pattern. They wander widely in fall and winter and some migrate as far east as Florida.

Range: S. W. California to S. W. Utah and central Texas, south to Honduras; winters in breeding range and east to Florida. *Characteristics:* male has flaming vermilion crown and underparts, with dark back. Female and young have brownish-gray back, streaked white breast, pink or yellow lower belly.

Male (left) and female vermilions, length 5½-6½"; Eliot Porter

RARE IMMIGRANT # The Rose-throated Becard

Family Cotingidae

ONLY THE EYE-CATCHING throat patch of the male rose-throated becard (*Platyp-saris aglaiae*) hints at the glories of its tropical relatives among the Cotingidae — such beauties as the cock-of-the-rock, the pompadour cotinga, the lovely cotinga, the ornate umbrella bird, and the three-wattled bellbird.

And yet the sight of this dark-capped gray bird, or its brownish mate, is a rare treat in the United States. The country's first becard was taken in the Huachuca Mountains of Arizona in 1888. Nearly a half-century passed before another sighting was reported — near Harlingen, Texas, in 1937. Of the 90 members of this New World family, only the rose-throated becard ventures north of the Mexican border.

Master builders, the becards erect distinctive castles in the air. From slender, drooping branches of sycamore or cottonwood they hang an airy cradle shaped like a teardrop. One found in Arizona measured 29 inches long and 15 inches in diameter at the thick lower end. Six inches from the bottom, an elliptical opening about two by three inches led to a short passage which turned down sharply into the nesting cavity. To build their spacious home the becards loosely weave dried grass, plant stems, long strips of inner bark, and occasionally some long feathers. The male brings some of the nest material and may even take a turn at construction, but the female does most of the work. As they go about their task, they chatter and call to each other with a whistled *seeoo*.

Swinging in the breeze from the very tip of a branch as high as 60 feet above ground, and with the entrance hole well down from the limb, the lofty becard mansion is well-nigh inaccessible to tree-climbing predators. Becards may return to the same nest site year after year. Sometimes they rip into the old structures for nest material; at other times they build completely anew.

The nest holds four to six white or creamy eggs with brown or purple streaks and spots. After the female incubates the eggs about 18 days, the male joins in feeding the nestlings. The parents may sound their call repeatedly but do not defend their territory aggressively against jays.

Becards tend to keep hidden in the thick foliage of tall trees. Like the flycatchers, these thick-billed, large-headed birds perch quietly until they spot an insect, then dart out to capture it in the air. They also glean twigs and leaves, and vary their diet with fruit. *Range:* S. Arizona and S. Texas to Costa Rica. *Characteristics:* male has black cap and cheeks, gray back, pale underparts, rose throat. Female has dark cap, brownish back, buffy collar and underparts.

Male (left) and female
rosethroats, length 6½"
Walter A. Weber
National Geographic
staff artist

117

BLITHE SPIRITS OF THE COUNTRYSIDE # The Larks

Family Alaudidae

U P FROM the greening field he whirls, a small brown bird singing a song of gold. In undulating spirals that show now dark-streaked wings and now white-trimmed tail, he bores high into the azure sky. And still his song continues: a high, clear, driving river of runs and rills that floods the day with joy. This master of song is the skylark (*Alauda arvensis*), a native of Eurasia and northern Africa, the "blithe spirit" of Percy Bysshe Shelley's immortal ode.

The skylark's American admirers have often tried to transplant him. In the 1880's they almost succeeded in establishing a colony in Brooklyn. A group of the imported birds survived and bred, but only briefly. Today no skylark sings in Flatbush. The only ones in all North America dwell on Canada's Vancouver Island.

Yet a lark can be heard on the mainland. The horned lark (*Eremophila alpestris*) is the only native American of the family's 75 species (meadowlarks are in a different family). The horned lark's song does not match the skylark's, but the irregular notes make tinkling music.

Twenty-one subspecies of horned lark range from Mexican deserts to Alaskan tundra. Most have the same general appearance: brown with light underparts, black head stripes and chest shield. The "horns," sometimes hard to see, are tufts behind each ear. Though duller, females and young resemble the males.

Besides their dull garb and bright music, horned larks share a number of other

SKYLARK, *famed Old World songster, sings in North America only on Vancouver Island.*
Length 7-7½", Eric Hosking

characteristics with the Eurasian and African members of the family. They hunt their food of weed seeds and insects on the ground, walking or running, never hopping. The hind toenails of these terrestrial birds grow out straight and extra long. Larks generally tend to flock. Most races migrate.

The male horned lark goes all out at courtship season. The appearance of a rival means a short strutting contest, then a thrashing battle, usually a few feet above the ground. To the victor belongs the female, and he treats her to an aerial display. He climbs high to sing threats and promises, then dives almost into the ground before leveling off and landing. Finally he marches around her with his small crest puffed, tail spread, and wings adroop.

Like the skylark, the horned lark seems to avoid trees and bushes. He inhabits pastures, plains, and flats, from ocean beaches to tablelands above timberline. Breeding pairs prefer patches of completely bare earth. Plowing, lumbering, even soil erosion work to their advantage. The female lays three to five spotted gray eggs in a grass-lined depression. She guards her young tenderly. If an intruder draws near, as Audubon noted in 1833, "she flutters away, feigning lameness so cunningly, that none but one accustomed to the sight can refrain from pursuing her."

Skylark—*Range:* Vancouver Island. *Characteristics:* small, rounded crest, strongly streaked brown back and wings, buff-white underparts; tail with conspicuous white border feathers; high-pitched, liquid, long-sustained song.

Horned Lark—*Range:* Alaska and Canada's Arctic coast south to S. Mexico and N. Georgia. *Characteristics:* black "horns," black head and chest stripes, brown back, light underparts, blackish tail edged with white; may have yellow throat.

HORNED LARK, *named for its head tufts, is heard over most of North America.* 119
Male, length 7-8"; Eliot Porter

LIKE BEADS ON STRINGS, *bank swallows*
assemble on northern power lines for their
autumn migration to South America. Sociable birds,
swallows nonetheless like a little privacy—
hence the spacing between most individuals.
Cliff swallows (inset) shuffle and flutter in puddles,
filling bills with mud balls for nest building.

STREAMLINED HARBINGERS OF SPRING

The Swallows

Family Hirundinidae

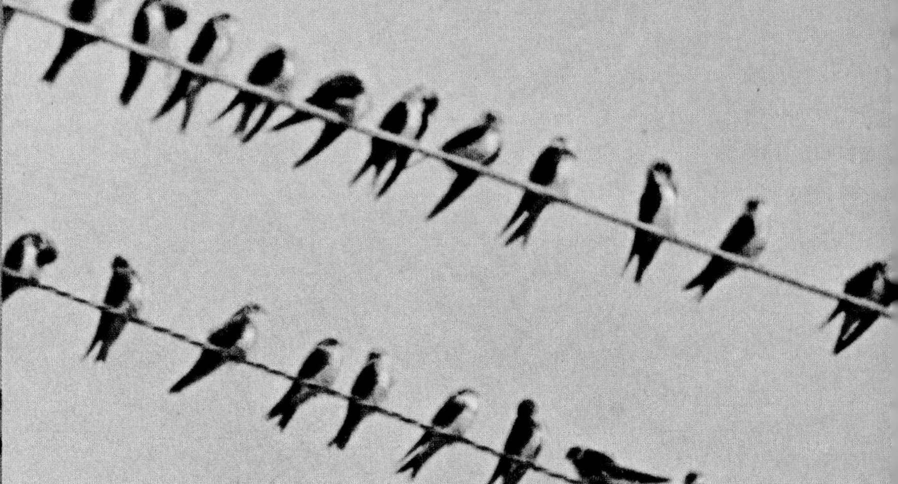

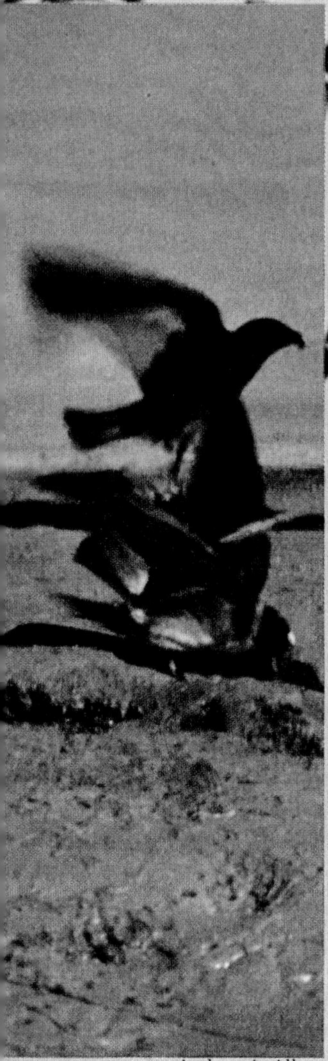

Arthur A. Allen

By PHILIP S. HUMPHREY

Everywhere I have gone in the New World, I have seen swallows perched on power and communication lines. Wherever man has settled, building homes and stringing wires, the swallows have gone too. One wonders what they did before there were barns and martin houses and the irresistible wires.

Still, the ultimate limitation for most swallows is aerial insect food, not wire. Graceful fliers with slender bodies and saber wings, they spend much of their time darting in pursuit of mosquitoes, flies, wasps, beetles, and other insects. This probably accounts for the absence of swallows in the Antarctic and the relatively insect-free areas of the Arctic. Otherwise, they are found the world over except on a few oceanic islands. In the western hemisphere 8 of the 75 species in the family occur regularly north of Mexico.

Our North American swallows are migratory, wintering from the southern United States to Central and South America. In late summer and early fall hundreds of these sociable birds space themselves evenly along the wires in great premigration flocks. Most don't re-

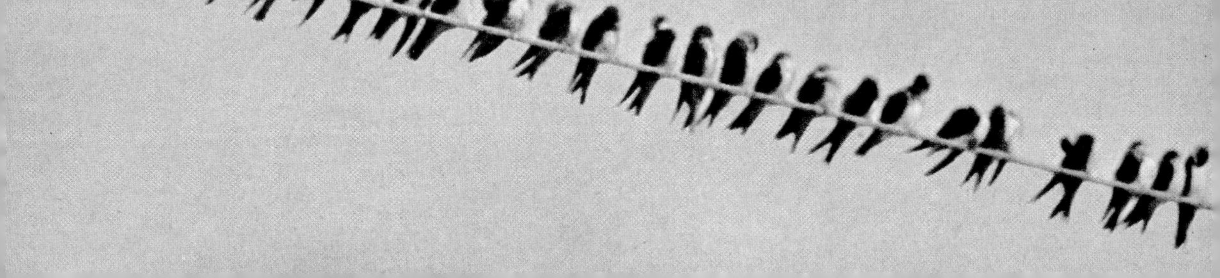

turn until late April, when the hard edge is off winter. Swallows are popularly thought to be quite precise in their homecoming dates. Actually, it all seems to depend on the weather. If swallows are harbingers of anything, it is the first warm spell and the accompanying hatches of flying insects.

Arrival of swallows, however, is by no means proof that spring is here. A sudden cold snap, during which most of the insects die or go back into hiding, can be disastrous to the newly returned swallows. Cliff swallows may die of starvation and exposure by the hundreds. Other species huddle in cavities or behind shutters, where many of them succumb to the cold. The tree swallow, not as susceptible to shortages of insect food, survives on bayberries and sedge seeds. In fact, some have been seen plucking seeds from the snow. Perhaps this is why they are the earliest swallows to return north in the spring.

I spent one of my most memorable spring mornings watching swallows at a lake outside New Haven, Connecticut. It was light, though the sun had not yet peeped over the treetops, and wisps of mist blurred the mirror surface of the water. At the far end of the lake stood packed regiments of cattails.

Suddenly the whole scene came to life as the mist was cut by dozens and now hundreds of swallows, dipping and wheeling, rising and falling. They swept in graceful arcs close to the surface, sometimes dimpling it for a drink and quartering back and forth in disorder as they searched for food. I tracked them eagerly with my binoculars—here a tree swallow, there a rough-winged or bank or barn swallow. In the cattail marsh hundreds more perched on bending stalks.

These aerialists, hardly capable of walking, are poor songsters, given only to brief notes in flight or soft twittering at the nest. Neither are they colorful in their sooty blues and browns. More striking is the South American white-winged swallow, with its glossy green back and white wing patches. I saw it for the first time at Iguazú Falls on the Argentine-Brazilian border, swooping so low over the obsidian waters that it looked as though it were being pulled into the roaring cataract.

THE NESTING HABITS of swallows have long fascinated me. The closely related tree and violet-green swallows will share a martin house along with bluebirds and others but will not tolerate the presence of a purple martin. Curiously, the larger — and one would think more powerful—purple martin has more bluff than spunk and turns tail when challenged by a tree swallow.

I used to think that martins, tree swallows, and violet-green swallows were the only North American species which could be attracted to specially built nests. Then I learned that a man-made plaster mold coated with mud successfully lured cliff swallows. Characteristically, they added some mud of their own to make it seem like home. Ordinarily these industrious birds gather hundreds of mud pellets to build their unique bulb-shaped nests.

As a boy in rural Connecticut I learned firsthand about barn swallows. Every morning I would put on rubber boots and get to work with shovel and hose in a cow barn. I remember watching the birds at their squat mud nests plastered to the tops of whitewashed beams. Sometimes two or three swallows were in the air at once, shuttling back and forth from outdoors with food for their ravenous offspring. The ugly hatchlings, sparsely covered with down, had to be fed as often as once every minute. But they grew rapidly, and in about three weeks I was amazed at their remarkable transition—from helpless, almost naked little creatures to fully feathered birds ready for their first adventure in the air.

A FILIGREE *of cliff swallow nests clings to California's Carmel Mission.*
Warming weather determines when swallows return to their homes.

B. Anthony Stewart, National Geographic photographer

Barn swallow, length 5¾-7¾"; Frederick Kent Truslow

Barn Swallow
Hirundo rustica

A SOFT AND JOYFUL TWITTERING—*kvik kvik, wit wit*—breaks the peace of deep summer. The sleek singers flash gracefully across the sky, in and out of the barn, or circle to snap at insects stirred up by cattle or the farmer's plow. The delightful *rustica* is at his work.

The brilliant flyer with his deeply forked tail and dark blue back has been welcomed in the countryside ever since the colonists discovered that he was nearly identical to the beloved swallow they had left behind in the Old World. Thomas Pennant, an 18th century naturalist, wrote that some swallows returned to ancestral nesting sites in caves and cliff crevices. "Others, since the arrival of the Europeans, affect the haunts of mankind," he observed, "and make their nests in barns, stables, and out-houses; in some parts they are, on that account, called Barn Swallows." The name has stuck.

The westward spread of farming helped the bird extend its range. With their wide doors always left open, the lofty haymows of old-fashioned barns offered ideal homes. The swallows find it ever more difficult to homestead in today's tightly closed farm structures. Garages are acceptable substitutes in many areas.

In the spring barn swallows leave South America on a journey that takes some of them to northern Alaska. Some may forage on ocean beaches, catching flies at high-water mark.

Skillfully they skim over open country for winged insects, sometimes deftly picking their prey from the grass tops. At moonrise they join bats hawking for mosquitoes. But when a long, cold rain drives insects to cover, barn swallows face death from hunger and cold.

Season after season the swallows return to the same nest site. Courting begins as the birds interlock bills and preen each other's plumage.

Preparing a home, they may choose to repair old nests rather than build new ones. In either case they need a supply of mud and straw. From the edge of farm ponds or barnyard puddles the birds gather beakfuls of mud, rolling it to form pellets. Using bills as trowels, both sexes tamp the pellets into place. They build up the cup with alternate layers of mud and straw. The nest usually rests on a beam, but the birds sometimes plaster it against the side of a wall. They line it with feathers and animal hair.

The male shares the 15-day incubation of the four or five white eggs marked with reddish brown. Sometimes fly larvae fatally pierce the skin of the nestlings. Sometimes nestlings get tangled in the nest lining and strangle. If the youngsters survive three weeks, parents entice them from the nursery by flying back and forth beyond reach with food in their bills. While the father trains the fledglings to forage, his mate lays another set of eggs. Juveniles of the first brood may help feed the later nestlings.

As summer wanes, families form flocks that twitter and preen on telephone lines. For a few weeks they roost in fresh- and saltwater marshes before starting the long journey south.

Range: N. Alaska to Newfoundland, south to central Mexico; winters from Panama to S. South America. *Characteristics:* blue-black back, buffy underparts, deeply forked tail with white spots. Female and young are duller.

Cave Swallow
Petrochelidon fulva

SCATTERED IN DEEP CAVES from Carlsbad Caverns National Park, New Mexico, to south Texas, these rare migrants raise their young in air-conditioned comfort during the hottest months of the year. Summer's end sends them south to wintering grounds as yet unknown to science.

From mud pellets collected beside a spring or a desert stream, the swallows mold their cup-shaped nests to niches in caves. Each year they enlarge old nests until the added weight brings them crashing to the floor.

Indolent members of the colony often try to steal finished homes from the builders. The owners resist furiously in aerial grapples and nearly always win. Eventually each female lays two to five white eggs with purplish mottling.

Pale cheeks and throat and a chestnut forehead distinguish the cave dwellers from the similar cliff swallow. The two species sometimes nest side by side in adobe buildings in Mexico.

Range: S. E. New Mexico and south central Texas to S. Mexico and West Indies. *Characteristics:* chestnut forehead, buffy throat, underparts, and rump; white-streaked back, square tail.

Cave swallow, length 5-6"; James K. Baker

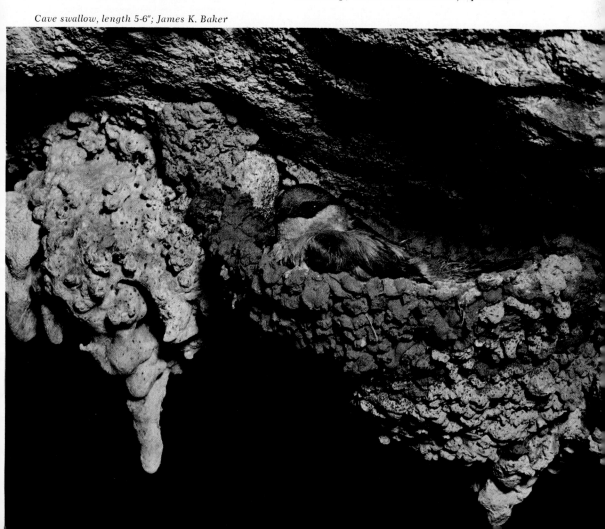

Cliff Swallow
Petrochelidon pyrrhonota

EACH SPRING colonies of master masons come winging up from deep in South America. After thousands of miles of arduous travel, they seek homesites. Their wants are simple – damp clay and an overhanging bluff or sheltered eave to keep the rain away. They'll settle for the walls of a remote mountain gorge, an isolated barn, a city house, or a tall office building.

At the chosen location the male cliff swallow stakes a nesting claim and drives off hovering neighbors. Then the female alights, and the pair begin building their bottle-shaped nest with the entrance at the neck. Wings aloft and feet barely touching the ground, the birds form a ring around a puddle. As pioneer ornithologist Elliott Coues observed, each rolls a gob of mud in its mouth and sticks "the pellet against the wall, as carefull as ever a sailor, about to spin a yarn, deposited his chew on the mantelpiece."

Clusters of nurseries grow out from vertical bases. Bickering swallows steal mud from one another's nests, and birds that fail to breed form roving gangs that harass other members of a colony, even taking adobes by force. But house sparrows are the most inveterate nest thieves. Sandy soil also impedes home building; pellets crumble and nests come crashing down.

The cliff swallow's building techniques have won it such nicknames as eave swallow, jug swallow, pipe swallow, and mud dauber. Audubon called it the Republican swallow, "in allusion to the mode in which individuals associate." Some colonies have numbered thousands of birds. One Wisconsin farmer, who had carefully kept the house sparrows away, counted 2,015 cliff swallow nests on his barn.

Before a pair builds the roof on a new nest, the female lays four or five brown-spotted white eggs. A colony often raises its young in the same nests year after year until these decay and fall apart.

Cliff swallows carry on their intensely social habits in all they do. They preen together at dawn assemblies amid squeaking and guttural gratings. They wheel and crisscross in flocks, hawking flying beetles and other insects. They glide in long, elliptical patterns, following each glide with a steep climb like a roller coaster. They perch by the hundreds on telephone wires.

In August and September, before cold weather drives away their insect food, the cliff swallows start south, following one of the longest migration routes of American land birds. *Range:* central Alaska to S. Quebec, south to central Mexico; winters from S. Brazil to central Chile and Argentina. *Characteristics:* pale forehead and rump, black crown, dark brown throat and cheeks, streaked back, square tail.

Cliff swallow, length 5-6"; Frederick Kent Truslow

Violet-green Swallow
Tachycineta thalassina

SWIFT AND GRACEFUL, this exquisite bird skims western fields and canyon streams, hunting leaf bugs, flying ants, and beetles. On clear, warm days when the insects fly high, it circles at great heights. Flocks at rest perch in long rows on telephone wires or sun themselves in the treetops. Glossy green and violet hues blend in the birds' backs, contrasting sharply with the snow-white of breast and rump.

The violet-green swallow's ordinary call is a thin *chip* or *chit chit*. In the predawn hours during the courtship season the call becomes quicker, shriller, more excited.

Through much of its range this dainty swallow

makes its home in the wilderness, settling into a woodpecker hole or cliff crevice. But it also nests readily in bird boxes and under house eaves. Unafraid of man, it has been known to snatch feathers from a bird lover's fingers, using them to line its twiggy bedstead. The white eggs usually number four or five.

Sensitive to weather, these swallows are often decimated by cold spells in spring and fall.

Range: central Alaska to S. W. Alberta, south to central Mexico; winters to Central America. *Characteristics:* glossy green and purple above, pure white below; two white rump patches.

Tree Swallow
Iridoprocne bicolor

THE GREAT HOST darkens the sky. Thousands upon thousands of white-breasted, dark-backed birds twist this way and that, like a living cloud tossed by gusty winds. The autumn flocking of tree swallows is a sight to behold.

Delta-shaped wings flutter as the birds dive and climb and veer together. They alight on telephone lines and fences and cover them for miles. Or the vast concourse sweeps down on a beach until the sand seems black. They feed in coastal marshes and roost on swaying reed stalks.

The hardy tree swallow is one of the last migrants to leave the northern breeding grounds. He is also one of the first to arrive in spring, sometimes finding sustenance in seeds pecked from frozen ponds. By June mated pairs have moved into tree cavities and bird boxes as far north as northern Alaska. The birds favor a homesite in an open field near water.

On a base of dried grass they pile a lining of feathers, often arranging them artfully to curl over the clutch of four to six white eggs. The brown backs of the youngsters resemble the plumage of the bank and rough-winged swallows.

One of the earliest of the morning singers, the tree swallow utters a sweet, liquid twitter, a rapid variation of *weet trit weet.*

This swift forager crisscrosses wet meadows and ponds to snatch flying insects on the wing. It eats more vegetable food than other swallows, and a diet of bayberries and other fruits enables some individuals to winter as far north as Long Island and Cape Cod.

Range: N. Alaska and Canada to Virginia and California; winters S. United States to Central America. *Characteristics:* pure white underparts, blue- or green-black back.

Violet-green swallow, length 5-5½"; Allan Brooks
Right: tree swallow, length 5-6¼"
Allan D. Cruickshank, National Audubon Society

Bank swallows' breeding colony and (inset) a nestling; Allan D. Cruickshank, National Audubon Society

Bank Swallow
Riparia riparia

MANY SWALLOWS switch easily from natural cavities to man-made shelters. But *riparia*, "the dweller in stream banks," sticks to his primitive nesting habits. He burrows his hole in a river border, a gravel pit, or a sandy bluff often fronting a lake, a bay, or the ocean.

In spring migration, colonies of up to several hundred bank swallows search the coast northward for good sites; many follow rivers inland. When space is tight, contending birds peck fiercely at each other for a favored spot. Then they begin excavating, often less than a foot apart. They loosen earth with bill and claws, whipping it back with vigorous kicks and wingbeating. As the work proceeds, others circle above, twittering with harsh, reedy sounds. A finished burrow measures up to four feet long and often slopes up at the inside end. This keeps rainwater from running into the nest. Both sexes brood four or five white eggs on a bed of feathers and grass.

Bank swallows get along well with kingfishers, which also tunnel out nests. The swallows often build in the same banks with the rattling, crested fishermen and even, on occasion, use the kingfishers' tunnels to get to their own nests.

But their enemies are legion. Along western streams badgers dig out the nestlings. Crows seize them before they learn to fly. And one observer found a Minnesota roadway black with bank swallows slaughtered by fast-moving automobiles. He estimated the toll at 1,000 birds.

This cosmopolitan species breeds throughout the northern hemisphere. Its unsteady, butterfly-like flight reveals a brown back and clear white belly. When perched, it clearly shows the dark chest band that distinguishes it from the slightly larger rough-winged swallow.

Coursing above a stream, the bank swallow devours mayflies and midges as they emerge from the aquatic stage. The bird also eats flies and beetles and dragonflies. Like other swallows, *riparia* flocks to coastal and inland marshes before heading south in late summer.

Range: Alaska to Quebec, south to California, Alabama, and Virginia; winters in central South America. *Characteristics:* brown back, white throat, dark chest band.

Roughwing, length 5-5¾"; Arthur A. Allen

Rough-winged Swallow
Stelgidopteryx ruficollis

THIS NONCONFORMING MEMBER of the gregarious swallow family usually prefers to breed in solitary pairs rather than in a colony.

But the roughwing is not particular about its dwelling place and provides an excellent example of a species that readily adapts to any kind of cavity. Usually it tunnels into steep banks of clay, sand, or gravel; the burrow's entrance is often larger than the holes made by bank swallows and not as neat. Roughwings also build in masonry holes, drainpipes, crannies under bridges and culverts, and in the abandoned tunnels of kingfishers and ground squirrels. Home can be anywhere from Canada to Argentina.

A sober-looking bird of brown and gray, the male roughwing impresses prospective mates by spreading the white feathers under his tail coverts during courtship flights. The female usually incubates the six or seven, rarely eight, white eggs in a nest of grass and rootlets. Spring tides and freshets sometimes flood the burrows made in riverbanks, destroying eggs and young.

The roughwing does not zigzag erratically as the barn swallow does while snatching insects. It glides and sails more and courses more directly. The roughwing also sounds a rougher note, a rasping *trit trit*.

Range: S. Canada to Argentina; winters from S. United States southward. *Characteristics:* brown back, dusky throat.

Bank swallow, length 4¾-5½"
Arthur A. Allen

Purple Martin
Progne subis

EVERY YEAR the same scene takes place in countless towns and villages across the nation. Pleased citizens look skyward and the warmth of springtime is in their voices as they exclaim, "The swallows are back!"

Wheeling overhead, alternating rapid wingbeats with periods of sailing, is a throng of purple martins, largest of our swallows. Glossy blue-black both above and below, these are males. They usually arrive a few days before the females, which are gray on forehead and underparts. Their pleasant twittering fills the air as they hunt the flies, wasps, and other insects which comprise their entire diet. Some descend to eat ants on the ground, then rise again, beautifully proportioned birds lifting on sable wings.

Purple martins breed in colonies. When the country was wilderness, they nested in natural cavities in trees and cliffs. A few western martins still prefer old woodpecker holes in tall pines, but elsewhere most have long since given up such shelters for those provided by man.

In colonial days Choctaw and Chickasaw Indians used to attract martins to their villages by hanging up hollowed-out gourds and calabashes for the birds to nest in. They welcomed these birds because the martins fearlessly drove hawks and crows away from crops and chickens.

The custom spread to southern plantations, and before long people everywhere were erecting all kinds of martin houses in their backyards. The birds are not fussy. They'll accept structures with accommodations for one pair or twenty. Dealers offer models of varying size attractive to the birds, with instructions for location and suggestions for annual care.

Many towns are proud of their martins and put up boxes for them in their parks or even in business areas. Martins have been nesting in boxes in Greencastle, Pennsylvania, since 1840, except for one mysterious gap of 15 years after the Civil War, when they did not return.

The earliest martins reach the United States in January; the last stragglers appear in April. When a colony needs a new house, male scouts reconnoiter the countryside for suitable accommodations. A structure out in the open, about 20 feet from the ground, seems ideal to martin tastes.

The first claimants in any martin house, old or new, are the males who battle fiercely for compartments. Successful squatters fly in wide arcs, then dive to the property, which they enter and re-enter, chattering all the while.

When females arrive to join the flock they choose the most pleasing combinations of suitor and apartment. Aggressive couples try to grab and hold all the real estate they can. Their supremacy may be brief. Often late arrivals take over, throw out the earlier tenants, and monopolize the choicest compartments.

When housing disputes have been resolved, the colony settles down to a month or more of sporadic nest building. Both sexes drag in piles of grass, leaves, crawfish claws, rags – anything that will serve. The materials vary with the locality. The female lays four or five white eggs and incubates them for two weeks. A rim of dirt in front of the nest keeps them from rolling out.

Both parents feed and care for the young birds, which eat prodigious numbers of insects – flies, mosquitoes, wasps, bugs, beetles, even dragonflies. In one house occupied by nine families, some parent bird was observed returning on an average of once every 30 seconds during daylight hours with food for hungry mouths. The adult martins periodically bring in green leaves as fresh nesting material.

Purple martins must cope with danger in several forms. Cold spring rains clear the air of insects, and whole colonies starve. Excessive heat kills nestlings. The swallows fiercely repel crows and other large birds, but starlings and house sparrows often usurp the martins' nests.

IN AUGUST AND SEPTEMBER, after the young are on the wing, martins abandon their boxes. Ranging the countryside during the day, they gather in large flocks to roost at night, often in trees right in the center of a city. Martins for miles around Washington, D. C., gather into larger and larger flocks as sunset approaches and head for the community roost. The location varies from year to year. By the end of August 40,000 or 50,000 martins may be circling over downtown Washington. Elsewhere in the country concentrations of up to 100,000 martins have been noted, their voices blending in a roar like escaping steam. Sometimes tree branches snap under the weight of roosting martins.

Migrating at a leisurely rate, purple martins start south in September for their winter home in South America. When they head north again in January, many birds make for the very same houses they nested in the year before.

A related species, the Cuban martin (*Progne cryptoleuca*), comes occasionally to Florida. The male is also blue-black, and the female has a brown throat and brown sides.

The gray-breasted martin (*Progne chalybea*) of tropical America wanders to southern Texas. Both sexes resemble the female purple martin, but they are smaller and have dark foreheads.

Range: S. British Columbia to Prince Edward Island, south to Baja California and S. Florida; winters in South America. *Characteristics:* male is uniformly blue-black; female has gray throat, belly, and forehead.

HANGING GOURDS *lure martins to an Alabama garden; nesters drive off crows.*
Male (foreground) and female purple martins, length 7¼-8½"
Walter A. Weber, National Geographic staff artist

Jays, Magpies, and Crows

Family Corvidae

By OLIN SEWALL PETTINGILL, JR.

To ME AS A YOUNGSTER in the farming country of inland Maine, the blue jay was a spirited companion of the long winter—a welcome call from the silent woods and a flash of azure across the snow-banked dooryard. The common crow was a harbinger of spring. Its *caw caw caw*, heard long before the carol of the first robin, heralded the softening March days. Possibly the liking for jays and crows in my youth has influenced my regard for them as an ornithologist. Even though some raid cornfields and the nests of songbirds, I am among their staunchest champions.

The family Corvidae also includes the ravens of the sea cliffs and mountain crags, the magpies of the western plains and intermountain valleys, and Clark's nutcracker in the coniferous forests of the high western mountains. Of the 100 species of Corvidae in the world, 15 are found in North America north of Mexico.

Jays monopolize the bright colors in the family, being especially prone to blues. With one exception they are *always* colorful regardless of season, sex, and age. The exception is the fluffy-feathered gray jay of the cool evergreen forests. Its attire is a conservative gray, black, and white. As in other jays, the male and female look identical, but young gray jays are surprisingly different—a fact driven home to me one day years ago on

"GHASTLY GRIM AND ANCIENT RAVEN" —
Poe's words connote no ordinary bird.
Large and powerful, with wings
spanning more than four feet,
Corvus corax can kill a young deer or lamb.
Mainly it feeds on smaller prey and
picks the bones of carrion clean. Like all corvids,
the hardy raven possesses large feet for
perching, grasping, running, and hopping.

Robert C. Hermes, National Audubon Society

the west side of Hudson Bay. There among dense spruces I saw two uniformly slate-colored forms sitting quietly and looking for all the world like catbirds. Catbirds in the north country? Fortunately I was saved from recording this familiar species far north of its range when a gray jay suddenly appeared and proceeded to stuff my "catbirds" with food.

Corvids eat practically anything, thanks to their all-purpose bills. Stout, sharp-pointed, almost as tough as steel, they can be used to hammer, crush, crack, probe, split, and tear. If a man could invent a tool as simple and powerful, he would make a fortune. No acorn is too hard for a corvid bill to crack.

I have watched a blue jay working on an especially stubborn acorn, first holding it down with a foot and pounding it without success, then wedging it in a log where it could be given a more effective blow. And I remember observing a flock of Clark's nutcrackers, in the foothills of the Grand Tetons in Wyoming, extracting nuts from the cones of ponderosa pines. Cleverly each bird worked – sometimes upside down – inserting its bill under the tightly pressed "shingles" and pulling out the nuts, which were at once crushed between the mandibles, shelled, and swallowed.

All corvids are courageous and aggressive. Woe unto any squirrel or other four-legged tree climber intruding upon a jay's nesting territory. He is immediately threatened with earsplitting screams and painful thrusts from sharp beaks. Except in the nesting season, corvids band together and take a special delight in mobbing would-be predators. Time and again their raucous harassment has called my attention to an owl or hawk that I might easily have overlooked. Sometimes, too, I have been tricked by corvids. Thinking that they were raiding something worth seeing, I have investigated only to find nothing whatever. What was all the fuss about? Were they just being noisy for the fun of hearing themselves?

The flight of corvids is strong but unspectacular. More important to survival are their keen eyesight and their ability to perceive and escape danger. Though crows frequently feed on road kills, they seem to sense when to take off before oncoming traffic and never risk the "one more mouthful" that could be fatal. Rarely is a crow hit by a car.

Good fliers that they are, corvids are nonetheless sedentary, inclined to stay put. Common ravens are seen in the Far North throughout the white, frigid months, sometimes the only dark spots visible for miles around. White-necked ravens endure the blistering summer heat of the arid Southwest. Clark's nutcrackers remain in their mountain forests through the dead of winter, rarely moving to the sheltered valleys a few miles below. Black-billed magpies ride out prairie blizzards. Jays are no less hardy. My wife and I once arrived in the Chisos Mountains of Big Bend National Park, Texas, after an unprecedented snowfall. About our cabin a flock of Mexican jays busily dislodged snow from cactus and century plants as they searched for seeds and fruits. We scattered the crumbled remains of our lunch on the porch, and in minutes they were about our feet, snatching up the bits.

M UCH HAS BEEN SAID about corvid intelligence. I gained some insight into the family's mental capacities when I raised four blue jays, starting on their 15th day, just before they were ready to leave the nest. I kept them in a large wire cage. The first dish of water I gave them elicited no attention – even when they stepped in it. But on the 20th day one youngster inadvertently hopped in and, touching the water with its tongue, drank for the first time! The others followed. Five days later they were bathing. After that the young jays showed increasing curiosity. They

STRONG ENOUGH TO PERCH, *this young black-billed magpie can't fly yet. Age will strengthen his wings and blacken his bill.* 135

Allan D. Cruickshank, National Audubon Society

tasted a lemon peel, dropped it, and never touched it again. They carried about bottle caps, cork stoppers, and buttons—or stood on them and whacked them with their beaks as though attempting to break them open. Often they merely pecked at the wire of the cage, ran the edge of the floor paper through their beaks, or nibbled at their toes, just to play, just to be doing something.

Crows and ravens are known to be more intelligent than jays. A pet common raven belonging to Bowdoin College students was taught to pick pockets. I shall never forget that black monster suddenly alighting on my shoulder and poking its bill into the pocket of my jacket. It pulled out a pencil, tested it between the mandibles—for edibility, I suppose—then flung it scornfully to the ground.

Of all the peculiarities of corvids, none is more outstanding than their adjustment

CURIOUS, ADAPTABLE, INTELLIGENT, *corvids make themselves at home around the haunts of man. The tame crow (right) learned to rouse his master and even call his name. The pet headed straight for the refrigerator when hungry. A relative, a Tibetan raven (left) begged handouts—at 21,000 feet!—from the 1963 American Mount Everest Expedition. Jays mix fun with thievery. The blue jay perched on the camera later snatched a shiny quarter off the ground and whisked it away. The blue jay foundling (below) shares a girl's sympathy with a young robin.*

Robert F. Sisson and (left) W. Robert Moore and (upper left) Barry C. Bishop, all National Geographic staff

Alice Martin

to civilization. Blue jays are as common around my parents' home in suburban Boston as they are in Sapsucker Woods, 175-acre sanctuary at Cornell's Laboratory of Ornithology in upstate New York, where the habitat is ideal. Gray jays actually thrive on man's invasion of their wilderness, pilfering anything digestible from his campsites and earning such names as "camp robbers" and "meat birds."

Other jays have the same habit. While my wife and I lunched one spring in Bentsen-Rio Grande Valley State Park, Texas, green jays in trees overhead waited hopefully for leftover morsels. And those Steller's jays where we camped in Yellowstone National Park! It was September, after the exodus of tourists, and we were the sole occupants of a big campground. Eyeing us were a score or more of these cocky, crested, deep-blue birds, anxious for any handout. We were the last resort.

The ingenuity of corvids in obtaining food explains why they still flourish. In Maine we used to put up a scarecrow as soon as we planted the garden. The ragged coat, frayed overalls, and old hat all draped on a post—to me that scarecrow flapping in the breeze was a frightful thing. But not to the crows. They were in the garden the next morning. I suspect the scarecrow indicated the presence of food as much as the freshly tilled soil did. The benefits from corvids as destroyers of weed seeds and obnoxious insects, however, far outweigh their harm as depredators.

Jays, magpies, crows. They are to be lived with, understood, appreciated. What our American outdoors would be like without their vitality I cannot imagine!

Blue Jay
Cyanocitta cristata

"THAT NOISY COXCOMB, in his gay light blue coat and white underclothes." Thus Washington Irving dismisses the blue jay in his *Sketch Book*. But 19th century ornithologist Charles Bendire found more: "Cunning, inquisitive, an admirable mimic, full of mischief; in some localities extremely shy, in others exactly the reverse, it is difficult to paint him in his true colors."

Most people don't try. They just look at and listen to this handsomely crested, healthy-looking bird—one of the most easily recognized and best known in eastern North America. Here it lends a flash of bright color to a barren, snow-laden thicket when all the land seems asleep. There it rends the air with joyous shouts, domineering at the feeding tray. Originally a bird of the wild woods, the blue jay has adapted itself to settlements of man.

One of the bird's outstanding characteristics is its noisiness. It shrieks singly and in chorus. It screams at hawks, cats, and snakes, or merely for the pleasure of making a din.

The blue jay displays its wide vocal repertoire most often in autumn, when other birds are quiet. Head bobbing up and down, *cristata* graces a soft Indian summer day with a bell-like *tull-ull* call. Roving companies keep in touch with soft conversational chatter. Well known for its mimicry, the species is particularly adept at imitating the harsh screams of several hawks. In the concealment of a dense conifer, the blue jay delivers its whisper song: a barely audible but exquisite medley of sweet, lisping notes resembling those of such small birds as the chickadee, wood pewee, and winter wren.

Most familiar of all is the petulant shriek of *jay jay jay*. Henry Thoreau remarked on the "unrelenting steel-cold scream of a jay, unmelted, that never flows into a song, a sort of wintry trumpet, screaming cold; hard, tense, frozen music, like the winter sky itself."

Curiosity aroused, a blue jay may silently follow a man through the woods. At other times its raucous shouts warn all animals of potential danger; this bird is the bane of deer and squirrel hunters.

Nothing arouses the ire of a jay more than the discovery of a roosting owl. Bluff and bluster reign as an azure clan rallies to hector its enemy. Their high, pointed crests shooting upward, the jays drive the owl from tree to tree. Bird watchers following the angry mob are sometimes rewarded: The jays may flush a rare bird.

Blue jays become silent and furtive during the nesting season. After a courtship in which the male ceremoniously feeds his mate while they exchange low whistles, the pair collect twigs.

They haul these around until a suitable nest site is found. In the South they say, "the jaybird carries sticks to the devil."

In a coniferous tree or thicket both birds fashion a platform of twigs, bark, grass, and paper. Sometimes they forcibly appropriate robin nests, remodeling them under the eyes of the wrathful owners. A bed of fine rootlets, sometimes laid on a base of mud, cups four to six eggs, olive or buff and marked with brown spots. The male hops silently up the tree along an invisible "spiral staircase," bringing morsels to his brooding mate and later to the young. The pair defend their nest vigorously and may peck at encroaching humans. The offspring hatch in about 17 days; they are ready to leave the nest 17 to 21 days later.

BLUE JAYS PREFER to forage in mixed woodlands with nut-bearing trees such as oaks and beeches. They depended heavily on the American chestnut for food before a blight wiped this noble tree from eastern forests. These birds eat three times as much vegetable as animal matter and store acorns and other nuts for winter use. They often bury their provender and, with gray squirrels, are responsible for white oak reforestation in some regions. In Florida the blue jay feeds extensively on palmetto seeds.

During warm weather *cristata* samples spiders, snails, salamanders, and tree frogs. It eats many insects and is one of the few avian predators on hairy caterpillars; it even rips open cocoons to get at the pupae. And it preys on mice at every opportunity.

Blue jays have a somewhat tarnished reputation as devourers of the eggs and young of songbirds. Occasionally, the jays also attack and kill birds as large as hairy woodpeckers. However, the damage is usually insignificant; jays do not menace the survival of any species.

The blue jay is not always the aggressor. From the protection of thick woods it can afford to taunt dangerous enemies like the sharp-shinned hawk. But in the open the predators waylay the slow-flying jays. Scattered clusters of feathers here and there testify to a jay's capture. Sometimes these feathers appear later in the nesting material used by birds whose eggs and young the blue jay has been known to eat.

Noisy family groups explore the woods as summer wanes. They troop from one grove to another, crossing open areas a few at a time. A group may travel miles in quest of a more ample supply of beechnuts and acorns. Some blue jays remain in the north through the winter, but many spend the colder months in the south.

Range: S. Canada to Gulf states, east of Rockies. *Characteristics:* wings and tail bright blue with white spots; paler blue crest, black neckband, pale gray underparts.

Blue jay, length 11-12½"; John H. Gerard

Gray jay, length 10-13"; Frederick Kent Truslow

Gray Jay
Perisoreus canadensis

SOME WANDERERS in the cool evergreen forests welcome the companionship of this somber gray bird. But many would rather suffer loneliness, for the "camp robber" of the north steals anything he can carry away.

When "Whiskey Jack" calls, loggers and trappers look to their stores. This bird seizes bacon from the frying pan, pecks at fresh meat hung up to cool, and shows special fondness for baked beans. He filches chunks from fresh-caught fish and steals the bait from traplines. He invades a tent to snatch a cracker from an open box, and makes off with matches, pencils, cigarettes, and chewing tobacco. He pecks to pieces candles and bars of soap. A gunshot brings *canadensis* winging, for he knows great feasting is in store when a moose or deer is killed.

Gray jays, also known as Canada jays, can make do with what nature provides: grasshoppers, wasps, mice, berries. As suggested by their generic name *Perisoreus*, meaning "heap up" in Greek, they cache food at every chance. This enables them to feed their nestlings on days when foraging is meager.

These birds nest early, sometimes in the face of deep snows and temperatures down to 30° below zero F. Between February and April the female fashions a neat cradle, usually concealing it in the foliage of a small spruce. Sticks, moss, spider webs, and bark form the framework. On this she lays a luxuriant bed of fine grasses and feathers. The rim of the nest fits her body snugly,

trapping heat around the clutch of three or four, occasionally five, eggs. These are gray or greenish white marked with brown and lavender.

After raising the season's single brood, adults lead their soot-colored youngsters on foraging expeditions through the deep coniferous forests. Using branches as a ladder, they explore a tree from bottom to top, then parachute gently to the base of another one. The first winter's molt garbs the juveniles in fluffy gray plumage. This, combined with the short bill, makes the gray jay look like an overgrown chickadee.

This jay's sounds vary from shrill, hawklike cries through a series of whistles and cooing notes to a gentle whisper song reminiscent of the purple finch's warbling.

Range: N. Alaska to Newfoundland, south to N. California, S. Rockies, and New England. *Characteristics:* white forehead, black head patch, gray back, lighter gray underparts, small bill.

Mexican Jay
Aphelocoma ultramarina

OAK TREES and Mexican jays form a smoothly working alliance for survival. The trees furnish the birds with acorns for food, twigs for nests, rootlets to line them, and forks to place them in. The jays in turn bury surplus acorns and often forget where they are stored, helping ensure the start of new groves.

This blue jay without a crest inhabits the foothill country along the Mexican border. It ranges to the edge of the pine belt at 7,000 feet, but the favorite habitat embraces the parklike forests of blackjack oak where canyon mouths open out toward the plains.

Highly gregarious, the Mexican jay nests in loose colonies. Three or four birds pitch in to help each other build platforms of green twigs. They make many false starts but usually end up with more than one inhabited nest in the same oak or pine. In May female jays brood four or five eggs in a bowl of rootlets lined with fine grasses or animal hair. The eggs vary in color from plain green to spotted green.

The whole colony helps feed and guard the hatchlings. Within a month the young follow foraging parties to feed on acorns, grasshoppers, and eggs stolen from other birds' nests. In these wanderings they often visit feeding stations.

These bold, blue rowdies, known too as Arizona jays, scold at rattlesnakes with raucous cries of *wink? wink?* They also vent their noisy wrath upon skunks, foxes, and wildcats.

Range: central Arizona to S. W. Texas, south to S. Mexico. *Characteristics:* pale blue crown and back, gray underparts.

Mexican jay, length 11½-13"; Eliot Porter

Steller's Jay
Cyanocitta stelleri

SHOOK SHOOK SHOOK. Shattering the silence of the evergreen forest, this brazen call identifies the only western jay with a crest. The black-and-blue Steller's replaces the blue jay in the coniferous belt that stretches from the Rocky Mountains to the Pacific.

Like its eastern counterpart, Steller's jay is a superb mimic. It can reproduce the scream of the red-tailed hawk, the falsetto song of the crow, or the tremolo call of the loon. A sanctuary of dense foliage usually muffles a whisper song.

In the mountains Steller's jay ranges the forests between the timberline domain of Clark's nutcracker and the foothill oaks inhabited by the scrub jay. The Steller's does much of its foraging in the treetops. Pine seeds and acorns contribute heavily to its diet. Family groups invade the lowlands in winter, searching backyards for food and often stealing from the storehouses of acorn woodpeckers. This marauder also eats the eggs and young of songbirds and may destroy nests.

The Steller's usually nests in a conifer. The bird builds a foundation of twigs, sinks a deep cup of grass or moss, plasters the structure with mud, and lines it with pine needles or rootlets. The nest holds three to five greenish-white eggs specked with brown and lavender.

Range: S. Alaska to Nicaragua, east to E. New Mexico. *Characteristics:* foreparts, including long crest, blackish; wings, tail, and belly blue. Rocky Mountain races wear white line over eye.

Steller's jay, length 12-13½"; Eliot Porter

Scrub Jay
Aphelocoma coerulescens

BLUE WINGS and tail spread wide, a crestless jay sails down the side of a brushy western hillside to a perch in an oak tree, uttering a harsh *tschek tschek tschek.* Alighting, he bows deeply in several directions before settling down to observe the countryside. If alarmed, the bird dives straight into the dense shrubbery found throughout most of his habitat.

The habitat names the bird, but the scrub jay is also known by several other names. At one time various forms of this brownish-backed, white-throated bird were considered distinct species; today science classifies them as subspecies. The California race ranges in the coastal region of that state. The Woodhouse's dwells among the nut-bearing trees of the lower mountain slopes from Oregon to Texas. The Texas jay lives in the center of the Lone Star State. Xántus' jay, a pale form, resides in a somewhat different habitat—the deserts and mountains of Baja California. The Santa Cruz race, largest and handsomest of all, is restricted to rugged Santa Cruz Island, off the California coast.

Centuries ago the scrub jay is believed to have ranged from coast to coast. For reasons unknown it disappeared from the East except in Florida. And this race is truly isolated. It never leaves the central portions of the state.

Where sandy soil produces scrub growth—impenetrable thickets of saw palmetto, sand pine, and scrub oak—the Florida jays are a familiar sight. Their habit of letting the tail hang down while perched in repose offers a good field mark. These birds are quieter and seem to have better manners than many of their quarrelsome relatives. They may come to the hand for food.

The situation is far different in the West. The scrub jay is one of the noisier birds of California and is widely disliked. Sportsmen and bird watchers resent its habit of following them around with such loud shrieks that every creature within hearing disappears.

This handsome villain also preys on the eggs and young of smaller wild birds and domestic poultry. It even plunders the nests of other scrub jays. Although the small birds usually lay another set when their eggs are stolen, the damage nonetheless can be serious. Sometimes songbirds of several species band together to mob an attacking scrub jay.

Man has reacted too. Farmers and fruit growers have shot large numbers of these jays, and in some parts of California hunters have organized annual jay shoots. But these assaults have had no appreciable effect on the scrub jay population, and the species remains abundant.

These birds also feed on mice, shrews, insects, and acorns and other nuts, usually foraging close to the ground. They often store nuts in shallow pits, covering them with leaves or stones. To get at the meat, the birds wedge the nut into a limb crevice, then hammer it open. Other birds sometimes benefit from the leftovers.

Scrub jay nest sites range from hillside bushes to high tree limbs. Fine roots and animal hairs line the twiggy bowl, which is often well concealed. The eggs, usually three to five, are among the most attractively colored of any North American birds' eggs—green with reddish-brown spots. The background color of the California jay's eggs, however, frequently is red.

Fledglings take wing at the age of 18 days. With a little coaxing they quickly learn to love the water and frolic at the nearest creek. In the Rockies scrub jays often move up to heavy timber after the nesting season.

In the Southwest this species may be confused with the Mexican jay. The Mexican's plumage is plain underneath while the scrub displays a streaked throat above a faint blue breastband.

Range: S. W. Washington to Colorado, south to S. Mexico; also central Florida. *Characteristics:* crestless blue head, blue wings and tail, gray or brownish back, white throat, blue breastband, black eye patch.

Green Jay
Cyanocorax yncas

PÁJARO VERDE—green bird—the Mexicans call this brilliant gem of the forest. Despite the vivid contrast of green body, blue crown, and black throat, it is surprisingly inconspicuous in the lights and shades of thick foliage. In open glades the yellow sides of its tail merge with the dappling of sunlight.

The first descriptions of this species were based on birds from Peru, the land of the Incas. The only green-colored jay resident in the United States, *yncas* brings a touch of the tropics to the live-oak groves and chaparral of the lower Rio Grande Valley.

Green jays chase each other through the trees in small troops. Any human intrusion into their haunts quickly brings them out of the dense cover to investigate. They scream and caw and toot for a while, then melt silently into the bush.

On a platform of rootlets and twigs the female deposits three to five brown-spotted eggs. The base color may be gray, greenish, or buff.

After nesting, green jays resume their roaming, even scavenging in towns or on ranches. They hold acorns in a claw, jay fashion, and chop them open with the bill.

Range: S. Texas to Honduras, also in N. South America. *Characteristics:* blue head, black throat, green back; underside of tail yellow.

Upper: scrub jay, length 11-13"; B. Max Thompson, National Audubon Society
Lower: green jay, length 10-12"; Lyman K. Stuar

Black-billed Magpie
Pica pica

THIS STRIKING BLACK-AND-WHITE bird, native to Eurasia as well as America, has stirred man's imagination for centuries. Also his temper.

In English folklore the magpie is a bird of omen. One magpie, they say, is for sorrow, two for mirth, three for a wedding, four for a birth, five for silver, six for gold, seven for a secret not to be told, eight for heaven, nine for hell, and ten for the devil's own sel'.

In the western United States the black-billed magpie has long been despised as a thief and scavenger. Members of the Lewis and Clark expedition told of magpies invading their tents and seizing meat from the dishes. Cattlemen today complain that these birds attack weak or injured stock and peck at open branding scars, preventing their healing. Magpies kill young chickens and eat hens' eggs. They feed the eggs and young of swallows to their own offspring. European magpies are the bane of estate keepers because they destroy the nests and young of game birds.

The blackbills perform some useful services too. They thrive on carrion and help rid the roads of rabbits, squirrels, and other small animals killed by cars. They pick ticks from the backs of larger animals and consume offal, grasshoppers, noxious rodents, and weevils.

Strangely, while magpies have been killed by the thousands in organized campaigns, they also have long enjoyed favor as pets. The bird can imitate the human voice, and sometimes one delights its owner by learning to repeat phrases.

Man's enmity has not noticeably decreased the magpie's numbers, and the bird is still a familiar sight in the range and pasturelands west of the prairies and north of the deserts. It needs open stretches for foraging on the ground, with nearby shrubs and low trees for cover and nesting.

The magpie walks about with short, jerky steps. Its "sidewheeler" wings—short and rounded, with large patches of white—are unsuited

Blackbills, length 17½-22"; Helen Cruickshank and (inset) Walter A. Weber, National Geographic staff artist

for rapid flight. The long, wedge-shaped tail of iridescent green seems to get in the way when the bird tries to fly in a strong wind.

Magpies mate for life and use the same nest year after year. They build a home with two entrances in thick brush. They line a mud cup with rootlets, surround it with a wall of sticks, and cover it with a twiggy dome to fend off hawks. The female incubates six to nine greenish-gray eggs, heavily blotched with shades of brown.

Range: S. Alaska to S. W. Manitoba, south to central California, N. New Mexico, and W. Kansas. *Characteristics:* black-and-white body; iridescent green and greenish-blue feathers in wings and wedge-shaped tail.

Yellow-billed Magpie
Pica nuttalli

EXCEPT FOR ITS YELLOW BILL, a bit of bare yellow skin behind the eye, and slightly smaller size, *nuttalli* looks exactly like the black-billed magpie. But the difference in range and distribution of these two birds is one of the mysteries of ornithology.

The blackbill is found, in one or another of several closely related subspecies, over much of the northern hemisphere. But the yellowbill is confined to a strip less than 150 miles wide and measuring 500 miles north and south, west of the Sierra Nevada in California. And where the yellowbill ranges—the Sacramento and San Joa-

quin valleys and the coastal valleys south of San Francisco Bay—the blackbill is unknown.

In conspicuous flocks, *nuttalli* roves the pastoral interior valleys where groves of tall trees stand etched against a golden landscape of rolling hills. Small streams and cattle troughs provide water. The birds haunt ranches because food to their liking is usually plentiful there. When cattle or sheep are butchered, the magpies gather round to glean the refuse, uttering a variety of squawks and throaty squeals.

Competing for a scrap, two birds puff out their chests, aim yellow bills skyward, then walk toward each other. The successful bluffer wins the food, though they sometimes bump chests before one concedes. Yellowbills are always on the lookout for the eggs of other birds. They also eat grasshoppers, worms, and grubs.

These magpies nest far out on the limbs of tall trees. Sometimes they hide their home among clumps of mistletoe. They build a bulky, covered cradle of twigs, leaving two openings for escape when danger threatens. The frame holds a cup of mud or cow dung lined with pine needles, rootlets, and sometimes horsehair. The five to eight eggs are pale olive-buff with brown or grayish-olive spots. Sparrow hawks often usurp a yellowbill nest, then peacefully raise a family in the midst of the host colony.

Range: interior and coastal valleys of central California. *Characteristics:* yellow bill, black-and-white body; iridescent green and greenish-blue feathers in wings and wedge-shaped tail.

Yellowbill, length 16-18"; Allan Brooks

White-necked Raven
Corvus cryptoleucus

THE SKY IN SPRING is a playground to the white-necked raven. High above a desert or cattle range of the Southwest, 50 or more performers soar skyward until nearly out of sight. Amorous males impress prospective mates with a display of sideslipping, wheeling, and tumbling. As if for fun, whitenecks even plunge into the swirling funnel of a dust devil. Perched in a tree yucca or mesquite, courting birds rub bills or bow to each other with wings elevated.

White-necked ravens are slightly larger than common crows and have a strong bill that looks like a Roman nose. The white bases of the feathers on the breast and shaggy throat show only when ruffled. These birds utter a hoarse *kraak*, less resonant than the common raven's.

In flat, open country the white-necked raven's nest can be spotted a quarter of a mile away. The female builds it in a tree, an old windmill, or on a telephone pole. She cushions a platform of thorny twigs with bark, wool, or rabbit fur. Then she lays five to seven eggs, green with purplish or brown streaks and spots.

A resourceful scavenger, *cryptoleucus* visits towns and ranches for scraps, follows railroad tracks for refuse from the diner, and patrols highways for animals killed by cars. It also feeds on grasshoppers, small reptiles, mice, and the eggs and young of smaller birds. Juicy cactus fruits sustain whitenecks in waterless regions.

More sociable than the common raven, this species sometimes forms large winter roosts in streamside timber.

Range: S. E. Arizona to S. Nebraska, south to central Mexico. *Characteristics:* wedge-shaped tail; throat feathers show white when ruffled.

Common Raven
Corvus corax

ABOVE THE FLANKS of Appalachian ridges, where cliffs thrust up through the blanket of forest, one may see a pair of large black birds riding the thermal currents on motionless wings that spread more than four feet. The same birds might well be soaring over a canyon in the Rockies or a sea cliff in Bering Strait. The raven is a symbol of wilderness. Sagacious and adaptable, he has retreated before man but still thrives across a vast expanse of North America.

Shaggy throat feathers, the rounded tip of his tail, and the "Roman nose" effect of his stout beak distinguish the common raven from the crow. The raven is also longer and nearly twice as heavy. And no crow ever matched the raven's skill as an aerial gymnast. Using the fan-shaped tail as a rudder, he can circle for hours in a flat, eagle-like glide. He rides the wind, hovering and sideslipping adeptly. From a height of some 500 feet ravens dive to earth like falcons or tumble in a series of somersaults.

Tradition pictures the raven as a dour and somber bird. Through the centuries his hoarse croakings have been considered portents of evil. The shadow of his sable wings falling across the path of a bride foretold disaster. Many have credited him with supernatural powers. Ravens have been kept in the Tower of London for centuries. Charles II, the story goes, predicted that England would fall if they ever left. But in his natural haunts the raven is often a playful creature. He sometimes seems to challenge hawks in the air, easily evading each pass.

The raven is not a talented vocalist, but he utters a variety of sounds, mixing a melancholy croak with lisps, buzzing noises, and gulps. In late summer a small group of birds may gather in a secluded patch of woods to hold a concert. They face each other while taking turns performing solos in a low warble.

In the Arctic ravens are mainly carrion eaters, though they gorge on berries during the brief fruiting season. They search tundra, seacoast, and riverbanks for the carcasses of whales, walruses, and seals, and they shadow wolves to glean leftovers from caribou and moose kills.

Whiteneck, length 19-21"; Thase Daniel

Common raven, length 21½-27"
Robert C. Hermes
National Audubon Society

The crafty birds may cooperate to kill young seals trapped on floe ice. One raven blocks the mammal's escape hole while the other dispatches the victim with blows on the head. Raven teams sometimes steal food from dogs. One bird attracts the dog's attention by tweaking its tail; the other grabs the morsel. These vandals also take a heavy toll of eggs from seabird colonies.

Once common on the Great Plains, ravens declined with the disappearance of the buffalo, on whose carcasses they fed. Many perished from eating poisoned bait put out for wolves and coyotes. But ravens still thrive in the mountains, deserts, and forests. This diverse terrain offers a menu of insects, reptiles, and small animals.

Ravens often range in pairs and are reputed to mate for life. They return to the same cliff for many years to breed on a sheltered ledge over a sheer drop. Some nest in trees. Peregrine falcons are sometimes neighbors, the two species tolerating each other.

The raven builds its bulky nest of sticks lined with fur, seaweed, or any soft material. The four to seven eggs, green with olive or brown dots, hatch in three weeks.

Ravens show enough boldness to mob golden eagles and rout such fierce birds as gyrfalcons. In these encounters *corax* usually wins. Only man is a serious enemy, because of the raven's reputation as an attacker of domestic animals and poultry, wildfowl, and other game.

Range: Alaska, Canada, north central states, and Greenland; south in western United States to Nicaragua; in East through mountains to Georgia. *Characteristics:* black, longer and heavier than the crow; "Roman nose," shaggy throat feathers, rounded tail.

147

Young common crows; Allan D. Cruickshank, National Audubon Society

♪♪ Common Crow
Corvus brachyrhynchos

HENRY WARD BEECHER, the 19th century American preacher, remarked that if people wore feathers and wings, very few of them would be clever enough to be crows. These canny rogues have found terrain altered by man just to their liking. Croplands furnish year-round feeding grounds; woodlots provide nesting areas. But the crow's fondness for corn and other crops has hardly been to man's liking.

By wit and adaptability these raucous black birds have survived such retaliation as bombing of their roosts, shooting, and poisoning, and today are more numerous than ever. They have also learned the range of guns and usually keep a safe distance from anyone with a weapon. Scouts often precede a flock into new feeding territory. When danger threatens a feeding flock, sentinel birds sound the alarm. And crows long ago learned to live with scarecrows.

In the Far West crows often form loose colonies to nest in streamside timber. Elsewhere solitary pairs seek out tall trees, frequently pines. On the plains and prairies crows have nested in windmills and even on the ground.

Between February and May a mated pair fashions a platform of sticks around a deep bowl lined with shredded bark, leaves, wool, or other soft material. Four to six eggs, greenish with brown spots, comprise the usual set. Both male and female share the task of brooding during the 18-day incubation period. Fledglings leave the abode at about five weeks.

In some regions crows devour the eggs and young of other birds. They can be especially destructive to nesting waterfowl. Yet the crow does not threaten the existence of any species. To its credit, the bird devours immense quantities of grasshoppers, beetles and their grubs, and moths. It also feeds on crustaceans, reptiles, small mammals, and carrion.

Young crows make interesting pets. They frolic with their owners, try to imitate words and human laughter, and carry off and hide bright trinkets about the house.

In fall and winter the sable wanderers scour wide areas for food, especially waste corn. Toward sunset they head directly – "as the crow flies" – for their roosts. There, amid a tumult of cawing, they gather by the thousands. These vast assemblies include crows that breed locally as well as others that have moved down from nesting grounds farther north.

Range: British Columbia to Newfoundland, south to N. Baja California and S. Florida. *Characteristics:* large, solid black, glossed with purple in strong sunlight; tail square-ended.

Fish Crow
Corvus ossifragus

FROM THE INLAND EDGE of tidewater country to the sea along the Atlantic and Gulf coasts, many crows sound as if they are suffering from bad colds. A hoarse *car*, clearly different from the common crow's *caw*, identifies *ossifragus*.

Fish crows soar like ravens or hover with rapid wingbeats while searching for floating food.

Common crow, length 17-21"; John H. Gerard, National Audubon Society

They often drink while skimming the water and sometimes seize surfaced minnows in their claws. They dive-bomb gulls and terns, forcing these birds to drop their catches. They scour shorelines and tidal marshes for small crabs, crawfish, shrimps, and carrion, and forage far inland along the larger rivers, eating a variety of fruits, berries, and seeds.

The fish crow preys heavily on the nests of herons, terns, rails, and other waterbirds. And in Washington, D.C., *ossifragus* is an urban nemesis, stealing the eggs and young from pigeon nests in the nooks of government buildings.

Fish crows usually nest in pines near a salt marsh or in tall hardwoods on a riverbank. They fashion a platform of small sticks lined with shredded bark to receive the four or five eggs, green or greenish blue with brown spots.

The northwestern crow, *Corvus caurinus*, which ranges from southern Alaska to Puget Sound, resembles the fish crow in many ways.

Range: coastal areas and major rivers, Rhode Island to Texas. *Characteristics:* black with faint greenish gloss; smaller than common crow.

Fish crow, length 16-20"
Allan D. Cruickshank, National Audubon Society

Piñon jay, length 9-11¾"; Eliot Porter

Piñon Jay
Gymnorhinus cyanocephalus

THESE RESTLESS "BLUE CROWS" forage endlessly in the Far West at altitudes of 3,000 to 8,000 feet where juniper and piñon clothe the foothills and mesas. Their nickname is well earned. They have the color of jays, but they look, walk, and fly like crows.

At one time the piñon jay was also known as Maximilian's jay in honor of the German naturalist Maximilian, Prince of Wied, who discovered the species in Montana in 1833.

Piñon jays descend on a feeding ground in flocks of hundreds. Those in the rear continually fly over the birds in front. Thus, a flock goes rolling across the countryside in a kind of flattened, hooplike formation.

Feeding largely on piñon nuts, these nomadic jays move on as they exhaust a piñon grove. With constant squeaks, clucks, and harsh, rasping calls, the wandering flocks seize grasshoppers and sample the seeds of other pines as well as berries in season. Where their favored nuts or other foods run scarce, these short, stumpy birds may sweep down on cultivated fields and do considerable damage to crops of beans and corn or other grains.

Long flights in fall and spring suggest migrations, but the species is not truly migratory except in the northern portions of its range. The flocks are usually searching for breeding sites or moving from one feeding ground to another.

Piñon jays breed in colonies of up to 100 birds, settling anywhere from the edge of the desert up to 8,000 feet. Each pair places a bowl of twigs, lined with grasses, in a juniper, piñon, or scrub oak. About the nest the harsh jay sounds become low and soft. The four or five eggs are specked with brown dots on a base of light blue, green, or gray. In June the newly fledged youngsters go about the flock, flapping their wings and clamoring incessantly for food. The older birds respond with grubs and insects.

Range: central Oregon to W. South Dakota, south to N. Baja California and W. Oklahoma; wanders widely to central Washington, S. W. Saskatchewan, Nebraska, Kansas, and N. Mexico. *Characteristics:* dull blue body, short tail, long, sharp bill.

Clark's nutcracker, length 12-13"; L. R. Owen, National Audubon Society

Clark's Nutcracker
Nucifraga columbiana

LIKE LEWIS' WOODPECKER, Clark's nutcracker was named for one of the leaders of the great expedition which crossed the continent in 1804-06 and incidentally discovered the two birds.

Capt. William Clark described the nutcracker as a "new species of woodpecker"; the early 19th century ornithologist Alexander Wilson called it "Clark's crow." Both had a point. This gray bird with black-and-white wings has the build of a small crow and walks sedately about much as a crow does. It also clings to tree trunks, pecking in the bark for grubs, as woodpeckers do.

A bird of the Rockies and Sierras, Clark's nutcracker ranges from juniper- and piñon-covered foothills through open yellow pine forests to heights up to 13,000 feet. In summer you find him along the tree line. Sometimes he plunges headlong down a deep canyon, wings folded. Just as he seems about to be dashed to pieces, he opens his wings to brake the dive and shoots upward. As the day wanes he follows the shadows back up to sunlit evening peaks.

Bills serve as crowbars to pry seeds from stunted, wind-beaten evergreens in the alpine zone, or as pickaxes to hammer open cones. The birds often cache conifer seeds for winter, especially the sweet nuts of the piñon. Before the piñon nuts ripen, the nutcrackers hunt moths on the wing and scour the ground for beetles, ants, grasshoppers, and black crickets.

The nutcracker also eats carrion and indulges in the family habit of robbing smaller birds of their eggs and young. He even preys successfully on chipmunks and ground squirrels. In winter he visits western camps for food scraps, though he is rarely as bold as the thieving jays.

Nutcrackers exhibit another family trait: They make a fearful racket. The harsh call, *khraa*, sounded by a nearby flock, grates on the ears and nerves of some listeners. Close to the nest the birds are quieter.

Both sexes build the nest, often starting it in February. In a juniper or pine they form a platform of twigs bound by bark strips and lined with pine needles and shredded bark.

The two share incubation duties, persisting on the nest even in the face of raging snowstorms and below-zero temperatures. The clutch is two to four, rarely six, eggs. Pale green and dotted with brown, gray, or olive, they hatch in about 18 days. During their three weeks in the nest, the young thrive on regurgitated pine seeds.

Range: central British Columbia to S. E. Wyoming, south to N. Baja California and W. New Mexico; wanders to Alaska, Manitoba, and S. W. Texas. *Characteristics:* gray body, white patches on black wings and tail, long, sharp bill.

Arthur A. Allen
BLACK-CAPPED CHICKADEE *shares a peanut with a friend.*

PLUMP LITTLE ACROBATS

Titmice, Verdins, and Bushtits
Family Paridae

L EAVES DRIFT SLOWLY down through the cool October air, rustling underfoot on the path through the river woods. A low call, *chick-a-dee-dee-dee,* announces a plump little gray-and-white bird with black crown and throat. Swinging upside down from the tip of a twig, he searches with his short bill in the roll of a curling leaf for hidden insects. Other chickadees flit through the branches, calling softly to maintain contact in a loosely organized flock. Gleaning insects from the bark as they go, they soon pass from view, their low notes lost in the rattling of the leaves.

Through most of the year these little birds or their relatives in the family Paridae —titmice, verdins, and bushtits—brighten our forests, orchards, and backyards. Bright-eyed and fearless, they rank with the friendliest of creatures. Suet, peanut butter, or a crumbled doughnut will bring them chattering to your feeding station while other species are still thinking over the idea. If you show patience, they may become bold enough to eat sunflower seeds from your hand.

Representatives of the family's more than 60 species live in Europe, Asia, and Africa as well as in North America. They are among our hardiest birds, the chickadees ranging to the limits of forest growth in the Far North. The distribution of titmice in part parallels that of the crow family and suggests a similar Old World origin. The vernacular family name "titmouse" comes from the Anglo-Saxon: "tit" means a very small object, and "mouse" is a corruption of *mase,* an ancient name for small birds of the titmouse group.

American titmice range in length from 3¾ to 6 inches; an Old World species may reach 8 inches. Drably colored in the main, they wear grays, browns, and olives. Most of them sport bold markings of black, white, chestnut, or, in the case of the verdin, yellow. The sexes usually look alike, and often the young wear duller shades of their parents' colors. Some titmice are crested, much like jays.

Most of the Paridae nest in cavities. Some chip their own holes out of rotten stubs and fence posts; others move into secondhand woodpecker holes or natural tree cavities. In some species male and female share the labor of hewing out the nest cavity and lining it with soft materials; in others the female works alone. Verdins and bushtits differ by building sacklike nests that hang from a branch. In most species incubation is the female's job, but the male sometimes helps. He brings her meals during her confinement and later helps feed the young.

Titmice commonly roost within their nesting cavities, partly as a defensive measure and also, in winter, for shelter and warmth. Their quickness and agility also serve them well in escaping enemies. Nevertheless, they are often attacked by hawks, jays, owls, and four-legged predators, and the family has a mortality rate estimated at about 75 percent. Perhaps to offset this, titmice sometimes brood twice a year and usually lay large clutches—normally five to ten eggs, but as many as 13.

Though mainly nonmigratory, titmice may wander widely in search of food. Northern species sometimes retreat southward a few hundred miles during especially bitter winters, and those found on high mountains drift down to the valleys below. But they seldom follow other birds south to sunnier climes. Through the frigid months they enliven the bleak woodlands. And since these birds stay on the job all winter long, feeding upon hibernating insects and eggs hidden in bark crevices, they rank with the best of man's allies in pest control.

NIPPING *a sunflower seed, a tufted titmouse feasts at a backyard feeder. Young tit (right) will boast smoother plumage at maturity.*

Blackcaps, length 4¾-5¾"; Arthur A. Allen

Black-capped Chickadee
Parus atricapillus

THIS GENTLE LITTLE BIRD takes its name from its clearly enunciated call note, *chick-a-dee-dee-dee*. With the approach of spring it also whistles a plaintive, high-pitched *fee-bee*. Sometimes two blackcaps whistle a *fee-bee* duet, the second bird answering the first a tone lower.

Blackcaps are year-round residents in the northern states and Canada. They rove the winter woodlands in small flocks, minutely examining bark, twigs, and branches for spider eggs, cocoons, and other dormant insect life. They can usually be found with woodpeckers, nuthatches, brown creepers, and kinglets. The chickadees can easily be distinguished from the other small birds. Their white cheeks shine out, separating the solid black cap above from the fringed black bib below; their backs are gray.

In summer they feed mainly on insects, seeds, wild berries, and other fruits. Because they can alight upside down on the underside of a twig and perform similar gymnastics, they often find food missed by other birds.

The blackcap ranks as the most trusting and least pugnacious bird among those that visit feeding stations. It feeds in amity, yielding to bullies without argument and returning unobtrusively when the way is clear. At the same time this amiable bird wages incessant war on insect pests. Maine and Massachusetts have named it their state bird.

At the start of the spring courting season blackcaps grow agitated and begin their *fee-bee* song. Gradually the flock breaks up as the birds pair off. To build a nest both sexes work at chipping out a cavity in a dead stub. The female lines the nest with moss, plant down, feathers, animal fur, and insect cocoons. She lays five to eight white eggs speckled with reddish brown and incubates them for about 12 days.

The young birds soon may weigh as much as or more than their hard-working parents, who deplete their own strength by feeding the offspring. Blackcaps raise one or two broods each season; some adults remain mated for life.

Northern shrikes and fast-moving hawks prey on chickadees, but the little birds are so quick and alert that they often escape. Sometimes they dive for cover in a network of evergreen twigs.

Range: central Alaska to Newfoundland, south to N. California, N. New Mexico, and W. North Carolina. *Characteristics:* black cap and bib, white cheeks and breast, gray back, buff sides, wing feathers edged with white.

Carolina Chickadee
Parus carolinensis

THE CAROLINA replaces the black-capped chickadee in the southeastern states. Nearly identical
to the blackcap, it is noticeably smaller and
shows less white in its wing feather edgings and
sharper separation between black bib and white
breast. Its chickadee call is more hurried and
higher pitched, and it sings a four-part song: *fee-
bee, fee-bay, tsee-dee, tsee-dee.*

First described by Audubon from birds taken
near Charleston, South Carolina, *carolinensis*
lives most abundantly among the great swamps
of the Atlantic and Gulf coastal plains. It is attracted to woodlands too, and comes freely to
backyards. Bird lovers who want to get acquaint-
ed with this tame, inquisitive bird often get a
quick response by putting suet, cheese, or bones
with bits of meat or gristle in their feeders.

In natural haunts Carolina chickadees eat
moths, caterpillars, insects, and spiders. Clinging to the undersides of branches, they hunt
insect pupae and eggs to vary a diet that also
includes small berries.

Early breeders, they may begin nest building
in mid-February if the season is advanced. They
build in old woodpecker holes, fence posts, de-

*Carolina chickadee, length 4¼-4¾"; Walter A. Weber,
National Geographic staff artist. Upper: juveniles,
Allan D. Cruickshank, National Audubon Society*

cayed stumps, iron pipes, bridge supports, and
small birdhouses. They form their nests of grass
and bark and line them with fur, feathers, and
thistledown. Often they build one side of the nest
higher than the other. This makes a flap which
serves to cover the five to eight brown-speckled
white eggs when the parents are away. A pair of
Carolina chickadees may remain mated for several breeding seasons.

Range: S. E. Kansas to central New Jersey,
south to central Texas and Florida. *Characteristics:* black cap and bib, white cheeks and breast,
gray back, buff sides.

Mountain chickadee, length 5-5¾"
B. Max Thompson, National Audubon Society

Grayhead, length 5½"
Walter A. Weber, National Geographic staff artist

Mountain Chickadee
Parus gambeli

WHEN THE MOUNTAIN CHICKADEE clings upside down to search a pine twig for insects and larvae, the white eyebrow that distinguishes it from other chickadees shows to good advantage.

Like the black-capped chickadee, it chips out a cavity in a dead tree for its furry nest or looks for an old woodpecker hole. The female lays large sets of white eggs, usually seven to nine in a set, sometimes as many as 12. They often lack the speckling found on other chickadee eggs.

During the breeding season this chickadee is common throughout the coniferous forests of the western mountains. In the fall the adults and their young range up to tree limit and even beyond. One specimen was taken in the mountains above Taos, New Mexico, at 12,500 feet – a thousand feet above timberline. In winter the mountain chickadee comes down out of the heights and joins the blackcaps in stands of willow and cottonwood along valley streams.

The mountain chickadee's call – *tsick-a-zee-zee-zee* – sounds more guttural than that of the blackcap. It whistles the *fee-bee* song high and clear, and its cheerful chatter is one of the commonest bird sounds heard in the forests of the Sierra Nevada. Like her relatives, the nesting female sends forth snakelike hissings to keep marauding squirrels at a distance.

Range: N. W. British Columbia and S. W. Alberta, south to N. Baja California and S. W. Texas. *Characteristics:* black cap with white line over each eye; black bib, white cheeks and breast.

Gray-headed Chickadee
Parus cinctus

THE GRAYHEAD makes its home in the scattered stands of spruce, birch, and willow that mark the upper limits of the boreal forest along the riverbeds in Alaska and northwestern Canada. Most northern of the chickadees, it is an Old World species that has crossed the Bering Strait from Siberia. It has also been known as the Alaska chickadee.

Grayheads feed voraciously on insects, insect eggs, and larvae. Scraps of food about forest settlements attract flocks of these little birds. Unafraid of the cold, they have been observed nibbling nonchalantly on the fat of a frozen caribou carcass at 20° below zero F.

These chickadees build their nests in natural tree cavities or chip out a home in a dry or rotten tree stump. They have been known to eject a woodpecker from its hole and move in. On a soft bed of moss and rabbit or lemming fur the female lays seven to nine dull white eggs, finely sprinkled with reddish-brown spots that are often concentrated at the larger end.

The grayhead's most characteristic call is a low-pitched, two-syllable *dee-deer, chee-ee,* or *pee-vee.* Few ornithologists have had a chance to hear it. One who did, Olaus J. Murie, thought the tone and accent implied a "peevish and complaining state of mind." Others have described it as a hissing sound.

Range: N. Alaska and N. W. Canada. *Characteristics:* dark gray cap, black bib, white cheeks, dusky sides and back.

Boreal chickadee, length 5-5½"; David G. Allen

Boreal Chickadee
Parus hudsonicus

THE VAST NORTHERN FORESTS in Canada and
Alaska are the year-round home of boreal chickadees, which sport "brown derbies" to go with
their brown coats and black bibs. Sporadic southward movement brings them into New England
and even to Pennsylvania during the winter. In
1954 the first specimens ever noted so far south
were recorded in nearby Maryland by members
of the Audubon Society of Washington, D. C.

Also known as Hudsonian chickadees, these
birds are partial to coniferous trees but seem
equally at home in birch and willow thickets,
particularly in the vicinity of peat bogs and mus-
kegs. In winter they wander through the woods
in company with black-capped chickadees, nuthatches, and woodpeckers, feeding on hibernating insects and insect eggs.

The boreal builds a nest of fur, bark, and moss
in tree cavities, as do other chickadees. It raises
a brood of five to seven young, hatched from
creamy white eggs sparingly stippled with reddish brown. One pair were observed feeding
their young 362 times within a 15-hour period—
an average of 24 times an hour!

The *chick-a-dee* call of the boreal is slow and
drawling and sounds more like *chick-che-day-
day-day*. The bird also has a number of distinctive *chip* notes, uttered in a sharp, petulant tone,
and a short, warbled song.

Range: tree limit in N. Alaska and Canada to
N. United States. *Characteristics:* dark brown
cap, buffy brown flanks, black bib.

Chestnutback, length 4½-5"; Arthur A. Allen

Chestnut-backed Chickadee
Parus rufescens

A BIRD of the deep forests of the Pacific Northwest, this chestnut-and-black chickadee is inconspicuous in the somber shade of redwood,
fir, spruce, and pine. It lives, in large part, remote from human settlement but shows no fear
when man invades its solitude. It may venture
into open woods along quiet roads and trails,
feeding on conifer seeds, fruits, spiders, caterpillars, and other insects.

Chestnutbacks dig their own nest cavity, usually starting with some natural advantage—
a place where the bark has been torn away or
a hole excavated by the larva of a large beetle.

The birds line the nest with moss, feathers,
and fur, and the female lays a set of six or seven
white eggs speckled with reddish brown. Bum-
blebees, which also live in tree holes, seem to
like this chickadee's soft nest material and may
drive away the brooding bird.

The chestnutback has many notes, among
them a hoarse *tsick-a-see-see* or *zhee-che-che*
and a harsh *zze-zze*. It flutters up with a loud
hiss when disturbed in its dark nest chamber.

Range: Pacific coast from S. Alaska to S. California and inland to Montana. *Characteristics:*
chestnut back and sides, white cheeks, sooty
cap, black bib.

157

Tufted titmouse, length 6-6½"   *Male blackcrest, length 5-6"; Allan Brooks*

 ## Tufted Titmouse
Parus bicolor

IN A FAMILY of gentle, friendly birds the saucy "tomtit" of the South seems more active and vivacious than the others, an impression heightened by his jaunty crest.

The tufted titmouse makes so much noise that he is generally heard before he is seen – especially since his quiet gray suit of feathers blends easily into forest shadows. The bird's favorite haunts are groves of deciduous trees where he flits among the branches feeding on insects, their eggs, small acorns, and meaty seeds. In recent years he has expanded his range northward.

He comes fearlessly to feeding shelves for offerings of suet, bread, doughnuts, and sunflower seeds. The visits are quick and purposeful. The bird nips up a seed, takes it to a branch, whacks it open, then flies back for another. When he arrives on his daily call and food is not ready, the tomtit scolds insistently.

The bird can easily be attracted by placing the fingers against the lips to make a kissing sound. And an intruder – a cat, a screech owl, or a snake – will bring the tomtit to the scene with raised crest and scolding notes that alert all other small birds in the vicinity. The tomtit varies his harsh, chattering calls with a clear, whistling song, *peter peter peter*.

Tufted titmice build their nests of moss, hair, and bark shreds in a tree hollow, sometimes in a bird box. Bold scroungers, they have been known to collect hair from living mammals – including humans. The nest holds a clutch of four to eight white eggs dotted with brown.

Range: S. E. Nebraska to S. Ontario and S. W. Connecticut, south to E. Texas and central Florida. *Characteristics:* gray crest and back, whitish underparts, rusty flanks.

Black-crested Titmouse
Parus atricristatus

THIS HANDSOME BIRD is distinguished from the tufted titmouse by its jet-black crest. Common wherever trees are plentiful in its limited southwestern range, it feeds largely on caterpillars, insects, their eggs, and larvae. In fall and winter it shells pecans and starchy seeds by holding them against a branch and cracking them open, woodpecker fashion, with sharp blows of its stubby bill.

The blackcrest whistles a cheery *peter peter peter* or rasps out a scolding *eck-eck*. The female lays four to seven chestnut-spotted white eggs in a well-lined nest built in a tree cavity. After the breeding season, when the young take wing, these titmice roam in family parties. In winter they often visit towns. The blackcrest hybridizes with the tufted titmouse in central Texas.

Range: Texas and E. Mexico. *Characteristics:* black crest, whitish forehead and underparts, rusty sides. Female and young have duller crests.

Bridled Titmouse
Parus wollweberi

NAMED FOR THE CURIOUS MARKINGS on its head and throat—black-and-white stripes that suggest a horse's bridle—this titmouse is quieter and less agitated in its movements than other titmice or chickadees. But it is no less sociable, flitting through the woods in family groups of a dozen or more. In early fall the flocks often number 20 or 25 birds.

Dwelling in the southwestern mountains and Mexican highlands, the bridled titmouse shows a preference for oak groves, where it spends much of its time foraging in bark crevices on trunks and branches for insects, their eggs, and larvae. At times in winter these striking birds wander down from their mountain canyons to wooded river valleys.

The notes of this titmouse resemble those of chickadees but are higher in pitch. The song has many variations, each a two-syllable phrase repeated rapidly four or five times. The call notes suggest those of kinglets, beginning high and ending in a series of jarring sounds.

In natural tree cavities the bridled tit builds a nest foundation of coarse weed and grass stems and lines it with cottonwood down, fern fronds, and cocoons. Here the female lays five to seven immaculate white eggs.

Range: central Arizona to S.W. New Mexico, south to S. Mexico. *Characteristics:* black crest and throat, black-and-white "bridled" head.

Bridled titmouse, length 4½-5"; Eliot Porter

Plain Titmouse
Parus inornatus

WITHOUT A TRACE of contrasting color in its gray dress, this titmouse is plain indeed. But what it lacks in appearance, *inornatus*—meaning "un-adorned"—makes up in a vivacious manner and melodious voice. An inquisitive small bird with a jaunty crest and alert bearing, it looks like a miniature jay.

The plain is the western counterpart of the tufted titmouse. It favors the foothills' sunny slopes where evergreen oak, juniper, and piñon provide shelter and food the year round. This bird hunts insects but eats more vegetable matter than other members of the family.

Plain titmice usually keep the same mate from year to year. They often nest in boxes when these are available but normally build in woodpecker holes or natural tree hollows. Their nests, warmly felted with moss, feathers, and spider webs, hold six to eight white eggs, plain or spotted with reddish brown. The fledglings are driven away from home as soon as they are self-sufficient. Sometimes the scrub jay perches outside the nest and pounces as they emerge.

The plain titmouse sends a variety of notes echoing through the woods. Its commonest call is *tchick-a-dee-dee* and its song a whistled *weety weety weety* or *tee wit tee wit.*

Range: S. Oregon to S.W. Wyoming, south to Baja California and W. Texas. *Characteristics:* gray crest and back, lighter gray underparts.

Plain titmouse, length 5-5½"; Lyman K. Stuart

Verdin
Auriparus flaviceps

A HARDY DESERT DWELLER unafraid of heat, cold, or thirst, the verdin lives in the arid regions of the Southwest. He seems to have little need for water for either drinking or bathing. Apparently he may get all the liquid he needs from insects and berries. Some verdin nests have been found ten miles from the nearest water source.

Although most common in dense thickets, the verdin lives wherever he finds scattered thorny desert shrubs and cacti. He builds his nest, a bristling fortress of thorny twigs, in the fork of a spiny branch. An accomplished architect, the bird lines the nest with leaves, grass, spider webs, and feathers. Sometimes he camouflages the side entrance with a projecting canopy of twigs. The male does all the work and often builds several nests to give his mate a choice. Verdins also build roosting nests where they spend cold winter nights in safety and comfort.

The female lays four or five greenish-white or bluish eggs dotted with brown. The gray youngsters, lacking the yellow head of the adults, may be confused with bushtits. Adult verdins also wear chestnut shoulder patches, but these are usually inconspicuous.

Although not so gregarious as bushtits, verdins rarely travel alone. They roam the desert in pairs or small family groups that often associate with cactus wrens and curve-billed thrashers. The pugnacious verdins, active as chickadees, will scold and chatter and hop about if you venture into their haunts. Poke a finger into their warm nests and you take a double risk – severe lacerations from the spiny bush and vigorous pecks from the birds.

Verdins whistle a song of three or four clear notes all in one key: *tswee tswee tswee tsweet.* They boast unusually powerful voices for their small size. The notes of their rapidly repeated short call– *tsit tsit tsit* –are so penetrating that mates can hear each other while foraging for food a hundred yards or more apart.

Range: S. E. California and S. W. Utah to S. Texas and central Mexico. *Characteristics:* yellow head, brownish-gray back, pale gray underparts. Female is duller; young are all gray.

Black-eared Bushtit
Psaltriparus melanotis

YOU CAN DISTINGUISH this tiny gray bird from the common bushtit by the black cheeks of the male. In the female the dark jowls are much less distinct. Like the common tit, the blackear prefers the oaks, junipers, and pines of the mountainous country; but it is usually found at higher altitudes than its companion species.

The blackears have a light *tsit*ing voice and keep up a continual conversation while foraging for insects in flocks of 50 or more.

The female lays four to eight white eggs in a gourd-shaped nest cunningly felted of plant down, spider webs, moss, and lichens. The nest hangs from twigs 6 to 25 feet above the ground. Blackears often raise two broods a year.

Range: S. New Mexico and W. Texas to Guatemala. *Characteristics:* gray head and back, lighter underparts. Male has black cheeks.

Common Bushtit
Psaltriparus minimus

IN A FAMILY of small birds *minimus* ranks as the tiniest of all. He flits from bush to tree, constantly exchanging soft, twittering calls with others in the straggling flock.

If one member spots a hawk nearby he sounds an alarm note. Suddenly every member of the flock joins in a "confusion chorus" of shrill pipings. All stand motionless as the monotonous sound intensifies, making it extremely difficult to locate any individual. The din continues until

Verdin, length 4-4½"; Eliot Porter

Male blackear, length 4-4½"; Allan Brooks

Common bushtit, length 3¾-4¼"; Eliot Porter

the enemy passes through the scattered band.

These bustling bushtits frequent the oak, juniper, and piñon groves of the mountainous Far West. They swing from leaves and twigs seeking the small insects and plant scales that make up the bulk of their diet. Their nondescript gray coloring blends so well with their surroundings that they would be hard to spot were they not always on the move.

In late winter and early spring the flocks break up into pairs for breeding. The nests are works of art — long, hanging pockets swung from slender twigs, with a small entrance at one side near the top. The bushtits may take five or six weeks to build their beautiful nurseries — using moss, lichens, leaves, spider webs, and feathers. The nest holds five to seven white eggs, much favored by marauding jays. Compensating for their losses, bushtits often raise two broods in a season.

Range: coast ranges, S. British Columbia to Baja California, east to Idaho, W. Colorado, and central Texas. *Characteristics:* gray back, brownish head, pale underparts, long tail.

161

The Nuthatches
Family Sittidae

CENTURIES AGO Europeans watched a stub-tailed, thickset, nervous little bird wedging nuts into tree crevices and hacking them open with its long, sturdy bill. The English called the bird "nuthack," the French "notehache." The name stuck, but later observers were more impressed by another nuthatch trait. They saw this woodland gnome scurrying down tree trunks headfirst, and dubbed it "topsy-turvy bird," "upside-down bird," "devil-down-head," or "tree mouse."

The nuthatch, observed American naturalist Herbert Brandt, "runs fearlessly about any bark surface, assuming every conceivable position, all with the nimbleness and the apparent disregard of a fly for the laws of gravity. It proceeds with hops, jerks, and short jumps as though it were responding to uncoiling springs. In fact its whole life seems a series of abrupt starts and stops."

Woodpeckers and creepers, climbing heads up, brace against their tails for support. Nuthatches depend entirely upon their claws. They stretch one foot forward under the breast and the other back under the tail, and hitch nimbly down the trees, digging in with their strong hind toes to support themselves.

Some 30 species of nuthatches are known in a family widely distributed over the earth except in South America, Central America, and central and southern Africa. Four members of the family reside in North America; their names describe them. The white-breasted nuthatch, the largest and most widespread, ranges the continent from southern Canada to southern Mexico. The red-breasted, or Canada nuthatch, inhabits coniferous forests and does not venture south of the Rio Grande. The brown-headed nuthatch is a bird of the open pine woods of the southeastern United States. The pygmy also prefers the pines, but its domain is the mountainous yellow pine belt that extends from British Columbia through the Rockies to the highlands of southern Mexico. Most nuthatches live the year round where they breed. The redbreast, however, may winter as far south as the Gulf Coast.

North American nuthatches measure from 3¾ to 6 inches in length, and the sexes generally resemble each other in plumage. These birds may breed in bird boxes but most often choose a tree hole. Both sexes prepare the nest. For some a natural cavity will do; others invariably dig their own chamber. Incubation lasts 12 to 14 days and is largely the female's chore.

Low, nasal calls and pipings identify the nuthatches as they comb the woodlands for nutmeats and bark-dwelling insects. Up and down the trunks they search, round and about the limbs, ever on the go. Often their relatives, the titmice and creepers, and perhaps a woodpecker or two, join the party. Seeds and suet bring them readily to the feeding tray. But they carry off much more than they eat, for nuthatches are great rainy-day birds. They spend long hours taking provender from bird feeders and wedging it in walls, under shingles, or behind loose bark, despite the fact that the food supply is constantly replenished. This hoarding instinct rewards the nuthatches when ice coats the trees and foraging is lean. Frequently it also benefits the squirrels and jays and other birds that constantly seek these caches.

CLINGING TO THE BARK *in a topsy-turvy stance that only nuthatches manage so well, a whitebreast (about 1½ times life-size) holds a tasty morsel. His sharp bill also probes for insect eggs and hacks open nuts.*

Eliot Porter

White-breasted Nuthatch
Sitta carolinensis

THE WHITEBREAST loses none of the family's acrobatic prowess by being the largest member. He can catch a falling nut in midair or rush headfirst down a trunk and overtake it. He can hang upside down, swinging from a tiny branch.

A bird of short neck, broad shoulders, beady eyes, and glossy black cap, *carolinensis* also likes to get his rations the easy way—at a feeding station. He calls regularly at the shelves, especially if sunflower seeds and suet are set out. Remarkably unafraid, he will take food from a hand after a little patient coaxing.

Industrious hoarders, the whitebreasts airlift much of the fare from the trays to hiding places. They spend most of their waking time gathering food, climbing over the bark of trunks and main branches of large trees. They thrive on spiders, insects, insect eggs, and acorns, shelling the nuts with their bills. Generally they forage with other woodland birds. The whitebreasts remain paired the year round and keep in touch with a piglike, nasal *yank yank* call unlike that of any other bird. They also chatter with a soft conversational *hit hit*.

With the approach of spring the whitebreasts begin to whistle pleasantly, and the male, rather indifferent during the winter months, pays more attention to his mate. He bows before her, sings to her, and brings her food. They usually nest in tree holes, but a bird box covered with bark may attract them. The warmly felted cup of feathers, hair, and vegetable fibers receives five to nine white or pinkish eggs with reddish-brown spots.

Range: S. Canada to S. Mexico. *Characteristics:* black head, white face and breast, gray back, black-and-white wings.

Redbreast, length 4¼-4¾"
Allan Brooks

Whitebreasts, length 5-6"; Allan Brooks

Red-breasted Nuthatch
Sitta canadensis

BOBBING THROUGH the evergreen forest, working over the boles in typical nuthatch fashion, the redbreast strikes the observer as a busier, more stylish bird than the larger whitebreast.

Rusty underparts and a distinctive dark line through the eye enhance the redbreast's plumage. It moves at a quicker tempo, winding all the way out to the ends of the little twigs.

Redbreasts are more sociable, too, chattering constantly among themselves. They ring innumerable changes on their high tin-whistle note and sound like a band of merry penny trumpeters. They also utter a squealing note and a short, explosive *kick*.

This species ranges through the coniferous forests of the United States and Canada. Redbreasts in the north migrate but rarely come to the central region that extends from Saskatchewan to Texas. They may be drawn far to the south by a heavy growth of spruce and pine seeds, a prime source of food. The birds deftly pry under the scales of the cones, probe with their bills, and draw out the seeds. They also fly out to capture insects in the air.

Redbreasts usually excavate a nesting place

Brownhead, length 4-5"; Allan Brooks

Pygmy, length 3¾-4½"; Allan Brooks

in a dead stub or limb. Invariably, even when settling into a bird box, they smear pitch at the entrance. They bring little globules on the tips of their bills and tap the pitch around the hole — science does not know why. On a mattress of soft fibers the female lays four to seven white, creamy, or pinkish eggs with reddish-brown spots.

Range: S. E. Alaska to Newfoundland, south to S. California and North Carolina; winters irregularly to Gulf Coast. *Characteristics:* black cap, black eye stripe on white cheek, gray back, tawny underparts.

Brown-headed Nuthatch
Sitta pusilla

THESE TALKATIVE SPRITES travel through the lonesome pine barrens of the South in little flocks. Sometimes they pore over the needles in the summits of the tallest trees. Or they may sweep close to the ground, examining minutely the nooks and crannies in buildings, telephone poles, and fence posts.

What are they looking for? Pine seeds, grasshoppers, moths, beetles, ants, and spiders. As they forage they offer a medley of soft *pit pit* sounds and harsh, reedy pipings. The flock often scolds vociferously at intruders. If really alarmed, the birds hide by freezing against the bark that they match so closely in color.

Mated pairs dig a nest hole in a post or utility pole, but more often in an area of dead pines — stubs riven by lightning, blackened by fire, or killed by impounded water. On a soft nest lining the female lays a set of five or six creamy eggs spotted with reddish brown. After breeding, the birds roam the woods in family groups with wood-

peckers, kinglets, pine warblers, and titmice.

A pale subspecies of the brownhead, the gray-headed nuthatch, resides in Florida.

Range: S. E. Oklahoma to S. Delaware, south to Gulf Coast. *Characteristics:* brown cap down to the eye, white nape spot, gray back, white throat and underparts.

Pygmy Nuthatch
Sitta pygmaea

THE GRAY MIDGETS of the nuthatch family follow the yellow pines all the way up to 10,000 feet in the western mountains. Their strong bills crack the pine nuts or pry hidden insects from trunks and the very topmost limbs. The birds flutter in front of terminal twigs to pick off insects and dart out to snatch one on the wing.

Rubbing against the rough bark, the birds may be smeared with pine pitch, and whitish breast feathers often become worn.

The pygmy usually nests in a conifer stub, preparing a felted mass of plant down and fur or feathers. The six to nine white eggs are lightly spotted with reddish brown.

In the fall pygmies gather in small flocks and troop through the forests with titmice, warblers, and creepers. The most conspicuous bird sounds are the shrill twitters and rapid *kit-kit-kit* of the nuthatches. In winter many of these birds retreat from the yellow pines to the lower oaks, junipers, and piñons.

Range: mountainous areas from S. British Columbia to W. South Dakota, south to S. Mexico. *Characteristics:* gray-brown cap down to the eye, white nape spot, gray back, whitish underparts.

The Wrentit
Family Chamaeidae

WINTER AND SUMMER, spring and autumn, the song rings through the lowland chaparral and brushy stream borders up and down the West Coast. Staccato at first, then running into a trill: *yip-yip-yip-yi-ytr-tr-tr-r-r-r*.

The loud, whistle-like song is often heard, but the singers are hard to find. For the wrentit (*Chamaea fasciata*) rarely leaves the thick brush. When he does he is easy to recognize: a brown bird with a long, rounded tail tilted up from the body. He climbs about the twigs like a wren and takes to the air with his tail pumping to cross little openings, but he doesn't fly far.

The wrentit chooses one homesite and one mate—both for life. On their acre or so of brushland the two birds, which wear similar plumage, do almost everything together. They forage for berries in season. In summer they gather insects, sometimes hanging upside down, titmouse fashion, as they hunt among the leaves. They roost together, lean-

ing against each other with feathers interlaced and inner legs drawn up. They build a nest of cobwebs, bark shreds, and feathers, hiding it in a low bush under a screen of leafy twigs. Jays sometimes take the three to five pale blue eggs and the nestlings.

The Chamaeidae are the only family of birds restricted to North America, and the wrentit is its only member. Its nearest relatives are among the babblers (Family Timaliidae) of the Old World.

Range: western Oregon to northern Baja California. *Characteristics:* white eye, grayish-brown back, streaked cinnamon-brown underparts; long legs and long, tilted tail.

Wrentits, length 6-6½"; Arthur A. Allen and (below) Allan Brooks

The Brown Creeper
Family Certhiidae

BARK and the brown creeper (*Certhia familiaris*) go well together. Bark provides food, shelter, and a protective background. And as the creeper spirals up the boles, it eats insects and eggs that may threaten the life of the trees.

Nature endowed the creeper superbly for this partnership. The bird's long claws and bracing tail hold it to the trunk. Its curved, needle-sharp bill extracts the food from crevices. Alarmed by a hawk or shrike, the creeper flattens against the trunk; the bird's brown, streaked back blends with the bark pattern.

The creeper builds a hammock-shaped nest of twigs, fibers, and moss behind a loose shingle of bark. The four to eight eggs are white with brown spots.

Usually inconspicuous, the creeper often makes itself known by a thin, high-pitched call or a delicate warbling. Male and female look alike. Seven similar forms of this species are found in North America; others dwell in Europe and Asia.

Range: S. E. Alaska to Newfoundland, south in west to Nicaragua, in east to S. Appalachians; winters to Gulf Coast.
Characteristics: brown back with gray streaks; white underparts, curved bill.

Brown creeper, length 5-5¾"
Allan D. Cruickshank
National Audubon Society

HERMIT AT THE WATERFALL

♪♪ The Dipper

Family Cinclidae

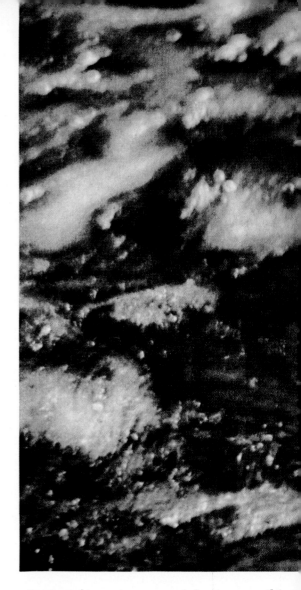

FORAGING *in western mountain streams, the*

P ERCHED ON A ROCK in a mountain stream, a slate-colored bird with pale legs and white lower eyelids bobs rapidly up and down, then chirps a sharp *zeet*. Compact body, strong feet, and a short, upturned tail make the dipper (*Cinclus mexicanus*) look like an oversized wren.

Rushing waters swirl about it, and spray dashes against its toes. Suddenly it plunges into the torrent and disappears. The dipper, or water ouzel, is "flying" underwater, propelled by stubby, rounded wings.

Seizing an insect from the gravelly bottom, it pops back to the surface some 20 feet from the original perch. Now, swimming across the surface, it heads for the bank and clambers ashore. Again it bobs vigorously—some 40 to 60 times a minute. This characteristic motion inspired the common name of dipper or "teeter bird." At last it takes to the air, skimming along just above the water with rapid, whirring wingbeats.

A solitary bird, the dipper always lives near water—foaming rapids being its preference. "Find a fall, or cascade, or rushing rapid, anywhere upon a clear stream," advised naturalist John Muir, "and there you will surely find its complementary Ouzel, flitting about in the spray, diving in foaming eddies, whirling like a leaf among beaten foam-bells; ever vigorous and enthusiastic, yet self-contained, and neither seeking nor shunning your company."

The dipper is the only purely aquatic perching bird in North America. Movable flaps or scales close over each nostril when the bird goes underwater, and an enlarged preen gland supplies oil for dressing and waterproofing the plumage. Beneath the outer feathers lies a warm, protective coat of underdown. Besides diving and swimming in search of food, the ouzel also walks on the bottom of streams. It eats caddis fly larvae and other aquatic insects, snails, and the fry of fish.

The dipper is one of four species comprising the family Cinclidae, all similar in form to the wrens. They inhabit mountainous areas of Europe and Asia, as well as the western highlands of North and South America, to altitudes of 12,000 feet. All

Dipper, length 7-8½"; Alfred M. Bailey and Patricia Bailey Witherspoon
dipper may remain submerged 30 seconds. Both sexes wear identical gray plumage.

are quite similar in general appearance, and males and females look alike. The juveniles have spotted breasts, revealing the family's kinship with the thrushes.

The dipper does not migrate but merely moves to lower altitudes to find running water. Its burbling wrenlike song—clear and sweet, with many trills and cadenzas —may be heard at any time of the year.

The female builds her nest near the water—on a ledge, a rock in midstream, or among the tangled roots of a waterlogged stump. Sometimes she hides it behind a waterfall. Considered by Muir "one of the most extraordinary pieces of bird architecture," the globular weave of moss and grass measures about a foot in diameter and has an arched entrance at one side. A dipper may raise two broods a year. The three to six white eggs hatch after 16 days of incubation. After a nest life of 15 to 24 days, the young take to the water.

Range: mountain areas of western North America from north central Alaska and Aleutian Islands to Panama. *Characteristics:* slate plumage, short tail, bobbing motion; swims underwater. Young have spotted breasts.

BROWNIES WITH BIG VOICES The Wrens
Family Troglodytidae

Acording to an ancient fable, the birds of the world decided to choose as their ruler the one that could rise highest from the earth. In the competition the great eagle mounted steadily upward until he had outdistanced all the others. The other birds were about to acclaim him king when from his back came a burst of song. The little wren had concealed himself among the eagle's feathers. Having been borne so far aloft without labor, the bird flew out and easily won the crown!

The wren of the fable is the Old World species, closely allied to the winter wren of North America. It is the only wren found outside of the New World, where the family is believed to have originated. Representatives of the 63 species penetrate into Patagonia and thrive in the dense vegetation of the tropics and on the bleak slopes of the Andes. Ten breed north of Mexico.

They combine timidity, curiosity, and aggressiveness. From its hiding place in a vine, thicket, or weed clump, a wren may hop out to chatter at an intruder or to sing, then dash back to cover at the slightest alarm. Cherokee Indians in their mythology considered the wren a busybody who slipped about learning everybody's business and reporting it to the birds' council. When a baby was born in the tribe, the wren brought the news. If the papoose was a boy, the birds were sorrowful, for they knew he would grow up to hunt them. If it was a girl they were glad, for she would not harm them.

In the United States some of our wrens are year-round residents; others leave the colder regions to winter in the southern states, Mexico, or Central America. In the spring these wide-ranging birds seek nesting sites on the eroded tablelands of the Southwest, in the cool forests of the North, in the brackish swamps along the Atlantic, Gulf, and Pacific coasts—and often in your neighborhood.

Many of the wrens nest in cavities fashioned by nature or man. This trait explains the family name Troglodytidae, or "cave dwellers." These little birds may make their home in an abandoned woodpecker hole, a canyon crevice, the twig-filled hollow of a cactus, a domed thatching of bog grass, or a homemade, backyard birdhouse.

Perky and brown, with tail cocked over his back, the wren defends his territory fiercely, sometimes puncturing or rolling out the eggs of competing birds. His powerful song ranks high in bird music. Females of many species sing too. Mates put on duets, one starting, the other finishing the tumbling, bubbling phrases.

HOUSE WREN *brings home an insect to feed her young. A gourd is her castle; she stuffed it with twigs to bar intruders and shaped a nest amid the clutter. Feathers cradle the clutch of eggs below.*

Arthur A. Allen

171

House Wren

Troglodytes aedon

A BUSTLING BUNDLE of nervous energy, the house wren shows up in spring in garden trees and roadside shrubs throughout southern Canada and most of the United States. Brief acquaintance dispels any illusion that this bird is as self-effacing as small size and drab plumage suggest. Early settlers, reminded of the wren they knew in Britain, named this one "jenny" after it. A strange name it is, for there is nothing feminine about this jaunty, belligerent mite.

Spring brings the male to his breeding grounds to stake a territorial claim before the females arrive. He seeks a low, wooded tract, preferably deciduous, perhaps at the far edge of a yard. Finding it, he proclaims his rights.

His song is a torrent of liquid notes, delivered with driving vigor. He may repeat it four times a minute. Listening to this vocal cascade, the Chippewa Indians named the bird *O-du-na-mis-sug-ud-da-we'-shi:* "a big noise for its size."

Should the big noise fail to halt trespassers, the house wren may try a smaller one — a grating scold, full of dark threats. And if this and menacing displays do not drive away a claim jumper, the wren may attack. He fights off incursions by his own species and by Bewick's wren. Another close relative, the Carolina wren, he tolerates though its nest may adjoin his own.

The male house wren is a habitual nest starter. He stuffs any likely nesting cavity with twigs, grass, and other materials, perhaps to mark his territory and perhaps as an inducement to the females when they arrive.

As soon as they appear, the busy male sings to draw their attention. He courts one ardently, wings quivering, tail flicking straight up. If she proves receptive, he escorts her around his prospective nest sites.

The female almost always disapproves of her mate's homebuilding efforts. After she selects one of his sites she usually removes all the materials and starts the nest over again. Sometimes she collects strange items. One nest contained 52 hairpins, 188 nails, 4 tacks, 13 staples, 10 pins, 11 safety pins, 6 paper clips, 2 hooks, 3 garter fasteners, and a buckle. Another was largely built of chicken wire.

Controversies rage during the rejection and rebuilding of nests. Pairs of house wrens often fight like fury, but the job gets done. The female lines the nest to suit her; the male stands guard and sometimes starts another nest which may be used later for a second brood. He also may take up with a second female, for just as his mate is a shrew, he is a philanderer.

In the wilds house wrens nest in natural hollows or old woodpecker holes. They have been known to appropriate hornet and wasp nests and to live in bleached cattle skulls. But near man's habitat the birds make full use of whatever civilization may provide: a soap dish, a weathervane, old farm machinery, a bag of feathers. Amazingly adaptable, they may set up housekeeping in a tin can in a garbage dump, or in a mailbox, a basket, even an old hat (page 48). And of course they welcome boxes and birdhouses that people put up for them.

To bar house sparrows, wren houses should have an entrance hole no more than 1¼ inches across. A slit this high and several inches wide may provide a better door, for it permits wrens to carry in twigs held crosswise in their bills. House wrens often leave sticks jutting out from their entrances to help bar larger birds.

The six to eight eggs, finely sprinkled with reddish-brown dots, hatch in 13 days. House wrens have a strong feeding instinct and are tireless parents. One male, working from 4:15 a.m. to 8:00 p.m., made 1,217 trips in a single day with food for his family. He averaged a trip every 47 seconds, not counting the sorties that he made to satisfy his own hunger.

Sometimes when a house wren has not found a mate and raised a brood, he will gratify his parental urge by feeding the young and even the parents of other species. Observers have seen the birds feeding a family of grosbeaks, also a nestful of house sparrows, which are among the house wren's worst enemies.

An even greater danger to the birds is the farm cat. Since wrens both young and old feed almost exclusively on insects destructive to crops, many nest near cultivated fields. Farmers welcome them — and so does tabby.

Young house wrens leave the nest about two weeks after hatching. As fall approaches, the birds grow shy and desert farm and backyard to find seclusion in the woods. Soon they migrate.

T HE HOUSE WREN can be distinguished from his relatives because he lacks the pronounced eyeline of other North American wrens. The western house wren is slightly larger and paler than the eastern race but shares all its habits.

The brown-throated wren of Mexico (*Troglodytes brunneicollis*) was not recorded north of the border until 1945, when it was discovered nesting in Arizona. This bird is so closely related to the house wren that many scientists consider it another subspecies. The brownthroat wears a buffy eye stripe, however, and to the ears of an expert his voice is distinctly different.

Range: S. British Columbia to New Brunswick, south to N. Baja California and N. Georgia; winters to S. Mexico and S. Florida. *Characteristics:* brown upperparts, buffy underparts; blackish bars on rounded wings and tail.

SHORT-TAILED BABY HOUSE WRENS *clamor for a tidbit outside their custom-built home.*
Adult, length 4½-5¼"; Walter A. Weber, National Geographic staff artist

Short-billed marsh wren, length 4-4½"; Eliot Porter

Cañon wren, length 5½-5¾"; Alfred M. Bailey

Long-billed marsh wren, length 4¼-5½"
Allan D. Cruickshank, National Audubon Society

Long-billed Marsh Wren
Telmatodytes palustris

CUT-CUT-TURRRRR-UR. You may hear this song, day or night, in brackish coastal marshes or in sloughs far in the interior. It sounds like pebbles being struck together and signals the presence of *palustris*. Look for him creeping down a cattail stem to pluck mosquito larvae from the water, or rising swiftly in song from the rushes, only to flutter slowly down.

He arrives first in spring and begins building dummy nests. When the females come some ten days later, he woos one by perching above her, fluffing out his breast feathers, and cocking his tail over his back so far that it almost touches.

The female builds the true nest, a coconut-shaped home of leaf strips, stems, and grasses lined with down and fine fibers, with an opening near the top. Usually it is attached to several reed stems, one to three feet above the water. The spotted brownish eggs normally number three to seven, but there may be as many as ten. Longbills raise two broods a season, and the males are often polygamous.

Not all races of *palustris* migrate. Those that do go no farther in fall than southern Mexico.

Range: central British Columbia to New Brunswick, south to S. Mexico. *Characteristics:* brownish upperparts, white stripe over eye, black-and-white streaks on back; dull white underparts.

174

Short-billed Marsh Wren
Cistothorus platensis

PERCHED on a swaying sedge stem, a male short-bill serenades his hidden mate with a dry *chap chap chap chap chapper-rrr*. If you approach, he hops down and scurries off like a mouse.

These shy, tiny wrens lurk in the drier, grassy marshes and wet meadows, feeding almost entirely on insects. They build several false nests. The true one, a ball of grass with an opening in the side, is hidden deep in a tussock. The female alone incubates the four to seven white eggs.

Range: S. E. Saskatchewan to New Brunswick, south to Arkansas and Virginia; winters to the Gulf Coast and S. Florida. *Characteristics:* streaked brownish upperparts, buffy underparts.

Rock wren, length 5-6¼"; Eliot Porter

Cañon Wren

Catherpes mexicanus

SUDDENLY THE CANYON rings with song, a silvery cascade of descending notes followed by an upward flourish. You look up and see a brown bird creeping along a rock ledge. Soon this star vocalist of the western gorges pauses and throws back his head. The gleaming white throat swells, and again the rock walls resound with the cañon wren's wild and lovely song, so powerful that it can be heard a quarter of a mile away.

Nature has adapted *mexicanus* to canyon haunts. With his sharp claws he climbs up and down the steepest surfaces as he hunts insects and spiders. His short legs and flattish body enable him to squeeze into nooks and crannies.

But you may meet him in town too. He frequents the chimneys of abandoned houses and probes among piles of brush and old tin cans. He may also invade an occupied home. One pair nested over a window in a Texas ranch house. The wrens would hop about the floor and sing from a table when the owners were in the room!

Usually cañon wrens nest on a rocky ledge or in a crevice inside a cave. On a foundation of twigs they form a cup of leaves, moss, and spider webs. The five or six white eggs, dotted with reddish brown, rest on a lining of wool or feathers.

Range: S. British Columbia to S. W. South Dakota, south to S. Mexico. *Characteristics:* brownish head and back with whitish dots; white throat and breast, reddish-brown belly.

Rock Wren
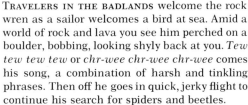
Salpinctes obsoletus

TRAVELERS IN THE BADLANDS welcome the rock wren as a sailor welcomes a bird at sea. Amid a world of rock and lava you see him perched on a boulder, bobbing, looking shyly back at you. *Tew tew tew tew* or *chr-wee chr-wee chr-wee* comes his song, a combination of harsh and tinkling phrases. Then off he goes in quick, jerky flight to continue his search for spiders and beetles.

This wren builds its cuplike nest of grasses, straw, and rootlets on a foundation of small flat stones. Usually it is placed in a rodent's abandoned burrow or in a crevice or hole in a cliff or gully. Nearly always a stone pathway eight to ten inches in length leads to the nest. Sometimes pebbles are piled up at the entrance like a barrier. The five or six eggs, rarely ten, are glossy white sprinkled with reddish brown.

Range: central British Columbia to S. Saskatchewan, south to Costa Rica; migratory in the north. *Characteristics:* grayish-brown head and back, dull white underparts with dusky streaks on throat and chest; cinnamon rump, black band and buffy patches at end of tail.

Walter A. Weber
National Geographic staff artist

Allan D. Cruickshank, National Audubon Society

Winter wren, length 4-4½″

Bewick's wren, length 5-5½″

Winter Wren
Troglodytes troglodytes

A TINY, SECRETIVE BIRD, the winter wren summers in the forest depths. In these dark, still haunts his enchanting song fairly bursts upon your ears. The notes tumble over each other in a long succession of tinkling warbles and trills.

Bobbing up and down, he gathers insects in brush, windfalls, and shrubbery. The female, who looks like her mate, usually builds the nest of moss and twigs in the earth-encrusted roots of a fallen tree or in a stump. She also incubates the five or six white eggs dotted with brown.

Most winter wrens head south in fall and may visit gardens in migration. Nine races, however, dwell the year round in the islands off Alaska. This species also inhabits Europe and Asia.

Range: S. Alaska to Newfoundland, south to central California, Idaho, Massachusetts, and in the mountains to N. Georgia; winters to S. California and S. Florida. *Characteristics:* brown upperparts, paler eyebrow stripe and underparts; barred wings and belly; short, barred tail.

Bewick's Wren
Thryomanes bewickii

LONG, FAN-SHAPED TAIL twitching, this friendly bird creeps along fences and under the eaves of buildings hunting insects. Now and then he throws his head back to deliver a sweet, powerful song. Little wonder *bewickii*, named by Audubon for the English engraver, Thomas Bewick, is often adopted as the "house" wren in its range.

These wrens may nest in a woodpecker hole, a brush pile, a barrel, or even a mailbox. The five to seven white eggs are spotted with brown. The female incubates them for about 14 days.

Range: S. British Columbia to S. Utah, S. Ontario, and Virginia, south to S. Mexico and northern sections of the Gulf states; winters to the Gulf Coast and S. Florida. *Characteristics:* brown upperparts, white eyebrow stripe and tail spots, whitish underparts; long, barred tail.

Carolina Wren
Thryothorus ludovicianus

THIS CHUNKY CHARMER is apparently not content to keep his whistling in Dixie. He has been moving north. Today he may breed as far as Minnesota or Maine. But such ventures can be fatal. Nonmigratory, he frequently fails to survive a severe northern winter.

One of our more persistent bird musicians, the Carolina wren sings the year round, rain or shine. Often he sings as he darts about thickets and yard shrubbery searching for insects. His rich, whistled notes sound like *teakettle, teakettle,* or *sweetheart, sweetheart.*

He and his mate may build a domed nursery in a tree fork or nest in almost any kind of cavity or receptacle. The four to six white or pinkish eggs are spotted with brown.

Range: S. E. Nebraska to S. Ontario and S. Massachusetts, south to N. Mexico and S. Florida. *Characteristics:* white eyebrow stripe, rusty upperparts, buffy underparts, barred tail.

176

Cactus wren, length 7-8½"

Carolina, length 5¼-6"; Arthur A. Allen

Cactus Wren
Campylorhynchus brunneicapillus

SWIFTLY the huge wren with the blotchy throat feathers runs across the cracked earth to a fallen cactus joint. Lifting it with the side of his bill, he peers under and spies an ant. Snap! Snack swallowed, he flies to a shaded yucca limb and sings a coarse *chuh-chuh-chuh-chuh*. In the heat he holds his bill open as if panting and lifts his wings for ventilation.

The nights are cool, however. At sunset he retires to one of several retort-shaped nests he has fashioned from plant fibers amid the spiky desert shrubbery. With cozy feather lining and tunnel-like side entrances, they provide snug year-round homes. In one of them the female incubates four or five pinkish eggs dotted with reddish brown.

This wren, the state bird of Arizona, often settles around dwellings. The young birds squawk at each other and race playfully about buildings and lawn furniture. In fall the youngsters build their own roosting nests.

Range: S. California to S. Utah and central Texas, south to central Mexico. *Characteristics:* largest U. S. wren; brown head and back, white eyebrow stripe, back streaks, and tail edges; light underparts heavily spotted with black.

Courtship and Nesting Behavior

By ROBERT M. McCLUNG

CAROLING HIS SPRING SONG from the limb of one of our apple trees, a male robin tells the world that he claims our backyard as his own. Suddenly his bright eyes spot another robin, an interloper, on the lawn.

Down he swoops. Head feathers bristling, tail high, he hops toward his rival. For a moment the two square off like small boys, toe to toe, each daring the other to strike the first blow. Then they hurl themselves at one another and collide in midair in a flurry of beaks, legs, and fluttering wings.

Tumbling to the ground, they separate, then tangle again and again until the intruder calls it quits and flies away.

I know that the victorious cock robin would attack with equal fury the stuffed skin of another male (left), or smash into his own reflection in a window. He might even fight a tuft of feathers colored like a male robin's breast. For this is his courtship time and, like most male songbirds, he is vigorously defending the territory he claims for courting, nesting, and feeding a family.

This aggressive behavior is one phase in a series of instinctive activities that follow one another like links in a chain. All lead to the robin's primary goal—the propagation of his species. And the whole cycle is triggered by the lengthening, warming days of spring. "For, lo, the winter is past, the rain is over and gone;

DEFENDING HIS TERRITORY *in the fervor of the spring courting season, a cock robin pounces on an intruder. Though his rival is only a stuffed bird skin placed there in a scientific experiment, he attacks it furiously.*

Arthur A. Allen

179

the flowers appear on the earth; the time of the singing of birds is come. . . ." How beautifully the Bible's Song of Solomon expresses the feeling of joy and new life that springtime and the glimpse of the first robin bring!

In contrast I recall a short, cold afternoon when Christmas was in the air. The house was warm and bright, filled with smells of cooking and the murmur of children decorating the tree. Through the window I watched juncos and sparrows gather at the feeder, their feathers fluffed against the chill. They ate their fill, and as the leaden sky darkened they fluttered off to find shelter from the bitterness of night and the threat of snow. This December day, I realized, was the year's shortest in the northern hemisphere. At this time, when the sun's path lies farthest to the south, survival is the only concern of the wintering species.

Just as the sun affects the growth of a plant, it guides the inner workings of a bird. In midwinter the creature spends the few sunlit hours searching for food and water. But as the new year dawns the days grow longer. The sun's path approaches the equator, crosses it on March 21, and swings farther north each day.

At my home in Amherst, Massachusetts, the snow melts, the earth seems to stir, slowly awakening to spring. Furry catkins appear on pussy willows. Skunk cabbages thrust their purple hoods through the thawing ground. Swelling buds show color as sap rises in the trees. Spring peepers call from the swamp behind the meadow. Then one day I glance out at the lawn and see a robin hopping briskly about, as though he had never been away.

Again, I have the sun to thank for the return of my robin friend. Increasing light stimulated the bird's pituitary gland to give off hormones. These activated the reproductive organs. They in turn secreted into the blood stream other hormones which set up the pattern of behavior for the robin – a series of urges for him to obey in regular sequence. One of the first of these urges was to get back north to his breeding ground – which happened to be my backyard.

M IGRATING FLOCKS of robins follow the leading edge of spring northward, taking advantage of favorable weather to fly. They keep pace with their food supply as it is freed from winter's grip. The birds often advance as much as 40 miles a day as they move with the thaws that bring out their favorite food, earthworms.

Storms or sudden freezes may hold them back for a time, but even these delays help to coordinate their movement. For like other migrating birds, robins follow a timetable that brings them to their breeding grounds to court, mate, and raise broods when their food supply is increasing. Ideally, the supply will be greatest when the robins need it most.

In many kinds of birds the sexes migrate separately. Adult male red-winged blackbirds, for example, reach their northern haunts first: adult females follow about two weeks later; immature birds – last year's nestlings – come last. This schedule allows the males to set up their territories so that they may concentrate on courtship when the females arrive.

Around Amherst male redwings usually appear during the blustery weather of late March. Swaying on stalks of winter-killed cattails, they display their bright red epaulets and utter their characteristic *ok-a-lee* over and over again. Robins dot the greening lawns about the same time, and I hear the year-round resident cardinals whistle their loud *cheer cheer cheer* from lofty singing posts. By this time hardy English sparrows are already incubating eggs in their untidy nests under the eaves

(Continued on page 184)

YELLOW-HEADED BLACKBIRD *in Utah's Bear River marshes pours forth his love call. It sounds like a rusty gate, but it's music to the female's ears. She arrives, is entranced by his plumage display, and succumbs to his courtship antics.*

Frederick Kent Truslow

SOUND AND FURY *signify the breeding season
for these yellow-shafted flickers.
Strident calls, wicker wicker wicker,
ring out above the new fields of spring.
Loud drumming echoes through the
budding forest as the birds
chisel out nest holes.*

*Propped on her stiff tail
feathers, a female (right)
dares her rival to approach,
while the male, apex of
this courtship triangle,
hammers away at his nest.
Black moustache beside
his lower mandible is
the badge of his sex.*

*Two wary females (below)
square off, beak to beak. One is
apparently backing down, while
the other seems to say, "Go steal
a mate from some other bird!"*

*The male ignores the bickering
and works on until the winning
female arrives. They indulge in
mutual display (top right), then
fly off into the woods. Returning
to inspect the nest, she finds it too
bare and reams the inside to provide
chips as a bed for the eggs.*

*Next on the flickers' schedule:
a clutch of 6 to 8 lustrous white eggs
and 11 or 12 days' incubation before the
ugly, blind, helpless nestlings are hatched.*

Frederick Kent Truslow

SOMETHING COZY FOR THE NEST, *cotton tied to a branch, attracts a diligent female*

of an old shed. Not before April, however, do I hear the house wren's cascading music as he inspects a nest box in the front yard maple tree. By then migration has quickened. New birds arrive every day. Skirmishes over territories increase.

Nesting territories vary in size. Birds that gather in colonies—chimney swifts, purple martins, and cliff swallows, for example—may defend only the few square inches that their nests occupy. They gather food on the wing and share the same aerial hunting grounds. But most songbirds stake out claims from a few square yards to several acres in extent and defend them with battles royal.

At this time our backyard robin becomes thoroughly conditioned to fighting. Yet another kind of bird with dissimilar requirements for its life may share his territory without any fuss. I have seen different species that do not compete nest peacefully within a few feet of each other.

Many birds proclaim the boundaries of their territories from certain perches—limbs, rocks, or posts—often the same ones year after year. Our robin has many such vantage points and pours out his song from each of them in turn. He sings more

yellow warbler. She can expect no homemaking help from the male "yellowbird."

or less throughout the day, but the peak periods are likely to fall in early morning and late afternoon. Song sparrows have been heard singing almost constantly for nine hours a day—more than 2,000 separate songs! By trumpeting their claims and indulging in a good many fights, male songbirds finally reach agreement on borders that all can respect. Then the females arrive.

Attracted by the songs (the sunrise serenade can be almost deafening to the human householder), female birds wander through various territories. In many species their plumage is almost identical to that of the males, so the arrival of a female brings a male bird swooping down, feathers abristle, ready for instant warfare. Here's an intruder! Throw the scoundrel out!

But the trespassing bird neither offers resistance nor flies away. Her response is typically feminine, and suddenly all the fight drains out of the male bird. Before he knows it the next instinct in that pattern of behavior has taken hold, and he is courting this oddly attractive stranger. Of course, in those species where the two sexes wear quite different plumage there is no problem of identification.

Courtship to a male prairie chicken means dancing and strutting before the fe-

ATTENTIVE GOLDFINCH *perches beside his nest-bound mate, who has just hatched* *the eggs. He feeds her by regurgitating crushed milkweed seeds into her bill.*

She will pass the predigested meal on to her young; they get it third time round!

male on an open display ground. Cranes, storks, and herons do the same thing, but both sexes take part.

Among most songbirds the male takes the initiative. He may sing to the female, then spread his tail and show off his fine breeding plumage. He may offer her a bit of food or drop a twig before her, presumably a symbol of the nest. Bobolinks and meadowlarks sing and display on the wing, but most species do their courting with both feet on the ground or on a handy perch.

Once a female accepts the attentions of a posturing male, the two become mates. Some waterfowl and birds of prey are believed to mate for life, but most birds stay together for only one breeding season. Some nest more than once in a season and may take a new partner for each nesting.

In most species, if anything should happen to one of the mates, the other quickly finds a replacement. One female indigo bunting accepted ten males in rapid succession. Each time her current partner was removed she took a new one.

Certain species like the blackbirds often practice polygamy. Dominant males take several mates and help raise the young of each. Still other birds are completely promiscuous and form many temporary and casual liaisons. This is the way with many game birds. One lusty sage grouse was observed mating with 21 different females in the course of a single morning!

A FTER COURTSHIP and mating comes the serious business of nest building and egg laying. Most songbirds build a new nest each year, sometimes a new one for every brood. Just as the male bird usually selects the territory, the female generally chooses the nesting site within it. More often than not she does the actual building as well, though her mate may help gather the material. Female hummingbirds and vireos do the whole job themselves. Male and female woodpeckers, kingfishers, and swallows share the task.

By the time the nest is finished, the hen bird is ready to lay her eggs. In practically

The birth of a bird

INTO THE WORLD *struggles a baby blue jay (upper), tiny egg tooth that pipped the shell still in place on its bill. Parents cram food into the helpless young (left). Blind and naked at birth, the nestlings open their eyes within a few days (right); pinfeathers sprout. In about two weeks (opposite) the four lusty youngsters fill the twig nest to overflowing. Orange-red mouths gape as they clamor for food. Well feathered, the fledglings soon will leave home and begin to fend for themselves.*

every species she has only one functional ovary—the left one—and it is active only during breeding season. At egg-laying time it is greatly enlarged, and the developing eggs give it the shape of a bunch of many-sized grapes. Scientists believe that hormones from the pituitary gland regulate the growth of each egg and the time when it will be discharged into the oviduct.

The egg is a single giant cell—mostly yolk. When it reaches the proper stage of development, it moves into the open end of the oviduct and is fertilized by waiting sperm. Then it starts its journey to the outside.

On its way down the narrow passageway the fertilized egg receives a layer of albumen from glands in the walls of the oviduct; farther on it picks up membranes which will line the inside of the shell. The shell is formed by limy secretions in the uterus. As these harden they remain plain or are marked or tinted with color from pigment glands. At last the finished egg emerges, usually big end first.

Many large birds produce only one egg every two or three days, but most small kinds lay an egg daily until their clutch is complete. With many species the number of eggs in each clutch is almost invariably the same. The rare California condor

breeds only every other year and lays just one egg each time. Hummingbirds and doves ordinarily lay two eggs, and many sandpipers four. Most songbirds in temperate regions average four to six eggs in each clutch. Weather, abundance of food, or other external conditions may influence the number.

Certain birds have been known to lay day after day, almost indefinitely, when something happened to their eggs. The flicker usually lays a clutch of six to eight, but in one experiment an egg was removed from a flicker's nest each day, so that the bird never had more than one to show for her trouble. Trying to complete her clutch, the long-suffering female laid 71 eggs in 73 days!

SOME BIRDS begin to incubate as soon as the first egg is laid. But most wait until the clutch is complete, with the result that all their eggs hatch at about the same time. Thus the parents can devote undivided attention to their young.

Among buntings and sparrows the female bears the full burden of incubation, while her mate stands guard and may bring food to her. But in the case of many other songbirds the male and female share the job, taking turns sitting on the eggs.

With my family I have watched the pair of catbirds that nest amid the tangled shrubbery near the back porch. During incubation the male sometimes arrives to spell the female. He slips into the nest, inspects the eggs, turns them over with his bill, then settles down on them with many a wriggle.

Incubating birds develop brood patches—areas on the abdomen that are bare of feathers. Here networks of fine blood vessels lie close to the surface. These distribute body heat directly to the eggs and keep them at their normal incubating temperature—about 93° F. The royal albatross incubates its single egg about 80 days. Waterfowl sit on their eggs about 28 to 35 days. Crows incubate 18 to 20 days, jays 16 to 18. For small songbirds incubation usually lasts only 12 to 14 days.

The embryo grows atop the yolk, nourished by it and by the albumen, which also cushions shocks. The porous shell allows air to enter and gaseous wastes to

pass out. At the large end is the air sac—air that the baby may breathe just before it hatches. When its time has arrived to face the world, the hatchling pips the shell with a tiny egg tooth at the tip of its bill. This hard protrusion drops off a few days later. The baby cracks the shell, eventually breaks it in two, then struggles free. Most parent birds either eat the egg shells or remove them from the nest.

Songbirds are blind, practically naked, and utterly helpless when they hatch. In the beginning they are too weak to be fed, so they rely on all they have absorbed from the yolk. They are cold-blooded—unable to control their body heat—for the first three or four days. So their parents must shade them from the sun, shield them from night's chill, and of course feed them constantly. The infant's total existence is a steady round of gaping for food, swallowing what is pumped down the gullet, digesting, defecating, and sleeping.

The inside of a baby songbird's mouth is bright-colored—red, orange, or yellow. Instinctively, he raises his wobbly head and opens his bill wide when he feels the nest jiggle as his father or mother lands on the rim, or when he hears their food call. His bright mouth makes a prominent target for the parent birds. The sight of it sets off a response in them—a strong desire to cram food into this gleaming cavity. Sometimes the impulse gets so overwhelming that adult birds will forget their own young and spend time feeding larger, more active gapers in a nearby nest.

Songbird hatchlings get plenty of protein food for rapid growth—usually insects, with some seeds and berries thrown in. A parent bird often predigests the meal, then thrusts its beak far down the infant's throat to activate the impulse to swallow. Then the adult regurgitates into the baby's gullet.

As soon as the little bird has been fed, he automatically raises his body and discharges a neat sac of waste material. If this is not forthcoming immediately, the parent may prod him in the rump. The parent swallows the sac or flies off with it.

When the nestling is four or five days old, he goes through what might be called the feather explosion. Blue-sheathed feathers erupt, sprouting as spiky quills, then quickly growing and expanding. In several days he is pretty well covered.

As his eyes open fully and his senses register, the baby bird becomes increasingly aware of the wonderful world around him. Before long he will show fear at the

THESE BLUEBIRDS *(above) were hand-raised for six months in a sound-isolation chamber in Cornell's Laboratory of Ornithology at Ithaca, New York. Then songs of various birds were piped in. The observer, tape-recording their response, noted that the young bluebirds showed little interest. Finally he played the bluebird song. Reacting strongly to these unfamiliar notes, they quickly learned to sing them.*

CORNELL SCIENTISTS *record bird activity on a graph. At every call, flutter, or scratch by the parrots caged in the background one of 20 buttons is pressed, and a squiggle of ink marks the paper roll.*

A syringe replaces mother's bill for a test of diet (left). Formula for this baby bluebird: cottage cheese, fruit, vitamins, and antibiotics, mixed with earthworms and chick starter in an electric blender.

James M. Hartshorne. Upper: Robert B. Goodman

Bruce R. Young

sight of an intruder. He cheeps in panic or crouches silently in the bottom of his nest.

At last the day comes when the young bird leaves the nest. He may tumble out on his own, launching himself on unsteady wings, like the fledgling robin that made his first flight right before me as I prepared to mow the lawn. He took off from a branch above my head and came down, wings flapping frantically, without the slightest control. But he landed successfully in the thick grass and seemed mighty proud of himself—like a novice skier who has just completed his first awkward, arm-flailing run down the golf-course slope and stood up all the way!

Sometimes the parents must persuade a baby bird to leave, perhaps refusing to feed him so that he will venture out for dinner. Even after he has taken the big step, his parents' duties are not done. In some species such as the robin the father now takes charge while the mother goes about raising another brood. The solicitous male disperses and hides his young in sheltered places so that predators won't snap them up or severe weather wipe them out. And he continues to feed them until they learn how to forage for themselves. Their wings grow stronger. Soon they are able to handle themselves both in the air and on the ground.

Experience teaches the young bird which foods are good, where they can be found and when, and what dangers must be avoided. Many lessons are learned only by trial and error—and if a young bird makes an error he may not live to repeat it. But many of the actions that a bird learns strike us as strange, often amusing. In England many titmice have picked up the habit of removing the tops of milk bottles to get a drink. Scientists suppose that the birds learned the trick partly because of their instinct to pry up loose bark and dry leaves in their search for food.

I HAD HEARD OF ANTING, that intriguing behavior of so many birds that still puzzles naturalists. But not until I saw a starling indulging in it did I fully appreciate the fascination of this mysterious performance.

Starlings are enthusiastic anters, and the one I saw had gathered a beakful of writhing ants. While I watched he spread his wings wide, thrust his tail awkwardly between his legs, and with his beak rubbed that cluster of ants the length of his feathers. Seemingly drunk with ecstasy, the bird teetered, eyes half closed. Finished at last, he swallowed his "brush" of ants.

Naturalists have watched hundreds of anting incidents in nearly 150 species of birds but have failed to come up with any clear-cut explanation. Some have suggested that the formic acid secreted by ants may be a deterrent to lice and mites in the feathers. This seems doubtful. A more likely proposal is simply that birds like the feeling of that ant secretion on their bodies.

They react the same way to such things as smoke, vinegar, mustard, raw onions, cigarette butts, and mothballs. One of my gardening friends puts mothballs around her flowers to discourage rabbits and chipmunks. We've seen grackles hold these pellets in their bills and use them to dress their feathers, reacting the same way that they do with ants. When the mothballs fall, the birds keep on preening.

IN THE ECSTASY OF ANTING, *a blue jay and a robin (right), ant in bill, rub the insects along their outspread feathers. Veiled eyes and contortions suggest that the birds experience exaltation like a cat's over catnip—but no one knows why.*

Robert F. Gunn. Right: Sherbourne Drake

FLOCKING *after the nesting season, many birds migrate in company. It is February,*

Are bird songs instinctive or are they learned by listening? Mockingbirds, catbirds, and other mimics certainly must be born with the ability to imitate, but they have to learn their repertoire of sounds by hearing them. The mockingbird cannot instinctively know the loud clear call of the cardinal, the rasp of a squeaky gate, or the warble of a bluebird. But what about the bluebird's own song?

To answer this question a Cornell University ornithologist raised young bluebirds in isolation where they could never hear the notes of other songbirds. For six months the bluebirds did not utter any song – only call notes of distress or alarm, indicating that these are inherited. Then recorded songs of the robin, the Baltimore oriole, and the wood thrush were piped into the chamber. The birds paid little attention.

At last the typical bluebird song was played. The effect was amazing. The young birds crouched, cocked their heads, listened raptly – then attempted to repeat what they had heard. In five minutes they were singing recognizable bluebird music!

Parasitism intrigues naturalists. How did this trait develop in such birds as the cowbird and the European cuckoo? The females of these species slip into the nests of other birds and quickly lay an egg while the rightful owner is away. They fly off, leaving their eggs to be incubated and their young to be raised by involuntary foster parents. Many birds accept the cowbird's egg and care for the young cowbird as they do their own. Others abandon a nest with a cowbird egg in it. Robins may push the offending egg out. Yellow warblers often build another story to their nest, covering both their own and the intruder's eggs, then lay a new clutch. One warbler nest had five layers, each of them with a cowbird egg (page 296).

Other features of bird behavior are just as strange – for example, the use of tools. The Galapagos woodpecker finch uses a sharp twig or cactus spine to pry insects from crannies. And the Australian bowerbird paints his bower with a frayed stalk. Possibly the tools were first used – untold ages ago – entirely by chance. Proving of worth, they may have been adopted gradually by the whole population of the species until their use became habit. Now this behavior seems to be largely instinctive.

194   But the behavior of hooded crows in Norway, which pull fishermen's lines through

and these cedar waxwings have winged their way south to Daytona Beach, Florida.

holes in the ice, seems to show real insight and reasoning ability. Grasping the line in his bill, a crow hauls it a convenient distance out of water, then walks back for a new hold, treading on the line to prevent it from slipping back. Finally he pulls up the end of the line and eats the bait or hooked fish. Such an action cannot be instinctive. The young crows must learn it by watching their elders.

As they mature, young birds gradually exhibit the behavior patterns of their kind. Soon after they leave the nest, the young of many species gather in bands. They feed and roost together while their parents are busy raising second or third broods. Juveniles of other species go their solitary ways.

After the breeding season, when all the cares of parenthood are over for another year, some birds fly about the countryside in family groups or small flocks. Whenever birds congregate in any sort of group, they adhere to that hierarchy called the peck order (since the birds establish it by pecking one another). Each bird quickly

learns which of his fellows he can dominate and which can bully him. So his rung on the status ladder usually depends on how aggressive he is.

As late summer turns to fall, many songbirds gather in larger and larger flocks. Martins scatter over the countryside to feed during the day but join in immense hordes at dusk and spiral down into their communal roosts. Bluebird families flit about the fields, filling the autumn air with soft warbles. And flocks of sleek cedar waxwings cluster on the branches of mountain ash to feed on the orange berries.

The days are now shorter; the weather here in Massachusetts is crisp and cool. Insect food for the birds has diminished, and our backyard friends must look elsewhere for their meals. Some roam the nearby woodlands, but most gradually wing their way southward, following their food supplies to their wintering grounds.

A sign has been placed in an Amherst store: "Do your Christmas shopping early!" Seeing it, I visualize those short, bleak days of December when the few remaining songbirds throng our feeder, finding sustenance at the low point of their life cycle. But then I look beyond, and my heart warms and quickens at the thought of spring – even as the bright new days to come will warm and quicken my backyard tenants. 195

Mockingbirds and Thrashers

Family Mimidae

By ALDEN H. MILLER

ONE MORNING IN MAY at my camp in a mesquite thicket near Casa Grande, Arizona, I awoke to the dawn chorus of thrashers. I was out among them before the sun was up, while the desert was still pleasantly cool. Listening carefully, I could pick out the song of each species.

From the sandy flats in the distance drifted the sweet, smooth-flowing songs of Le Conte's thrashers. On the stony mesas curve-billed thrashers whistled ecstatically, most of their notes very abrupt and penetrating. Closer at hand in the mesquite I heard the melodic phrases of the crissals. After sunup the Bendires, out among the scattered bushes, joined in with their hurried, driving songs.

Song gives the thrashers and mockingbirds the color their plumage generally lacks. Inconspicuous in browns and grays, they command attention with a seemingly endless variety of sounds. The flight song of the sage thrasher is unforgettable. Many a spring I have heard its clear cascade of notes on the plains of the Great Basin. Unlike the mockingbird, which may spring briefly into the air while singing, the sage thrasher undulates in a wide circular course, bounding lightly and swiftly over the aromatic sage tops, all the while pouring out its continuous melody. It also sings while perched, but to my mind its musical sweeps over its broad territory are more impressive.

Allan D. Cruickshank, National Audubon Society

YOUNG CURVE-BILLED THRASHERS *in Texas display their spotted breasts and present in profile the sturdy beaks they'll swing like pickaxes to unearth grubs.*

FOUNDLING MOCKER, *welcomed into a Virginia family and raised to a fledgling on eyedropper rations, follows a young friend around like Mary's little lamb.*

I trace my earliest recollections of birds to members of this family, the Mimidae, particularly to the California thrasher and the mockingbird. They dominated our yard on the then wooded and smog-free slopes of the Arroyo Seco near South Pasadena. It was a common sight to see the California thrasher running rapidly across an opening and through the brush, its tail uplifted as a balancer. Now and then it would stop to search for insects, digging in the soft ground and flicking aside loose matter with its great curved beak.

Seen at close range the bill looks like an awesome weapon. We were amused to see these thrashers hop up to the food tray in our yard and bluff away all other birds, including large jays. I have never seen a thrasher strike with his bill in combat, but it looks as if he could and perhaps that's the most important thing. Wouldn't you retreat if a sickle-shaped bill the length of your own head were suddenly aimed at you from six inches away?

The mockingbirds in our yard were almost continually in our ear as they proclaimed their territories, their urges, and their dislikes. Every day they sang for hours on end and sometimes through long stretches of the night. In the height of springtime excitement a male pours forth his song from a high perch, often a tree-

197

top. I have seen a mocker vault three to ten feet in the air without a break in voice, his white-marked wings and outspread tail suggesting the turning of cartwheels.

Every spring a pair of mockingbirds built their nest in a cedar in our front yard. Boldly they guarded it against cats and me. Nevertheless I scrambled up to it to look in and admire the blue-green eggs well spotted with brown.

Later in the spring when the young mockers were about, I was awakened daily by the parent birds harassing a neighbor's cat. Their tirades went on endlessly as they dashed over the cat's back, sometimes ticking it and jabbing it. When the cat didn't move on, the birds stepped up the attacks and finally made it run for cover.

Mockingbirds have great skill in imitating sounds they hear about them, which they build into continuous outpourings of song. At my boyhood home I have heard them perfectly imitate certain calls of scrub jays, the very peculiar *ja-cob* notes of acorn woodpeckers, the neighbor whistling for his dog, and the call of the Pacific tree frog. And none of these imitations have I heard from the mockers around my desert camps in Joshua Tree National Monument in southern California, where the various sounds of home are lacking. Instead I awake to the perfect imitation of the cactus wren's guttural song.

Why does the mocker mimic? And why to a lesser extent do thrashers and catbirds? What purpose is served?

My answer is that a continuous singer of the mockingbird type borrows songs for no other purpose than to have something to sing. He weaves together and repeats song motifs of his own invention and others that he hears. And why shouldn't he borrow a sound if it suits his own vocal equipment?

Despite his marvelous ability to mimic, the mockingbird originates more phrases than he borrows. I estimate that only about ten percent of the phrases are mimicking efforts, even less in winter.

R ENOWNED for their excellent voices and fascinating actions, the 32 species of the family Mimidae are found only in the Americas. Ten of them occur on the North American continent north of Mexico.

In the East and Northeast catbirds and brown thrashers abound in gardens and in the understory shrubs of woods and stream borders. Strongly migratory birds, they leave their nesting grounds to winter in the South. But in the arid Southwest thrashers remain throughout the year.

Le Conte's thrasher lives the year round in sandy wastes. No other American bird is exposed so fully to intense light and heat – and without water to drink.

One April in the Pinto Basin of the California desert country I discovered where the Le Conte's gets at least part of its moisture. A flurry of rain weeks before had brought a growth of desert flowers and with them a

Washington Evening Star

hatching of large caterpillars – juicy thrasher food. I saw Le Conte's thrashers gorging on these reservoirs of moisture, spilling yellow stain out the corners of their mouths and over their pearl-gray throats. This sand-colored desert dweller – to me the most striking of the thrashers – runs smoothly, like a faint, swift shadow, from one cactus bush a hundred yards to the next with little or no pause. It relies on running rather than flight for escape.

Birds' eggs often are things of beauty, and those of the mockingbirds and thrashers rank among the best. In color they range from the startling glossy greenish blue of the catbird's eggs to light blue, and even to greenish gray or cream as in the Bendire's eggs. They may be clear and unmarked like the catbird's and the crissal thrasher's, or richly spotted with reddish brown like the sage thrasher's.

In southern Arizona I can often determine which species of thrasher built a nest, though the parents are nowhere in sight, for each species that breeds there has a distinctive nest architecture and differently colored eggs.

ANGRY MOCKINGBIRD, *white markings flashing like a dive bomber's insignia, drives a tabby away from the nest. Dogs and snakes also trigger the bird's wrath. But the mocker at right lives in peace with an Irish setter.* 199

Photomontage by Joseph Spies

Mockingbird
Mimus polyglottos

NIGHTFALL BRINGS a fragrant hush to a Georgia garden. As the light of the rising moon gilds the leaves of a magnolia, the bird called by naturalist John Burroughs "the lark and the nightingale in one" begins his rapturous nocturne. Moonlight, magnolias, and the mockingbird—these are enduring symbols of the Old South. Indeed, Tennessee, Florida, Mississippi, Arkansas, and Texas have named this matchless minstrel their state bird.

But the mocker ranges far beyond the borders of Dixie. The moon that shines on Georgia evokes the same music among clumps of cholla cactus in the Arizona desert and blossom-laden lemon groves in California. Americans enjoy the song of the mockingbird from coast to coast, especially where the climate is balmy.

The colonial naturalist Mark Catesby heard it in the low country of South Carolina more than 200 years ago. First scientific chronicler of the mockingbird, he reported that "The Indians, by way of eminence or admiration, call it *Cencontlatolly*, or four hundred tongues." A bit more cautious, science named the mocker *Mimus polyglottos*, "many-tongued mimic."

Two researchers in Ohio demonstrated that it imitates other birds so expertly that only electronic analysis can detect the difference. They measured rhythm, loudness, and pitch with an audiospectrograph to distinguish between the original melodies and the mocker's imitations.

Another listener heard a mocker change his tune 87 times in seven minutes—all repeated several times. The famed mocker of Boston's Arnold Arboretum was credited with the ability to reproduce 39 bird songs, 50 bird calls, and the sounds of a frog and a cricket!

A mocker's repertoire may include squeaky gate hinges, a dog's bark, and the postman's whistle. One bird joined the National Symphony Orchestra during an outdoor concert in Washington, D. C. He imitated the flute which imitated the bird calls in "Peter and the Wolf."

The master mimic also sings at great length in phrases that are pure mockingbird and nothing else. He repeats each theme rapidly up to half a dozen times or more. The rollicking outpouring is distinctive; no other member of the family Mimidae repeats a phrase so often.

Mockingbirds start tuning up in late January and reach their vocal peak in spring, singing almost any hour of the day or night. Quiet during the August molt, they return to form in the fall. At this time the females deliver a soft but beautiful song, usually from the seclusion of a bush.

At one time mockingbirds were widely sold as cage birds in the South. The practice has been stopped, but the mocker is still a familiar sight around the settlements of man, as he has been since colonial times. Today his vocalizing competes with mid-city traffic noises. Suburbanites hear him singing on the ground, in garden shrubbery, and from house eaves, television antennas, and lofty tree perches. Occasionally he bounds into the air as he sings.

White patches wink boldly in wings and tail as he flies to his station with a rowing motion that looks somewhat labored. Perched, the trim, long-tailed bird displays his gray back and white underparts. He resembles the loggerhead shrike but is slimmer and his face lacks the shrike's black mask.

INTENSELY TERRITORIAL, the mocker stands ready to attack any creature that invades his domain, especially his own kind. "Dogfights" involving six or more mockingbirds are not uncommon. So quick is he to pick a fight that he frequently assails his own image reflected in a window, car hubcap, or other polished surface.

Sounding a harsh *tchack tchack*, he swoops down to repel dogs, cats, and sometimes even human trespassers. Snakes that try to rob the mocker's nest often meet a hail of vicious pecks aimed at their heads.

Both male and female take part in building the nest of twigs, grass, and rootlets, and sometimes bits of string. Usually located within ten feet of the ground in a shrub, small tree, or porch vine, the cup holds four or five bluish or greenish eggs heavily splotched with brown. They hatch in about 12 days and the young take wing about two weeks later. Their parents generally build a new nest for a second brood.

Male and female adults wear similar plumage, but the youngsters look different, with brownish backs and spotted underparts.

Wild berries make up more than half the mocker's diet. He has at times been accused of damaging grapes, citrus, and other cultivated fruits. He also eats beetles, caterpillars, grasshoppers, and other insects.

Mockingbirds have been spreading northward in recent years; some have reached as far as southern Canada. Those that breed in the colder climates may migrate and a few individuals wander considerable distances, but the species in general is nonmigratory.

Range: N. California to S. South Dakota and central New Jersey, south to S. Mexico and the West Indies; occurs casually in N. United States and S. Canada. *Characteristics:* gray head and back, paler underparts, large white wing and tail patches conspicuous in flight; long tail; sings great variety of phrases for long periods. Young have brown backs and spotted breasts.

DEFENDING *territorial rights in a holly tree, a mocker dive-bombs the challenger.*
Mockingbirds, length 9-11"; Walter A. Weber, National Geographic staff artist

Opposite: Louis Agassiz Fuertes, American Museum of Natural History

Catbirds, length 8-9¼"; Woodrow Goodpaster, National Audubon Society

Brown thrasher, length 10½-12"; John H. Gerard, National Audubon Society

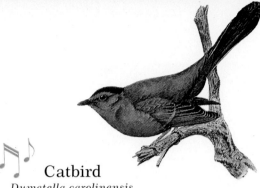

Catbird
Dumetella carolinensis

HIDDEN IN THE TANGLE of a rosebush, a trim gray bird with a black skullcap pours forth a wild medley of songs and calls — sounds that approach the mockingbird's in richness and mimic artistry. The catbird can echo many of the birds in his neighborhood, but unlike the mocker he doesn't repeat his notes.

Often he leaves his hiding place to continue his lengthy, disjointed concert from the top of the bush. Tail depressed and body held close to the perch, he looks as if he were skulking. The one bit of color in his plumage — the chestnut undertail coverts — is difficult to detect.

If an intruder approaches, the song stops, the tail flips up, and the bird voices a querulous *mew*. This distinctive catcall identifies the catbird. Several catbirds may band together to mob a snake or other predator.

A good neighbor, the catbird responds quickly to a cry of distress from another bird. He has been known to care for the orphaned young of other species. People consider him a good neighbor too, for his playful ways and entertaining mimicry.

Catbirds migrate at night. The males arrive on the breeding grounds first and quickly announce their territorial claims. When the females arrive a few days later an animated courtship begins. The male dashes through the thick greenery in hot pursuit of his chosen female. He struts about with wings lowered and tail high; often he pauses to deliver a burst of song.

After a few days of this whirlwind courtship nest building begins, usually close to the ground in dense thickets, vine tangles, or small trees. While the male gives vent to his joy by singing morning and evening and often far into the night, the female does most of the work. She forms a foundation of sticks, grass, and leaves and lines it with bark shreds and rootlets. The three to five blue-green eggs hatch in 12 or 13 days.

The young are fed mainly insects. Adult birds also dine on fruit. After the nesting season the catbird often delivers a clear and lovely whisper song, much softer than the caroling of spring.

Range: S. British Columbia to Nova Scotia, south to central Arizona and S. Georgia; winters to Panama. *Characteristics:* slate-gray body, black cap, chestnut undertail coverts.

Brown Thrasher
Toxostoma rufum

APRIL'S ON THE WANE in New England when the brown thrasher arrives from the South. Gold-tasseled pussy willows nod and swamp maples glow with red blooms. The bird with the bright brown back and streaked breast comes quietly, reconnoitering the ground in short, easy strides.

He hops about, thrashing among the fallen leaves, his long bill pitching them in all directions with sidewise strokes as he searches for insects. Some believe the thrasher was named for this habit. Others think he may have been named for the way he thrashes large insects to death or for the way he switches his long tail.

Having chosen his territory, he mounts a tall bush near a grove or a lofty perch on a wayside tree. Head high, bill open wide, tail down, and body vibrating, he delivers a spectacular spring song. He is less of a mimic than the mockingbird, more of a musician than the catbird. His short, loud phrases are full of sparkle. Farmers hearing him during spring planting say he's giving them advice: *drop it drop it, cover it cover it, pull it up pull it up.*

When a female joins him and they court in the shrubbery, the song becomes soft and subdued. In the South, where brown thrashers live the year round, and in the Midwest the nest site is in thickets, brush heaps, hedges, and vine tangles, sometimes near human habitation. In New England thrashers nest away from dwellings, often on the ground.

The female builds a bulky outer basket of twigs and successive inner layers of leaves, stems, and rootlets. She lays four or five white or bluish eggs finely dotted with brown.

An alarm call like the sound of a loud smacking of the lips may bring her off the nest to join her mate in a swift stabbing attack against an intruder. With fierce courage they assail dogs, cats, weasels, foxes, and even people. Soon after the young leave home the female begins building a nest for a second brood.

Beetles, caterpillars, and other insects make up about two-thirds of the diet of this ground-feeding bird. He also eats fruit and acorns. In the South and Midwest, where he seems less shy than in the East, the brown thrasher may visit feeding stations and birdbaths. He is Georgia's state bird.

Range: S. E. Alberta to W. Maine, south to N. Texas and S. Florida; migratory in the north. *Characteristics:* reddish-brown head and back, yellow eyes, white wing bars and dark-streaked whitish underparts; slightly curved bill, long tail.

Longbill, length 10-12"; Arthur A. Allen

Long-billed Thrasher
Toxostoma longirostre

IN THE CHAPARRAL and in the forests along the stagnant watercourses of southern Texas dwells the long-billed thrasher.

Also known as Sennett's thrasher, the longbill was at one time considered a form of the wide-ranging brown thrasher, which it resembles. But as its name suggests, *longirostre* has a longer, more curved beak. It lacks the reddish tinge in its back and has a grayer head.

Yellow eyes glowing, the longbill hops up through the bushes to an open perch, then dives back to the ground. There it dines on beetles, ant lions, and grasshoppers. The fare also includes hackberries and other wild fruit.

The beautiful and varied song rings out in typical thrasher fashion—a series of short, sparkling phrases repeated once or twice. The longbill also sounds a mellow *too-ree* call note.

Pairs conceal their nest in the heart of a thorny bush, in cactus plants, or in the forest undergrowth four to ten feet above ground. Built of thorny twigs, grass, and straw, the nest holds two to five eggs. These are greenish- or bluish-white speckled with brown. Like other thrashers, male and female longbills wear similar plumage.

Range: S. Texas and E. Mexico. *Characteristics:* grayish head, brown back, whitish wing bars, whitish underparts streaked with black; long black bill, long tail.

Curve-billed Thrasher
Toxostoma curvirostre

OVER THE SOUTHWESTERN mesas skims a slender gray-brown bird with long tail and curved bill. He flies from bush to bush, occasionally moving along the ground to pick at parched soil and flick aside leaves in his hunt for insects.

A thrasher, surely. But which one? Bendire's, curve-billed, Le Conte's, and crissal thrashers all roam the desert and all look similar. If the bird has faint breast spots and the curve of his bill is well defined, he's a curve-billed thrasher. The Bendire's also has a spotted breast, but his bill is shorter and not strongly curved.

The curve-billed thrasher whistles a sharp *whit-wheet* call. He also sings ecstatically in short, clear phrases.

He and his mate stay together the year round and may remain paired for life. They build a nest of thorny twigs and grass in a cholla cactus bristling with barbed spines. Observers often are amazed at the birds' ability to pick their way in and out without getting impaled. The two to four blue-green eggs are dotted with brown. The birds may raise two broods each season.

Curvebills are fond of water and frequently approach ranch houses to drink and bathe.

Range: N. W. Arizona to S. Texas, south to S. Mexico. *Characteristics:* strongly curved bill, gray-brown head and back, orange or yellowish eyes, faintly spotted breast; dull white tips sometimes show on outer feathers of long tail.

California Thrasher
Toxostoma redivivum

THIS SWIFT-FOOTED THRASHER never leaves his namesake states in the United States and Mexico. And there he usually shuns deserts and mountain heights. The California thrasher favors dense chaparral slopes and stream borders. Residents of the foothill towns know him well.

On the ground he moves quickly and easily, tail uptilted. In the air he looks awkward; his head and tail droop and the flight is jerky. When alarmed he usually runs to cover. When he feeds he swings his bill into the soil, picking and shoveling until he gets his fill of insects. He also eats berries and seeds.

Despite his affinity for the ground, he often chooses a high tree limb when he delivers his rich song—musical phrases mixed with harsh notes and occasional imitations of other birds.

In a bush or scrubby tree the bird builds a nest of twigs, lined with rootlets and grass, for the three or four speckled blue eggs. The nest is less well cupped and coarser than that of the mockingbird, which often nests nearby.

Range: California and N. Baja California. *Characteristics:* dark gray-brown head and back, brown eyes, pale cinnamon belly and undertail coverts; long curved bill and long tail.

California, length 11-13"; Lyman K. Stuart   *Above: curvebill, length 9½-11½"; Eliot Porter*

Crissal, length 10½-12½"   *Le Conte's, length 10-11"; Allan Brooks*

Crissal Thrasher
Toxostoma dorsale

THE CHESTNUT PATCH in the undertail coverts, or crissal area, gave this thrasher his name. The daub of color helps distinguish him from his relatives in the desert if he will stay put long enough for you to see it. For here is another thrasher that usually darts for cover at the first sign of anybody in his territory.

Shunning the open desert, the crissal thrasher frequents the mesquite tangles along streams and arroyos and on sloping canyon sides. The bulky nest of twigs, lined with grasses, is usually placed in a thorny bush. Both adults incubate the two to four blue-green eggs.

Moving through the thickets with long, graceful strides, the crissal thrasher feeds on wild fruit and digs for insects with his sharply curved bill. When food is most abundant in spring and fall this fine musician hits his top vocal form. From a favorite perch high in a thorny tree he sends forth a sweet, rich melody.

Range: S. E. California to S. W. Utah and W. Texas, south to central Mexico. *Characteristics:* dark gray-brown head and back, brownish eyes, pale gray breast, chestnut patch under tail; long sharply curved bill, long tail.

Le Conte's Thrasher
Toxostoma lecontei

IN THE HOTTEST, driest, most barren reaches of the desert southwest dwells the wraithlike Le Conte's thrasher. His pale gray-brown plumage blends so well with the sandy flats that he is almost invisible, even in the sparsest cover.

He welcomes the new day with a fine sweet song. Then, despite the wilting heat, he dashes swiftly from bush to bush searching for insects. When pursued, he dodges with startling suddenness to disappear from view, or makes short flights close to the ground.

At midday he rests silently in the partial shade of a scrawny plant. In the evening he resumes his concert, perched with head thrown back, tail drooping, and curved bill open wide. He may sing for hours in the cool, starry desert night.

Male and female join in building the bulky nest of twigs and grass in a cholla cactus or, in the San Joaquin Valley, in a saltbush. The male also helps incubate the two to four bluish-green eggs dotted with brown.

Range: central California to S. W. Utah and central Arizona, south to N. W. Mexico. *Characteristics:* pale gray-brown body, dark eyes, long dark tail, long curved bill.

206

Bendire's, length 9-11"
Allan Brooks

Sage, length 8-9"

Bendire's Thrasher
Toxostoma bendirei

THIS SWEET-SINGING DESERT BIRD lurks among the spiny bushes. His voice provides a good clue to his whereabouts, but he may remain silent in the presence of unwanted company. Naturalist Herbert Brandt spent six seasons in the parched haunts of Bendire's thrasher before he heard this timid bird's clear, unbroken warble—"like mountain brook music rushing over the sands of the desert."

The Bendire's feeds on caterpillars, beetles, and other insects. Like his close relatives in the arid Southwest, he probes the ground with his bill to dig out morsels of food. But unlike their long, sickle-shaped bills, his bill is short and relatively straight.

His faint breast spots are most distinct in fresh fall plumage; after a season of wear and fading they may not show at all.

Despite his shyness he may nest near a farmhouse. More often a pair sets up housekeeping in a desert cactus bush. Skillful artisans, they fashion a small basket of twigs and grass and line it with soft fibers. In it the female lays three or four gray-green eggs spotted with brown.

Range: S. E. California to S. Utah, south to N. W. Mexico. *Characteristics:* gray-brown head and back, yellow eyes, faintly spotted breast; relatively short, slightly curved bill; white-tipped tail less notably long than in other thrashers of the Toxostoma group.

Sage Thrasher
Oreoscoptes montanus

A DAWN MIST shrouds the sea of pale green sage. All is still. As the rising sun burns through the haze a gray-brown bird with streaked breast takes wing to greet the new day. A flood of music breaks over the western mesas. Ecstatic whistlings, low trills, and burring calls pour out.

The sage thrasher delivers his morning song from the top of a tall bush or on the wing. His pose, flight style, and habit of repeating phrases suggest the mockingbird; indeed he was once known as the sage or mountain mockingbird.

But watch him scurry along the ground, tail high, and vanish in the bushes when you approach him. He's a thrasher, no doubt, though he lacks the long curved bill seen in others.

Sage thrashers breed on sagebrush plains and juniper-clad foothills. Usually placed in a low bush, the twiggy nest holds four or five blue or greenish-blue eggs boldly splotched with brown. The cup may be arched over with twigs.

Like other ground feeders, this thrasher devours huge quantities of beetles and grasshoppers. In late summer he loses much of his shyness and visits ranches and gardens to dine on fruit.

Range: central British Columbia to S. Wyoming, south to S. California and N. W. Texas; also breeds in S. W. Saskatchewan. Winters to N. Mexico. *Characteristics:* dark gray-brown head and back, yellow eyes, streaked breast, white tail corners; relatively short bill and tail.

The Thrushes

Family Turdidae

By E. THOMAS GILLIARD

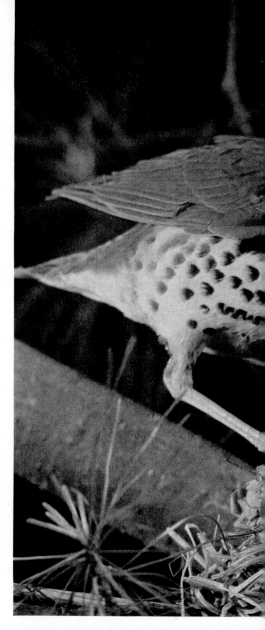

I N THE MISTY FORESTS of the Pocono Mountains in Pennsylvania I love to hear wood thrushes tuning up at the earliest trace of dawn. Their flutelike songs, combined with the voices of other birds, build to a cascade of melody timed to greet the rising sun. Exuberant, bursting with the joy of living, the swelling chorus never fails to stir me deeply.

Imagine the eloquence of this wave of song as it sweeps westward just ahead of the sun, breaking all the way in a crescendo of purest music. Though only 14 species of thrushes live in North America, they contribute the dominant sounds to this early morning phenomenon. Imagine, too, what it sounds like in the Old World where most of the 304 species, including the celebrated nightingale, dwell!

What manner of birds are these songsters, so widely acclaimed as the finest of nature's musicians? To know them we have only to look in our backyards at the robin, the bluebird, and the wood thrush.

The robin probably is the best known and most widely loved American songbird. To me it is a top-notch lobbyist for all living things. Running over a lawn, pausing, tilting its head, watching for a

SPOTTED BREASTS, *russet backs camouflag*

slight movement, then grasping and tugging an earthworm—this fascinating behavior never ceases to amaze me. Nor does the fact that a large robin nestling requires about 14 feet of earthworms per day.

What more delightful way is there to study nature than to peer out a window at a family of robins a few feet away? They may nest on a windowsill, porch post, limb, or in a mailbox. Sometimes the nests are stacked, new on old; sometimes they are lined up like exhibits on a shelf. Often broods are raised year after year on the same easily seen ledge, providing their human admirers with a dramatic source of amusement as well as natural science education.

I learned early about another popular North American thrush—the bluebird. I was investigating a woodpecker hole in a Maryland apple orchard when, to my surprise, out flew a bluebird. I was expecting a downy woodpecker. Nesting in holes,

Woodrow Goodpaster, National Audubon Society

lump wood thrushes, denizens of forests and wooded yards. Nest blends with habitat.

I learned, is one way bluebirds differ from other thrushes. Taking advantage of this practice, many people provide nest boxes to attract the birds to their yards.

The third thrush species in North America which commonly nests in our gardens is the wood thrush. And of the three it is the most reluctant to leave the woodlands, as its name implies. Yet countless thousands of these birds raise their young close to man. They build their nests on shaded limbs, often near houses, and with aplomb bathe in the spray of lawn sprinklers.

Other thrushes, however – among them the hermit, gray-cheeked, olive-backed, and the veery – disdain our company. Dressed in olives and browns with pale, spotted underparts, they lose themselves in the dim recesses of the forests they love. All are superb musicians. The finest of these songsters, the hermit thrush, sings its haunting melodies deep in northern forests, far from human ears.

Only during migration are these woodland species apt to visit our gardens. We then might be favored by a call from the veery, en route to winter quarters in central Brazil. Or the graycheek from, say, Hudson Bay might drop in on his way to Ecuador. Such visitors probably will leave our gardens at night. For of our North American thrushes only robins and bluebirds migrate during the day.

Not all thrushes which breed in North America migrate to winter quarters in the warmer parts of America. The shy Townsend's solitaire of the Rocky Mountains merely moves down the slopes from summer homes as high as 12,000 feet to protective valleys and gorges. And Old World wheatears breeding in Alaska and Greenland fly across Europe or Asia to winter in Africa!

Some of the younger robins tend to get lost and wander long distances, even to Europe. This ability to cross broad water barriers may have contributed to the dispersal of robinlike birds all over the world. The traveler to distant lands is amazed ever and again to find himself eye to eye with a familiar bird.

In 1937 near the brink of Angel Falls in Venezuela, the world's highest waterfall, I saw the rare Roraima thrush, a gray-and-black robin with cadmium-yellow bill and legs. I watched it fly swiftly from boulder to boulder, searching in the sodden moss for insects.

In 1950, above the tree line on Mount Hagen in the interior of New Guinea, I saw another bird incongruously similar to our robin. After hunting my heart out for many days in trackless alpine grasslands, I finally secured a specimen. This New Guinea thrush proved to be an unknown race.

Another indelible memory is of finding a black chat-robin's nest in the Telefomin region of New Guinea where Stone Age tribes still dwell. The sturdy cup—typical form of robins' nests all over the globe—lay under a tussock of grass close to the wooden crosses of men recently killed in ambush. An indelible memory? I'd almost been included in that ambush!

Most thrushes lay oval-shaped, bluish eggs, sometimes marked with browns. The average clutch numbers five. Many species raise second and third broods, but as a rule in North America all the young have fledged by August. Juvenile plumage is always more or less spotted, both above and below. Relatively long, slender legs and bills characterize adults.

Thrushes feed chiefly on insects and other animal food, but some species also eat fruit. I well remember a cherry orchard in Kashmir where fruit-stealing thrushes found slim pickings. There was no wind, yet the trees were swaying. The birds couldn't have been more puzzled than I. Then I found the answer in a sharp-eyed boy tending a maze of ropes which radiated from the treetops like spokes in a wheel. He yanked the lines to flush the robber birds.

A thrush's protein-rich larder is gathered in many niches. Woodland species hunt insects on the forest floor. Others search amid shrubbery, undergrowth, and growing leaves. And some thrushes forage for snails and even crustaceans.

Such feeding habits seem less surprising when you scan the bill of fare that an eastern bluebird presents to its young: grasshoppers, crickets, katydids, caterpillars, spiders, moths, beetles, centipedes, millipedes, and praying mantises.

As consumers of insects, thrushes prove their economic worth. As songsters they rank among the most admired of all birds. How fortunate we are that some of the most interesting species in North America have found that man is good company.

SYMBOL OF HAPPINESS, *the bluebird is welcomed at nest boxes. Small entry hole—1½ inches across—lets pale-hued eastern female in, keeps starlings out. Albinos like this robin (inset) are not uncommon in some thrush species.*

210

Frederick Kent Truslow. Inset: New York Zoological Society

Robin
Turdus migratorius

RESPLENDENT in his brick-red vest and charcoal-gray coat, black head thrown back, the herald of springtime carols *cheerily cheerily cheerily*. The beloved robin is back in the north and winter's spell is shattered.

He hops and runs across a lawn, pauses, cocks his head, and looks – or does he listen? Suddenly his sharp beak stabs the ground and recoils, clutching an earthworm or beetle grub.

Within a few days after the males appear in northern yards the females arrive, looking somewhat paler. Soon the cockbirds rend the air with cries as they stake out nesting territories and grapple with rivals (page 179). Amazed onlookers have watched an infuriated male challenge a reflection of himself and bang away at a windowpane until he's exhausted.

A successful suitor and his mate immediately start building a nest, usually in a bush or on a tree limb 5 to 15 feet above ground. Fence posts, window ledges, even the girders in half-built skyscrapers may do as well. Every year newspapers tell of builders stymied by robins in a family way. Once in a while a daring pair nests on a merry-go-round or other moving structure.

After laying a platform of twigs and grass, the female builds up the walls with mud and more grass. Turning round and round inside the cup, she smooths and shapes the inner walls with her breast and half-extended wings. Then she adds a lining of soft grass and perhaps a few feathers.

While her mate stands guard against invaders, the female incubates the three or four eggs of robin's-egg blue for 11 to 14 days. As soon as they hatch, the parents spend their days from dawn to dusk hunting food for the hungry brood.

The nestlings grow rapidly. At two weeks they are well feathered and show the spotted breast of their juvenile plumage. Only in youth do robins wear these markings that indicate their kinship to other thrushes.

The fledglings face a critical time when they quit the nest. Before they can fly well they must run a gauntlet of enemies – cats, dogs, hawks, snakes, and other predators. For a few days the male parent looks after them while the female prepares for a second brood. Then the youngsters are on their own. The old birds may even raise a third brood later in the season.

Some robins breed as far north as the tree limit in Canada and Alaska. One pair observed 100 miles south of Point Barrow, Alaska, brought their young from egg to first flight in just 10 days. In the almost continual daylight of the brief Arctic summer, the hard-working parents were able to gather food 21 hours a day.

Although a few robins may winter in sheltered areas as far north as New England and Ontario, most seek milder wintering grounds. In southern states flocks of many thousands congregate at night to sleep in thickets or wooded swamplands.

Audubon reported in 1841 that these roosts caused a "sort of jubilee" among hunters who went after the birds with "bows and arrows, blowpipes, guns, and traps of different sorts."

"Every gunner," he went on, "brings them home by bagsful, and the markets are supplied with them at a very cheap rate. Several persons may at this season stand round the foot of a tree loaded with berries, and shoot the greater part of the day, so fast do the flocks of Robins succeed each other. They are then fat and juicy, and afford excellent eating."

Through protective laws this unhappy slaughter has long since been stopped. Because of the clearing of forests robins are probably more plentiful now than they were when the first colonists arrived in North America and named them after another thrush, the familiar robin red-breast of Europe.

A modern threat to the robin, however, has been the widespread use of DDT and other insecticides for spraying shade trees, lawns, and golf courses. When rains wash the chemical to the ground it mixes with the soil and is eaten by earthworms. Robins, in turn, eat the earthworms and may consume fatal amounts of the pesticide.

These earthworms, as well as insects and fruit, make up the bulk of the robin's diet. The cherry grower may grumble at crop losses, but most peo-

HATCHLINGS *stretch wide for father's worm. Speckled breasts mark older juveniles (right).*
Male (upper) and female robins, length 8½-11"; Walter A. Weber, National Geographic staff artist

ple appreciate the bird's joyous, liquid song and friendly ways. Connecticut, Michigan, and Wisconsin have named it their state bird.

A similar species, the San Lucas robin (*Turdus confinis*), is paler and has a creamy buff breast. It inhabits southern Baja California.

Range: northern tree line in Alaska and Canada, south to S. Mexico; winters to Guatemala. *Characteristics:* brick-red breast, yellow bill, black head, gray back, streaked whitish throat. Female is duller. Young have spotted breasts.

Varied Thrush
Ixoreus naevius

SHAFTS OF SUNLIGHT filter through dripping branches of spruce and fir, dappling the ground with flecks of gold. From the underbrush comes an eerie song that breaks the silence of the northwestern rain forest — one long quavering whistle, a pause, then another note in a changed pitch. The haunting music of the varied thrush matches his somber surroundings perfectly.

As he hops into view the singer reminds you at first glance of a robin. His shape, stance, and general color scheme resemble the robin's, but there are significant differences. A broad black band stretches across the varied thrush's rusty breast. He also has prominent orange eye stripes and matching wing bars. Westerners often call him the banded, or Oregon, robin.

In a nearby nest sits the female, paler than her mate and wearing a gray breastband. Snuggled against the trunk of a young spruce and supported by small branches, her nest is fashioned from twigs, rootlets, moss, and other plant fibers and bound together with mud. On a grass lining rest the three to five blue eggs marked with brown. The female incubates them for about two weeks. Sometimes she raises two broods in a season.

Breeding in dense woodlands from Alaska to northern California, the varied thrush seems equally at home at sea level or high in the mountains. He combs the forest floor for earthworms, sow bugs, thousand-leggers, and beetles. He also dines on seeds and fruit in season. Drifting southward or down from the mountains as winter approaches, he may spend the cold months in a sheltering ravine where acorns and berries are available for the picking.

In migration varied thrushes have been found far east of their normal range, usually in company with robins. On rare occasions some have ventured as far as the East Coast.

Range: N. Alaska and N. W. Canada, south to N. California and N. W. Montana; winters to N. Baja California. *Characteristics:* gray-black head and back, rusty breast, black breastband, orange eye stripes and wing bars. Female is paler. Young have speckled underparts.

Fieldfare
Turdus pilaris

CHANCES ARE that you will never see the fieldfare in the United States. Before the spring of 1937 this Old World thrush had been reported only twice in the western hemisphere—both times in Greenland. Since then the bird has established itself as a nesting species in southern Greenland. And in 1939 an old Eskimo woman produced a specimen taken in Arctic Canada.

Distinguished by its gray head, chestnut back, and streaked breast, this bird customarily breeds in the forests of northern Europe and Asia. The nest of mud and grass holds five or six blue-green eggs speckled with reddish brown.

The fieldfare feeds on insects and berries. It sings a medley of warbles and squeaks; its call is a loud, harsh *chack chack chack.*

Range: S. Greenland to N. Europe and Siberia; winters to the Mediterranean Sea and N. India. *Characteristics:* gray head and rump, chestnut back, black tail, streaked rusty-yellow breast.

Wood Thrush
Hylocichla mustelina

A RUST-COLORED HEAD and large spots on snowy breast and sides mark the wood thrush. Slightly smaller than his cousin the robin, this plump bird usually nests in cool deciduous forests, often near water. But sometimes he invades towns and cities. Here he usually keeps close to thickly shaded areas, in contrast to the robin, which prefers wide lawns with plenty of sunshine. After a time he may lose much of his timidity and come out on the lawn to forage or enjoy a shower under the sprinkler.

The wood thrush transforms the woodlands with a melody of great beauty and power. Serene, suggestive of bells and flutes, the song consists of a series of varied phrases broken by rather long pauses. The notes sound like *ee-oh-lee . . . ee-oh-lay* and are repeated many times in many different keys.

The wood thrush sings most often at dawn and dusk but may begin his daily concert half an hour before daybreak. If alarmed or excited, the vocalist raises and lowers his head feathers and sounds a sharp *pit pit pit* call.

After wintering in the brushy woodlands of Mexico and Central America, the wood thrushes spread through the eastern half of the United States and southern Canada. The males arrive on the nesting grounds first and immediately begin claiming territory. Some chase off rivals. Others greet a challenger with a magnificent burst of song that may last as long as ten minutes.

Mated pairs build their nest of grass and weed stalks in the fork of a sapling or on a horizontal

Above: fieldfare, length 10"

Wood thrush, 7½-8½"; Woodrow Goodpaster, National Audubon Society

Male varied thrush, length 9-10"

Female varied thrush, Bob and Elsie Boggs

limb. The cup has a middle layer of mud or leaf mold and a lining of rootlets. From its base may dangle streamers of paper, cloth, or cellophane. The female, who looks like her mate, incubates the three or four blue-green eggs, which are slightly darker than a robin's eggs. The male helps the female feed the young a varied diet — mulberries, honeysuckle berries, caterpillars, and small insects. Sometimes a pair raises two broods in a season.

The wood thrush and its relatives in the Hylocichla group of thrushes are all expert songsters. They all have spotted breasts and brown upper parts. As a result they are often difficult to tell apart. Slightly longer and plumper than the others, the wood thrush has larger, rounder spots and a reddish-brown, or rusty, head. The hermit thrush has a rusty tail. The Swainson's and gray-cheeked thrushes have uniformly gray-brown upper parts, while the veery has a warmer, reddish tone in its back.

Range: S. E. South Dakota to S. Quebec, south to S. E. Texas and N. Florida; winters from S. Texas to Panama. *Characteristics:* bell-like song; rusty head, brown back, white breast and flanks with large rounded spots.

Hermit thrush, length 6½-7¾"; Lyman K. Stuart　　*Swainson's, length 6½-7¾"; Eliot Porter*

 ## Hermit Thrush
Hylocichla guttata

CLEAR AND FLUTELIKE, the haunting music of the hermit thrush floats through the twilight – a serene benediction to the wilderness sunset. One after another the beautiful notes ring out in varied phrases, some high, some low, some blending in tremolo effects. The sweetest singer of his family, the hermit thrush is often called the American nightingale.

A true hermit, this peerless songster inhabits the lonely northern and western evergreen forests. His monk's cowl of brown, his rusty tail, and his spotted breast all blend with the fallen leaves that conceal such delicacies as beetles, caterpillars, and ants. Silent most of the time, he offers liquid cadences at dawn and dusk. Disturbed, he sounds a scolding *kuk-kuk-kuk*. In repose he cocks his tail and then slowly drops it.

The snug nest of plant fibers and rootlets is usually located on the ground. Porcupine hair may furnish a soft inner bed for the three or four greenish-blue eggs. Fed by her mate, the mother bird incubates them for 12 days. Many of the young fall prey to weasels, skunks, foxes, owls, and other woodland predators.

Most hermit thrushes migrate from their northernmost breeding areas. Vermont claims this fine vocalist as its state bird.

Range: central Alaska to Newfoundland, south to N. New Mexico, Wisconsin, and Maryland; winters to Guatemala. *Characteristics:* clear, sweet song; brown head and back, rusty tail, spotted white breast.

Swainson's Thrush
Hylocichla ustulata

BUFFY EYE RINGS, cheeks, and breast are the only quickly recognizable field marks which distinguish the Swainson's from the gray-cheeked thrush. Both birds have spotted breasts and dull gray-brown upper parts. This conservative coat gave Swainson's thrush the alternate common names of olive-backed or russet-backed thrush.

Usually breeding in far northern or remote mountain forests and wintering in tropical America, this thrush is seldom seen by most of us except as a migrant. We sometimes hear its sweet, plaintive whistle in September as it wings through the darkness. It travels as much as 200 miles a night. By day it rests and feeds in the woodlands. Next spring we may see it returning with the warblers and other late migrants.

In a small tree or bush mated birds build a bulky nest of grass, leaves, and moss. It holds three or four blue eggs dotted with brown.

A versatile forager, Swainson's thrush gathers food – mainly insects and wild fruit – on the ground, on tree limbs, and on the wing.

Not as gifted a singer as the hermit or wood thrush, the Swainson's has a melodious song of breezy phrases rising in pitch. One exuberant bird in Michigan was heard pouring forth 4,360 songs between the dawn and dusk of one day.

Range: central Alaska to Newfoundland, south in the mountains to California and West Virginia; winters from S. Mexico to Argentina. *Characteristics:* gray-brown head and back, buffy eye rings and cheeks, spotted whitish breast.

Graycheek, length 6¼-8″

Gray-cheeked Thrush
Hylocichla minima

RANGING FARTHER NORTH than any other species in the Hylocichla group, the graycheeks breed in spruce and tamarack forests of Alaska and Canada. Many push on into the tundra and nest during the short Arctic summer in streamside groves of stunted willow, alder, and birch. Others cross the Bering Sea to raise their young in northeastern Siberia.

Another race of the gray-cheeked thrush, slightly smaller and often called Bicknell's thrush, nests in the mountains of New York and New England. Extremely shy, it is seldom seen. Indeed it was not recognized as a distinct race or as a breeding bird in this region until the 1880's. Like the larger form, Bicknell's thrush winters in tropical America.

Usually placed close to the ground, the graycheek's nest of mud and grass contains three to five greenish-blue eggs faintly marked with brown. The female occasionally sings when on the nest, while her mate may engage in flight songs over his territory. The soft, sweet song sounds like the veery's but ends on a rising note instead of spiraling downward.

The graycheek has a slurred *quee-a* call note, much longer than the abrupt *whit* or *peep* of its close relative the Swainson's thrush.

Range: N. E. Siberia and Alaska to Newfoundland, south to N. British Columbia and W. Massachusetts; winters from Nicaragua and West Indies to N. South America. *Characteristics:* gray-brown back, gray cheeks, spotted breast.

Veery
Hylocichla fuscescens

A CASCADE of silvery notes fills the air — *vee-ur-vee-ur veer*. The phrases spiral downward, each weaker and lower than the one before. The veery's continuous, whirling melody sounds wild and far away as it rings through the deep woods.

Some listeners say the veery sings the finest of all thrush music. Others consider the melody second rate. Whatever its ranking, the veery song, once heard, identifies the singer thereafter.

Often the song may be the only clue to the veery's presence, for he dwells in the thick shade of moist woodlands with deep underbrush. A quick glimpse reveals a tawny-brown back, richer and warmer than the gray-brown coat worn by the Swainson's and gray-cheeked thrushes. The veery also has less spotting on its breast.

The bird builds a nest of leaves and grass on the ground or very close to it. The three or four blue eggs spotted with brown hatch in 10 to 12 days. The parents soften grubs and hairless caterpillars between their mandibles before feeding them to the nestlings. Later the young may be offered dragonflies and butterflies.

Range: S. Canada and N. United States, south in the mountains to N. Arizona and N. Georgia; winters from Central America to Brazil. *Characteristics:* down-spiraling song; tawny-brown head and back, whitish breast lightly spotted.

Veery, length 6½-7¾″; Eliot Porter

Male (upper) and female eastern bluebirds, length 6½-7½"; juvenile at right

Eastern Bluebird
Sialia sialis

BRILLIANTLY ARRAYED, gentle in manner, the bluebird delights all who see it. The bird "carries the sky on its back," said Henry Thoreau. The settlers of Plymouth Colony noted the rusty breast and called it the "blue robin."

With the first warm days of February or March the migrating eastern bluebirds start for their northern breeding grounds. "In New York and New England the sap starts up the sugar maple the very day the bluebird arrives, and sugar-making begins forthwith," wrote John Burroughs. At this time their soft *chur-wi* calls can be heard as they fly overhead. They also warble three or four delicate gurgling notes.

Like the robin, the bluebird shuns the deep forest. He prefers open country, roadside trees, orchards, trees in cities and towns, and cutover woodlands with plenty of tree hollows for nesting. A mated pair may place its loose grass nest in an abandoned woodpecker hole. Suitable accommodations are in great demand, and bluebirds must compete aggressively with house wrens, house sparrows, and starlings.

Fortunately, bluebirds will readily settle into nest boxes. These should be set on poles from 8 to 12 feet above the ground in open areas. Since bluebirds seem to prefer large territories, the boxes should not be too close together. An entrance hole measuring 1½ inches in diameter will keep starlings out.

The female incubates the four to six bluish-white eggs for about 12 days. The father takes charge of the fledglings, feeding them and teaching them to feed themselves while his mate is busy renovating the nursery or building a new one for a second brood.

Young bluebirds have mouse-gray backs and spotted white breasts; only a tinge of dull blue in the wings and tail hints at the bright colors they'll wear when they grow up.

Bluebirds pore over the ground for grasshoppers and beetles. They dart about foliage hunting flying insects and caterpillars. From trees and bushes they pick berries and other fruit.

In early autumn the family groups wander about the countryside. Soon they join other families and start a leisurely journey southward. A few hardy individuals brave northern winters.

Deceived by prematurely mild weather, bluebirds may return north too soon. Many are killed by sleet and ice storms. An entire small flock may take shelter in a tree hole and freeze to death.

In recent years conservationists have voiced alarm at the virtual disappearance of the bluebird from vast portions of its range. They cite various reasons: widespread use of insecticides, severe winters, growing competition from starlings, and the disappearance of old orchards that furnished favored nest sites.

There have been several campaigns to provide more housing for this beautiful species, which has been named the state bird of Missouri and New York. Recently the junior edition of the Campfire Girls of America—the "Bluebirds"—engaged in a nationwide program of erecting new homes for bluebirds.

Range: S. Saskatchewan to Nova Scotia, south to Honduras; migratory in the north. *Characteristics:* blue back, rusty breast. Female is duller. Young have gray backs, spotted white breasts, some blue in wings and tail.

Western Bluebird
Sialia mexicana

THIS HARDY WESTERNER wears the same pleasing colors as its eastern cousin but has them arranged differently. The male's throat is blue and the rusty red of his breast extends to shoulders and back. The female is much paler.

Frequenting open woodlands and mountain glades, western bluebirds generally nest in old woodpecker holes or natural cavities in oaks and yellow pines. They are as easily attracted to bird boxes as the eastern birds and defend their man-made homes vigorously against house wrens and violet-green swallows. When tree holes and bird boxes are lacking, these bluebirds may raise their family in a building or even in a cliff swallow's nest. One determined pair, whose eggs were systematically taken by an oologist, built six nests in a single season. In each the female laid a clutch of six eggs.

Usually two sets of four to six pale blue eggs are laid in one year. The female incubates them alone on a bedding of grass. The young birds are grayish and wear the telltale markings of the thrush family—spots on their breasts.

A western bluebird often perches quietly on a limb which commands a wide view of the countryside. He darts out to snatch flying insects, flutters down to capture them on the ground, or skims over the herbage, picking off morsels.

In late summer and fall he eats a heavy proportion of berries. Seeds of the mistletoe berry pass through the bird's body undigested; thus the bluebird helps spread the parasitic shrub.

At this time bluebirds gather in family flocks, sometimes in company with robins and mountain bluebirds. Attracted by abundant supplies of berries, the western bluebirds may drift up the mountains as winter draws nigh. But most descend to lower altitudes for the cold months.

The loose bluebird formations sometimes fly so high that only their call notes give notice of their passage overhead. This *mew* note, repeated over and over, becomes the song. The westerner, unlike the eastern bluebird, earns few bouquets for his music making.

Range: S. British Columbia to central Montana, south in mountains to S. Mexico. *Characteristics:* blue head, wings, and tail; rusty breast and back. Female is paler. Young are gray with spotted breasts and some blue in wings and tail.

Male (right) and female western bluebirds, length 6-7½"
Walter A. Weber, National Geographic staff artist (also opposite)

Male (right) and female mountain bluebirds, length 6½-7¾"; Walter A. Weber, National Geographic staff artist

Mountain Bluebird
Sialia currucoides

HERE IS THE BLUEBIRD without any rusty red in his plumage. Except for a whitish belly, the male in breeding finery is all turquoise blue.

Flashing through the air in undulating swoops or hovering over a field on rapidly beating wings, he seems like a living model for the beautiful turquoise jewelry fashioned by some of the western Indians. In fall and winter his plumage has touches of dull brown, the predominant color of the female all year.

The mountain bluebird sings its sweet warble in high meadows at altitudes up to 10,000 feet or more. The state bird of Idaho and Nevada, it may venture as far north as central Alaska and is sometimes called the Arctic bluebird. Nesting in tree holes and bird boxes, this species incubates two sets of five or six blue eggs in a season. Its diet includes insects and fruit.

Range: central Alaska to S.W. Manitoba, south in the mountains to S. California and W. Oklahoma; winters to N. Mexico. *Characteristics:* male is turquoise blue with whitish belly. Female is pale brown with blue tinge on wings, tail, and rump. Young resemble the female.

Townsend's solitaires, length 8-9½"; Bob and Elsie Boggs

Male wheatear, length 5½-6¼"; Eric Hosking

Townsend's Solitaire
Myadestes townsendi

THIS LONELY WESTERN TROUBADOUR makes ringing mountain music – clear, loud, and sweet. But until you hear his glorious voice you may find it hard to think of the solitaire as a thrush.

The slim gray bird snaps up insects in midair with an audible click of the mandibles in the manner of a flycatcher. In flight the light wing patches and white outer tail feathers stand out, suggesting a mockingbird.

Unknown to science before 1834, Townsend's solitaire was described by Audubon from a specimen taken near the Columbia River by the pioneer ornithologist John Kirk Townsend.

As its name implies, the solitaire often plays a lone hand. In the breeding season pairs and family groups may be found in open mountain forests up to 12,000 feet.

Breeding birds place their nest of twigs and evergreen needles on or near the ground. The three or four white eggs are blotched with brown and may have a blue, green, yellow, or pink tinge. The juvenile plumage is heavily spotted.

In winter the solitaire moves to sheltered canyons to feed on mistletoe and other berries.

Range: Alaska to S. W. South Dakota, south to N. W. Mexico; migratory in the north. *Characteristics:* gray body, light eye rings, white tail sides, buffy wing patches; long tail, short bill. Young have buff spotting.

Wheatear
Oenanthe oenanthe

A NATIVE OF EURASIA, the wheatear long ago invaded far northern regions of the New World, coming both from the east and west. Now only about 1,000 miles of Arctic wastes separate the two forms found in America.

The wheatear is easily identified by the inverted black "T" on the upper part of his white tail. Constantly bowing and bobbing, he flits from rock to rock or dashes into the air to seize insects. He sings a short warble and sounds a scolding *chak-chak* like pebbles struck together.

Usually located in a rock crevice or an abandoned rabbit burrow, the nest of grass and feathers contains five or six blue eggs.

Wheatears that nest in Alaska migrate across Asia. Greenland wheatears fly east across Europe in the fall. Some may wander as far south as Long Island. Both forms winter in tropical Africa.

Another wide-ranging thrush species of Eurasia, the bluethroat (*Luscinia svecica*), ventures into Alaska to breed. Only the breeding male of this brown-backed species has a blue throat.

Range: N. Asia to N. Alaska and N. W. Canada; also Europe to Greenland and N. E. Canada; winters to tropical Africa and India. *Characteristics:* brown back, buff underparts, white rump, white tail with black center and tip. Breeding male has gray back, black wings and mask, white stripe over eyes.

221

TINY FORAGERS OF THE FOREST

Gnatcatchers and Kinglets

Family Sylviidae

By AUSTIN L. RAND

Each spring in my garden near Chicago the ruby-crowned kinglet passes through on his way to nesting grounds in the spruce forests of Canada. The plump, short-tailed little bird usually travels alone. He hops through the leafless barberry bushes and the green-budding lilacs, flitting his wingtips nervously.

His ruby crest is usually concealed, but white eye rings give him a curious staring expression. Every now and then he offers snatches of his distinctive song: *li-ber-ty, li-ber-ty, li-ber-ty.* These would serve as loud notes for many birds, but for this feathered mite they are barely more than whispers, mere hints of the full song he will sing later at home in the spruces.

Others may interpret the rubycrown's song differently, but the loud, rollicking phrases still say "liberty" to me the way they did when I first learned them many years ago. I remember the

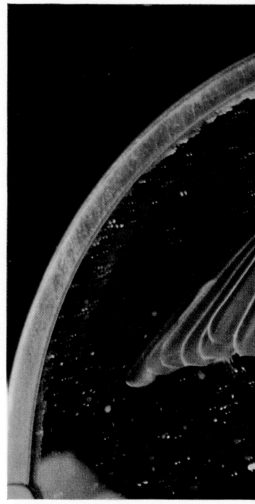

BLOWING HIS RED TOP *at a fancied rival,*

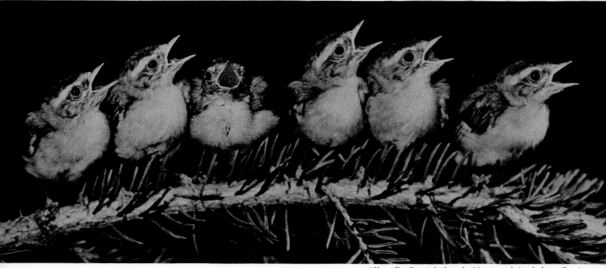

Allan D. Cruickshank, National Audubon Society

NOISY SEXTET *of golden-crowned kinglets clamors for food. These juveniles fatten on insects brought by their parents. They will retain the light eye stripe when they are grown.*

Arthur A. Allen

bristling ruby-crowned kinglet asserts territorial rights before a snow-flecked mirror.

line of spruces on the edge of a Nova Scotia pasture where on an April day I first heard a rubycrown. I say heard rather than saw—though I did see the tiny greenish bird in the treetop—for the song is his most remarkable feature.

Song gave the sylviids the name of warbler in the Old World—and they merit it far more than our thin-voiced American wood warblers, an entirely different family for whom the name was borrowed.

In Europe's gardens and hedgerows I have heard the black-capped warbler's clear, rich notes; the garden warbler's sweet, even-flowing melody; the marsh warbler's strikingly beautiful song, sometimes delivered at night when other birds are still. On board ship in the Mediterranean I have seen the migrating chiffchaff that repeatedly says its name, and the willow warbler that sings a rippling series of notes —rising in volume, then dying away.

In New Guinea's lowland forests I have seen the brilliant blue wren-warbler come popping through the bushes, tail cocked, singing its pleasant trills and warbles. And in Madagascar, in a scraggly tree in a little gully, I collected a grayish warbler so different it *had* to be new. Now known as *Randia pseudozosterops* Delacour, it was a genus and species unknown to science.

223

The Sylviidae are a family of quite small birds. One with a body larger than the end joint of my thumb is a big one. They have slender bills and feet, and most wear dull colors to match their habitat. They eat mainly insects.

Two gnatcatchers and two kinglets are the only widespread sylviid species in North America. Each group has special traits that proclaim its identity. The golden-crowned kinglet displays the same wing-flicking habits as the rubycrown. The blue-gray and the black-tailed gnatcatchers have the habit of cocking up and twitching their tails. Some people see in these rather slender, long-tailed, elegant little birds dressed mostly in gray a striking similarity to the much larger mockingbird.

The gnatcatchers and kinglets also differ in the way they build their nests. In their northern habitat the kinglets weave a bulky, semipensile nest amid a dense cluster of conifer twigs. Made of moss and spider webs and lined with fur and feathers, it provides warmth and concealment for the parent and the seven to nine eggs or young. Some gnatcatchers, dwelling in deciduous woods of warmer climates, build a neat little cup like that of a hummingbird. Made of plant down and spider webs and decorated with bits of lichen, it could easily be mistaken for a knot on a branch. The nest hollow is only large enough to hold the four or five speckled eggs.

Other gnatcatchers and a few species called "gnatwrens" inhabit the American tropics. The Arctic warbler, a member of another sylviid group, breeds in Alaska. These sylviids are all immigrants from the Old World. The rest of the 400 or so species flourish in Europe, Asia, Africa, and the Australian area. The gnatcatchers and the gnatwrens, whose ancestors are believed to have crossed from Siberia to Alaska ages ago, have evolved such differences while occupying the warmer parts of the New World that it is impossible to say which are their nearest Old World relatives. The kinglets, on the other hand, came comparatively recently. They still nest in the evergreen forests of the north, the same as their close relatives in northern Asia and Europe. The Arctic warbler arrived but yesterday, geologically speaking, and its Alaskan outpost is only an extension of its Eurasian range.

Looking back over the sylviid warblers I've seen, I'd group them in three cate-

Arctic warblers, length 4¾"; Adolph Murie

Arctic Warbler
Phylloscopus borealis

AN IMMIGRANT from across the Bering Sea, this lively little bird has established a summer outpost in western Alaska. Like other leaf warblers of the Old World, this greenish-brown bird flits and hops about the foliage. In dwarf willows it hunts insects and sings over and over a short trill preceded by a *tzick*.

The Arctic warbler, also called Kennicott's willow warbler, usually nests at the base of a shrub. Using leaves, moss, and grass, it builds a domed chamber with a side entrance. The female, who looks like her mate, broods the five to seven white eggs spotted with brown.

Though Arctic warblers breed from Finland to the slopes of Mount McKinley National Park in Alaska, they all funnel down to ancestral wintering grounds in southeast Asia.

Range: N. Eurasia to W. Alaska; winters in S. E. Asia. *Characteristics:* greenish-brown head and back, whitish underparts tinged with yellow; pale eye stripes, wing bars, and legs.

FINELY WROUGHT NEST *of the blue-gray gnatcatcher is camouflaged with lichens.*

gories: Some flit and hop in trees and among shrubbery, some skulk in underbrush, and some live in grasslands. The gnatcatchers and kinglets are part of the flit and hop brigade. They are continuously and nervously active as they pick a spider off a twig, hover in front of a leaf to snatch a tiny caterpillar, or dart after a passing fly. Some sing as they feed.

Like most northern insect-eating birds, the gnatcatchers and kinglets move south for the winter, visiting gardens from which they've been absent all summer. Some go as far as Central America, although the golden-crowned kinglet may only move to southern Canada. On their winter grounds they tend to join chickadees, nuthatches, wood warblers, and vireos. You may walk for miles through the winter woods, seeing only an occasional crow or woodpecker. Then suddenly you come upon a mixed flock of these birds, flitting and hopping, gleaning through the forest.

225

Ruby-crowned kinglets
male (upper) and female, 3¾-4½"

Golden-crowned kinglets
male (upper) and female, 3¼-4"

Male blue-gray gnatcatcher
length 4-5"

Male black-tailed
gnatcatchers, length 4½"

Female blacktail

Ruby-crowned Kinglet
Regulus calendula

IN THE EVERGREEN WILDS of western mountains and the north, the restless rubycrown comes into full voice. Here on his breeding grounds he sends forth a song both beautiful and loud—remarkably loud for his size. The melody opens with a high-pitched *tee tee tee*, drops to a low *tew tew tew*, and ends with a tinkling, repeated chant of *ti-da-dee* or *li-ber-ty*.

In courtship males flare their brilliant scarlet crown patches, which are usually hidden. Mated pairs hang a mossy cup among the twigs of a conifer branch. The female broods the seven to nine tightly packed white eggs dotted with brown.

These tiny birds turn, hop, and flick their wings continually as they search for insects. White eye rings, broken at the top, give them a staring look. While breeding, rubycrown pairs prefer a solitary life. In migratory foraging they may join warblers, nuthatches, and other birds.

Range: N. W. Alaska to Newfoundland, south to Baja California, New Mexico, N. Michigan, and Nova Scotia; winters to Guatemala. *Characteristics:* broken white eye rings, olive back, buffy-gray underparts, pale wing bars, stubby tail; flicks wings. Adult male has red crown patch.

Blue-gray Gnatcatcher
Polioptila caerulea

A THIN TWANG, like that of a plucked banjo string, heralds his presence—somewhere among the twigs of a tree. You look up to see a tiny blue-gray bird with a white belly and a long tail that twitches busily. He flies out to seize an insect winging past, then makes a short, undulating flight into an open grove where he sings a wheezy but melodious warble, so soft it is barely audible a few yards away.

His proportions and movements—especially that active tail—resemble the mockingbird's. His size and colors identify him as a gnatcatcher.

The blue-gray favors a different environment in different parts of his range: woods and wooded residential sections in the south, watercourses and timbered swamps in the north, hillside bushes and mesquite in the west.

On the horizontal limb of a tree blue-gray gnatcatchers fashion a beautiful cup of plant down and fibers, bound with spider webs and decorated with lichens. It holds four or five bluish eggs spotted with reddish brown.

Range: California to S. Ontario and N. New Jersey, south to Guatemala; winters from S. United States southward. *Characteristics:* blue-gray head and back, white eye rings and underparts, long black tail with white sides; swishes tail. Adult male has black forehead band.

Golden-crowned Kinglet
Regulus satrapa

ONE OF THE SMALLEST BIRDS of the coniferous forests, this olive-gray kinglet with the glowing crown is a friendly creature. Humans sometimes get close enough to touch him.

Wings opening and closing in a characteristic flicking motion, the goldencrown flits about the bushes and evergreen trees picking out insects and their eggs. In winter he may even glean branches partly buried by snow.

He sounds a call note so high-pitched many people cannot hear it. The song also begins high, then drops to a staccato chatter.

Mated birds build a globular nest of moss, lichens, and spider webs and line it with feathers and fur. Suspended from conifer twigs, the nest holds eight or nine creamy eggs speckled with brown. The young do not acquire the bright crowns of their parents until late summer.

In winter many of these stub-tailed mites roam northern woods with chickadees, brown creepers, and woodpeckers instead of migrating south.

Range: S. Alaska to Newfoundland, south in western mountains to Guatemala, in East to W. North Carolina; winters to Gulf Coast. *Characteristics:* black head stripes, white eye stripes, olive-gray back, whitish underparts; flicks wings. Crown patch orange in male, yellow in female; young lack the crown patch.

Black-tailed Gnatcatcher
Polioptila melanura

MESQUITE THICKETS in the southwestern desert country and the Rio Grande Valley provide a year-round home for the black-tailed gnatcatcher. Once he finds a mate and a few acres of brush to his liking he seldom leaves either.

The male wears a black cap from February through the breeding season. Otherwise he and his mate look much like the blue-gray gnatcatcher. As his name indicates, the blacktail shows much more black on the underside and a thinner band of white at the sides. His thin *chee* call is harsher than the blue-gray's.

The blacktail hops through the shrubbery to pick insect food from twigs. Despite his name he does not catch many gnats.

In the twiggy tangle of a small bush blacktails build a deep cup of grass and bark and line it with fur and feathers. The four brown-spotted eggs have a greenish hue when freshly laid; later the ground color turns pale blue.

Range: S. California and S. Nevada to S. Texas and N. Mexico. *Characteristics:* blue-gray head and back, white or gray underparts, long tail with white sides and blackish underside; flicks tail. Breeding male has black cap.

SMALL PEDESTRIANS
OF PASTURE AND MEADOW

Wagtails and Pipits
Family Motacillidae

YELLOW WAGTAIL *guards its nursery*

L IKE A WIND-UP TOY, a little bird with long toes and a golden belly runs through the snow-starched grass. An icy wind from the Bering Sea sighs across the tundra, but the bird only flicks his white-edged tail. Cold weather is routine to the yellow wagtail.

He is one of a family of 48 species that ranges from the Arctic to the island of South Georgia in the Atlantic, 15 degrees north of the Antarctic Circle. The family originated in the Old World; only seven of its species are seen in North America.

Of these, four appear on far northern islands and are accidental elsewhere in the western hemisphere. The white wagtail, common in Europe and Asia, shows up in eastern Greenland; two Siberian races have appeared in the Aleutian Islands of Alaska, and one of these has been found in Baja California. The Pechora pipit of Siberia has been reported on Alaskan islands. The meadow pipit breeds in eastern Greenland. And the red-throated pipit of northern Europe and Siberia has been observed in Alaska and Baja California.

The other three species breed regularly on the North American mainland—the yellow wagtail in northern Alaska and northern Canada, and the water pipit and Sprague's pipit through much of Canada and the United States. The water pipit on migration is a common sight in the United States. A farmer will see a large flock wheel over a plowed field. Suddenly the pipits will land and scamper along the furrows searching for insects. They are especially welcome in the cotton country, for they attack the boll weevil.

Though strong fliers, wagtails and pipits stay on the ground when they can, running and walking rather than hopping. They generally dwell close to water and prefer open country, clear of trees and underbrush—except for the yellow wagtail, which seems to frequent groves of willow trees. The birds are slender, with long, pointed wings, long legs, and thin bills. They have nine primary flight feathers instead of the usual ten. And their hind claws are long in proportion to their sparrow-sized bodies. An African pipit, the longclaw, has 1½-inch hind toes.

228

in Alaska. A feather, below blossoms of Labrador tea, reveals the moss-cupped eggs.

The wagtail's plumage is clear and boldly differentiated—the yellow of the Alaskan bird's breast is unmistakable. But the pipit is a drab, streaked bird, hard to see against the terrain. Both wag their tails when they pause in their endless scuttling about, but the wagtail does so with vehemence, shaking like a hula dancer. Both birds sing their unremarkable songs on the wing, but the pipit flies higher. Rising, he calls incessantly; then as he circles at 200 feet or so, his song changes emphasis.

Finally he drops earthward, often in sudden, dramatic silence, the descent sometimes ending in a "falling leaf" maneuver. Because of this singing in flight Audubon dubbed the birds "larks" or "titlarks." Sprague's pipit, which Audubon named for Isaac Sprague, a companion on his Missouri River journey of 1843 during which the species was discovered, is still sometimes called the Missouri skylark.

Yellow Wagtail
Motacilla flava
(Picture on preceding page)

EARLY JUNE in western Alaska finds the yellow wagtails arriving from Asia for the brief summer. The slim, restless birds are a common sight, but usually at long range. Before you get close, one rises on nervous wings and swings back and forth before you, crying his indignation with a metallic *ple-ple-ple*. Now you can see the bright lemon underparts – a splash of gaiety in the bleak landscape of boggy meadow and tundra.

Seemingly always on the move, the birds scuttle briskly across meadows and coastal mud flats. At every abrupt, momentary pause they flirt their tails up and down or back and forth. Their heads bob in accompaniment.

They feed on beetles, spiders, flies, sometimes on salmonberries and crowberries, and on tiny invertebrates that are washed ashore. Until flushed, they stay near the ground. They would rather slip into a tangle of riverside brush than fly.

When courting, however, the male puts on a marvelous aerial display. He angles up from cover to about 100 feet, then stiffens his wings and spreads his tail, raising it nearly perpendicular to his body. In this position he floats down to within a few feet of the ground while singing a series of jingling notes. He lands in a bush, then rises again to repeat the performance.

Though usually seen around willows, wagtails nest away from trees, often in the side of a turf-covered hummock. The nest is woven of grass and moss, lined with tufts of hair and perhaps ptarmigan feathers, and concealed by grass curling down from the tussock. The four to seven eggs are pale green with brown and gray splotches.

About mid-July the fledglings leave the nest. Within two months most yellow wagtails have migrated, heading west across Bering Strait, then southward along the coast of Asia to their wintering grounds. Thus they return annually to the Old World.

Range: N. E. Siberia across N. Alaska to N. Yukon, south along west coast of Alaska; winters in Java, New Guinea, and the Philippines. *Characteristics:* white eye stripe and throat, olive-gray upperparts, yellow underparts; dark legs, long dark tail edged with white. Wags tail.

Sprague's Pipit
Anthus spragueii

SPRAGUE'S PIPIT is an elusive bird, as Audubon discovered after collecting it. He and his comrades on his Missouri River expedition kept looking for the bird on the ground, for its song seemed to spring from the prairie grass. Then, says Audubon, "we at last looked upwards, and there saw several of these beautiful creatures singing in a continuous manner, and soaring at such an elevation, as to render them more or less difficult to discover with the eye. . . ."

Ornithologists still note the pipit's ventriloquism as he sings his soft, sweet flight song:

ching-a-ring-a-ring-a-ring-a, the notes dropping about an octave down the scale. The bird utters it while flying in wide circles high in the air. When the pipit finally descends – and Audubon timed one singing and flying for 36 minutes – his song ceases. Once he alights he becomes just another slight little brown-striped bird. He blends so well with the grass that often only the flick of white as he twitches his tail gives him away.

Walking and running rather like a starling, Sprague's pipit scours the short-grass prairies of southern Canada and the northern United States for insects. He also eats weed seeds.

The settlement of the prairies destroyed much of this bird's habitat, and individuals have been found far from the usual range – in the flat, jack-pine country of Michigan, for example, and on an Ohio airport. Perhaps the species is gradually adapting to a new environment.

The grass nest, sometimes concealed by a frail arch, rests in a depression in the ground. It is hard to find, but one searcher noted that when a male pipit drops to earth after singing on high, his mate darts off the nest to meet him. Her appearance furnishes a good clue to the whereabouts of the four or five eggs, pale gray with purple-brown speckles and dark lines.

Range: N. Alberta to central Manitoba, south to Montana and N.W. Minnesota; winters from S. Arizona, S. Louisiana, and N.W. Mississippi to S. Mexico. *Characteristics:* streaked grayish-brown upperparts, buffy underparts; tail edged with white; thin bill, pale legs.

Water Pipit
Anthus spinoletta

Wave on wave, the brown birds rise from the sun-lit field and turn northward, dipping and gliding across the sky. The water pipits, or American pipits, are migrating–an unforgettable sign of spring.

Instinct draws the birds toward cold bleak lands for their breeding season. They head for the tundra of Arctic Canada, the barren coast of Labrador, the treeless slopes of western mountains. On Mount McKinley in Alaska they are found at heights of 4,000 to 5,000 feet. Farther south they seek higher elevations.

Walking daintily, swinging his white-edged tail, the slender water pipit plucks insects and seeds from the grass or looks for invertebrates in shallow pools on tidal flats. From high in the air his flight song rings out – a series of trilling notes: *chwee chwee chwee chwee chwee.*

The mated pair build a nest of grass and twigs, usually on the side of a hummock or half under a rock. The four to seven pale eggs are marked with brown. The male brings food for his mate as well as for the young.

Late August finds the birds flocking, with many calls of *pi-pit.* Then they are off for the wintering grounds, keeping close to beaches and salt flats.

Range: Alaska, N. Canada, and W. Greenland, south in western mountains to New Mexico; winters to Guatemala and Florida. *Characteristics:* gray-brown upperparts, buffy underparts, white tail edges; slender bill, dark legs. Nods head.

Water pipit, length 6-7"; Eliot Porter

CEDAR WAXWINGS *perch amid pyracantha berries in California. Red "wax" marks the wings of one of this look-alike pair. Irregular migrants, the sleek birds visit almost any state any time of year. Mottled gray young (opposite) leave the untidy nest when about 16 days old.*

Adults, length 6½-8"; D. E. Williams

SLEEK, CRESTED BERRY PICKERS # The Waxwings
Family Bombycillidae

THEY SWEEP over the yard in purposeful, undulating flight, then swerve and plummet toward a tree where the fruit is ripe—a cherry or mulberry, perhaps. Quickly the small flock settles into the foliage. Efficiently each bird harvests berries, conversing with his neighbors in a wheezing, lisping voice, high pitched yet soft. This is the cedar waxwing (*Bombycilla cedrorum*), a handsome and amiable visitor to gardens and orchards. He belongs to a family of three species, two of which breed in North America, the third in eastern Asia.

Crested and black masked, he has sleek brown plumage, yellowish in front, and a yellow band at the tip of his tail. In some birds certain wing feathers and occasionally tail feathers are tipped with glossy red, as though touched by sealing wax. This explains the family's common name.

The cedar waxwing eats avidly but seldom bickers with his fellow diners. Before his flock wings off, he may join half a dozen other waxwings in a charming ritual. They sit on a limb, facing the same direction, and pass a cherry or perhaps a caterpillar back and forth several times until it is consumed. No one knows the purpose of this rite, but during courtship a male and female may pass petals back and forth as though exchanging gifts. One hops forward to pluck the offering from the other's bill, then hops back to offer it in turn.

Waxwings feed on insects, cankerworms, and such delicacies as apple blossom petals. But their addiction to fruit explains their restless wanderings over much of the United States and their late nesting. Not until the berries are ripening on northern breeding grounds do they mate. In a tree or bush they build a nest of twigs, grass, and moss for the three to six speckled blue-gray eggs. They carry off twine and ribbon that people leave, and are so trusting that they continue feeding the hatchlings even if human hands have touched the young.

Bohemian waxwing, length 7½-8¾"; C. G. Hampson

THE BOHEMIAN WAXWING (*Bombycilla garrulus*) is slightly larger than the cedar waxwing and even more elegantly groomed, wearing white and yellow on his wings and chestnut under his tail. Gypsylike, he roams the northwestern forests, sometimes in huge flocks. He thrives in sub-zero cold—as long as there is food. A winter shortage of berries may send him into the Southwest or eastward into New England. He shares the red markings and many habits with the cedar waxwing and may join its flocks, blending his rough buzzing voice with his cousin's lisping calls. The Bohemian lays four to six dull blue eggs with black spots.

Cedar waxwing—*Range:* S. E. Alaska to Newfoundland, south to N. California and N. Georgia; winters to Panama. *Characteristics:* sleek, crested; brown back, yellowish front, yellow-tipped tail. Most adults have glossy red marks on secondary wing feathers. Young are gray with soft streaks on breast.

Bohemian waxwing—*Range:* W. Alaska to Manitoba, south to Washington and N. Montana; winters to California, Arkansas, Nova Scotia. *Characteristics:* grayish body, larger than cedar waxwing; white-and-yellow wing markings, rusty under tail.

SLENDER COUSIN OF THE WAXWINGS # The Phainopepla
Family Ptilogonatidae

WHITE WING PATCHES flash against glossy black plumage as a male *Phainopepla nitens* rises from the top of a southwestern pepper tree. With mincing flight he crosses a desert wash to a mesquite tree where mistletoe clings. He bows his crested head to eat a berry, then raises it to warble wheezily.

During his long flights he often snaps up an insect, flycatcher fashion. His crest, build, and the silkiness of his plumage resemble the waxwing's.

Phainopepla means "shining robe." The name fits him but not his dark gray mate. The birds nest in trees or bushes, the male building a shallow cup of twigs for the two or three speckled whitish eggs.

Of the four silky flycatcher species this is the only one that breeds in the United States; the other three are denizens of Mexico and Central America.

Range: central California to W. Texas, south to S. Mexico. *Characteristics:* slender, crested; long flaring tail. Male is blue-black with white wing patches that show only in flight. Female is dark gray. Young resemble the female.

Male and (inset) female phainopeplas, length 7-7¾"; Eliot Porter

BUTCHER BIRDS

The Shrikes

Family Laniidae

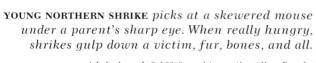

IMPALED ON THE THORNS of a sweet locust tree, the torn bodies of a sparrow and a goldfinch swing stiffly in the winter wind. The wan sun falls on the tree's grisly fruit and touches its crown, where – still as a stone – sits the harvester. Black bars mask his eyes; his hooked beak curves above a finely lined white breast. This motionless sentinel is *Lanius excubitor*, "butcher guard," called the northern shrike. He kills, then hangs his prey in his larder tree for future meals.

Now, in a nearby gully, a mouse is running.

The bird drops with a flutter of short dark wings. His head cocks to deliver a lethal chop – and the mouse swerves. Many times, by breaking backs and necks, the small horny scimitar has dealt swift death. This time it goes a fraction awry – cutting, not killing. Teeth bared, the mouse turns and lunges.

One, two, three times the bird dodges. He does not flee – shrikes rarely do. Finally it is the mouse that flees – but too late. Midway in his second leap the bird is upon him, and he falls. Shaking, twisting, choking, the shrike stills his victim, and then the beak strikes home again and again, hacking and ripping until the mouse dies in the blood-soiled snow. The killer, clutching the carcass tenuously – for a shrike's claws are not overly strong – flaps heavily back to his tree to spike the fresh meat, then to carve and eat.

Sixty-seven species of butcher birds compose the family Laniidae. Two dwell in the New World: the northern and loggerhead shrikes. The northern breeds in Alaskan and Canadian spruce forests and normally ranges south of Canada only in winter. The loggerhead shrike (*Lanius ludovicianus*) generally ranges through open and semiopen country over most of the United States.

Perched high with black tail tilting, or flying low on white-splotched wings, the loggerhead looks much like his northern cousin, except that his mask is continuous from eye to eye, not broken by the beak. To some observers he resembles a masked mocker, hence the name "French mockingbird." Loggerhead sexes are alike, whereas the female northern shrike has a dark, sometimes olive-tinged back, and duller tail and underparts than her mate.

Shrikes are undeniably bloodthirsty. Reports tell of their invading homes to kill canaries, and slaughtering every bird in a bird banding trap. Yet grasshoppers, locusts, crickets, and other large insects are their staple diet. With their superior eyesight shrikes can spot a moving insect as far away as 70 yards.

The loggerhead sings such light phrases as *queedle, queedle* and *tsurp-see, tsurp-see*. The northern butcher bird, on the other hand, gives better indication that "shrike" came from the same root word as "shriek." His song, though interspersed with occasional trills, resounds with squeaks, mews, and caws.

Courtship for the male loggerhead appears quite frustrating. The female apparently tires quickly of his wing spreading and tail fanning, and he has to chase her to regain her attention. Having mated, both partners construct a deep, well-lined cup of twigs and grass in a bush or tree. The female lays four to seven white, gray, or buff eggs marked with gray, yellow, or umber spots. Within hours of hatching, the young are fed insect bits. In their third week infant loggerheads leave the nest. They weigh nearly as much as their parents.

Northern shrike — *Range:* N. Alaska to central Labrador, south to N. British Columbia and central Saskatchewan; winters to N. California, New Mexico, and Maryland. *Characteristics:* large head with broken black mask, curved bill fringed with light feathers; gray back, barred white breast; dark, white-edged wings and tail. Female has darker back, duller tail and underparts. Young have barred brown breasts.

Loggerhead shrike — *Range:* S. British Columbia to New Brunswick, south to S. Mexico; winters throughout range but generally south of Canada. *Characteristics:* same as male northern shrike except for smaller head, eye-to-eye mask; smaller, less-hooked bill with dark fringe; unbarred breast. Young are gray.

LOGGERHEAD SHRIKE, *builder of long-lasting nests, utters grating calls and repeated pairs of whistled notes. Like the mocker, he can mimic other birds.*

Length 8-10", George M. Bradt, National Audubon Society

AGGRESSIVE BANE OF SONGBIRDS

The Starling 𝅘𝅥𝅮𝅘𝅥𝅮

Family Sturnidae

T HE FATEFUL DAY was March 16, 1890. The place, Central Park in New York City. Overhead circled 60 European starlings (*Sturnus vulgaris*) released by a zealous group that planned to introduce into the United States all the birds mentioned by Shakespeare. Anxious eyes followed the birds' every flit and hop. Would they survive? Previous attempts to establish them in this country had failed.

Within weeks came the answer: A pair were nesting under the eaves of the American Museum of Natural History. The eggs hatched. The next year 40 more immigrant starlings were freed in Central Park. A Pandora's box had been opened.

From these 100 starlings sprang the unnumbered millions that now inhabit North America. Hardy, prolific, aggressive, they have pushed far northward into Canada, southward to southern Mexico, westward to California, Vancouver Island, and even

238

Alaska. In many areas they assemble each fall and winter in mighty flocks — sometimes miles long — that blot out the sun.

A dense flight of starlings, wheeling and maneuvering almost as one bird, is a marvel to watch. At sunset the black armada descends to favorite roosts, often on ledges of buildings or in trees along sidewalks. Pedestrians in Washington, D. C.,

STARLINGS IN FEBRUARY DRESS *home in on a feeder. Bills turn yellow in winter, speckles fade by summer. Starlings at roost (lower) give bare trees a winter foliage.*

Length, 7½-8½"; Richard F. Baxter, National Geographic staff. Lower: New York Zoological Society

wise to the ways of perching starlings, detour around the laden trees.

Irate city officials constantly wage war on such roosting flocks, but so far the adaptable birds have defied rattles, balloons, whistles, fireworks, blank shells, fire hoses, stuffed owls, and other bogies. They also pay little heed to supersonic sounds and recordings of the starling's distress call. They do shy away from electrified wires and sticky chemical repellants—only to regroup in nearby areas.

Gunners find the starling—one of the few species not protected by law—an elusive, spindle-like target in flight. Its top speed approaches 50 miles an hour.

A plague to other birds as well as to people, starlings evict bluebirds and swallows from nest boxes and tree holes, often destroying eggs and young in the process. But they will accept almost any site for their bulky nests of twigs and trash.

The parents take turns incubating the four to six pale blue eggs, and both adults grub for worms and insects to feed the nestlings. They rear two, sometimes three, broods a year.

The starling molts its juvenile feathers completely. The mouse-gray plumage of youth is shed for glossy black with iridescent flashes of green and purple.

A born noisemaker, the starling squeaks, rattles, wheezes, and whistles. It mimics the songs of other birds and even the sounds of barking dogs, mewing cats, and human "wolf whistles." Indeed, Shakespeare's Hotspur in *King Henry the Fourth* declared: "I'll have a starling shall be taught to speak nothing but 'Mortimer.'"

THE FAMILY STURNIDAE, represented now on every continent except South America, includes 111 species. Some, such as those found in Africa, are brilliantly colored. Others, in Asia, make interesting cage birds; talking hill mynas imitate human speech better than parrots.

The only species besides *vulgaris* to gain a foothold in North America is the Asiatic crested myna (*Acridotheres cristatellus*),

MAN VERSUS STARLING—*and the score,
as many a harried city official will
tell you, is in favor of the bird.
In Washington, D. C., electricians strung
wires atop the Capitol's Corinthian
columns (right) and turned on the current.
A shocking experience here causes starlings
to relocate—on ledges of nearby buildings.*

*On the White House grounds trees were wired
for sound. The President's Press Secretary points
to a loudspeaker (below) that broadcast the wail
of distressed starlings. Unnerved, the birds regrouped
in stately sycamores along Pennsylvania Avenue.
Soon they were back. Nicotine sulfate and molasses
were smeared on tree limbs to give the birds a hotfoot.
They now cluster on more hospitable boughs.*

*In Providence, Rhode Island, city fathers lit up the sky
with Roman candles (opposite). The result: Shell-shocked
starlings fled, only to flock back with friends to
witness the display. Scare the starling with fireworks,
splatter him with water, and he will go, all right—
for reinforcements. Residents of Englewood,
New Jersey, came up with a drastic solution:
They cut down many of their shade trees.*

Wide World (also opposite). Above: United States Capitol

a chunky, short-tailed bird with white wing patches and a bushy crest on its forehead. Introduced at Vancouver, British Columbia, this myna straggles into western Washington and Oregon. Orchardists there keep their fingers crossed, for the bird loves fruit. Unlike its European cousin, it shows no sign of a population boom.

What to do about starlings? The problem has been debated in Congress and in civic meetings across the land. Farmers point to crop losses amounting to millions of dollars, attributable to starlings. Defenders reply that the bird's diet consists largely of insects, much of it the devastating Japanese beetle. But, for good or ill, the starling population keeps right on exploding.

Some southerners, taking a cue from the French, have discovered one way to control the starling—eat him. Wrap the birds in bacon, spit them, roast in a hot oven, serve on toast. "Delicious," say gourmets.

Range: central Alaska and Canada to S. Mexico and West Indies. *Characteristics:* dark plumage, yellow bill, short tail; speckled plumage in winter, dark bill in fall.

POPULATION EXPLOSION! *Starlings by the thousand descend on a feedlot at Caldwell, Idaho, competing with cattle for potatoes. The ravenous horde devours a ton an hour — 15 to 20 tons a day! Stockmen complain that the starlings eat more than the steers. Long a bane to eastern cities, starlings have rapidly expanded westward to farms and villages. Since World War II vulgaris has spread across the Rockies and now is solidly entrenched as far north as Alaska.*

U. S. Fish and Wildlife Service

TIRELESS SONGSTERS
OF THE WOODLANDS

The Vireos

Family Vireonidae

By GEORGE MIKSCH SUTTON

O N THE CAMPUS at the University of Oklahoma I listen every April for the first warbling vireo of spring. I know the very tree, a big hackberry, in which the bird is likely to be singing. The cheerful song has a special meaning for me. A few weeks hence it will, if I want it to, lead me straight to a nest. I will listen carefully to determine what part of the treetop the song comes from. Then I will scan the leaves with my binoculars until I see the neat little suspended cup and the head of the singing male poking over the rim.

The warbling vireo is a small, dull-colored bird. This description fits most of the 35 species comprising the Vireonidae, a family found only in the New World, with 11 of the species breeding in north temperate areas. Shades of olive, gray, and yellow make up the family colors, and some species have light eye rings and wing bars. I consider the vireos "interesting" rather than pretty.

As if to make up for what they lack in bright colors, vireos are persistent and enthusiastic singers. The yellow-throated vireo's song, delivered at times with a beak full of dragonfly, never fails to remind me of the remarkably apt imitation by the great bird artist Louis Agassiz Fuertes – a drawled, carefully timed "Mary, Mary, come 'ere!"

Some vireos, notably the male redeye, sing from morning to night during the breeding season. No matter how hot the air, how drowsy the noon hour, the redeye must sing. I listen to his conversational, slightly monotonous, at times almost melodious phrases and wonder whether these are not a kind of soliloquy rather than warnings uttered in defense of nest territory. Who would be invading *anyone's* territory at such a time? Who, indeed, would be doing anything except taking a nap?

While the redeye nests, much of its singing is surely territorial. But after the young fledge and the adults complete their late summer molt, what purpose does this vocalizing serve? Can it be anything more than an expression of good health and spirits? I have often pondered this while listening to the fall songs, less persistent than those of spring but still delightfully exuberant. The fall pronouncements of the adult birds, full-voiced and sure of themselves, contrast with the raspy, wheezy, sputtered first attempts of the young.

A vireo's most noticeable structural feature is its rather heavy, slightly hooked bill, a characteristic that many believe relates the bird to the shrikes. In this connection, I vividly recall painting a yellow-green vireo from life some years ago in

MORE! MORE! *Young yellow-throated vireos in New York open wide as mother strives to fill them up. Her cuplike nursery is the handsomest of the vireo nests. Cousin redeye (above) likes to sing all day.*

Frederick Kent Truslow. Above: Olin Sewall Pettingill, Jr., National Audubon Society

San Luis Potosí, Mexico. I held it in my left hand and painted with my right. It could, and did, bite hard! As I watched it chewing on my thumb, I was ready to argue that shrikes and vireos were the closest of cousins.

Many vireos are deliberate in their movements. The redeye slowly raises its crown plumage to express curiosity or concern. The solitary vireo, on the lookout for caterpillars, always perches on a large twig — as if to make sure of its footing — and slowly turns its head from side to side. The sight of a caterpillar finally stirs it to action. The bird flies to a leaf to make the capture, returns with squirming prey in beak, whacks it to a pulp, and swallows it thoughtfully.

Such behavior has led to the belief that vireos in general are sluggish. But generalities are to be avoided. The black-capped vireo, common among the scrub oaks and junipers of Oklahoma, is an active, energetic bird, almost warbler-like in behavior. Red-eyed vireos, darting at a blue racer snake moving toward their nest, can become veritable furies. And I shall never forget the ferocity and swiftness of a pair of yellow-throated vireos pummeling a blue jay whose beak held a baby vireo.

MOST VIREOS suspend their nests from a fork at the end of a branch — well above ground in many cases. A warbling vireo nest that I found in Michigan was hung about 35 feet up in a huge elm. I could not climb the tree to the nest, for it was near the tip of a slender, overhanging bough. Nevertheless, I was determined to reach the nest, for I wanted to find out if incubation started before all the eggs were laid. So I borrowed a truck equipped with an extension ladder and drove it under the tree. I raised the ladder, climbed to the topmost rungs, and gingerly reached for that all-important branch. When I felt inside the nest, it was empty. Two days later I found one egg. In all I discovered four eggs on successive days.

I was surprised by the tolerance of the birds. Not once did they dive at me while I was climbing the ladder, and they scolded very little even when my hand was at the nest. Their manner reflected incredulity rather than hostility. Their bright eyes seemed to ask: "How in the world has *he* managed to get here?"

I was surprised in a different way when I watched a pair of red-eyed vireos that were obviously about to nest. Or were they? While the male sang, his silent partner appeared to show special interest in a certain spot on an oak branch. Here she stood high, looking downward as if measuring distances between twigs. Wriggling and twirling, she fitted herself into the fork of a twig and went through motions of nest building that would have astonished me had I realized they were only motions. That bird passed a make-believe strand over a twig, grasped it on the other side, and fastened it securely — all by way of making certain, I suppose, that a nest *could* be built there. Naturally, I believed she had put a cobweb in place; but when I examined the twig I could not find a shred of material.

A yellow-throated vireo nest that I found near the end of a long oak branch was real enough, however. It contained four nestlings. These were fed during the early morning hours almost exclusively on dragonflies. Dragonflies? I had never seen a yellow-throated vireo chase a dragonfly, much less catch one in flight. I eventually solved the mystery by following the parent birds to a leatherleaf bog not far away. There among the leaves they caught the roosting insects, easy prey before the sun had had a chance to warm them up.

The birds pulled the wings off each dragonfly and battered the head and thorax before giving it to the young. Sometimes this resulted in an alarming sight. An inch or so of unswallowed dragonfly abdomen looked for all the world like a piece of old wire sticking straight up from the mouth of the nestling.

Most of the vireos whose nesting habits I have studied suffer from the parasitism of the cowbird. Many times I have found vireo eggs that it had jabbed and thrown to the ground. So heavily parasitized is Bell's vireo in central Oklahoma that I often wonder how the species manages to survive there. A Bell's nest that I saw in a persimmon sapling held two dead baby vireos, two barely alive, and a vigorous young cowbird almost ready to fledge.

Newly hatched vireos of most species have thin gray down on their upper parts. The Bell's and black-capped vireos, however, are born stark naked – perhaps not a bad idea considering the high temperatures throughout most of their breeding range.

Young vireos are wonderfully winsome. I have painted many of them. A nine-day-old yellowthroat that I "kidnapped" in Michigan had the amusing vireo way of sidestepping on its perch. Between sittings – often on my finger – it fed on crushed grasshopper and caterpillar from my forceps, then resumed its quiet pose.

NOT ABOUT TO BUDGE, *this solitary vireo in Colorado tolerates a visitor rather than abandon its eggs. Both parents share incubation and feed the young.*

Alfred M. Bailey

Black-capped Vireo
Vireo atricapilla

THE BLACK-HOODED, white-goggled males arrive on their southwestern breeding grounds in late March or April. Along canyons and low ridges they threaten one another with harsh, bubbling calls and darting flights, each bird staking a claim to about four acres of scrub-oak growth.

They hop about, picking up the larvae of butterflies and moths and make short, fluttering flights from branch to branch, often hanging head down for a moment before moving on. The quiet demeanor and leisurely movement of most vireos are lacking in this one.

The gray-capped females fly in from their winter quarters in Mexico a week or so after the males arrive. With flutters and dives that display his olive back and yellow-barred wings, each suitor pays court. His success, however, may depend on whether the female likes his territory.

She also makes the final decision on the homesite, sometimes bypassing a place he has chosen. Both birds build the nest, a cup of bark strips and plant fibers suspended from the crotch of an oak branch or a low bush. In it the female lays three to five spotless white eggs.

Range: N. Oklahoma to N. Mexico; winters in W. Mexico. *Characteristics:* white "spectacles" and underparts, olive-green back. Male has black head, pale yellow wing bars; female has slaty head, white wing bars. Young are brownish.

Male blackcap, length 4¼-4¾"; Jean W. Graber

White-eyed Vireo
Vireo griseus

FROM THE DEPTHS of a tangled thicket comes an outpouring of songs. Most begin and end with a sharp, emphatic *chick*. In the course of a song the white-eyed vireo produces a striking variety of sounds – whistles and mews and melodic fragments reminiscent of the catbird, chat, robin, flicker, song sparrow, whippoorwill, house wren, wood thrush, goldfinch, or summer tanager.

The medley stops and the shy bird is nowhere in sight if you invade his retreat for a glimpse of the versatile songster. Soon the singing resumes from a distant bush.

If the nest is near, the green-and-white bird may stand his ground fearlessly and scold, or approach to within a few feet and look you over closely. At this distance his white irises, surrounded by yellow "spectacles," are easily seen.

As he hops from one low twig to another through brier bushes, vines, and swampy undergrowth, the white-eye feeds on moths, spiders, beetles, grasshoppers, wasps, and flies. When insects are scarce he turns to berries – sumac, dogwood, wild grape, and wax myrtle.

White-eyed vireos nest close to the ground. From the slender fork of a tree or bush they hang a cone-shaped nest of leaves, bark, grasses, and moss, bound and secured with spider webs. Both parents incubate the four white eggs dotted with brown or black. Cowbird eggs are often found in the clutch. The young vireos hatch in 12 to 16 days; their gray irises do not turn white until the following spring.

Range: E. Nebraska to New York, south to central Mexico and Florida; winters to Honduras and Cuba. *Characteristics:* olive head and back, white irises, yellow "spectacles," yellowish sides, white underparts, light wing bars.

White-eye, length 4½-5½"; Eliot Porter

Yellow-throated Vireo
Vireo flavifrons

MOST BRILLIANTLY COLORED of all our vireos, the yellowthroat summers in the shade trees of the eastern United States. Like the solitary, white-eyed, and Bell's vireos, the yellowthroat has eye rings, wing bars, and light underparts. But no other vireo in the United States has such a bright yellow throat and breast.

The leisurely yellowthroat frequents open stands of tall, deciduous trees near streams and along roadsides in residential areas. Moving slowly through the treetops, it feeds on cater-pillars, bugs, beetles, and moths.

The yellowthroat builds the prettiest nest in the vireo family. Using huge quantities of spider webs, it hangs a cup of moss, plant stems, and fine grass from a forked twig as high as 60 feet off the ground. Lichens decorate and camouflage the outside. Deep and thick-walled, the cup bulges below the rim, providing added security for the eggs or young as the nest sways in the breeze. The four white or pinkish eggs, heavily spotted with shades of brown, hatch in about 14 days.

This vireo sings a distinctive song: rich, reedy notes with definite pauses between phrases. A persistent vocalist, the yellowthroat continues singing into September as it prepares to head south, a time when many birds are silent.

In recent years the yellowthroat has disap-peared from many urban areas in the Northeast. Whether due to widespread spraying of shade trees, as some have maintained, or to some other cause, the loss has saddened bird lovers.

Range: S. Manitoba to S. Quebec, south to cen-tral Texas and central Florida; winters S. Mexico to Nicaragua. *Characteristics:* olive-gray head and back, yellow "spectacles," bright yellow throat and breast, white wing bars.

Bell's Vireo
Vireo belli

PERCHED in a streamside willow, warming his faintly bespectacled face, olive-gray body, and barred wings in the southwestern sunshine, a Bell's vireo sputters, scolds, and squeaks.

Cheedle cheedle chee? he seems to ask in one fragment, and answers with falling inflection: *cheedle cheedle chew.* None of it sounds like music, but this vireo sings on and on – all day, all summer, even into September. In top form he may pour out as many as 20 songs a minute.

Often found with white-eyed vireos, Bell's vir-eo forages in desert and bottomland thickets for grasshoppers, locusts, and caterpillars. No other vireo eats so many bulky insects. One Bell's vireo was seen to carry large black flies to a branch and hold them down with a foot while he nibbled them with his stout, slightly curved bill.

These vireos nest in a tree or bush, almost al-ways within a few feet of the ground. Suspended from a forked limb, the purse-shaped cradle is built of leaves, bark strips, cottony fibers, grass, and spider webs. Hatchlings without a shred of down emerge from the four brown-dotted white eggs after 14 days of incubation. Both parents cooperate in brooding and feeding the young.

Normally shy, Bell's vireos bravely stand fast when a human intruder approaches their nest. But the cowbird frequently invades the nursery, throwing out the vireos' eggs and leaving its own. The vireos often abandon their home when the parasite bird moves in. Cats and other preda-tors also destroy the eggs and young in the low-hanging cradle.

Range: California to N. E. Illinois, south to S. Texas and N. W. Louisiana; winters Mexico to Nicaragua. *Characteristics:* gray head and back, whitish wing bars, indistinct white "spectacles." 249

Yellowthroat, length 5-6"; Eliot Porter

Bell's, length 4¼-5"; Allan D. Cruickshank
National Audubon Society

Solitary, length 5-6"; Allan D. Cruickshank, National Audubon Society

Solitary Vireo
Vireo solitarius

HANDSOME RECLUSE of evergreen and hardwood forests, *solitarius* calmly scans his territory from a shaded twig. He swings his dark gray head slowly, looking first to one side, then to the other. Sighting a caterpillar or beetle, he leaves his lookout post to gather the snack.

Sometimes he darts out to seize a flying insect. As he passes from shadow into strong light his white "spectacles" and yellowish sides stand out and his snowy underparts gleam; his head color seems to change from slate-gray to blue-gray. Many know him as the blue-headed vireo. In the Rockies a subspecies has a gray back without the olive tones generally found in this vireo.

The solitary vireo shuns the habitations of man. Except when migrating it rarely visits gardens or city parks. But one of this bird's most remarkable traits is its tameness—some call it fearlessness—when man invades its forest solitude. Without fuss or scolding, a brooding bird may continue to sit calmly as a man draws near, may even allow itself to be stroked and lifted off the nest. Freed, the bird settles confidently back on its eggs; sometimes it breaks out in song. As its confidence grows it may even take food from the hand of an observer.

The song is one of the most tuneful in the vireo family—short, whistled phrases interrupted by pauses, a pattern somewhat like the red-eyed vireo's but higher pitched and much sweeter.

The male solitary hauls the material for nest building—bits of bark, leaves, moss, grass, and vegetable down. The female, who looks like her mate, weaves and shapes the basketlike cradle and binds it to the fork of a low limb. The three to five white eggs are dotted with brown or black. The cowbird frequently leaves eggs in the nest, but the female vireo sometimes thwarts the parasite. If the unwanted eggs are left before the vireo produces any of her own, she may cover them up and lay her eggs on top.

Range: British Columbia to Nova Scotia, south to El Salvador; winters from Arizona and South Carolina to Nicaragua and Cuba. *Characteristics:* gray or blue-gray head, olive or gray back, yellowish sides; white eye rings, underparts, and wing bars.

Gray Vireo
Vireo vicinior

To GLIMPSE this nondescript bird in the parched southwestern foothills you rarely have to look up. The gray vireo ordinarily rises no higher than five feet as it hunts insects through the chaparral and mesquite. It hops about the bushes with jerky wrenlike movements and wags its longish tail like a gnatcatcher.

The sexes look but don't sound alike. The male sings a loud *chee wi chee wi choo*. The female utters a harsh *churr*. Their nest, hung from a forked twig in a thorny shrub, holds three or four white eggs dotted with brown.

Range: central California and N. Baja California to W. Oklahoma and W. Texas; winters in N. Mexico. *Characteristics:* gray back, narrow eye rings, indistinct wing bars.

Gray vireo, length 5-5¾"; George Miksch Sutton

Hutton's Vireo
Vireo huttoni

PEERING under foliage and bark scales, this inconspicuous little vireo spends all seasons in the western live oaks and other evergreens.

When the ruby-crowned kinglet arrives in fall to share the insect food, the two birds may be hard to tell apart. Hutton's vireo moves more slowly and has a stouter, slightly hooked bill. The persistent vireo song, *zu weep* or *day dee dee*, is also distinctive. The Hutton's hanging, mossy nest holds four brown-dotted white eggs.

Range: S. W. British Columbia to Baja California; also central Arizona to W. Texas, south to Guatemala. *Characteristics:* olive head and back, white wing bars, incomplete eye rings.

Hutton's, length 4¼-4¾"; Allan Brooks

Philadelphia Vireo
Vireo philadelphicus

PHILADELPHIA is not the most likely place to look for *philadelphicus*. He summers well to the north and winters in the tropics. But he may pass by in migration. The species was described from a bird collected near the city in 1842.

He looks like a warbling vireo but has more yellow on his breast. He sounds like a red-eyed vireo but sings the abrupt, double-noted phrases less often and in a higher pitch.

In the tops of deciduous trees the Philadelphia hunts insects in the air or hangs head down to pick them off leaves. This vireo builds a hanging nest of bark and vegetable fibers which holds four white eggs spotted with dark brown.

Range: N. E. British Columbia to Newfoundland, south to N. North Dakota and Maine; winters from Guatemala to Colombia. *Characteristics:* gray head, olive back, light stripe over eye, dark line through eye, yellowish breast.

Philadelphia, length 4½-5"; George Miksch Sutton

Blackwhisker, length 6½"; George Miksch Sutton

Black-whiskered Vireo
Vireo altiloquus

PAINT A sooty stripe on each side of a red-eyed vireo's throat and you have a black-whiskered vireo. An offshoot of a West Indian species, this summer resident of southern Florida and the Keys has the appropriate subspecific name of *barbatulus* — "with a slight beard."

Bird watchers must slosh through swamp waters up to their knees to find the blackwhisker in its coastal mangrove haunts. It may be sighted from the Overseas Highway in the Keys — but not during the winter vacation season. The bird is in the West Indies or South America then.

This vireo slowly gleans trees from top to bottom for insects; it also eats berries. Its song seems to vary with locale. Jamaicans hear the notes as *whip-tom-kelly*. Others say they sound like *sweet-john-to-whit* or *cheap-john-stir-up*.

Hung from a mangrove fork, the nest of grass, leaves, fragments of palm fronds, and other plant fibers holds three white or pinkish eggs spotted with brown.

Range: S. Florida and West Indies; winters mainly in N. South America. *Characteristics:* gray cap, black-bordered white stripes over red eyes; black whisker stripes, olive-green back, white underparts. Young are brownish.

Warbling Vireo
Vireo gilvus

WITHOUT A SONG the warbling vireo would hardly be noticeable. With no conspicuous mark of adornment, not even the "spectacles" or wing bars worn by other vireos, this leisurely grayish-green bird blends into the high foliage of elms and poplars in the east, aspens and cottonwoods in the west.

With his song the warbling vireo ranks as a charmer. His simple melody complements the summer calm of village streets and countryside. Hour after hour he sings, through the scorching days of July and August on into September. His song is a true warble unbroken by the pauses typical of other vireo melodies. The slow notes undulate gently in pitch, building to the highest and most forceful phrases at the end. Pronounced slowly, the phrases sound like *brig-a-dier brig-a-dier brigate.*

In the east these vireos stay mostly in the leafy tree crowns, feeding on beetles, caterpillars, and moths. At the end of a high, slender limb they hang a cradle of bark strips, stems, grass, leaves, and spider webs. In it the female lays four white eggs speckled with brown. Soon after fledging, the brownish youngsters start singing.

Western warbling vireos, slightly smaller and darker than the eastern race, may nest much

Warbling, length 4½-6"; Patricia Bailey Witherspoon

Redeyes, length 5½-6½"; Eliot Porter

closer to the ground, in bushes or in low trees.

Range: British Columbia to Nova Scotia, south to Baja California and E. Virginia; winters from central Mexico to El Salvador. *Characteristics:* gray-green head and back, faint eye stripes, buffy or whitish breast. Young are brownish.

 ## Red-eyed Vireo
Vireo olivaceus

SPRING GREEN has spread through the northern trees and the bird choir is already in fine voice when the "preacher" arrives from his winter home in South America.

The red-eyed vireo's "sermon" is well-nigh endless. From dawn through the long day he exclaims, asks rhetorical questions, answers them —*cherr-o-wit, cheree, sissy-a-wit, tee-oo,* and on and on. He may sound as many as 40 different phrases in a minute, then start over.

The short, emphatic phrases usually end with a rising inflection. To some the song seems monotonous, to others cheerful. Everyone agrees the sermon is long-winded. "I have always thought," wrote ornithologist Bradford Torrey, "that whoever dubbed this vireo the 'preacher' could have had no very exalted opinion of the clergy."

Despite his incessant vocalizing the redeye is hard to spot as he hops about the high, slender branches of leafy trees in eastern woodlands and along stream borders and town streets. Unless he is close by, his red irises cannot be distinguished; the white eye stripes, gray cap, green back, and white underparts are more helpful.

The redeye eats about six parts animal matter to one part vegetable. His menu includes moths, caterpillars, beetles, flies, and bugs, as well as wild berries and other fruit.

The dainty pensile nest is finely wrought from bits of bark, grass, and rootlets. Mated pairs secure the cup to the fork of a shrub or low tree limb with spider or caterpillar webs.

The four white eggs marked with brown or blackish dots hatch in about 11 days. The young wear the same plumage colors as adult birds, but their irises are brown through fall and winter.

Squirrels, chipmunks, and hawks sometimes attack the redeye's nest. Cowbirds frequently deposit their own eggs in the hanging cup. Redeyes have been known to rear a brood consisting solely of cowbirds.

As summer draws to a close and the redeyes prepare to head south, their song diminishes. Often they forage for berries in complete silence except for a petulant, snarling *queee.*

Range: British Columbia to Nova Scotia, south to central Texas and central Florida; winters in N. W. South America. *Characteristics:* gray crown, black-bordered white eye stripes, red irises, olive-green back, white underparts.

The Wood Warblers

Family Parulidae

By JOHN W. ALDRICH

IT WAS A CRISP MAY MORNING in Ohio, and I was leading a public bird walk sponsored by the Cleveland Museum of Natural History. A cold front had moved in the night before, putting a bite in the air. We could see the white vapor of our breath.

With jacket collars turned up and hands jammed deep in our pockets, we wandered past the still leafless oaks, looking, listening for some telltale sign of birdlife.

At first we were disappointed, for the day seemed unusually quiet. Not one bird song. Then suddenly we saw them. Dozens of brilliantly colored warblers soon were literally at our feet—dazzling orange-and-black redstarts, Blackburnian warblers glowing like embers, and a host of bright yellow-breasted species.

Hopping about on the gravel walks, they busily picked up insects which, numbed by the cold, had fallen from the air and the budding foliage and now lay easy prey. To those of us in the habit of craning our aching necks to catch a glimpse of a warbler uttering its buzzy song high in a tree, seeing these birds so close at hand was indeed an amazing sight.

These northbound migrants had arrived during the night. The cold spell had checked their progress, precipitating them over the countryside. The patches of green parkland in the city must have seemed like oases in a desert to these tired and hungry little birds.

I think we incline to link birds with places where we have known them best. Thus there is a certain nostalgic association for me between the misnamed prairie warbler, with its lazy, ascending *ze-ze-ze-ze-ze,* and the hot, sweet, fern-scented pastures of southern New En-

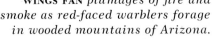

WINGS FAN *plumages of fire and smoke as red-faced warblers forage in wooded mountains of Arizona.*

254

Length 5-5¼", Eliot Porter

gland; the hooded warbler, with its snappy *pleased to, pleased to-meet-you,* and the cool, green deciduous forests of Ohio; and the prothonotary warbler, with its flashing blue-and-yellow plumage, and the willow-bordered streams and swamps of the South. There always seems to be a warbler to symbolize every situation in outdoor America, so great is their variety of form, voice, and environment.

During my high school years I was invited to a school for nature counselors on Cape Cod. There I met the idol of my boyhood, Edward Howe Forbush, author of the great three-volume work, *Birds of Massachusetts and Other New England States.*

I was in the magnetic presence of that kindly old gentleman with the twinkling eyes and gray beard when I saw my first black-throated green warbler. At first it was just a buzzy song in the pines. Then the bright golden-cheeked, black-bibbed songster appeared at the tip of a wind-tossed branch. Actively moving about over the green needles, peering into terminal buds, it never ceased searching for insects.

"Listen," remarked Dr. Forbush. "He says *pines, pines, murmuring pines.*" And sure enough, the song did sound like that to me. To this day I always associate black-throated green warblers with pines. Indeed, this species is one of the most characteristic inhabitants of the cool, fragrant forests of pines, hemlocks, and hardwoods in northeastern America.

Many other species of warblers also favor the northern coniferous forests. The summers I spent as a nature counselor at Camp Chewonki on the Maine coast gave me many opportunities to observe a variety of forest-nesting warblers. At a hemlock-shaded pool rippled by water dripping from mossy rocks, I made the acquaintance of three summer residents that came there to drink and bathe—the magnolia, Canada, and Blackburnian warblers. Dripping water seems to attract warblers, and bird banders have used it to bait the birds into traps.

Arthur A. Allen

THE FASCINATING and strictly American birds we know as warblers are more exactly called wood warblers to distinguish them from the sylviid warblers of the Old World.

Our warblers belong to the family Parulidae. They number more than 100 species, about half of them nesting in temperate North America.

As in most large families, the warblers have members whose existence is threatened, apparently because they need particular habitats. The Kirtland's warbler, numbering only about 1,000 birds, nests solely on the lower peninsula of Michigan among young jack pines of a special density and age range.

The golden-cheeked warbler, confined to a relatively small area of central Texas on the Edwards Plateau, depends on

Photographed at the Burgundy Farm Country Day School, Alexandria, Virginia, by Roland Scherman

FLEDGLING ORNITHOLOGISTS, *matching warbler skins with field guide pictures, learn that some species look different in spring and fall. The magnolia warbler (in the girl's hand) loses its breast stripes in the fall. But the adult male hooded warbler (opposite) wears a black badge of identification year round.*

mature juniper growth there for success. Conservationists are concerned because elimination of these limited habitats could exterminate both species.

During graduate school days when I was studying ecology of bogs, I saw how an altered habitat affected northern waterthrushes. Pymatuning Bog on the Ohio-Pennsylvania border sheltered many wildlife species characteristic of northern climes, this warbler among them. One winter, when the northern waterthrushes were in tropical America, the forest of tamaracks and hemlocks was leveled in the construction of a reservoir. The following spring when the birds returned, I found them hopping about among the stumps of their former wooded habitat, looking extremely out of place. Their homing instinct had brought them back to their place of origin, but it was no longer suitable for nesting.

One kind of warbler that baffled me when I was a boy appeared each fall in the rambler rose outside our dining room window. It was a dull olive-green bird with a streaked, pale yellow breast; but most conspicuous were its two white wing bars.

Years later I learned that this was the blackpoll warbler in autumn plumage, strikingly different from the black-and-white spring pattern. I would have been more impressed had I known that this bird made one of the longest migrations of any songbird—from northernmost forests of Canada and Alaska to central South America.

Other warblers make similar journeys. In fact, while on a museum expedition in Panama, I found that these tiny migrants from the north make up a substantial part of the birdlife there. Time and again I thought I was about to identify some new tropical species flitting among the flowering tops of the forest giants, only to have it turn out to be a Tennessee, chestnut-sided, or other familiar North American warbler.

Not all the warblers in tropical America are northern migrants. To me one of the more impressive native species of those regions is the buff-rumped warbler; it seems to fill the same ecological niche as the Louisiana waterthrush of the eastern United States. Both frequent the banks of forest streams and flit about in the undergrowth, wagging their tails in exactly the same way.

There are many such parallels in habitat among the wide-ranging warblers. The pine warbler, at home in the pine woods of the southeastern states, reminds me of the olive warbler, which dwells in the pine forests of the mountains in Mexico and Central America. High treetop dwellers include the Townsend's and hermit warblers of the northwest, the bay-breasted and Cape May warblers of the northeast, and the cerulean warbler of the lofty beech and maple forests of the eastern states.

Although warblers vary in habit and appearance, there is one member so unwarbler-like that some experts question whether it belongs in the family. I first made the acquaintance of this big clown of the warbler tribe in the coal mining country of eastern Ohio.

From a thicket on a spoil bank came a startling, rasping outburst followed by loud, derisive laughter. I almost jumped out of my skin. Then

SPRAY FLIES *as Tennessee warblers refresh in a*

the cause of the commotion suddenly catapulted out of the thicket. Wings fluttering and legs dangling, the bundle of feathers almost somersaulted in the air. Before it settled back among the foliage with another burst of raucous chatter, I caught sight of its bright yellow throat and the conspicuous white markings around the eye. The strange bird could be no other than a yellow-breasted chat.

But my first real excitement in identifying birds came when I was a boy of ten. Playing near my home in Providence, Rhode Island, I heard a mysterious call coming from a thicket: *witchity-witchity-witchity-witch*. The staccato notes aroused my interest. I wanted to see as well as hear the maker of these sounds.

Patiently I stalked the bird, its elusive voice retreating before my advances

Paul Schwartz

Venezuelan pool. Come spring, these migrants wing northward as far as the Yukon.

through the dense shrubbery. Suddenly it flitted out from behind a screen of foliage. I saw its bold pattern in startling clarity—a tiny bird with head down and tail up, its bright eyes peering curiously from a jet black mask bordered with white. Its throat was brilliant yellow.

How many times had I seen this identical image staring at me from the thumb-worn pages of my Reed bird guide. How I had wished to see this intriguing warbler with the highwayman's mask—the yellowthroat. Now to glimpse it briefly as it flitted nervously from twig to twig, its *witchity* song replaced by a scolding *chit*, was one of the most exciting moments of my boyhood. Even now, half a century later, I can still feel some of the thrill of that early adventure in bird watching.

Male black-and-white, length 4½-5½"; Arthur A. Allen

Black-and-white Warbler

Mniotilta varia

LEAVES HAVE BARELY unfurled when a squeaky refrain sounds through eastern woodlands: *wee-see weesee weesee weesee weesee weesee weesee*. As he repeats his seesaw couplet seven times or more, the singer clambers up and down tree trunks and along large limbs like a creeper or a nuthatch. But the long stripes that cover his body reveal him as the black-and-white warbler.

Most warblers arrive in the temperate regions in mid-May when insects are swarming around blossoms and leaves. This bird arrives a month earlier to search bark crannies for insects and eggs. He moves along a limb with a switching motion; you see his tail on one side, then on the other. Later in the season he examines leaf clusters for beetles and caterpillars.

A pair usually nest against the base of a shrub or tree. Hidden under an arch of dead leaves, the cup of bark, rootlets, and grass holds four or five eggs dotted with brown. Unlike the young of some other warblers, fledglings do not remain on the ground very long after leaving the nest. Instead, they perch on tree limbs, where their parents feed them.

In late summer family groups forage quietly through swampy woods. Some move south at this time while a few linger until October. Their journey may take them across the Gulf of Mexico.

Range: N. E. British Columbia to Newfoundland, south to central Texas, S. Louisiana, and central South Carolina; winters from Baja California and central Florida to N. South America. *Characteristics:* striped black-and-white body. Female and young have white underparts.

Prothonotary Warbler

Protonotaria citrea

FEATHERED SPRITES in burnished gold battle for nesting territories amid swamplands in the East and Midwest. Their repeated *tweet* rises from the spring verdure. Claims settled, each bird patrols his domain, blue-gray wings beating against his gleaming body.

The female builds the nest of moss and twigs in a tree hole, stump, or bird box. She lays four to six creamy eggs spotted with brown and gray.

These striking swamp birds gather insects and their larvae from tree trunks and fallen logs.

Prothonotary (pronounced pruh-*thahn*-uh-terry) warblers received their name because their golden crowns seemed to resemble the yellow hoods worn by prothonotaries, or clerical officials, in earlier times.

Range: E. Minnesota to central New York, south to E. Texas and central Florida; winters from S. Mexico to N. South America. *Characteristics:* rich yellow head and breast, blue-gray wings. Female is duller.

Male prothonotary, length 5½"; Ralph E. Lawrence

Worm-eating warbler, length 5-5½"; Arthur A. Allen

Swainson's Warbler
Limnothlypis swainsonii

THIS GRACEFUL WARBLER summers in cane-brakes along streams that meander through southern piney flats, and in rhododendron thickets of the Appalachians. He whistles his rich song, *whee whee whee toot-tut-say bee-o*, from a favorite perch or while he hunts insects on the ground. His gait is an easy, gliding walk.

His mate, clad in the same dull brown colors, lays three or four creamy or bluish eggs in a leafy nest placed in a bush or tangle of cane.

Range: N. E. Oklahoma to S. Ohio and S. Maryland, south to S. Louisiana and N. Florida; winters in S. Mexico, British Honduras, and West Indies. *Characteristics:* olive-brown back, dingy yellowish underparts, whitish stripe over eye.

Swainson's, length 5"; Allan Brooks

Worm-eating Warbler
Helmitheros vermivorus

TAIL RAISED at a jaunty angle, the worm-eating warbler walks sedately over logs and fallen leaves in quest of beetles, spiders, and small caterpillars. He hardly ever eats a worm. But he still bears the name given him by early writers apparently misinformed about his diet.

After wintering in Mexico and Central America, he makes for the hillsides of the eastern half of the United States where second-growth deciduous trees rise above saplings and shrubs. If a stream bordered by brier and alder thickets runs nearby, so much the better. Modestly garbed in olive, he blends well with the shadows of the underbrush. But the bold black stripes on his buffy crown are easily seen.

Quarrelsome males chase each other through the thickets and in wild zigzag flights among the treetops. A pursuer eventually alights on a twig or a mossy log and, with body puffed out and bill aimed skyward, sounds a buzzy trill resembling the song of the chipping sparrow.

Mated birds usually hide their nest in a drift of leaves piled against the base of a tree or shrub. The female alone incubates the four or five white eggs dotted with brown.

If an intruder draws near while she's brooding, she flutters away with open wings and tail, feigning injury. If the young are well feathered she may try to shoo them off to a safer place.

Range: N. E. Kansas to N. Illinois and W. Massachusetts, south to E. Texas and N. E. North Carolina; winters from S. Mexico and West Indies to Panama. *Characteristics:* black stripes on buffy head, dull olive back, light underparts.

Golden-winged Warbler
Vermivora chrysoptera

THIS SPRIGHTLY BIRD clings upside down to twigs like a chickadee. He even has the chickadee's black bib and white breast. But the sparkling gold on his head and wings marks him unmistakably as the golden-winged warbler.

With his needlelike bill he probes for tiny insects among dense shrubs and on tree limbs in overgrown pastures or along the briery borders of swampy woodlands. From a lofty limb, often one bare of leaves, he sends forth a drawling, buzzy song of four notes: *beee-bz-bz-bz*. He sings most frequently from the time of his arrival in the north in May until mid-June.

Golden-winged warblers hide their nests on the ground within the shade of the woodland edge. A clump of grass or bunch of weed stalks screens a bed of leaves, grapevine bark, and grasses.

Often the growing plant stems lift the nursery off the ground. The four or five whitish eggs sprinkled with brown hatch after ten days. The youngsters leave the nest ten days later and soon flutter about in the thickets, learning to climb nimbly on grotesquely long legs. Their insistent cricketlike chirping keeps parents constantly on the go gathering insects for them.

Range: S. E. Manitoba to E. Massachusetts, south to E. Tennessee, N. Georgia, and N. W. South Carolina; winters in Central America and N. South America. *Characteristics:* yellow forehead and wing patches, white facial stripes and underparts, gray back. Cheeks and throat are black in male, gray in female.

Female Tennessee, length 4½-5"; Eliot Porter

Tennessee Warbler
Vermivora peregrina

WITH GRAY cap and white eye stripes, this warbler calls to mind an overactive vireo. In spring migration it darts through the treetops hunting insects and singing a loud, chippering song. It passes through Tennessee but neither breeds nor winters there. The species was discovered there, hence the name.

In boggy northern swales mated birds conceal their nest in sphagnum moss on the ground. The five or six white eggs are dotted with brown.

Range: S. Yukon to Newfoundland, south to central British Columbia and New Hampshire; winters from S. Mexico to N. South America. *Characteristics:* (in spring) gray head, white eye stripes and underparts, greenish back; (in fall) greenish head, yellowish breast and eye stripes. Female in spring has yellowish underparts.

Bluewing, length 4½-5"; David G. Allen

Blue-winged Warbler
Vermivora pinus

BEE-BUZZ BEE-BUZZ. The wheezy, weak, locust-like song of the blue-winged warbler drones through trees and thickets in overgrown pastures and woodland openings.

The singer wanders from high perch to sapling to underbrush, his bright yellow face and underparts contrasting with bluish-gray wings. Often he pauses to comb a weed patch or brier tangle for small insects. He searches slowly, somewhat like a vireo. He may examine a cocoon or leaf cluster while hanging upside down.

Bluewings place their bulky, cone-shaped nest of leaves and grass among weeds or bushes. The female incubates the five or six white eggs spotted with brown. Until they molt in July the young birds are much duller than their parents.

Closely related, blue-winged and golden-winged warblers interbreed freely over a wide area of eastern North America and produce two types of hybrids. One group generally resembles a goldenwing without the black bib. The other and much rarer group looks like the bluewing but has black cheeks and a black bib. Individuals of the two hybrid types vary widely, however. The song of a hybrid may resemble that of either or both parents.

Range: central Nebraska to S. E. Minnesota and S. E. Massachusetts, south to N. W. Arkansas, N. Georgia, and Delaware; winters from S. Mexico to Nicaragua. *Characteristics:* yellow face and underparts, black line through eyes; greenish back, bluish-gray wings with white bars.

Bachman's Warbler
Vermivora bachmanii

BIRD LOVERS spend years trying to catch a glimpse of Bachman's warbler. The yellow-and-olive bird is one of the rarest of our warblers.

The Rev. John Bachman discovered the species in a swamp near Charleston, South Carolina, in 1833. It was not reported again for more than 50 years. Toward the end of the 19th century there was a flurry of sightings, usually while the birds were migrating from Cuba across the Florida Keys to wooded river swamps in Missouri, Arkansas, Kentucky, Alabama, and South Carolina.

In recent years the Bachman's has also been recorded in other southeastern states during the breeding season and sighted in winter in Mississippi and in Georgia's Okefenokee Swamp.

Drainage and lumbering operations have removed some of this bird's breeding haunts. Bird watchers who brave the swamps must contend with muck, ticks, and water moccasins. The nests have been found close to the ground amid fallen logs, vine tangles, and blackberry brambles. They were made of leaves, grass, and rootlets and held three to five white eggs.

In migration *bachmanii* has been seen in the treetops in company with parula warblers.

Range: breeds, or formerly bred, from S. E. Missouri and N. E. Arkansas to S. Kentucky and S. E. South Carolina; winters in Cuba, rarely north to S. Mississippi and S. Georgia. *Characteristics:* olive-green back, yellow underparts. Male has black crown patch and bib. Female has grayish crown.

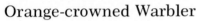
Orangecrown, length 4½-5½"; Eliot Porter *Nashvilles, length 4-5"; Bob and Elsie Boggs*

Orange-crowned Warbler
Vermivora celata

IN LATE AUTUMN a pall of snow spreads across jagged Cascade peaks. Driven to the foothills, swarms of greenish little birds sound a sharp *chip* as they flit through streamside thickets. Far to the east the same call punctuates the whisper of falling leaves in Pennsylvania woods.

Orange-crowned warblers forage through the underbrush on their way to winter quarters. This is the time of year they are most often seen—plain birds without prominent field marks. The specific name *celata* describes the usual status of the orange crown: concealed. Juveniles and some females lack it altogether.

Compared to many in his tribe, the orange-crown makes a relatively short journey. He may go no farther than the southern United States. During the winter, when insects are scarce, he dines on berries and such feeding station favorites as suet, doughnuts, and peanut butter.

In the spring eastern orangecrowns head mainly northwest, continuing as far as dwarf woody growth occurs along stream borders in Canada and Alaska. Western birds head north to seek shrubbery bordering alpine meadows. Hidden in a bush or on the ground among leaves, the nest of grass, bark strips, and plant down holds four to six white eggs with reddish spots.

In addition to their call note orangecrowns sound a weak trill with frequent changes in pitch.

Range: central Alaska to N. W. Quebec, south to Baja California, W. Texas, and central Ontario; winters to Guatemala. *Characteristics:* orange crown patch (usually hidden), olive-green back, faintly streaked olive-yellowish underparts. Young are more uniformly greenish or grayish.

Nashville Warbler
Vermivora ruficapilla

PIONEER ornithologist Alexander Wilson discovered this species near Nashville, Tennessee, in 1810, apparently during migration.

In the east migrating Nashville warblers stick to the middle story of open deciduous woods. For nesting, birds summering in the northern United States favor old fields overgrown with young birches. Those that keep going often settle in Canadian bogs covered with sphagnum moss and sprinkled with conifers. A western race, the Calaveras warbler, breeds in the chaparral and oak foothills of the Sierra Nevada and Cascades.

Woven from moss and bits of fern, the nest blends well with a moss hummock at the foot of a stump or bush. Rabbit hair often cushions the four or five white eggs dotted with reddish brown. The female incubates them for 11 or 12 days while her mate defends their nesting territory. His song starts slowly, then accelerates: *seebit, seebit, seebit, seebit, titititititi.*

Nashville warblers scour trees and underbrush for the eggs and larvae of small insects. They often hover on rapidly beating wings to snatch a morsel from a leaf.

Soon after molting in late summer, these sprightly birds begin a leisurely southward journey, and we see them once more in orchards and gardens, often in a mixed flock of warblers.

Range: S. British Columbia to Nova Scotia, south to central California and Pennsylvania; winters from Mexico and S. Florida to Guatemala. *Characteristics:* gray head, white eye rings, yellow throat and breast, olive back, yellowish rump. Chestnut crown partly veiled in male, often lacking in female. Young are much duller.

Female Virginia's, length 4-4½"; Eliot Porter

Lucy's Warbler
Vermivora luciae

MESQUITE THICKETS along the Colorado River and its tributaries shelter this tiny warbler, named in honor of Lucy Baird, daughter of the 19th century zoologist Spencer F. Baird.

This shy bird is the only member of the family likely to be found on his desert breeding ground. Modestly garbed in gray and white, he may be mistaken for a gnatcatcher or a verdin. The warbler's chestnut crown is difficult to see, especially in the female, and the chestnut rump patch can be seen only from certain angles.

The gorgeous blooms of mesquite, paloverdes, and ocotillos attract swarms of insects which provide sustenance for Lucy's warbler.

While the male flits about warbling a rapid *weeta weeta weeta che che che che che*, the female builds a nest of bark, weeds, leaf stems, and animal hair. For a site she may choose a tree cavity, an abandoned woodpecker hole, an old verdin nest, or the space behind loose bark. Her four or five white eggs are dotted with brown.

Range: S. Nevada to S. W. Colorado, south to N. E. Baja California and S. W. New Mexico; winters in Mexico. *Characteristics:* chestnut on crown and rump, white eye rings and underparts, gray back. Young lack chestnut patches.

Virginia's Warbler
Vermivora virginiae

THE GRAY-GREEN AND YELLOW of blossoming scrub oaks match the colors of Virginia's warblers arriving in the southern foothills of the Rockies from tropical wintering grounds.

The tiny bird ranges up to 9,000 feet in its semi-arid summer haunts, hunting insects near the ground among oaks and clumps of mountain mahogany and chokecherry. The species was named for Virginia Anderson, wife of Dr. W. W. Anderson who discovered it in New Mexico in 1858.

Virginia's warbler usually nests in a depression under a grass tussock on a steep hillside. The nursery of leaves, grass, bark, and moss is often lined with animal hair. The female incubates four white eggs spotted with reddish brown.

A close but larger relative, the Colima warbler (*Vermivora crissalis*), breeds on the dry hillsides or ravine bottoms of the Chisos Mountains in southwestern Texas.

Range: central Nevada to S. E. Idaho and N. Colorado, south to S. E. California and N. New Mexico; winters in Mexico. *Characteristics:* chestnut crown patch, white eye rings, grayish back and tail; yellow on breast, rump, and undertail coverts; flicks tail. Female and young may lack crown patch and yellow on breast.

Lucy's, length 3½-4", and (lower) male Virginia's; Allan Brooks

Parula Warbler
Parula americana

A SNOWY SPRAY of apple blossoms makes an exquisite setting for this dainty bird of blue and gold. And you can see the little insect hunter from all angles as he hangs from a blossom cluster like a chickadee or titmouse. Indeed, Parula means "little titmouse." And since this is considered the typical genus, the whole family is known as the Parulidae.

The parula is one of the tiniest of the warblers. In migration he often pauses in garden shade trees as well as in orchards of the eastern United States. But he may stay so high in the trees that his buzzy, rising trill is the only clue to his presence. He often ends his song with a sharp *yip*.

In the South parula warblers nest in a tangle of Spanish moss; in northern forests they seek out beard lichens hanging from conifers. The nest may be an unlined pocket or it may have a bed of grass. The four or five white eggs have reddish spots.

A tropical relative with black cheeks, the olive-backed warbler (*Parula pitiayumi*), reaches the lower Rio Grande Valley of Texas.

Range: S. E. Manitoba to Nova Scotia, south to E. Texas and central Florida; winters from central Mexico to Nicaragua. *Characteristics:* blue-gray head and back, greenish back patch, yellow breast, white wing bars and belly. Male has dark throat band. Female and young are duller.

Male and (left) female parulas, length 4¼-4¾"
Allan D. Cruickshank, National Audubon Society

Yellow Warbler
Dendroica petechia

LIKE A CAPRICIOUS sunbeam, the yellow warbler brightens garden shrubbery and shade trees over a wide expanse of North America. No other member of his family is so well known. Friendly and trusting, he may raise a brood of golden gems in a lilac bush outside your kitchen window.

The summer bird, or yellowbird, as this warbler is sometimes called, appears at a distance to be all yellow. His back, however, is yellowish olive and his golden breast is streaked with chestnut. The female and young are more greenish and may lack the breast markings.

The yellow warbler's cheery song complements his bright colors. The sweet, rapid melody sounds like *tsee-tsee-tsee-tsee-titi-wee*.

While we know this tame little bird best as a neighbor, he often breeds well away from the settlements of man—on the plains and prairies, in hot, semiarid country, and in subarctic wilderness. His simple habitat requirements include deciduous growth near a pond, stream, or lake. He favors willows but readily accepts alders, cottonwoods, elderberries, and a variety of bushes. In the Far North he breeds in dwarf shrubbery. A study of yellow warblers in Iowa showed that males stake out about two-fifths of an acre with commanding song perches, good feeding areas, and plenty of escape cover.

The female builds her nest in an upright fork, weaving the neat, solidly packed cup of milkweed fiber, grass, bits of rotten wood, and animal hair. The four or five grayish or greenish eggs are blotched with brown.

This gentle warbler is one of the most common victims of the parasitic cowbird. In many cases the yellow warbler tolerates the cowbird's eggs, incubates them, and rears the young. But at times the host bird goes to great lengths to frustrate its archenemy. It builds a new nest floor over the alien eggs. Nests of three, four, and even five stories have been found (page 296). In some instances the lower stories contained warbler as well as cowbird eggs. The warbler may also give up the fight and desert its homestead.

Both parents stuff the young warblers with small worms. Grown birds eat huge quantities of caterpillars as well as beetles and moths.

Yellow warblers start the southward migration as soon as the young are able to care for themselves. By the end of July many have vanished from their breeding haunts.

Range: N. Alaska to Newfoundland, south to N. South America; winters from central Mexico to Brazil. *Characteristics:* yellow head, underparts, and tail streaks; yellowish-olive back, chestnut breast streaks. Female (page 52) and young are darker, may lack breast markings.

Male yellow warbler, length 4½-5¼"
Frederick Kent Truslow

Male olive, length 4½-5"; Allan Brooks

Olive Warbler
Peucedramus taeniatus

HIGH IN THE MOUNTAINS of southern Arizona a hiker pauses among giant yellow pines rising above a dry, parklike glade. A burst of song descends from the lofty crowns overhead: *peter peter peter peter*. The ringing chant suggests a tufted titmouse. Gradually the singer maneuvers out to the small branches and reveals the rich orange-brown head and black cheeks of the olive warbler.

On a nearby limb sits the female, incubating three or four grayish or bluish eggs with olive-gray or brownish spots. With her yellowish or olive crown she looks more sedate than her mate. She sits on a beautiful nest, a thick cup made of moss, rootlets, flower stalks, lichens, and pine needles.

In April nuthatches and creepers join olive warblers in hunting the small insects that infest the mountain evergreens. In the fall these warblers sometimes forage with small flocks of western bluebirds. Some olive warblers remain in the Southwest through the winter. Others spend the colder months south of the border.

Range: central Arizona and S. W. New Mexico to Nicaragua. *Characteristics:* olive nape, mouse-gray back, white wing bars, whitish belly. Male has orange-brown head and breast, black cheeks. Female has olive crown, yellowish breast, dusky ear patch. Young resemble the female.

Female olive warbler; Eliot Porter

Male and (right) female magnolias, length 4½-5"; Eliot Porter

Male Cape May, length 5-5½"; Eliot Porter

Magnolia Warbler
Dendroica magnolia

DISCOVERED in migration among magnolias in Mississippi in 1810, this beautiful warbler breeds in northern evergreens. He feeds on insects and sings a short melody of *weeta* phrases.

The female incubates four speckled white eggs in a flimsy nest. Duller-hued than her mate, she has the same white band midway on the tail.

Range: N. British Columbia to Newfoundland, south to N. Minnesota and W. Virginia; winters from central Mexico and West Indies to Panama. *Characteristics:* gray head, white eyebrow stripe, wing patches, and tail band; black-streaked yellow underparts. Male has black cheeks and back; female has olive back. Young and fall adults are brownish and lack breast streaks.

Female Cape May
Louis Agassiz Fuertes

Cape May Warbler
Dendroica tigrina

BREAST OF GOLD and black gleaming in the sun, *tigrina* welcomes the cool northern morning with a thin, wheezy *seet seet seet seet*. For breakfast he darts out from his perch atop a towering fir to seize passing insects. Or he may search among the fir needles, hanging head down.

His brilliant garb and chestnut cheeks distinguish him from his duller-hued mate. Her nest of moss, twigs, and grass holds six or seven brown-spotted white eggs.

Once considered rare, Cape May warblers have been seen more frequently in migration in recent years. The species was discovered in a maple swamp in Cape May County, New Jersey, in 1811.

Range: N. British Columbia to Nova Scotia, south to N. E. North Dakota and S. Maine; winters in S. Mexico and West Indies. *Characteristics:* black cap, yellow eye stripe, neck patch, and rump; olive back, white wing patch, yellow-white underparts striped with black. Breeding male has chestnut cheeks. Female, young, and autumn male are much duller.

Female blackthroat
Louis Agassiz Fuertes

Black-throated Blue Warbler
Dendroica caerulescens

THE NEATLY DRESSED MALE, aptly described by his common name, is easily recognized. Not so the female, a plain-looking bird in olive and buff. A small white patch at the base of her primary wing feathers helps identify her.

Male black-throated blue warbler, length 5-5½"
Walter Dawn, National Audubon Society

Male (right) and female myrtles, length 5-6"; Eliot Porter

The birds hunt insects in parks and gardens as they travel through shrubbery en route to summer homes in moist woodlands from the southern Appalachians to southern Canada.

I am la-zy.... The husky drawl of these warblers floats up from the thickets of laurel and yew in which they breed. A nest of bark shreds and leaves holds the three or four white eggs spotted with brown.

Range: central Saskatchewan to Nova Scotia, south to central Minnesota and N. Georgia; winters to Gulf Coast and West Indies. *Characteristics:* male has blue head and back, black cheeks and throat, white breast and wing patch. Female has olive upperparts, buffy underparts.

Myrtle Warbler
Dendroica coronata

ABUNDANT, friendly, and conspicuous, the myrtle is perhaps our best known wood warbler after the yellow warbler. Among the earlier spring migrants, he heads for his breeding grounds in great numbers. An estimated 24,000 myrtle warblers flew by an observer on the South Carolina coast between 9 A.M. and 1 P.M. one March day.

In this season *coronata* is easily recognized, especially the male in his nuptial dress of blue-gray, black, and white with patches of gold on his crown, sides, and rump. The female is duller and has a brownish cast.

As they drift through the leafless treetops they sound a *check* note and a rather nondescript trill resembling a junco's song.

They settle for the summer in coniferous or mixed forests as far north as timberline in Alaska and Canada. They build their bulky nest of twigs, grass, and rootlets on the horizontal limb of an evergreen some distance from the trunk. The female incubates the four or five brown-spotted creamy eggs about 12 days. Her mate helps feed the young and clean the nest.

Myrtles are among the last in the warbler family to leave the breeding territory. Some fly all the way to Panama. Others go no farther south than Oregon or Nova Scotia. In the southern states myrtle warblers are familiar winter birds.

When insects are scarce these warblers can subsist for long periods on berries and seeds. Their common name stems from their fondness for bayberries, the fruit of the wax myrtle. Suet and doughnuts bring them to feeding trays. They visit sapsucker borings to drink the sap and eat the insects attracted to it. In Florida they drink the juice of fallen oranges.

Range: N. Alaska to Newfoundland, south to N. British Columbia, N. Minnesota, and Massachusetts; winters from N. W. Oregon, S. California, and Kansas to S. Nova Scotia, south to Panama. *Characteristics:* yellow crown, rump, and side patch; white throat, belly, and wing bars. Male has streaked blue-gray head and back; black cheeks, chest, and sides. Female is duller. Fall adults and young are brownish.

Audubon's Warbler

Dendroica auduboni

IN THE SPRING of 1834 ornithologist John Kirk Townsend set out from Independence, Missouri, with a group of settlers and missionaries bound for the Pacific Northwest. Food became so scarce along the way that some of Townsend's specimens were cooked and eaten. Nevertheless, Townsend preserved for his good friend Audubon some 70 specimens of birds which the artist-naturalist had never seen. One of these was a warbler new to science, secured in a forest near the mouth of the Columbia River. Townsend named it in honor of Audubon.

Throughout a large area of the west this warbler takes the place of its close relative the myrtle warbler. The handsome *auduboni* shows more white in its wings and tail, and its golden throat gives it five patches of yellow compared to four in the white-throated *coronata*.

Audubon's warbler does not range as far north as his relative but nests at higher altitudes – up to 12,000 feet in the Colorado Rockies – and extends much farther south, as far as central Mexico in summer.

In winter this hardy sprite may merely withdraw from the heights and spend the cold months almost as far north as he breeds. Now he flits through gardens, shade trees, eucalyptus groves, and hillside chaparral. His winter coat is streaky and brownish, his breast whitish; but in this as in all seasons the yellow rump stands out.

He pursues flying insects with all the skill of a flycatcher. Meeting a cloud of gnats, he plunges in, snapping up morsels in every direction; then, sounding his metallic *tchip* call, he races off after new prey. He gleans insects from decaying kelp on California beaches. He also dines on berries and weed seeds and may call at feeding stations.

As spring approaches, the male acquires his breeding finery of blue-gray and black, while the female takes on similar but less brilliant garb. They head for the mountain evergreens, and in the northwest their two-part song, *seet-seet-seet-seet-seet, trrrrrr*, is one of the first of the warbler melodies to be heard in spring.

The nest, usually placed on a horizontal limb well out from the trunk of a conifer, is formed of twigs and rootlets and lined with hair and feathers. The four grayish or creamy eggs blotched with brown hatch in 12 or 13 days. Audubon's warblers often raise two broods in a season.

Range: central British Columbia to W. South Dakota, south in the mountains to central Mexico; winters to S. Texas and Costa Rica. *Characteristics:* yellow crown, throat, sides, and rump patch; white belly. Breeding birds have streaked blue-gray back, black patches and streaks on breast and sides, white wing patches. Young and fall adults have streaked gray-brown back, whitish breast and wing markings.

Male Audubon's, length 5-5½"; Eliot Porter

"Audubon the Naturalist" by his sons John and Victor, c. 1841; American Museum of Natural History

JOHN JAMES AUDUBON
roamed the wilderness in
buckskin in stubborn pursuit of
his dream: to portray wildlife truly.
Born in Haiti in 1785, raised in France,
Audubon emigrated as a youth to
Pennsylvania, where he continued
to study nature at first hand.
Migrating to Kentucky in 1807,
he eventually failed as a merchant
and miller but made history with
his living portrayals of birds.
His monumental The Birds of
America, *completed in 1844,*
brought him world fame.
Its 500 engravings included
these Audubon's warblers.

Male (upper) and female Audubon's
Library of Congress

271

Male (upper) and female Townsend's, length 4¼-5"; Bob and Elsie Boggs

Townsend's Warbler
Dendroica townsendi

FROM THE CROWN of a giant fir a small bird dashes out to seize a flying insect. Up close the bird's distinctive black-and-yellow head pattern would quickly identify it as a Townsend's warbler. But at that distance and against the deep blue of the sky, its colors are difficult to make out.

As you crane, listen for the song. Soon a wheezy drawl comes drifting down through the shadowed hush of the evergreen forest: *dzeer dzeer dzeer tseetsee.*

The Townsend's warbler nests in the conifers, frequently high up. The shallow cup of bark, fir needles, and plant fibers is saddled on a horizontal limb. The three to five white eggs are spotted with several shades of brown.

During spring migration these warblers swarm northward along brushy stream banks, fluttering in the undergrowth like feathered butterflies. Often chickadees, kinglets, flycatchers, and nuthatches form part of the company.

Returning in the fall, many go no farther south than central California. A few drift to Kansas for the winter or remain as far north as Washington. One observer reported some Townsend's warblers wintering at Eugene, Oregon, on a feeding station menu of cheese, marshmallows, and peanut butter. The usual diet is mainly insects.

Range: S. Alaska to central Oregon and N.W. Wyoming; winters from central California to Nicaragua. *Characteristics:* male has black crown, cheeks, and throat; black streaks on back and sides; yellow face stripes and underparts, dark olive back. Female is duller with olive head markings, yellow face stripes and throat. Young and fall male resemble the female.

Male black-throated gray, length 4½-5"; Eliot Porter

Black-throated Gray Warbler
Dendroica nigrescens

IN THE PACIFIC NORTHWEST this trim warbler may breed in tall conifers. But here as well as farther south *nigrescens* favors dry brushy slopes where oak, piñon, and juniper grow. The grassy nest holds three to five white eggs spotted with brown. This bird gathers insects from trees and bushes and sings a drawling chant.

Range: S. W. British Columbia to central Colorado, south in the mountains to N. Baja California and E. New Mexico; winters to S. Mexico. *Characteristics:* black crown and cheeks, white face stripes, wing bars, and underparts; yellow spot in front of each eye. Male has black throat.

Black-throated Green Warbler
Dendroica virens

AMONG THE COOL EVERGREENS of the north, the lofty hemlocks of the Appalachian slopes, and the cypress swamps of the Carolina coast, *virens* sings its song of summertime.

The drowsy, sibilant song is one of the most pleasing in the family. For many listeners it evokes the fragrance of the forest and gentle summer breezes softly rippling the trees. "Trees, trees, murmuring trees," the little charmer seems to be saying, or "pines, pines, murmuring pines," or "sleep, sleep, pretty one, sleep."

These bright-cheeked birds nest on evergreen boughs from a few feet above ground to 70 feet high. The neat cup of twigs, grass, bark shreds, moss, and hair holds four or five grayish or creamy eggs marked with reddish brown.

In spring and fall black-throated green warblers migrate in vast congregations and can be seen in roadside trees, parks, and gardens tirelessly searching high and low for insect food. These trusting mites often allow people to approach them closely.

Range: N. Alberta to Newfoundland, south to central Minnesota, central Ohio, N. Alabama, and E. South Carolina; winters from S. Texas and S. Florida to Panama. *Characteristics:* olive head and back, yellow cheeks, black throat and side streaks, white wing bars and underparts. Female has yellow on throat.

273

Yellow-throated Warbler
Dendroica dominica

ALONG THE ATLANTIC COASTAL PLAIN this slow-moving warbler dwells in ancient live oaks draped with Spanish moss that once typified the plantation South. In the Mississippi Valley a subspecies sometimes called the sycamore yellow-throated warbler seeks out the large sycamores bordering streams. Pine trees and cypress swamps may also provide a summer home.

In his methodical search for food this warbler creeps along tree limbs, catching spiders, caterpillars, and scale insects. He often interrupts his feeding to sing a series of sweet descending whistles with an upturn at the end: *tee-ew, tew, tew, tew, tew wi.*

Where Spanish moss is available, the female almost invariably builds her nest in a hanging clump of it. Elsewhere she builds on a horizontal limb as high as 120 feet above the ground. The nursery of grass, bark shreds, plant down, feathers, and hair holds four greenish-white eggs splotched with purple and brown.

Ornithologist Alexander Sprunt, Jr., reported a bizarre hazard for this species. Twice he saw yellow-throated warblers entangled in the huge golden webs woven by Carolina silk spiders among the cypress lagoons of the South. In both instances the birds were dead.

The similarity in names makes it easy to confuse this species with the yellowthroat (page 286), a warbler different in looks and habits.

Range: Nebraska to S. W. Connecticut, south to E. Texas and central Florida; winters to Costa Rica and the West Indies. *Characteristics:* yellow bib, black-and-white head, wings, and sides; white wing bars and belly, gray back.

Yellow-throated, length 5-5½"; Arthur A. Allen

Hermit Warbler
Dendroica occidentalis

HIGH IN A DOUGLAS FIR a hermit warbler alights on a branch to begin an unhurried search for insects. He starts near the trunk and works his way to the outermost spray of needles. A tiny beetle is dislodged, the bird swoops after it, and now his yellow head gleams in the sun.

The hermit warbler is not really a recluse; he often forages near the ground. But he spends so much time high in the big firs and spruces that bird watchers are hard put to locate him.

On their way north in spring these warblers snap up flying insects among foothill oaks. They settle for the summer in the Sierra Nevada and western coast ranges at altitudes up to 7,600 feet. There in the middle levels of the evergreens they build their nests of plant fibers, twigs, pine needles, and lichens and line them with soft inner bark. The three to five white eggs are spotted with brown and lilac.

The hermit warbler's distinctive song consists of three high notes followed by two rapid lower notes: *seedle, seedle, seedle, chup chup.*

Range: S. W. Washington to central California; winters from central Mexico to Nicaragua, rarely in coastal California. *Characteristics:* yellow head, blackish nape, streaked gray back, white wing bars and breast, black throat. Female is duller, may have dusky throat.

Male (upper) and female hermit warblers length 4½-4¾", Allan Brooks

Blackburnian Warbler
Dendroica fusca

IN A COOL RAVINE twinflowers raise their delicate pink heads, and a brook flows through a corridor formed by stately hemlocks. In the upper limbs an orange ember flashes to life and brightens the shadows. "There is nothing to compare with the exquisite hue of this Promethean torch," wrote ornithologist Elliott Coues.

This beautiful warbler was named Blackburnian in the late 18th century in honor of Mrs. Hugh Blackburn of England. Her collection of birds included a specimen of the warbler that had been sent from America.

The Blackburnian breeds among the oaks and hickories on Appalachian ridges, but in the north he nests in hemlocks and other evergreens.

In his summer territory he sings from the spire of a tall tree. His extremely variable song is thin, high-pitched, and penetrating – a mixture of single notes and trills.

This warbler builds its nest well out toward the end of a high limb where it is safe from all but winged predators. Made of twigs, plant down, lichens, and bark shreds, it holds four white eggs spotted with brown.

The diet includes beetles, other small insects, and caterpillars gleaned from forest foliage.

Range: S. Saskatchewan to Nova Scotia, south to central Minnesota, Massachusetts, and in the mountains to N. Georgia; winters from Guatemala to N. South America. *Characteristics:* breeding male is black and white with orange head stripes, throat, and breast. Female, young, and fall adult are paler, more yellowish.

Golden-cheeked Warbler
Dendroica chrysoparia

BY THE END of March a hurried song seems to rise from everywhere on the dry upper slopes and eroded canyon sides of the Edwards Plateau, the stock-raising country northwest of San Antonio, Texas. The golden-cheeked warblers are back in their summer home after a winter spent in Mexico and Central America.

Tweeah, tweeah, tweesy – the song rings through the dwarf forest of Spanish oak and mountain cedar, a form of juniper. Ever on the go, the goldencheeks flit from tree to tree and pore over the limbs for insects.

Placed in an upright fork of a cedar 6 to 20 feet from the ground, the inconspicuous nest is built of cedar bark shreds, grass, and rootlets and lined with hair and feathers. The four white eggs are finely speckled with brown.

Range: south central Texas; winters from central Mexico to Nicaragua. *Characteristics:* yellow cheeks, black head, breast, eye stripe, and side streaks; white wing bars and belly. Back is black in male, olive-green in female.

275

Male (upper) and female Blackburnians, length 4½-5½"; Eliot Porter

Cerulean Warbler
Dendroica cerulea

A VOICE in the treetops, the cerulean warbler presents a tantalizing challenge to the bird watcher. *Zray zray zray zray zreeeee*, he trills over and over. You know he's there but you may strain for hours without catching sight of him in the woodland canopy.

And if at last he ventures out to an exposed limb, you'll probably see only his black necklace and white underparts. Rarely does an observer glimpse the crown of heavenly blue for which the cerulean warbler was named.

Quieter than her mate, the female is even more difficult to find. Her blue crown is similar to the male's, but her back may be olive-green rather than bluish, and her underparts may show a tinge of yellow with lighter side streaks.

After leaving the forests of northern South America, cerulean warblers migrate across the Gulf of Mexico and up the Mississippi Valley to settle for the summer in deep forests mainly west of the Alleghenies and east of the Great Plains. They breed most abundantly in the Ohio River Valley but seem to be increasing in the Northeast. They nest in scattered colonies in swamps and river bottoms among sycamores and oaks and in upland maples and beeches.

The female may build her nest 60 or more feet above the ground, or as low as 20 or even 15 feet. Usually placed well out on a substantial limb, the shallow cup of bark and weed stalks fastened with cobwebs often is decorated with lichens or

BIRD OF THE TREETOPS, *a cerulean warbler stuffs his young with a grub. The female (right) was discovered gathering bits of lichens for her nest saddled high in a linden tree near Jackson, Michigan. Photographer Eliot Porter*

bits of fungus. The four grayish or creamy eggs, rather heavily marked with reddish brown, rest on a lining of moss, hair, or feathers.

Foraging in the high branches, these birds feast on beetles and caterpillars. They also dart out to catch insects on the wing.

After a brief nesting season ceruleans wander for a time in family groups, then head south. Some reach the Gulf Coast in midsummer. A few may wander as far west as California.

Range: S. E. Nebraska to S. E. Minnesota and S. E. New York, south to E. Texas and central North Carolina; winters in N. South America. *Characteristics:* blue crown, whitish wing bars and underparts. Male has streaked blue-gray back, streaked sides, black necklace. Female has blue-gray or olive-green back, white eye line.

Red-faced Warbler
Cardellina rubrifrons
(Picture on page 255)

FACE AGLOW like a poppy in bloom and tail twitching constantly, this pretty little insect hunter flits about among firs, spruces, and aspens in the southwestern mountains. His clear, sweet song resembles that of the yellow warbler.

He breeds at altitudes up to 9,000 feet. The grassy nest, placed on the ground, holds three or four speckled white eggs.

Range: central Arizona and S. W. New Mexico, south to central Mexico; winters to Guatemala. *Characteristics:* black head patch, red face, breast, and sides of neck; white nape, rump patch, and belly; gray back and sides.

Length 4-5"

erected a 47-foot tower and waited many days to capture this scene. Despite the noise of construction, the flare of electronic flashes, and the presence of Porter only three feet away, the birds continued their daily rounds.

277

Chestnut-sided Warbler
Dendroica pensylvanica

IN THE EARLY 19th century this brightly garbed warbler was considered a rare bird. Audubon saw the species but once. Then, as men changed the landscape, the chestnut-sided warbler flourished. Today he is a familiar summer resident of the north central and eastern states.

He thrives in the brush and sprout growth of cut-over forests and neglected pastures. Tail high and wings drooping, he searches busily in low foliage for insect food. He makes a striking picture with his glowing cap and his puffed-out white breast framed by chestnut sides.

If he has just arrived on his breeding grounds, he may perch atop a bush to sing a distinctive territorial song. The loud, musical phrases sound like "please please please ta meetcha" or "sweet sweet sweet I'll switch you."

The female weaves a flimsy cup of bark shreds and grass in a bush or small tree. While she incubates the four brown-spotted eggs, her mate sings a nesting song more rambling and varied than his territorial melody. Cowbirds frequently leave their eggs in the nests of these warblers.

Range: central Saskatchewan to Nova Scotia, south to E. Nebraska, S. E. Minnesota, E. Pennsylvania, and in the mountains to Georgia; winters in Central America. *Characteristics:* yellow crown and wing bars, black-and-white face, yellow-and-white back streaked with black; chestnut sides, white underparts. Young and fall adults have green upperparts and white eye rings.

Chestnutsides, length 4½-5¼"

Grace's Warbler
Dendroica graciae

GATHERING INSECTS way up in the tall pines of the southwestern mountains, Grace's warbler exhibits an interesting change of pace. With quick, jerky flight he dashes out to seize a passing insect. Or he scrambles about the foliage, hovering occasionally to probe a cluster of needles at the end of a twig. At other times, however, he creeps along the limbs in leisurely fashion to examine the bark crannies. He may even descend almost to ground level to feed in the undergrowth. Now and then he pauses to sing a rapid *cheedle cheedle che che che*.

In the mountains of the Arizona border country this tiny warbler shares the pine tops with Audubon's and olive warblers.

Grace's warbler weaves a nest of plant fibers and down, fastens it with cobwebs to a conifer limb 20 to 60 feet high, and lines it with hair. The three or four white eggs are speckled with brown. After the young are fledged, they ramble through the forest with their parents until they are able to care for themselves. In late summer they leave the United States for the winter.

Ornithologist Elliott Coues discovered *graciae* in 1864 and named it for his sister Grace.

Range: S. Utah and S. Colorado south to Nicaragua; winters in Mexico and Central America. *Characteristics:* gray head and back, yellow eyebrow stripe, throat, and breast; white wing bars and belly, sides streaked with black. Female, young, and fall male are tinged with brown.

Adult Grace's, length 4½-5",
and juvenile (lower); Eliot Porter

Male (right) and female baybreasts, length 5-6"; Eliot Porter

Bay-breasted Warbler
Dendroica castanea

THE "LITTLE CHOCOLATE-BREASTED TITMOUSE," as pioneer naturalist William Bartram called this bird, may be hard to find as he moves up the Mississippi Valley in spring. He migrates rapidly, and his loud liquid song is hard to distinguish among the many migrating warblers.

In a northern conifer the bird builds a nest of twigs, grass, and rootlets for the five or six whitish eggs spotted with brown. One of the larger warblers, the baybreast bustles less as he feeds on insects than do many of his relatives.

Range: central Manitoba to Nova Scotia, south to N. E. Minnesota and S. Maine; winters from Panama to Venezuela. *Characteristics:* chestnut crown, breast, and sides; blackish face and streaked blackish back, white wing bars, buffy neck patches and belly, dark legs. Female is duller. Fall adults and young have olive-green backs.

Blackpoll Warbler
Dendroica striata

IN LATE SPRING, well after most of their family have passed through, blackpoll warblers suddenly swarm through eastern woodlands. Dense leaf canopies often screen their movements, but they sing a distinctive song. The insectlike *zi-zi-zi-zi* grows louder in the middle, softer toward the end. Attracted by city lights, these night migrants frequently pause in city parks and backyards to rest and hunt insects.

In the United States the blackpolls average about 30 miles a night. Then, as they near Canada, the nightly average increases to about 200 miles. Some go all the way to northern Alaska.

From there to the southernmost winter range in Chile the straight-line distance is some 8,300 miles. Blackpolls that breed in northern Alaska must travel at least 5,500 miles in spring. Many

Male (upper) and female blackpolls, length 5-5¾"
Louis Agassiz Fuertes

perish in storms as they cross the Caribbean; others collide with tall structures. Yet their numbers increase and the blackpoll ranks as one of our most abundant warblers.

While the male sings, the female fashions a feather-lined cup of twigs, weeds, and grass in a stunted northern spruce. The four or five creamy or greenish eggs are spotted with brown.

With the approach of fall, the blackpolls head south and southeast as they funnel down through Florida. Now all in greenish coats, they look much like bay-breasted warblers. If the bird has dark legs, buffy undertail coverts, and a trace of chestnut on its flanks, it's a baybreast. Pale legs and white under the tail identify the blackpoll.

Range: N. Alaska to Newfoundland, south to central British Columbia and N. Massachusetts; winters from Venezuela to central Chile. *Characteristics:* breeding male has black crown, streaked gray back, white cheeks, wing bars, and underparts. Female, young, and fall adults have streaked greenish upperparts, yellowish breast and wing bars, white undertail coverts.

279

Pine Warbler
Dendroica pinus

THE FIRST WARM BREEZES of the northern spring, spiced with the fragrance of pine, signal the coming of this cheerful warbler to the trees that provide it with food, a homesite, and a most appropriate name. Creeper fashion, it searches the pines from top to bottom for insects; often smudges of pine gum on the bird's feathers bear witness to its fondness for these trees.

The pine warbler is one of the earlier spring migrants in the family. Indeed, it may have eggs or young in the nest while the late warblers are still passing overhead.

The nursery of pine needles, weed stems, bark strips, spider webs, and feathers is often set out on a limb overhanging a road or path. In South Carolina these warblers have been found nesting 135 feet high in the tallest pines.

Male and female incubate the four speckled white, grayish, or greenish eggs. When these hatch, the parents gather spiders, flies, and caterpillars, mashing the larger insects against a limb before feeding them to the nestlings.

After the breeding season pine warblers may gather in flocks with bluebirds and chipping sparrows. At this time the warblers are quick to fight among themselves and occasionally bully the other birds. The warbler sings a trill much like the sparrow's but sweeter and slower.

Wintering among the southern pines, this warbler dines on pine seeds and wild berries.

Range: S. E. Alberta to central Maine, south to S. E. Texas, Florida, and the West Indies; migratory in the north. *Characteristics:* olive-green head and back, whitish wing bars, yellow underparts faintly streaked. Female is duller; young and fall female are brownish above.

Kirtland's Warbler
Dendroica kirtlandii

AMONG THE RAREST of our songbirds, the Kirtland's warbler is known to breed only on Michigan's lower peninsula in an area measuring roughly 60 by 100 miles. Even there it requires a very special habitat for nesting – thickets of young jack pines 5 to 15 feet high.

Forest fires produce this habitat by clearing and reforesting the land; the intense heat opens pine cones and frees the seeds. About 6 to 9 years after a fire the warbler may nest on the ground, sheltered by bushes and the limbs of the young pines, hatching its four or five speckled, creamy eggs. Within a few years the site is overgrown and the bird must seek a new breeding ground.

The first Kirtland's warbler nest was found in Michigan in 1903. In the heyday of lumbering there fires often swept the forests. Since then modern methods have controlled forest fires – and threatened survival of the species, now numbering only about 1,000 birds.

The Michigan Department of Conservation and the U. S. Forest Service have come to the rescue. They have set aside 11,690 acres for controlled burning, timber harvesting, and special planting to provide suitable habitat on a continuing basis. Scientists are also seeking some way to keep the cowbird from leaving its eggs in the warbler's nest. But no one expects that this finicky nester with the wagging tail and loud ringing song will ever become abundant.

Range: central Michigan; winters in the Bahamas. *Characteristics:* streaked bluish-gray head and back; broken white eye rings, grayish wing bars, yellow underparts with black side markings. Male has black mask. Young and fall adults have brown tinge on face, back, and sides.

Male pine warbler, length 5-5½"
Allan D. Cruickshank, National Audubon Society

Right: male Kirtland's, length 5¾"; Allan Brooks

Prairie Warbler
Dendroica discolor

THIS BOLD, LIVELY bird may venture out to prairie country to breed, but even there it looks for cover. The misnomer may be due to the fact that the bird has been found among scattered trees in southern grasslands.

Essentially an eastern warbler, this is a bird of partially overgrown clearings. It is also found in juniper-dotted pastures and open pinewoods with an understory of scrub oak.

Tails flicking nervously, these warblers flit and hop through the shrubbery, now snatching an insect in the air, now hovering with blurred wings to pick another from a leaf. If the day is bright and they allow a close approach, you may see the chestnut markings on the male's back; chances are you'll miss them on the paler female. The birds may fly to a perch in a tree to sound their thin, rising song, *zee zee zee zee zee*.

Usually located in a bush or small tree, the nest of weed stalks, leaves, grass, plant down, and feathers holds the four speckled white eggs. In Florida prairie warblers breed in mangroves.

Range: S. E. South Dakota to S. New Hampshire, south to E. Oklahoma, S. Louisiana, and S. Florida; winters from central Florida and the West Indies to Nicaragua. *Characteristics:* olive-green head and back, inconspicuous chestnut streaks on back; yellowish wing bars, yellow face and underparts with black markings. Female and young are duller.

Palm Warbler
Dendroica palmarum

IN THE NORTHERN BOGS and muskeg where it breeds, this warbler seems sadly misnamed. In the West Indies, where the species was discovered one winter, *palmarum* fits better.

His nicknames – "wagtail warbler" and "yellow tip-up" – fit in any season. This sprightly ground feeder bobs his tail incessantly as he hops and runs about picking up insects and weed seeds. His chestnut cap, yellow underparts, and feeble trill help identify him. But that constantly flicking tail is a clincher.

Two races of *palmarum* fan out over the north in spring. In both the sexes look alike. The eastern form, known as the yellow palm warbler because of its brighter breast, pushes up the Atlantic Coast to northern New England and eastern Canada. The western subspecies moves up the Mississippi Valley and spreads west across Canada.

The nest of moss or grass, placed in a sphagnum bog or on a hummock under a tree, holds four or five white eggs blotched with brown.

Palm warblers often visit southern gardens in winter. A few stay as far north as New England.

Range: N. British Columbia to Newfoundland, south to N. Minnesota and Maine; winters from Louisiana to North Carolina, south to the West Indies and Honduras. *Characteristics:* chestnut cap (grayish in fall), brownish back, yellow eye stripe, streaked yellow underparts; flicks tail. Western race has paler belly.

Male (upper) and female prairie warblers length 4½-5", Louis Agassiz Fuertes

Western (upper) and eastern palm warblers length 4½-5½"

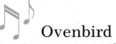 # Ovenbird

Seiurus aurocapillus

FREEZING WINDS or soft spring breezes may herald the northward migration of this ground-loving warbler. You can expect him pretty much at the same date every year at a given point along the flyways. He arrives in the northern states during the first week in May; by the end of that month and the first week in June he's settled in his northernmost summer territory in Canada.

Males and females usually return to the same nesting grounds in deciduous forests carpeted with dry leaves and scant underbrush. They resemble thrushes with their olive-brown backs and streaked white underparts, but the broad orange crown stripe makes them easily recognizable, if you can get a look at them (page 383).

Though they are hard to see they are often heard. Their notes grow louder and louder in a ringing chant which John Burroughs happily phrased as *teacher teacher teacher teacher*.

For a week or two after they arrive, this is their only song as they announce their presence and warn off trespassers. Then they begin singing their much more melodious flight song. The jumble of notes gushes forth — twitters and warbles and a few *teachers* thrown in — as the singer flits through the trees or skims the treetops. Often the wild outpouring is heard when twilight casts its spell or on warm starlit nights.

The male also sings in courtship. While serenading, he dashes this way and that, then rises high and flutters down toward his prospective mate, who sits in silence. Suddenly the male drops beside her and gives further evidence of his affection by a series of hops and dignified struts, by drooping his head and tail and elevating his wings. Finally the pair fly off.

With the male guarding the territory, the female selects the site for the unique nest from which ovenbirds get their name. From dead grass, leaves, and plant fibers she fashions an arched nest that looks like a Dutch oven; it has a side entrance and is so concealed amid the litter of the forest floor that it is nearly impossible to find. Upon a soft mattress of grass and hair she lays four or five white eggs speckled with hazel, purple, and reddish brown.

The eggs hatch in 11 to 14 days and both parents feed the young, approaching the nest along well-established runways. Snakes, red squirrels, and weasels prey heavily on the young.

Walking on pale pink legs, the ovenbird turns over leaves while searching for food on the ground and along fallen trees. He eats snails, slugs, earthworms, ants, crickets, and spiders.

Range: N. E. British Columbia to Newfoundland, south to E. Colorado and N. Georgia; winters from the Gulf Coast and South Carolina to N. South America. *Characteristics:* olive-brown head and back, black-bordered orange crown stripe, whitish eye rings, streaked white underparts, pinkish legs, short tail.

Ovenbird, length 5½-6½"; Eliot Porter

ing log or wade right into a swamp pool in quest of aquatic insects. As a rule he is less likely to be found around the rushing streams favored by his close relative. The northern waterthrush builds a mossy nest in a bank cavity or among upturned tree roots. Four or five eggs splotched with brown form the usual set.

This gifted musician sings a ringing melody which drops rapidly in pitch toward the end. In migration he visits city parks and gardens.

Range: N. Alaska to Newfoundland, south to N. Idaho, West Virginia, and Massachusetts; winters from central Mexico and West Indies to N. South America. *Characteristics:* olive-brown head and back, buffy eye stripe, streaked yellowish underparts.

Louisiana Waterthrush
Seiurus motacilla

OVER THE GURGLE of a swift mountain brook a wild sweet song rings out. It begins with a volley of three clear whistles and ends with a jumbled twitter of descending notes. Song over, the Louisiana waterthrush resumes his stroll by the water, body teetering. He may pause to snatch an insect or sound his sharp, metallic call note.

He sometimes forsakes running water for a stagnant pool or swamp. The nest of leaves, moss, and twigs, usually built in a stump or stream bank, holds four to six eggs. They are plain white or marked with brown and purple.

Range: E. Minnesota to S. New Hampshire, south to E. Texas and S. Georgia; winters from N. Mexico and West Indies to N. South America. *Characteristics:* grayish-brown head and back, whitish eyebrow stripe and streaked underparts.

Northern Waterthrush
Seiurus noveboracensis

IF IT LOOKS like a thrush, teeters almost constantly like a mechanical toy, and walks daintily along a lakeshore like a sandpiper, you're probably looking at a warbler called a waterthrush.

If the eyebrow stripes are buffy and underparts yellowish, it's the northern species. These marks are whiter in the Louisiana waterthrush.

The northern pokes under moist leaves in rock crevices for food. He may stride along a slant-

Connecticut Warbler
Oporornis agilis

ABOUT THE ONLY TIME this gray-hooded warbler visits the state in which it was discovered is during the fall migration to South America.

In spring the Connecticut warbler follows a different route. Heading northwest across the southern Appalachians, he pushes up the Mississippi Valley to the north central states and Canada.

He keeps to brushy shelter around swamps and meadows and rarely ventures more than a few feet off the ground as he hunts insects. He waits until observers are almost upon him, then scampers off to denser undergrowth or flies to a nearby tree and peers at them through large white "spectacles." In spring you may hear him sing *beecher beecher beecher;* it sounds like the ovenbird's song but without getting louder. In fall he sounds only his sharp *peek* note.

Journey's end in breeding season may be in muskeg country, in a spruce or tamarack swamp, or in a stand of poplar or aspen. A grassy cup, set in a mound of moss or in a hollow under a clump of grass, holds the four or five white eggs spotted with brown.

This bird resembles the MacGillivray's and mourning warblers but, unlike them, wears unbroken eye rings in both sexes in all seasons.

Range: E. British Columbia to N. W. Quebec, south to N. Minnesota and N. Michigan; winters in South America. *Characteristics:* gray hood, white eye rings, olive back, yellow underparts. Female, young, and fall male have indistinct hood of olive brown.

Kentucky Warbler
Oporornis formosus

A BLACK CAP, heavy "sideburns," and golden eyebrow stripes that curl down behind the eyes distinguish this ground-loving denizen of luxuriant eastern and midwestern forests.

In his moist, shaded haunts, as John Burroughs observed, the bird walks "rapidly along, taking spiders and bugs, overturning leaves, peeping under sticks and into crevices and every now and then leaping up eight or ten inches, to take his game from beneath some overhanging leaf or branch.... Draw a line three feet from the ground, and you mark the usual limit of the Kentucky warbler's quest for food."

His head pattern and tail-bobbing serve to identify him, but he is not easy to see in his dark summer home. His persistent singing, however, often provides a clue to his whereabouts. The loud chant sounds like *churry-churry-churry-churry.* Many observers have noted a resemblance to the song of the Carolina wren.

Male and female build a loose, bulky nest of dead leaves, grass, and rootlets. Placed on or just above the ground and well hidden in vegetation, the nest holds four or five white eggs spotted with brown. Cowbirds frequently lay their eggs in this warbler's nest.

Range: S. E. Nebraska to S. W. Wisconsin, central Indiana, and S. W. Connecticut, south to central Texas and N. W. Florida; winters from S. Mexico to N. South America. *Characteristics:* black crown and "sideburns," yellow eye stripe and underparts, olive-green back.

Male and (left) female Connecticut warblers, 5¼-6"

Kentucky warblers, length 4½-5¼"; Eliot Porter

Mourning Warbler
Oporornis philadelphia

TIMID AND UNOBTRUSIVE, the mourning warbler comes north late and leaves early. In passage he keeps to the dense shrubbery. On his breeding ground he spends a good deal of time skulking in underbrush; at the slightest disturbance he scurries off. Not many people get a look at him.

Some who have seen this bird think the black breast patch worn by the male is not enough to justify the somber name. The mourning warbler "seems as happy and active as most birds, and its song is a paean of joy," wrote ornithologist Edward Howe Forbush. The male in spring mounts to the top of a bush or small tree to sound a loud, ringing *chirry chirry, chorry chorry.*

For a summer homesite this warbler seems to prefer overgrown clearings and slash, or upland thickets where raspberry and blackberry bushes abound. Here the mourning warbler builds a bulky cradle of leaves and grass in a brier tangle, in a clump of ferns, or in goldenrod or other rank growth. The four white eggs are speckled with

Male MacGillivray's, length 4³⁄₄-5¹⁄₂"; Eliot Porter

MacGillivray's Warbler
Oporornis tolmiei

A WESTERN relative of the mourning warbler, this bird has the same shy ways. Its discoverer, ornithologist John Kirk Townsend, dedicated the species in 1839 to his friend W. F. Tolmie, a surgeon formerly of Fort Vancouver on the Columbia River. Audubon, however, named the bird for his associate, the Scottish naturalist William MacGillivray. Today the honors are split.

Where its range joins that of the mourning warbler, *tolmiei* can be told apart by its broken white eye rings. The breeding mourning warbler has no eye rings. In addition, the male eastern bird has a blacker chest.

MacGillivray's warbler hunts insects in new growth on burned-over lands, on dry, brushy hillsides, and among clumps of willow and alder that border canyon streams. He may deliver his rolling song—*chiddle-chiddle-chiddle, turtle-turtle* —from within a tangle of shrubbery or from a favorite perch some 30 feet above the ground.

The ragged nest of grass and weed stalks is usually placed on the ground or within a few feet of it in weeds or bushes. The four brown-spotted white eggs are often scrawled with black.

Range: S. Alaska to S. W. Saskatchewan, south to central California and central New Mexico; winters from N. Mexico to Panama. *Characteristics:* gray hood, broken white eye rings, olive back, blackish chest, yellow underparts. Female and young are much paler, with grayish chest.

Female mourning warbler, length 5-5³⁄₄"

brown; sometimes the eggs are also marked with black spots and scrawls.

In July and August these warblers begin a silent journey through the brush to the tropics.

Range: central Alberta to Newfoundland, south to N. E. North Dakota and W. Virginia; winters from Nicaragua to N. South America. *Characteristics:* gray hood, olive back, yellow underparts. Male has black breast patch. Fall female and young have broken eye rings.

Yellowthroat
Geothlypis trichas

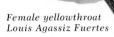

DARK EYES sparkling through his roguish mask, this excitable little bird diligently hunts for caterpillars, beetles, ants, and oth-

*Female yellowthroat
Louis Agassiz Fuertes*

er small insects. Invade his haunts and he scolds vigorously with chirps and chattering notes.

His vivacious ways may remind you of a wren. He darts here and there, disappears in thick brush, then reappears to berate you again. If he persists in keeping out of sight, try sounding a few squeaks. Often he or the plainer female will venture into sight to investigate.

Convinced you mean no harm, the male may rise to a singing perch in full view and deliver his loud, high-pitched song: *witchity-witchity-witchity*. The strongly accented syllables make the song easy to recognize.

The yellowthroat rarely takes to tall trees. He spends most of his time close to the ground, in briery tangles along little-used country roads, in streamside willow thickets, fresh and salt marshes, and fields overgrown with weeds. He breeds over most of the continent from Alaska to southern Mexico.

The female builds a large bulky nest of leaves, grass, bark strips, cattail shreds, weed stems, or animal hair, the materials varying with the site. She hides it so well in grass, shrubs, or reeds that you probably won't find a yellowthroat's cup-shaped nest unless you come close enough to flush a bird from one.

The four white eggs, spotted with brown, black, and gray, hatch in 12 days. In many areas yellowthroats frequently incubate cowbird eggs along with their own. Occasionally the warbler buries the parasite's eggs under a new nest lining.

Large numbers of migrating yellowthroats sometimes perish in storms and foggy weather. One misty September night in Washington, D. C., 189 of these warblers dashed themselves to death against the Washington Monument.

Science recognizes 12 subspecies of the yellowthroat. There are also two other closely related species. Belding's yellowthroat (*Geothlypis beldingi*) of Baja California is larger, with a yellow-bordered mask in the male. The ground-chat (*Chamaethlypis poliocephala*), which ranges from the lower Rio Grande Valley to Panama, has a stouter bill and longer tail.

Range: S. E. Alaska to Newfoundland, south to S. Mexico; winters to Panama and Puerto Rico. *Characteristics:* yellow breast, whitish belly, brownish flanks. Male has black mask with whitish upper border; olive-green upperparts. Female has olive-brown upperparts.

*Male yellowthroat, length 4½-5¾″
Woodrow Goodpaster, National Audubon Society*

Yellow-breasted Chat
Icteria virens

THE COLORS of this buffoon of the brier patch — olive-green, yellow, and white — are not unusual in his family. But his large size, thick bill, shorter wings, and odd behavior make him seem out of place among the wood warblers. He reminds some observers of a vireo. To others he suggests a catbird or a mockingbird.

The yellow-breasted chat breeds over most of the United States, especially where thickets surround small trees on low damp ground or in neglected pastures. If you come near him you'll know it though you may never see him. For he rends the air with an astonishing medley of cackles, whistles, barks, mews, and gurgles interspersed with distinctive *whoit* or *kook* notes.

Occasionally you can glimpse him peering at you through his white "spectacles" with tail pumping, or flying among the bushes with wings loosely flapping and legs dangling. If you retire he follows, scolding all the while.

Placed near the ground, the bulky nest holds three to five spotted white eggs. The female, who looks like her mate, incubates them alone.

Range: S. British Columbia to S. New Hampshire, south to central Mexico and N. Florida; winters to Panama. *Characteristics:* thick bill, broken white eye rings, olive-green upperparts, yellow throat and breast, white belly.

Male (upper) and female hooded warblers, length 5-5¾″

Hooded Warbler
Wilsonia citrina

To WELL-WATERED eastern woodlands and forested southern swamps this warbler brings his good looks and fine voice for the warm months.

Soon after he arrives in spring he begins to patrol his territory, whistling a loud *weeta wee-tee-o* as he goes. Frequently he spreads his tail, revealing distinctive white areas in it. Toward evening males often leave their haunts in the thickets to sing from the treetops.

The female, without her mate's dark hood and silent much of the time, is less conspicuous. But she may rise from the undergrowth to help the male drive an intruder from their territory.

The nest of dead leaves, secured with spider webs to the fork of a shrub or sapling, holds three or four creamy eggs blotched with brown.

These warblers feed mostly on insects caught in the air. Their diet also includes grasshoppers, caterpillars, and plant lice.

Range: S. E. Nebraska to S. Michigan and Rhode Island, south to S. E. Texas and N. Florida; winters from central Mexico to Panama. *Characteristics:* yellow face and underparts, olive back, white tail spots. Male has black hood; female has olive crown, yellow throat.

*Yellow-breasted chat, 6½-7½″; Allan D. Cruickshank
National Audubon Society. Upper: Eliot Porter*

Male (right) and female Wilson's, length 4¼-5″; Eliot Porter

Male Canada, length 5-5¾″; Frederick Kent Truslow

Wilson's Warbler
Wilsonia pusilla

THIS BRIGHT-EYED BUNDLE of energy, named for his discoverer, ornithologist Alexander Wilson, is also sometimes called the pileolated warbler. The black pileum, or cap, is worn by male birds and traces of it by some females. From the Arctic Ocean almost to Mexico the bird frisks through swampy thickets, shaking his wings nervously, jerking his tail and waving it from side to side.

Watch for him in remote bogs among willows, alders, and moss-grown evergreens. Look for the flash of his golden breast as he darts up to snatch an insect from a leaf or in midair.

During his spring migration he may be easier to see, for he often drops in at a city park. Here you may listen to his song—a series of short, bubbling notes that may drop in pitch at the end.

On his breeding grounds Wilson's warbler builds a ball-like nest of leaves and fibers on the side of a moss tussock or in the shelter of a clump of sedge. In the grass-lined nursery lie three to six white eggs with brown spots. *Range:* N. Alaska to Newfoundland, south to S. California, N. New Mexico, S. Manitoba, and central Nova Scotia; winters to Panama. *Characteristics:* olive upperparts, yellow underparts; male (and sometimes female) has black cap.

Canada Warbler
Wilsonia canadensis

NAMED for one country, equally at home in another, the Canada warbler breeds as far south as Georgia. In cool, moist Appalachian ravines where old deciduous trees grow tall above the rhododendrons, you may see him hop and dart in his search for insects. Often he picks them off in flight with a snap of his bill.

Yellow "spectacles" show brightly against his dark gray crown. But more distinctive is the necklace of short streaks—jet black in the male, less defined in the female—across the yellow breast. "Necklaced warbler" is another name for this handsome species.

In migration these birds frequent clearings with patches of second growth. They add their richly varied phrases to the medley of bird songs. But in the damp shade of their breeding grounds each pair keeps to itself.

In a rotten stump, a mound of moss, or the open roots of a fallen tree the Canada warbler hides its nest, usually a formless mass of dead leaves, bark shreds, and grass lined with such fine materials as rootlets and hair. The three to five white eggs are splotched with brown. The female probably does most of the incubating. Both parents feed the young. The family menu features the larvae and adults of moths, flies, beetles, mosquitoes, and other insects. *Range:* central Alberta to New Brunswick, south to central Minnesota, N. Ohio, S. E. New York, and in the Appalachians to N. Georgia; winters in N. South America. *Characteristics:* solid gray upperparts, yellow eye rings and underparts. Male has jet black necklace; female's is fainter. Young resemble the female.

Male (lower) and female Americans, length 4½-5¾″

Painted redstart, length 5-5¼″; Allan Brooks

American Redstart
Setophaga ruticilla

OF ALL THE WARBLERS that breed in the United States this is one of the most beautiful and abundant. Early settlers named him for the familiar redstart of England, a bird of another family.

Spanish imagination in the West Indies coined a more suggestive name, *candelita,* or little torch. Those who have seen this dainty bird fluttering after insects in a forest agree that the flaming color on wings and tail seems to light up the shadows. Like a big butterfly he whirls, floats, and dances in the air. Alighting, he fans his feathers and half opens his wings as if to show off their brilliant markings.

These spirited warblers wing northward in spring to breed in the forests of the United States and Canada. The males fight to set up individual territories nearly an acre in extent and greet the females with much strutting and display. They sing a high-pitched series of thin, sibilant notes.

With no help from her mate the female builds a compact nest of bark shreds and grass, bound with plant fibers and spider webs, usually in the crotch of a small tree. She incubates the three to five eggs, whitish with brown splotches.

Range: S. E. Alaska to Newfoundland, south to E. Oregon, S. Louisiana, and central Georgia; winters from central Mexico and West Indies south to N. South America. *Characteristics:* male is black with orange wing and tail patches, white belly. Female is gray-olive above, white below; yellow on wings and tail.

Painted Redstart
Setophaga picta

IN A WOODED southwestern canyon where a stream gurgles in the cool shadows, you may hear a rich contralto *weeta weeta weeta wee* and come upon this lovely little bird.

Flashing his contrasting black, white, and red, the painted redstart seems constantly in motion. Hovering, fluttering, he wheels and rises and spirals down, never far off the ground, as he chases insects. Even perching, he sidesteps and pirouettes, wings half-spread, an ever-restless kaleidoscope of color.

Primarily a Mexican bird, this warbler breeds north of the border in Arizona, New Mexico, and Texas. He and his mate, who wears similar plumage, are so tame they may approach you closely if you happen to be near their nest and sit still.

They build this large, shallow nest of bark shreds and grasses on the ground, usually under a projecting rock, between the roots of a tree, or cupped in a grassy bank. The three or four white eggs are speckled with brown. The young are quick to acquire the splendid adult plumage.

Range: N. W. Arizona to W. Texas, south to N. Nicaragua. *Characteristics:* black upperparts, bright red breast, white wing and tail patches and linings; white belly.

URCHIN AMONG BIRDS

The House Sparrow

Family Ploceidae

Male (upper) and female house sparrows, length 5-6⅓"
Walter A. Weber, National Geographic staff artist

A SHRILL, monotonous *cheep cheep cheep* outside the bedroom window greets the dawn. "Those blankety-blank sparrows!" we mutter. The twitterings swell as the familiar birds leave their roosts in ivied walls to roister on the porch roof. As daylight increases, jaunty males with white cheeks and black bibs, and drab females with eye stripes descend to the ground to feed.

Cocky street gamin and barnyard brawler, the house, or English, sparrow (*Passer domesticus*) is not a sparrow but a weaver finch and is native to the British Isles, Europe, Asia, and North Africa. He belongs to the family Ploceidae; of its 263 species, only two breed in North America. In 1850 eight pairs of *domesticus* were imported from England to help control cankerworms in Brooklyn. The birds failed to take hold. Later immigrants succeeded only too well.

House sparrows have become one of the most abundant and heartily detested birds. They steal food from other species. They often oust bluebirds or martins from bird houses and move in. Yet their rascality is frequently entertaining. Sometimes they follow along as robins search for earthworms. No sooner does the large bird uncover a beakful of breakfast than a small, cheeky sparrow snatches it away!

Grain and seeds are their staple foods, but house sparrows also take whatever insects abound in summer. They even dine on Japanese beetles, scanning the rosebushes, then swooping on their prey. And they pick dead insects from car radiators. They are not choosy about nesting sites either. A fire escape will do; so will a window ledge or the shade of a traffic light. They build untidy nests of grass or hay lined with feathers or soft scraps from the trash can. If the nest is in the open, they roof it. They rob each other of nesting materials; discovery of the theft leads to a free-for-all, tough little scrappers fluttering and rolling in the dust.

Courtship is also a rough-and-tumble affair, the promiscuous females encouraging the battling males. After mating, a female lays three to seven dull white eggs splashed with brown or gray. Incubation takes 11 to 13 days. Parents feed the young on insects, at first by regurgitation. If a baby falls from the nest, the adults will continue to feed and shelter it. They raise two or three broods a year.

Cheeping through the winter, house sparrows add a bit of cheer to bleak days. A handful of seed on the snow keeps them from monopolizing the backyard feeder.

The European tree sparrow (*Passer montanus*), a smaller, gentler cousin, was imported from Germany in 1870. A score of these brown-topped weaver finches were liberated in a St. Louis, Missouri, park and the birds have barely spread beyond the city since. In cavity nests they rear two broods of four to six annually.

House sparrow—*Range:* central British Columbia to Newfoundland, south to central Mexico and West Indies. *Characteristics:* streaked brown back, grayish belly. Male has gray crown, chestnut nape, black bib, white cheeks. Female has brown crown, whitish underparts, light eye stripes.

European tree sparrow—*Range:* St. Louis and adjacent areas in Missouri and Illinois. *Characteristics:* resembles male house sparrow but is smaller, with brown crown, black cheek spots.

HOUSE SPARROWS *collide as they noisily flee a feeder appropriated by a bobwhite. Their gentle cousin, the tree sparrow (below right), quietly feeds its young*

Above: European tree sparrow, length 6″; Eric Hosking
Left: Arthur A. Allen

Length 8-8½", Ray Fisher, Miami Herald

A DELIGHT TO THE EAR *as well as to the eye, a spotted-breasted oriole whistles a liquid stream of melody. The Florida immigrant is a tropical American species.*

Meadowlarks, Blackbirds, and Orioles

Family Icteridae

By ROBERT W. STORER

I HAVE SEEN red-winged blackbirds in the coastal marshes of New Jersey, the pot-holes of the Canadian prairies, and the mangrove swamps of southern Mexico; yet never have I glimpsed a tricolored blackbird outside the borders of California. I have searched no farther than the elms in my yard at Ann Arbor, Michigan, to find Baltimore orioles nesting; but I must hunt diligently in the hayfields for the bobolink and her young. I have heard the western meadowlark's loud, clear melody with ease through the closed windows of a speeding train; still I have to think twice to realize that the common grackle's squeaks are really a song.

Such diversity is common among the icterids. It's reflected in their names – black-bird, meadowlark, oriole, bobolink, grackle, cowbird – and in their appearance.

An oriole wears striking black and orange or yellow; the female bobolink is spar-rowy brown. And the meadowlark models both – the oriole's brilliance on its breast, the bobolink's drabness on its back. But a blackbird wins my vote as the handsomest icterid in North America. I vividly remember watching yellow-headed blackbirds stunting among the reeds along the Bear River marshes in Utah. Their white wing patches flashed amid the gleaming gold and black.

As songsters, some icterids have few rivals. The tinkling flight song of the bobo-link reminds me of glass wind chimes. To my mind the song of this American bird is so far superior to that of the European skylark that I wonder how Shelley might have described *its* "unpremeditated art."

Meadowlarks like to sing from a high perch so they can look over their territory, but they will sing from a clod of earth if they can find nothing higher. Baltimore orioles vary their rich songs. One which spent several summers in our neighborhood sang a particularly disturbing phrase, a syncopated "shave-and-a-haircut, two —,'' until I wanted to shout "bits" at him to finish it.

The icterids with less tuneful songs tend to accompany them with displays. Grackles erect their neck feathers when producing their unmusical notes, and male cowbirds spread their wings and lurch forward. The red-winged blackbird ruffs its plumage to reveal bright red epaulets as it sings its familiar *ok-a-lee*. The yellow-headed blackbird turns and sings its raucous song over its shoulder – always the left one, it has been observed.

The many sounds of the Icteridae are heard from Alaska to Tierra del Fuego. Nearly 100 species, with 19 resident north of Mexico, comprise this all-American family. Old World orioles, blackbirds, and larks belong to different groups.

The success of icterids in so many types of habitats is due partly to the diversity in their bills and in the muscles for opening and closing them. Meadowlarks obtain food by using specially powerful muscles for opening the bill. Probing for insects and worms, they insert the closed mandibles in the earth and then force them open. Handle a meadowlark and chances are that it will put its bill between your fingers and try to pry them apart. Another gaper, the orchard oriole, sticks its closed beak into soft fruits. When the beak opens, juices and pulp flow into the mouth.

Bobolinks and cowbirds are seedeaters, using strong jaw muscles to close their conical, finchlike bills. The thinner-billed grackle employs its bill-closing muscles and a cutting ridge in the roof of the mouth to shell small acorns (page 312).

The red-winged blackbird occasionally slits reeds with its pointed bill to get at succulent grubs, but usually it does not have to work so hard. One summer at a lake in central Alberta, Canada, I saw immense hatches of mosquitolike midges rise from the water to be snapped up by swooping gulls, crows, and magpies. But red-winged and yellow-headed blackbirds just perched on the ground, picking the insects off the vegetation one by one.

Blackbirds plait their closely woven nests among the reeds. Meadowlarks build on the ground, in grasslands, meadows, and pastures. They usually dome their nests, probably because ground-nesting birds need more protection than tree nesters.

There's a strong tendency for the orioles to hang their finely knit pouches from branches extending over roads. I've noticed it many times. I believe the pavement suggests water to them—and hanging the nest over a stream is, of course, characteristic of these birds.

Baltimore orioles favor elms for nesting, and they often fell victim to DDT when the trees were sprayed for Dutch elm disease. Poisoned birds fluttered in a pitiful manner. After they got the shakes they might not last an hour. Fortunately use of DDT now has been restricted.

REDWING AND CHIPMUNK *share a table under a canopy of marsh marigolds at Cornell's Sapsucker Woods. When dining in grainfields the blackbird risks the farmer's shotgun.*

Arthur A. Allen

Walter A. Weber, National Geographic staff artist. Below: W. V. Crich and (right) Hal H. Harrison

BATTLE FOR THE NURSERY *erupts
as a brown-headed cowbird tries
to invade a catbird's nest and
meets its furious defender (top).*

*Dependent on foster parents
to incubate her eggs and raise her
young, the cowbird jettisons
a chestnut-sided warbler's egg
(above) to make room for her own.*

*One unwilling host, a yellow
warbler, tried to foil the parasite
by roofing over its eggs. But
each time the cowbird ended up
on top. Cutaway view (left)
shows the five-story apartment.*

Grackles nest in a variety of places—in tree holes, in bushes, and, like blackbirds, in reedy marshes. When I was a boy growing up in New Jersey I saw a grackle claim squatter's rights in the base of an osprey's huge abode of sticks, lashed to the crossbar of a telephone pole.

Our cowbirds lay their eggs in the nests of other species, relying on the foster parents to raise their young. The bronzed cowbird most frequently selects other icterids as hosts. The brown-headed cowbird is far less discriminating; its eggs have been found in the nests of more than 200 species.

Though diverse in habit, song, and appearance, icterids do have some things in common. They are strong, direct fliers. The long lines of grackles, cowbirds, and blackbirds flying in to their communal roosts at sunset are familiar sights over much of the country.

Icterids share basic structural characteristics, such as the same number of flight feathers—nine attached to each wing hand—and the arrangement of the scales on the legs. Also, the females usually are much smaller than the males. The female boat-tailed grackle, for instance, differs so much from the male in size and color that the novice bird watcher may wonder if he isn't seeing two kinds of birds.

Some icterids are controversial. The redwings and bobolinks which we enjoy in the spring and summer may take their toll of grain in the fall. The fascinating cowbirds parasitize songbirds. And at times our grackles annoy me by robbing the nests of other birds and dropping the fecal sacs of their own young in our birdbath.

But these are minor complaints when weighed against the good points of this gregarious family. The abundance, conspicuousness, and adaptability of icterids make them favorites for study. I can expect to find eight to ten species almost anywhere I go in North America, and I welcome the sight of these dashing birds.

David G. Allen

RAVENOUS YOUNG COWBIRDS *beg "mother" solitary vireo for more food. The hulking interlopers often cause smaller species to starve in the nest.* 297

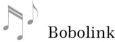

Bobolink
Dolichonyx oryzivorus

OVER THE FRESH GREEN GRASS of northern meadows the joyous song bubbles out, faster and faster, rising in pitch, each note tumbling over the one before. William Cullen Bryant phrased it:

Robert of Lincoln is telling his name:
Bob-o'-link, bob-o'-link,
Spink, spank, spink . . . .

In full voice and clad in breeding plumage, the male bobolink is readily recognized. His "bright black wedding-coat," as the poet describes it, contrasts sharply with his buff nape and large white patches on back and wings.

No other member of the family sings on the wing with such ecstasy. And no other icterid travels as far as the bobolink – some 5,000 miles from winter quarters in southern Brazil and northern Argentina to his summer territory in the northern United States and southern Canada.

Despite the distance, bobolinks return with great regularity to their nesting grounds. New England colonists found them breeding in coastal marshes and grassy river valleys. In succeeding centuries these birds adapted to the changes wrought by human settlement and found homesites in hayfields and damp meadows.

This adjustment proved disastrous. Early summer mowing of hayfields killed large numbers of nesting bobolinks and their young, and the species greatly declined in New England. But bobolinks followed the westward spread of grainfields and irrigated pastures and now breed as far as California and British Columbia. In late summer bobolinks that nested in the west return east to migrate along ancestral routes through Florida and the Gulf Coast. They fly high in open formation, much like other small blackbirds.

Bobolinks arrive in the north in May. Many use Caribbean islands as stepping-stones on their journey. Others cross the Gulf of Mexico from Yucatán to the United States.

The exuberant males reach the grasslands and clover fields first and fill the air with rapturous melody. Although they use weed stalks and tree limbs as song perches, these troubadours make their best music on the wing – the celebrated tinkling flight song.

When the females arrive a few days later, serenading males pursue them with great ardor. Often a retiring female dives into the grass for concealment. A suitor continues the courtship on the ground. He partly opens his wings, drags his tail, erects his buff nape feathers, and gurgles.

Yellowish with dark stripes, the female is nearly invisible on the ground and she fashions a nest just as difficult to detect. Her nursery is a depression walled with weed stems, lined with fine grass, and screened by thick grass. The female incubates the five or six gray or brownish eggs spotted with brown and purple. While brooding she seldom flushes from the nest but runs some distance through the grass before flying off.

By August startling changes have affected the boldly attired songsters of May. A complete molt has transformed the males to yellowish birds like the females. Most singing had ceased by early July; now the bobolinks gather in somber flocks, a metallic *clink* their only utterance. Congregating in marshes and on stream banks, they feed largely on seeds which they crack with strong, conical bills. Earlier in the year caterpillars, grasshoppers, and beetles had been their main sustenance.

No longer recognizable as the hero of *Robert of Lincoln*, the bobolink starts south along a flyway that once took him through the great rice fields of 19th century South Carolina. Planters dreaded the annual visitation of "rice-birds"; they descended by the millions on croplands, causing immense damage. In turn gunners slaughtered the well-fattened birds for the meat market. In one year 60,000 dozen were shipped to Philadelphia, New York, and Paris. Rice culture has declined along the bobolink's main migration route and the species is protected, but it has never recovered its former abundance.

Range: S. Canada to N. E. California and central New Jersey; winters in central South America. *Characteristics:* buff with dark stripes on head and back. Breeding male has black head, belly, wings, and tail; buff nape, white patches on back and wings.

DAPPER BOBOLINK *returns to nest hidden in grass. Young soon resemble mother (above).*
Male, length 6-8"; Eliot Porter. Above: Arthur A. Allen

Eastern Meadowlark
Sturnella magna

WINTER STILL GRIPS the fields and pastures when that eloquent herald, the eastern meadowlark, begins to vie for a breeding territory. Up from the grass he flies, a brownish, streaked bird with white feathers edging his stubby tail. Hurried wingbeats alternate with sailing.

Tee-you, tee-yair sings the meadowlark. To many a farmer the sweet, plaintive whistle sounds like "Spring is here."

The first meadowlarks heard are all-year residents that have wintered nearby and now are staking claims averaging seven acres of meadow to a bird. From a commanding perch, perhaps a power line, they watch for challengers. Soon other males arrive, migrants from far to the south. Their tails twitching and flitting with excitement, the squatters defend their claims with songs, alarm calls, and plumage displays. The birds may also battle fiercely in the grass.

Females begin to arrive about two weeks after the first migrant males. Suitors initiate a frenzied rivalry. The song tempo increases, and some performers spiral upward on rapidly vibrating wings while uttering a stream of chattering notes. Sometimes three males pursuing a single prospective mate may alight to put on a competitive display. An impassioned male springs from the ground, bill pointed upward, tail spread, wings beating. His puffed-out breast feathers form a flashing shield of gold and black.

Polygamy is not unusual among meadowlarks; a successful male may attract as many as three females to his plot of meadow. Construction of the cunningly concealed grassland nest is the female's job. She uses her beak as pick and forceps to dig a hollow or merely remodel a cow's hoofprint or other depression. Dried grasses with a lining of pine needles, horsehair, or other fine materials form the bedding. Over this the meadowlark interlaces a dome-shaped roof of growing grass stems. Sometimes a covered passageway leads to the hidden nest opening.

The eastern meadowlark lays three to seven eggs, though five is the most common set. They are white splotched with brown and lavender. The female alone incubates, leaving the eggs only to feed. Often she snatches insects from the grass without moving from the nest. Virtually invisible in her blind, she answers the flight song of the male with low, sweet, chuckling notes audible about 20 feet away.

Incubation usually takes two weeks. When the eggs hatch, the female removes the eggshells a considerable distance, then starts a routine of stuffing soft-bodied insects down the throats of her insatiable nestlings. In this she gets token assistance from her mate.

As they grow older the youngsters become so active they virtually demolish their nest and leave it before being able to fly. They jump about in the grass and call loudly for food. During the next two weeks father takes over the major role in caring for the youngsters while mother builds a new nest, lays a second set of eggs, and begins incubating them.

The meadowlark feeds on a variety of insects: cutworms, caterpillars, beetles, grasshoppers. He can seize prey on the ground or plunge his bill into the soil for a juicy grub. In autumn he eats weed seeds and waste grain.

Most meadowlarks leave the northernmost parts of their range with the approach of winter. Others gather in large flocks and spend the cold months in stubble fields and coastal marshes near the breeding grounds.

The farmer welcomes these birds for their sweet singing and their help in destroying insect pests. But his mowing machines kill great numbers of meadowlarks that nest unseen in clover and alfalfa fields. Others fall victim to hawks, cats, and snakes.

Range: N. W. Arizona to S. W. South Dakota and Nova Scotia, south to N. South America. *Characteristics:* streaked brown head and back, bright yellow throat and breast with black V; white outer tail feathers.

Western Meadowlark
Sturnella neglecta

IN 1844 Audubon commented on the "curious notes" uttered by meadowlarks along the upper Missouri River. He observed that although the species was known to members of the Lewis and Clark Expedition, no one had taken the "least notice" of these birds since. In consequence Audubon named the western meadowlark *Sturnella neglecta*.

Today the tag no longer fits. Kansas, Montana, Nebraska, North Dakota, Oregon, and Wyoming have picked *neglecta* as their state bird. His vibrant song brings a familiar message of cheer to open country from Illinois to the Pacific.

In plumage there is little to distinguish the western meadowlark from his eastern counterpart. Both have streaked upper parts, a yellow breast with a black V, and white outer tail feathers. The westerner, however, is somewhat paler.

In the realm of song all resemblance ceases. From his perch on a fence post or farmhouse roof the western meadowlark unleashes a bubbling medley of rich, flutelike phrases quite unlike the easterner's plaintive, whistled song; they contain hints of the wood thrush and the Baltimore oriole, with some of the bobolink's exuberance added for good measure.

Both species of meadowlarks overlap in the

Upper: eastern, length 8½-11"; Eliot Porter
Lower: western, length 8-11"; Allan D. Cruickshank, National Audubon Society

central states, but recent findings indicate that they do not hybridize. Females apparently choose their mates on the basis of call notes.

The western meadowlark favors the prairies and grassy valleys, but it also frequents sagebrush flats and the grassy glades within pine forests. In late summer it may reach an altitude of 12,000 feet in the open grasslands of the Rockies. Flocks of these birds wander in the fall, but they do not migrate very far. They winter in the desert and as far north as they can find snow-free feeding grounds.

The female usually builds her roofed-over nest of grass on dry ground in contrast to the moist depressions chosen by the eastern species. The westerner raises two broods a season, each with three to seven white eggs speckled brown.

After leaving the nest the young spend about two weeks with their parents, learning to hunt beetles, grasshoppers, and crickets. In winter the birds subsist on weed seeds and waste grain.

Range: central British Columbia to S. Ontario, south to central Mexico. *Characteristics:* streaked brown head and back, yellow throat and breast with black V; white outer tail feathers; paler than the eastern species, with yellow extending farther up into the cheek.

Yellow-headed Blackbird
Xanthocephalus xanthocephalus

ROCKING ON UPTILTED WINGS, a marsh hawk glides above the reed-choked borders of a prairie slough. Suddenly a cloud of black birds with yellow heads and white wing patches erupts from the marsh. The male yellow-headed blackbirds, joined by a few redwings, rush to the attack and the predator veers away across the uplands.

Noisy and conspicuous, always ready to defend his territorial rights, the yellowhead inhabits the reedy lakes and marshes that dot the valleys and plains of western North America.

In spring the males reach the breeding grounds first and stake out claims in tall aquatic vegetation well out from shore in several feet of water. They sometimes battle each other to decide territorial rights within a colony. When the females arrive a few days later, the males pursue them around the lake or bow their heads and spread their tails in courtship displays staged on reed perches (page 181).

The hardworking females – brownish birds with the yellow restricted to face, throat, and chest – handle all the nest building themselves. They use rotting vegetation retrieved from the water. Cleverly woven and lashed to growing reed stems, it forms a tight basket when dry. If the supporting plants grow unevenly, the nest tilts and the harried artisan must start again. Severe storms sometimes destroy the nest, and

mink, owls, marsh hawks, crows, red foxes, and muskrats prey on the eggs and young.

The female incubates the three or four eggs. These are grayish or greenish white heavily blotched with brown or gray. After they hatch, the mother also assumes most of the feeding chores. Within 12 days the hardy youngsters are learning to climb among the reeds. Eventually they become expert at alighting on the reed tips and balancing on the stems. Supported by their wings, they slide down to a firm foothold.

Their feet are large, with long, strong toes that help the birds walk on mud or floating vegetation. Yellowheads feed on aquatic insects among the cattails and sedges of marshy areas and fly to nearby uplands to devour beetles, grasshoppers, caterpillars, grain, and weed seeds.

No great musicians, the yellowheads sing a harsh jumble of notes ending in a rasping buzz. The songs are accompanied by twisting and writhing as if the birds were in agony.

As they prepare to withdraw from the northern portions of their range in late summer, the yellowheads wander over the plains country. Often the adult males congregate by themselves, the females and young moving in separate flocks.

Range: central British Columbia to N. W. Ohio, south to N. Baja California and N. W. Arkansas; winters to S. Mexico. *Characteristics:* male has yellow head and breast, black back, white wing patches. Female is smaller, has brown plumage, yellow throat and breast, white streaks on lower breast. Young resemble the female.

Tricolored Blackbird
Agelaius tricolor

AMONG THE MOST GREGARIOUS of North American birds, tricolored blackbirds breed in immense colonies through the great interior valleys of California. Singing their harsh, nasal *on-ke-kaaangh* song, they settle in streamside timber, rice fields, uncut alfalfa fields, and on tules and cattails fringing irrigation reservoirs. A single colony may hold as many as 200,000 nests.

The females, in streaked plumage, fasten the grass-lined nest of leaves to a cluster of reeds or branches. They also incubate the four greenish eggs spotted with brownish black. The adult males, black with scarlet shoulders, help feed the nestlings. In recent years scientists have found colonies nesting in spring and again in the fall, apparently stimulated by favorable feeding and climatic conditions.

Foraging in dense flocks, these blackbirds feed on beetles, caterpillars, weed seeds, and grain.

Range: S. Oregon to N. Baja California. *Characteristics:* male is glossy black with red wing patches edged in white. Female and young are sooty with light streaks.

Male yellowhead, Frederick Kent Truslow
Top inset: male (left) and female yellowheads, length 8-11″
Right: female and male tricolors, length 7½-9″; Allan Brooks

Red-winged Blackbird
Agelaius phoeniceus

UNDULATING LIKE A CLOUD of wind-whipped smoke, thousands of redwings descend on an Arkansas rice field. It is late summer, and the birds blacken the ground as they busily strip the ripening heads of grain. Irate farmers set off fireworks and other exploding devices. The flocks of black, red-shouldered males and brownish females reply with the thunder of their wings as they take off in search of undisturbed feeding grounds. The flock wheels and turns in unison, but the birds rise and fall independently, giving the whole a billowing effect.

Until the last fall harvests are in, this scene repeats itself not only in southern rice fields but among crops of corn and sorghum in the East and Middle West. New Jersey truck gardens also

suffer. In all, redwings—usually in company with grackles and cowbirds—inflict annual crop losses estimated at 20 to 30 million dollars. And the redwings are enjoying a population boom. They assemble at southern roosting sites in numbers that defy counting. The great winter blackbird roost in Virginia's Dismal Swamp held an estimated 15 million birds one recent year. And most of these were redwings.

Though locally destructive to crops, these birds compensate in many regions by eating quantities of such harmful insects as caterpillars, cankerworms, and beetles. The insect fare also includes mayflies and caddis flies seized in the wetlands during early summer.

When fields lie fallow after November, the great flocks scour the South and much of the West for weed seeds and waste grain in patches of stubble. Then the lengthening days of Febru-

Male redwing, length 7-9½"; Frederick Kent Truslow

ary impel the birds to start searching for nesting territory. As spring comes on, the sound of the redwing, the gurgling *ok-a-lee* so familiar to farm boys, is heard through the marshes.

Redwing breeding colonies flourish from Central America almost to the Arctic Circle – where thickets screen sluggish streams and cattails or tules stand densely in lake shallows. These birds breed as readily in the saw-grass wilderness of the Everglades as in the prairie sloughs of South Dakota, where they share the reeds with yellow-headed blackbirds.

Redwings nesting in the northern parts of the range arrive as spring migrants in three waves: old males, females, and first-year males. In the same order southern residents desert their winter quarters in fields and pastures for the nearest suitable marshy area. Male redwings establish a colony by staking out territorial claims. Bound-

Male (left), female, and (right) juvenile male redwings; Allan Brooks

ary disputes follow, with contestants flying at each other, epaulets blazing. Victors burst into song while parachuting gently to a perch. Often the folded wings conceal the red patches and only their yellow borders are seen.

When the females arrive they scatter quickly over the marshes, staying near the males but keeping out of sight among the sedges and cattails. Here they carve out their own nesting grounds, driving off intruders of the same sex.

With real estate needs satisfied, amorous females invade the territory of the nearest eligible male. If he is not ready for mating he drives the unwelcome visitors off his property. However,

a female set on raising a family accepts no rebuff. She keeps returning until the reluctant courtier accepts her attentions and permits her to stay. In courtship the perching male spreads his tail, ruffles his feathers, and half opens his wings. His gaudy shoulders flash in the sun as he sounds his gurgling song. In the reeds below lurks the brown female.

In a colony where the numbers of both sexes are approximately equal, red-winged blackbirds pair off and monogamy is the rule. But in many cases a surplus of females develops, and a male may have a harem of up to five females.

Last to reach the nesting colony are the outcasts of redwing society – the first-year males, dusky brown and showing signs of red on their shoulders. Capable of mating, they try their hand at courtship but are unsuccessful. The females shun them and the old males drive them off. Without territory they must wander for another year in bachelor flocks.

Though usually lashed to the stems of aquatic vegetation, redwing nests may be found on the ground, in waterside bushes, even well up in a tree. The female fashions the basket of rushes, filling in the chinks with peat or rotten wood. A lining of fine grasses cups the three to five bluish-green eggs spotted with brown and purple.

The male redwing does not help incubate, but he guards his breeding territory and boldly attacks crows and hawks that try to invade it.

Naked and blind when hatched, young red-winged blackbirds are ready to leave the nest ten days later. They become expert climbers and swimmers before they can fly.

With a host of enemies – including mink, foxes, weasels, water snakes, as well as avian predators – half the fledglings do not survive. But the species is prolific; two and sometimes three broods a year are not unusual.

In July, after the young of the second brood are strong on the wing, the redwings gather in flocks – the females and young in one, the males in another. The flocks forage in the uplands by day and return to roost in the marshes at night. After the August molt the redwings emerge from the wetlands to roam open country once more. Many of them remain in the north; others head for warmer regions and join the great congregations of southern redwings in winter quarters.

Scientists have divided this widespread species into 14 subspecies. In one, the bicolored redwing of California, the male has red epaulets without yellow edges.

Range: S. Yukon to Nova Scotia, south to Costa Rica, Cuba, and the Bahamas; migratory in the north. *Characteristics:* male is black with red epaulets bordered in yellow or buff. Female and young are brown with streaked underparts. Young male has mottled epaulets.

Baltimore Oriole

Icterus galbula

AMERICAN COLONISTS in the 17th century marveled at a brilliant orange-and-black bird. The "fiery hang-nest," they called it. Some noted that the male wore the family colors of the Lords Baltimore, colonizers of Maryland, and named him the "Baltimore-bird." Today this wide-ranging species is Maryland's state bird, known to all as the Baltimore oriole.

Old males arrive at their breeding grounds first, well after winter's final retreat. They settle into apple orchards in full bloom, at the edges of open deciduous woodlands, and in trees bordering streams and roads. To pioneer ornithologist Thomas Nuttall they seemed "like living gems intended to decorate the verdant garment of the new-clad forest."

Each bird announces his territorial claims from a chosen treetop. Ornithologist Alexander Wilson heard in these rich, piping notes "the pleasing tranquillity of a careless ploughboy, whistling merely for his own amusement." Henry Thoreau heard the oriole's whistle as "Eat it, Potter, eat it!" But the song is highly variable; no two orioles, it seems, produce identical tunes.

The females appear a few days after the males, who now have an opportunity to display their finery as well as their vocal talents. Lady Baltimore wears pleasing attire – saffron-olive on her back, yellow-orange on her breast, with perhaps some black about her head – but her prospective lord holds the center of the stage.

He perches near her, stretches to full height, then begins a series of low bows. His jerky movements impart a blinker effect; the female glimpses the flaming orange breast, then the black head and back, and once again the flash of orange, this time on the rump. All the while the male beguiles her with low, sweet whistles.

Soon after courtship the female begins planning her home. In New England, elms and breeding orioles seem to go together; the trees may border a hayfield or shade the streets of a village. Poplars, maples, old orchard trees, and conifers also serve as nest sites. In Minnesota, orioles favor the white birch.

A superb artisan, perhaps the most skillful among North American birds, the female usually locates her nest near the end of a drooping bough. It may be as high as 60 feet above ground. Hanging upside down much of the time, she twines long strips of plant fiber around the twigs. Her bill thrusts and pulls in rapid shuttle movements as she weaves the dangling mass together.

Before the age of the automobile, nests made largely of horsehair were common. In rural areas today the oriole uses dry plant fibers, Indian hemp, silk of milkweed, and grapevine bark.

Around towns she makes do with yarn, string, paper, or cloth; sometimes bird lovers put out a supply of such material. In Louisiana the bird collects Spanish moss for her hanging cradle.

After about three days the framework nears completion. Wings spread for balance, each foot on a separate limb, the oriole now starts working on the interior of the nest. She gathers the remaining loose strands and brings in another twig for support. Then she finishes the project by weaving in some more fibers.

The result is an exquisitely interlaced pocket from three to eight inches deep, usually open at the top. Occasionally a hole is left to serve as a side entrance.

Firmly attached by the rim to a fork, the nest sways safely in the stiffest breeze. The oriole weaves a new nest each year but may use a favored tree as a nest site again and again. This becomes evident in fall when several nests stretch from bare branches like pennants in a gale.

The female Baltimore oriole also undertakes incubation alone. Her four to six whitish eggs with brown tracings rest on a luxurious bedding of hair, wool, or fine grasses. Meanwhile the male continues to sing and even entices a few notes from his busy mate. He remains zealously on guard against interlopers. Like a wrathful flame he dives at squirrels, jays, and other intruders, driving them into retreat.

Both parents devote their energies to stuffing the nestlings with soft insect parts. The young at first remain quiet in their pouch nursery. But as flight time nears, they advertise their presence with petulant cries of *tee-deedee*. Crows and screech owls may follow the sounds and carry the nestlings off.

AFTER THE NESTING SEASON females and juveniles retire to thickets and woodland edges in search of ripening berries. Males become quiet and seem to disappear for a couple of months in the crown foliage of tall trees. In August they reappear, ready for the fall migration. They sing at dawn with the exuberance of spring.

Baltimore orioles feed heavily on caterpillars, often destroying whole infestations of the tent variety. They also eat beetles, ants, and parasitic wasps. Pairs of orioles explore a tree leaf by leaf, communicating at each discovery. On occasion these birds take nectar from the flowers of the trumpet creeper and rip open stingless male carpenter bees to extract their honey.

Range: central Alberta to Nova Scotia, south to N. E. Texas and N. Georgia; winters S. Mexico to N. South America. *Characteristics:* male has orange breast, rump, and tail corners; black head, wings, tail; white-edged wing feathers. Female (page 24) and young have orange-olive upperparts, yellow-orange underparts, white wing bars.

AGLOW WITH COLOR, *Lord Baltimore guards his hanging home in a Michigan apple tree.*
Male Baltimore oriole, length 7-8"; Eliot Porter

Black-headed Oriole
Icterus graduacauda

SCREENED FROM VIEW by dense thickets, a pair of black-headed orioles restlessly search for insects and hackberries. Year-round companions, they forage close to the ground and stay in the shade of trees while flying rapidly to another copse. In the underbrush of the lower Rio Grande Valley these shy birds, also known as Audubon's orioles, are hard to find despite their showy yellow backs and bellies.

They whistle a soft, sweet, halting song. The phrases may call to mind a young boy learning to whistle. These orioles are never very generous with their music, however, and are not often heard above the clamor of jays and flycatchers.

Blackheads attach their semipensile grass nest to the foliage of a shrub or low tree. The four bluish or grayish-white eggs are finely marked with brown and purple.

The cowbird frequently parasitizes the blackheads by laying eggs in their nest.

Range: S. Texas to Guatemala. *Characteristics:* black head, wings, and tail, wing feathers edged with white, yellow back and underparts.

Blackhead, length 8-9¼"
Allan Brooks

Female (upper) and juvenile male orchards
Allan Brooks

Orchard Oriole
Icterus spurius

FROM THE LEAFY SHELTER of shade trees or blooming orchards comes a rapid burst of song — whistles and harsh notes ending in *what-cheeer*. The singer is usually hidden, but sometimes sunlight catches the rich chestnut of rump and belly, identifying him as a male orchard oriole. His mate, attired in olive and yellow, is even more inconspicuous behind the screen of foliage.

An early observer of the species apparently mistook a female Baltimore for a male orchard oriole, and the orchard was known for a time as the spurious, or bastard, Baltimore.

Shunning the forests, orchard orioles usually breed near human dwellings. Mated birds weave a nest of grass, lashing it to tree limbs. The cup holds the four or five bluish eggs scrawled with brown and lavender. These birds seem to like eastern kingbirds as neighbors and may gain some protection from the kingbirds' aggressiveness in driving off nest marauders.

Orchard orioles feed on insects, mulberries, cherries, and other small fruit.

Range: S. Manitoba to N. E. Massachusetts, south to central Mexico and N. Florida; winters from S. Mexico to N. South America. *Characteristics:* male has black head, wings, and tail; chestnut rump and underparts, wing feathers edged with white. Female has olive head and back, yellow underparts, white wing bars. Young resemble the female; yearling male has black bib.

Male orchard oriole, length 6-7⅓"; Thase Daniel

Hooded Oriole
Icterus cucullatus

LIKE A WAYWARD FLAME, the bird with the bright orange cowl, or *cucullus*, flits through the foliage of a fan palm, the shrubbery of a desert watercourse, or among the blooms of an exotic garden in the Southwest. Restless, ever on the move but usually quiet, the striking male hooded oriole makes his way close to the ground.

Despite his shyness he frequently approaches human habitations, especially in California where he has extended his range with the spread of ornamental plantings. He probes the blossoms of aloes, lilies, agaves, and other tubular flowers for nectar and insects and responds readily to offerings of sugar syrup.

Sometimes he sings from the treetops, a medley of throaty notes interspersed with whistles: *chut chut chut whew whew.*

His flight is strong and swift, but when foraging for food he seldom uses his wings. Climbing through the shrubbery, he hangs upside down, chickadee fashion, to peer under leaves for caterpillars. He picks insect larvae from bark crevices and occasionally eats fruit.

During courtship in April several males may scold and fight each other while chasing a female. With the field to himself the winning male bows ceremonially to his prospective mate dressed in olive and yellow. She responds with a soft song while hopping around him among the branches.

A master at basket weaving, the female fashions her cradle in the foliage of cottonwoods, cypresses, sycamores, and mesquite,

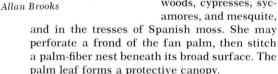

Female hooded oriole
Allan Brooks

and in the tresses of Spanish moss. She may perforate a frond of the fan palm, then stitch a palm-fiber nest beneath its broad surface. The palm leaf forms a protective canopy.

The female incubates the three to five dull white eggs marked with brown, purple, and gray. She may raise two or even three broods a season and build a new nest for each.

Lichtenstein's oriole (*Icterus gularis*), a similar but larger species, may wander into Texas from Mexico. The sexes are alike.

Range: central California to S. Texas, south to S. Mexico; winters mainly in Mexico. *Characteristics:* male has orange hood, belly, and rump; black throat, wings, and tail; wing feathers edged with white. Female has olive head and back, yellow belly, white wing bars. Young resemble the female; yearling male has black throat.

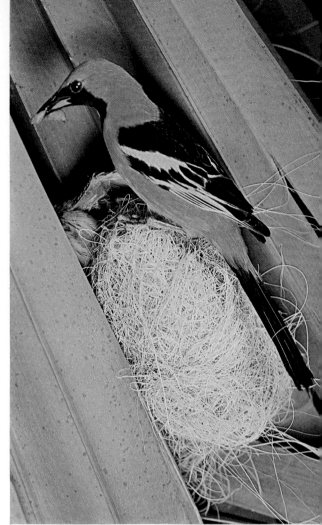

Male hooded, length 7-7¾"; Eliot Porter

Spotted-breasted Oriole
Icterus pectoralis
(Picture on page 292)

THIS MYSTERIOUS orange-and-black immigrant from tropical America brightens trees and gardens around Miami, Florida. No one knows for sure how the spotted-breasted oriole became a resident of the United States. Some were brought to Florida as cage birds and may have escaped.

First reported around Miami in 1949, *pectoralis* seems to be expanding his range. He has even become a bit of a nuisance, snipping off hibiscus blossoms to get at the nectar. But his good looks and delightful melody have won him friends.

Mated birds, alike in plumage, nest in a cup woven from palm fibers. The three or four eggs are heavily blotched with brown.

Range: S. Florida, and from S. Mexico to Costa Rica. *Characteristics:* orange crown and underparts, black throat, wings, and back; black spots at sides of breast, white wing patches. Young lack the breast spots.

Female Bullock's (left) and juvenile male, Allan Brooks   *Male Bullock's, length 7-8½"; Eliot Porter*

Scott's Oriole
Icterus parisorum

SINGING A CLEAR, whistled melody like that of the western meadowlark, Scott's oriole roams the foothills and dry plains of the Southwest.

The male cuts a striking figure in black and deep lemon yellow as he forages among the yuccas. He dines on nectar, insects, and some fruits.

Under the yucca leaves his olive-backed mate weaves a grassy pouch for the three bluish eggs streaked with black, gray, or brown.

Range: S. E. California to W. Texas, south to N. Mexico; winters to S. Mexico. *Characteristics:* male has black head, breast, back, wings, and tail; wing feathers edged with white; lemon-yellow belly and rump. Female and young have mottled olive back, yellow underparts, white wing bars; young male has black throat.

310

Male (left) and female Scott's, length 7¼-8¼"
Allan Brooks

Bullock's Oriole
Icterus bullockii

A FORAGING MAGPIE alights in a cottonwood, attracted by the calls of hungry nestlings. Out of the foliage darts a fiery orange-and-black bird to peck furiously at the intruder's head. As the magpie flees, the male Bullock's oriole returns to his vigil, his offspring safe for the moment.

Soon the female oriole, less striking in her olive, white, and yellowish plumage, arrives with a bill full of insects to satisfy the babies' hunger.

The Bullock's, most widespread oriole in the west, hybridizes with the Baltimore oriole on the Great Plains. The western species favors wooded river valleys, farmland, and lower mountain slopes. His chattering and piping are often heard high in the cottonwoods and sycamores, but he may nest in the lower branches or in a shrub or clump of mistletoe.

The female weaves the hanging nursery from vegetable fibers, bark, and horsehair, then lines it with wool and other soft materials. She builds so skillfully that her nest sometimes survives the winds and storms of several winters. She also incubates the four or five grayish eggs scrawled with black and brown.

Like other orioles, the Bullock's probes flowers for nectar. It eats insects, especially caterpillars, and in summer adds fruit to its diet.

Range: S. British Columbia to S. Saskatchewan and central South Dakota, south to central Mexico; winters to Costa Rica. *Characteristics:* male has black crown, eye stripes, back, and tail; white wing patches; orange cheeks, underparts, rump, and base of tail. Female and young have olive-gray head and back, yellow breast, white belly and wing bars; young male has black throat.

Rusty Blackbird
Euphagus carolinus

A FLOCK OF BLACKBIRDS walks sedately along the shores of a woodland pond in early spring, each member nodding its head. The males are black, the females slaty. The rusty feather edgings of fall that give these blackbirds their name have worn off during the winter.

Frightened by an intruder, the birds rise in a dense black cloud and fly off, the rippling mass rolling through the sky like a dark wave. Alighting in a distant grove, the birds face into the wind and almost immediately begin a "concert" of gurgles and squeaks.

Some may venture to the tree limit in Alaska and Canada. The flocks break up and solitary pairs nest in evergreens near a lake, bog, or stream. They build a cradle of moss, twigs, rotting vegetation, and grass. The four or five eggs, bluish green blotched with brown, hatch in 14 days.

Ground feeders, these birds eat insects, weed seeds, grain, and some fruit.

Range: N. Alaska to Newfoundland, south to central British Columbia and central Maine; winters to central Colorado and Gulf Coast. *Characteristics:* yellow eyes; winter plumage is rusty with barred breast. In spring male is black, female slate-colored.

Brewer's Blackbird
Euphagus cyanocephalus

ABUNDANT AND ADAPTABLE, Brewer's blackbirds have prospered with settlement of the West. In noisy flocks they forage across lawns, golf courses, and city parks, on irrigated pastures and freshly plowed cropland. Yet their harsh, squeaky notes are still heard along lonely Pacific beaches and in the mountain wilderness.

In contrast to the grayish female the male Brewer's is solid black. In strong light his iridescent feathers reflect purple tints about the head, green about the body.

These blackbirds flip over stones and chips of dried dung to get at the insects beneath. They also devour great quantities of Mormon crickets and some berries and waste grain.

In spring the birds pair off to nest in small colonies in trees or shrubs near water. In some regions the homesite is on the ground. The nest of twigs and grasses holds the three to six grayish eggs splotched with brown. The female incubates them about two weeks.

Range: British Columbia to Wisconsin, south to N. Baja California, N. Texas, and S. W. Michigan; winters to central Mexico and W. Florida. *Characteristics:* male is iridescent black with whitish eyes; female is grayish with brown eyes.

Allan Brooks

Brewer's blackbirds
male (right) and female, 8-10"

Rusty blackbirds
male (left) and female, 8½-9¾"

Female rusty
in winter plumage

Boat-tailed Grackle
Cassidix mexicanus

THE ENORMOUS keel-shaped tail that takes up half the bird's length would alone suffice to make this grackle conspicuous along the tidal marshes of the Atlantic and Gulf coasts and in the irrigated regions of the Southwest.

But the boat-tailed grackle, called "jackdaw" in the South, is also one of the noisiest birds in his range. He assaults the ear with a cacophony of rattles, grunts, groans, shrieks, yodels, and clacks. Occasionally he surprises listeners with a pleasant tinkling phrase.

The female is quieter, much smaller, and wears brown plumage unlike the gleaming black of the male. After settling into a breeding colony in rushes, shrubbery, or trees, she builds a nest of mud, sticks, and grass. While her mate roams the countryside pilfering and squalling, she incubates her eggs and rears the young. The three to five bluish eggs are spotted and scrawled with purplish-brown and black.

This grackle feeds on grain, berries, insects, and small lizards. He forages extensively near water and may wade in up to his breast to seize aquatic insects, shrimp, and minnows. On the ground he struts about with tail held high and a waddling gait. Sometimes a stiff gust catches the huge tail broadside and swings the bird completely around.

Boattails of Latin America and the Southwest range farther inland than do those of the eastern United States. Where the two forms meet along the Gulf Coast they do not interbreed, even in the same breeding colony. Hence some scientists regard them as two distinct species.

Range: S. Arizona to Florida, and up the Atlantic Coast to S. New Jersey, south to N. South America. *Characteristics:* long keel-shaped tail. Male has iridescent black plumage. Female is brown and much smaller; young resemble the female until the fall molt.

Common Grackle
Quiscalus quiscula

THE HANDSOME common grackle struts about a yard as if he owned it. When the sun hits his sleek black coat from different angles, the feathers gleam with wonderful iridescent hues.

These colors vary among subspecies. Across Canada and between the Rockies and the Alleghenies in the United States this grackle has a bronzy back. Another race that ranges generally east of the Alleghenies reflects purplish tints. Where the two meet and interbreed, hybrid offspring may show broken iridescent bars on their backs. A third form which inhabits the Southeast sports greenish highlights.

Wherever found, the grackle has yellow eyes and a long wedge-shaped tail which in flight looks like an airborne boat keel.

Large flocks of these grackles, widely known as crow blackbirds, roost in trees of city parks. Here they litter walks and raise a commotion with their rasping metallic chatter dubbed the "wheelbarrow chorus."

But the farmer, not the city dweller, complains most about common grackles. The birds sometimes swoop down in great black clouds on ripening cornfields, tear back the husks with their strong beaks, and devour the kernels. They feast at corncribs and damage other grains. They also eat small acorns but don't hammer them open with their bills the way jays do. Grackles grip the nut between their mandibles and crack it with the help of a ridge on the palate.

They gorge on crop-destroying insects and consume field mice. They stalk the shallows of a marsh or pond to snack on crawfish, minnows, or small frogs. They invade the nests of other birds

Male boattail, length 16-17"; Frederick Kent Truslow
Inset: female, length 12-13"; Allan Brooks

STRIPPING BACK THE HUSKS, *a bronzed (at left) and a purple grackle, two forms of the common grackle, feast on kernels in an eastern cornfield. A special "tooth" on the palate helps them shear through small acorns (below).*

Length 11-13½", Walter A. Weber
National Geographic staff artist

and eat the eggs and young. When other food is scarce, not even the adults of small species such as sparrows are safe from the grackle.

Grackles nest in colonies of from a dozen to a hundred pairs. They place their bulky platforms of dried grasses and weed stems in pine, cedar, and a variety of other trees. Some birds build in marsh reeds; others boldly set up housekeeping in the crevices of osprey nests and even steal food from their fierce hosts.

The four or five greenish or rusty eggs, handsomely scrawled with dark brown, hatch in about two weeks. Nestlings remain in the nursery for another 12 or 14 days. Their father guards them devotedly; his alarm note may bring the entire colony to the scene.

Range: N. E. British Columbia to N. Nova Scotia, south (east of the Rockies) to S. Texas and S. Florida; migratory in the north. *Characteristics:* large size, iridescent black plumage reflecting purple, bronze, or green; yellow eyes, long wedge-shaped tail. Female is smaller, less iridescent. Young are brown until the fall molt.

Brown-headed Cowbird
Molothrus ater

SCIENCE APTLY NAMES the brown-headed cowbird *Molothrus ater* — dark, greedy beggar. This parasite builds no home of its own. Instead the female reconnoiters her breeding territory, lurks about another bird's nest until the owner leaves, steals in, throws an egg out if there's one already there, lays one of her own, and takes off (page 296). Incubating the brown-specked white egg and rearing the nestling is none of *her* business. Let the host do it.

About half the host species do it. They raise the orphaned youngster as devotedly as they do their own. Of the other half, some species throw the strange egg out. Others bury it under a new nest lining and lay their own on an upper story. Still others desert their home.

Dr. Herbert Friedmann, who has long studied the ways of cowbirds, has compiled a list of 206 species victimized by the brownhead. Vireos, warblers, sparrows, and flycatchers suffer most.

The eggs hatch in 11 to 14 days, usually before the host's eggs. Larger than their nestmates, young brownheads often elbow the others aside in the quest for food. Sometimes the host's offspring are crowded out of their home.

The cowbird also deserves its common name. Flocks of glossy black, brown-headed males and gray females follow herds of cattle. They snatch insects stirred up by hoofs and alight on the backs of the animals to pick off ticks and other pests. They also feed on grain and wild fruit.

In the 1860's cowbirds accompanied Texas longhorns up the Chisholm Trail to Kansas; when

Male brownhead, length 6-8"
Allan D. Cruickshank, National Audubon Society

they followed the buffalo herds that once roamed the plains they were known as buffalo birds.

In late summer newly fledged cowbirds rejoin their kind in wandering flocks. By this time the brownheads have largely stopped singing their squeaky *weee-titi*. Most of them leave the northernmost breeding areas for the winter.

Range: central British Columbia to S. Nova Scotia, south to N. Mexico and South Carolina; winters to S. Mexico and S. Florida. *Characteristics:* small size, short bill. Male has brown head, iridescent black body. Female is gray. Until late summer young have olive-brown back, buffy throat, streaked whitish breast.

Female brownhead, B. H. Christenson, National Audubon Society

Bronzed Cowbird
Tangavius aeneus

IN A MIXED FLOCK of blackbirds along the Mexican border the bronzed cowbird can be singled out by the ruff of feathers on the nape that gives the bird a top-heavy look. At close range the blood-red eyes, bronzy back, and purplish wings and tail also help identify this parasite, sometimes called the red-eyed cowbird.

The bird roves croplands and pastures to dine on weed seeds and grain. Following grazing horses and cattle, it snatches insects from about their heads and backs.

The male does all the singing, a series of high-pitched, creaking notes. In spring courtship he struts before a prospective mate showing off his plumage and puffing out his neck ruff. He bows, bounces up and down, and may even flutter several feet off the ground.

Investigators have found the blue-green eggs of the bronzed cowbird in the nests of 52 species. Principal victims are blackbirds, orioles, and finches. Few of the legitimate nestlings survive,

Male bronzed, length 6½-8¾"
Allan Brooks

but the young cowbirds double their weight on the second day after hatching. They leave the nest at the age of 11 days, and their foster parents feed them about two weeks longer.

Range: central Arizona to central Texas, south to Panama. *Characteristics:* red eyes, black body with bronze hues on back and purple on wings and tail; neck ruff. Female is smaller and duller.

315

PARAGONS OF BRILLIANT DRESS The Tanagers
Family Thraupidae

LIKE SPRING MASQUERADERS, migrating tanagers bring a touch of Latin color to North America. Flecking the treetops with reds and blacks and yellows and greens, these bright and beautiful birds seem garbed more for the tropics than for northern landscapes. Named by the Tupi Indians of the Amazon region, who called them *tangará*, the tanagers are indeed warm-weather birds. All the Thraupidae — some 220 species — live in the New World, and most dwell in the humid forests of Central and South America. Only four species breed north of the Mexican border; even these wing south in fall toward their ancestral home in the tropics.

Given a spell of rainy, foggy April weather along the Gulf Coast, scarlet and summer tanagers will swarm into town parks and gardens and patches of woods. Buffeted by north winds as they cross the Gulf of Mexico, these migrants alight here to rest. Then on the first fair night they fly inland — the scarlet tanagers to scatter chiefly through the northern and eastern states and on into Canada, the summer tanagers to spread through the southern states. Coming overland from Mexico, the

western tanagers range from Texas all the way to Alaska, while the hepatic tanagers nest no farther north than Arizona and New Mexico.

Despite the resplendent plumage of the males, our tanagers usually remain unseen in the forests where they breed. For these are birds of the shadows, seldom venturing from their cloisters in the tree crowns where foliage screens them from the eyes of hawks and humans. Even the voices of tanagers serve to cloak their identity; their cheerful songs are often confused with those of robins and grosbeaks.

Insects are the tanagers' favorite food. With rather stubby, conical bills, notched at the cutting edge, they poke about under leaves for crawlers and probe the bark for borers. Like the vireos, tanagers are placid and observant feeders; they hop languidly from one perch to the next, ridding the trees of large quantities of harmful insects and larvae. But on occasion they move with great speed. They will dart out to snatch a fly in midair. And one observer saw a tanager drop a berry from its bill and recover it before it had fallen eight inches.

During the breeding season the male's behavior is as lordly as his plumage. The olive-and-yellow female must often build the nest without his help. And she alone tends the freckled, bluish-green eggs. The lustrous father keeps away during the 12 to 14 days of incubation, presumably so he won't draw predators to the nest, which is well concealed on a horizontal limb 10 to 60 feet from the ground. But when he spies the red mouths of his gaping brood, he returns to help his mate stuff them with insects and regurgitated food.

Sparsely covered with down at birth, the nestlings soon acquire plumage similar to their mother's. In two weeks they fledge. But another year must pass before the young males flit through these woods in the flaming dress of their fathers.

MALE SCARLET TANAGER *returns to the rickety nest with an insect for his downy young. Virginia student (above) examines a scarlet tanager netted and banded by his nature class.*

317

Male (left) and female
Allan Brooks

♪♫ Scarlet Tanager
Piranga olivacea

IT'S MAYTIME and from somewhere in the cool, dark oak canopy of a New England forest comes a hoarse, buzzing song: *querit, queer, queery, querit, queer.*

A robin? No, not lilting enough.

Where does the song come from? Far away, it seems. But no—the little ventriloquist is hidden in the foliage overhead. The experienced bird watcher locates him by walking past the sound and then returning to it.

Now the uppermost leaves are trembling. With a hop from shade to sunlight the singer appears —a fireball with sable wings and tail!

One of the most dramatic birds in North America, the male scarlet tanager seems to illuminate the foliage when the sun strikes the red pigment of his contour feathers. But the "firebird" is as shy as he is radiant—a recluse of the well-leafed treetops. He sounds his call, *chip-burr,* and disappears. No wonder a glimpse of him thrills even a veteran ornithologist.

Dr. Elliott Coues, a pioneer of the science, saw a scarlet tanager when he was a child and the experience had a great effect on him: "I hold this bird in particular, almost superstitious, recollection, as the very first of all the feathered tribe to stir within me those emotions that have never ceased to stimulate and gratify my love for birds."

The female scarlet tanager is not scarlet at all; her head, back, and tail are greenish, her wings dusky, her underparts yellowish. Thus it is not surprising that she often goes unnoticed. But the brilliant male remains almost equally inconspicuous because of his retiring ways. In fact, in many parts of its breeding range in the eastern United States and Canada this abundant bird is considered rare.

He arrives from his tropical wintering grounds during the height of spring migration when res-ident birds and migrants of many species are filling the woods. Lost in the crowd, the tanager makes a discreet entrance and heads for his favorite haunts in the treetops, where the leaves are growing fast. He generally stays there. He moves about with deliberation, stalking moths and caterpillars among the high branches, picking beetles off the leaves and bark. Even in the sheltering foliage he seems afraid to give himself away by making a sudden motion.

The tanager also eats berries and other small fruit, but insects comprise the major part of his diet. And though he hunts them almost lethargically, he eats them at an amazing rate. Ornithologist Edward Howe Forbush watched two scarlet tanagers in an apple orchard eat caterpillars of the gypsy moth for 18 minutes at the rate of 35 a minute. He calculated that if they kept up this pace for only an hour a day, they would consume 14,700 caterpillars a week—a great boon to the fruit trees.

In the oak forests that tanagers frequent, this appetite works wonders for tree conservation. The little bird feasts on literally hundreds of species of harmful insects.

Heavy spring rains, prolonged enough to flush insects off the foliage of trees and shrubs, will force scarlet tanagers to search out their meals on the ground. This is one of the few times they forsake their arboreal retreats.

In courting season the male goes about with red plumage fluffed, tail cocked, and wings adroop. Though he lacks any formal ritual, the female acknowledges his display with a husky whistle, *whee* or *puwee.*

In a saucer of twigs, stems, and rootlets, lined with grasses and pine needles, she lays three or four bluish-green eggs speckled with auburn. Placed well out on the limb of an oak, beech, or hemlock and as high as 45 feet above the ground, the nest is likely to be so loosely made that a person standing below can see through it.

The eggs hatch in about two weeks. In juvenile plumage the young birds resemble their mother. Scarlet tanagers are often victimized by the parasitic cowbird.

Beginning in midsummer the female becomes brighter on her upperparts and more orange-yellow below. At the same time the male grows duller, gradually exchanging his red coat for the olive-yellow colors of the female and adding new green-tinged black feathers in wings and tail. While this molt is in process, he is splotched with red, green-yellow, and black.

Range: S. E. Manitoba to New Brunswick, south to S. E. Oklahoma and N. W. South Carolina; winters in N. South America. *Characteristics:* male is scarlet with black wings and tail; female, immature, and winter male are dull green above with yellowish underparts, dusky wings.

SCARLET TANAGER *in nuptial array guards his squalling brood in a Michigan oak tree.*
Male, length 6½-7½"; Eliot Porter

Summer Tanager
Piranga rubra

AN ANGRY HUM and occasional crimson flashes in the top of a southern pine proclaim that the male summer tanager is hunting wasps. He takes several—breaking their stingers off against a limb—before the swarm leaves to their attacker the nest of juicy white larvae.

This rose-red bird (page 14) and his olive-and-yellow consort come up from the tropics each April to settle in open dry woods from California to the Atlantic Coast states.

In stands of oak, pine, hickory, and willow he sounds staccato *pi-tuck* calls and robinlike songs and in the unhurried tanager way consumes a little fruit and a lot of insects. Bees are a favorite food, so he can be the bane of beekeepers.

This tanager builds a shallow cup of bark, stalks, leaves, and grass 10 to 15 feet up in a tree. From the four dark-spotted blue or green eggs the young hatch in about 12 days, and both parents feed them. When grown, the males are often called summer redbirds. They resemble the male cardinal but lack his crest and black face.

Range: S. E. California to Delaware, south to central Mexico and S. Florida; winters from central Mexico to Bolivia. *Characteristics:* male is red; female and young have olive upperparts, yellow underparts. Immature male may show combinations of red and olive.

Western Tanager
Piranga ludoviciana

HIS RED HEAD and black-and-yellow body set off the male western tanager as one of the most colorful birds in the Rocky Mountain region. Daubing bold strokes on summer's canvas as he rockets straight up to snatch a flying insect or plunders an irate farmer's orchard, he is even more striking than his lustrous eastern relatives. And he is notably less shy.

A. Dawes Du Bois told of standing beside a Montana spring while a baby tanager bathed at his feet. The mother bird called warnings from a limb three feet away, but the little one paid no heed, looked the ornithologist over, bathed again, then sat and preened its feathers. When its father came, he showed no fear, even hopping between the observer's feet.

Despite occasional bold ventures, the western tanager generally stays in the sheltering canopy

Female summer tanager, length 7-7¾"
Karl Maslowski, Photo Researchers

Male western, length 6¼-7½"; Eliot Porter

of the mountain forest, ranging up to 10,000 feet. There amid the pines, oaks, and firs he sings his rough, robinlike song, repeats a *pi-tic* or *pit-i-tic* call, and hunts. Sometimes his insect hunting is aerobatic. More often it is a deliberate leaf-by-leaf search for wasps, ants, stinkbugs, caterpillars, and grasshoppers.

When berries begin to ripen, the bird ventures into the open to feed on them. About a fifth of his diet is fruit. The raids that bring him into disfavor with California cherry growers generally occur when the spring migration is unusually large and the birds leave their normal foothill routes. In partial compensation tanagers destroy many harmful insects.

Nest building begins the last of May and is the task of the better camouflaged female, who resembles the female summer tanager but has wing bars. Well out on a limb 10 to 65 feet up she braids a tureen of twigs, pine needles, and moss. Lined with rootlets and hair, it cups her three to five bluish, brown-speckled eggs.

During the 13-day incubation the radiant male rarely visits the nest. Afterward he works hard to appease the hatchlings' appetite for insects. *Range:* S. Alaska to central Saskatchewan, south to N. Baja California and W. Texas; winters from S. Baja California to Costa Rica. *Characteristics:* only tanager with wing bars. Breeding male is yellow with red head (the red fades in fall), black back, wings, and tail. Female has dull green head and back, yellow underparts. Young resemble the female.

Hepatic Tanager
Piranga flava

DURING CAPT. LORENZO SITGREAVES's exploration of the Southwest in 1854, the expedition naturalist, Dr. S. W. Woodhouse, often roamed away from camp. One day in the pines flanking the San Francisco peaks of Arizona he spied a brick-red bird with ash-brown upperparts. This was the first of the hepatic, or liver-colored, species reported in the United States. It had been considered a Mexican bird since its discovery there nearly 30 years before.

Both the red male and his dusky-and-yellow mate have dark ear patches and blackish bills. In parts of Arizona, New Mexico, and Texas these features help distinguish the male hepatic from the summer tanager and the female from the summer and the western tanagers.

In the deep shade of a forested mountain canyon the hepatic's song rings clearly from the tall trees—a warble like that of the black-headed grosbeak but less varied. He sounds his terse call: *chuck!* Then a pause, and he calls again.

High in the pines, firs, sycamores, and oaks the hepatic stalks his insect prey. Like the other tanagers, he tends to plod at foraging. But now and then he abandons his search of the leaves to whisk out and pluck a morsel on the wing. Come autumn, he often turns to wild cherries and grapes on the canyon slopes.

In the fork of a limb, perhaps 50 feet high, the hepatic tanager weaves a saucer of grass, weed stems, and flower stalks. Blossoms may adorn the nest. On a lining of fine grass rest the three to five bluish eggs marked with brown or often liver-colored spots.

Range: N. Arizona to S. Texas, south to Brazil; migrates in northern parts of range. *Characteristics:* blackish bill, dark ear patch. Male is dull red. Female has dusky upperparts, yellow underparts. Young resemble female; streaked breast.

Male (left) and female hepatics length 7½-8", Allan Brooks

THICK-BILLED SEEDEATERS

Cardinals, Grosbeaks, and Finches

Family Fringillidae, Part 1

By ARTHUR A. ALLEN

I WELL REMEMBER the first cardinal that came to Ithaca, New York. His cheerful whistle awakened me early one February morning in 1914. He had discovered the feeding log in my garden. His brilliant crest and fiery red bill thrilled me as I watched him busily shucking sunflower seeds among the juncos and white-throated sparrows. A pioneer from the South, he had pushed through snow and storm to help establish a new breeding ground for his kind.

I had no inkling of how common cardinals would become here in the next 50 years. Today central New York enjoys these birds the year round, and the flash of red against sparkling snow is a familiar sight.

The year 1914 was notable for another ornithological event – a visitation of evening grosbeaks. Every seventh year, it was said, we could expect a flight of these beautiful yellow-hued birds from the Northwest. Now they populate the north woods all the way to Massachusetts, but in those days they were rare visitors. Perhaps no cardinal had ever seen an evening grosbeak. So, with the coming of the cardinal, I contemplated photographing these two thick-billed birds together, uniting North and South in a most unusual picture.

Day after day I waited at the kitchen window. A cord at my hand stretched outside to my camera, which was focused on the feeding log. Finally came the day when I saw the cardinal on the log and at the same time heard grosbeaks calling in the branches overhead. Closer and closer came the grosbeaks. At last one of the males dropped to the feeder. Side by side gleamed glorious gold and brilliant red. What a picture! I yanked the cord to release the shutter. At the same instant the cardinal darted at the grosbeak and knocked him off the log. The photograph was largely a blur, but I still cherish it as a memento of that thrilling meeting.

The cardinal undoubtedly ranks as the favorite North American representative of the Fringillidae, which constitute one of the largest families of birds. The 426 species are distributed in practically all parts of the world except the Australian and Antarctic regions, and 79 of them breed in the United States and Canada.

Most of the North American members are small, dull-colored birds – the sparrows, towhees, juncos, buntings, and longspurs. They comprise the cast of characters for Part 2 of the Fringillidae, beginning on page 346. This chapter deals mainly with the more colorful species – the cardinal, pyrrhuloxia, grosbeaks, finches, crossbills, and those incredible painted and indigo buntings.

A male indigo bunting in his flashing blue breeding plumage is indeed hard to believe. One spring day I pointed out such a bird to a group of students on one of our field trips. He sat on a power line warbling his unmistakable song: *sweet, sweet – where, where – here, here – see it, see it*. But he was definitely black. Not one of the students believed this bird really was blue. To no avail I explained that blue as a pigment does not exist in bird plumage; that it is a structural color visible only when reflected at certain angles. A few minutes later the bunting flew down to

SNAP! *Viselike mandibles crack a seed, staff of life to the cardinal.*
Like many other male seedeaters, he wears bright colors all year.

322

Frederick Kent Truslow

a patch of dandelions on the lawn. The sunlight struck him just right. Never was a bird more blue, varying from intense indigo on his head and back to almost sky blue on his chest. Our little black bird was transformed before our eyes!

Later in the season we found his nest—or perhaps I should say *her* nest, since the male seemed to have nothing to do with it. Never did we see him carry food to the female while she was incubating. Never did we see him bring food to the nestlings. Not until the young left the nest did he show any interest in them, but then he made up for lost time. An insect in his bill, he would hover over the youngsters. Sometimes their enthusiasm for the food carried them right off the perch.

Cardinals, grosbeaks, and finches all make open, cup-shaped nests. Goldfinches use cottony materials and fibers in theirs and line them with thistledown. Indigo buntings usually weave in dead leaves for bulk. Cardinals and rose-breasted grosbeaks, on the other hand, build loosely woven nests, and the eggs often show through the base of roots and stems.

Years have passed since I found my first rose-breasted grosbeak's nest. I will never forget the experience, for I discovered the male sitting on the eggs. I had been led to believe that male birds didn't stoop to such menial work because their bright colors might attract attention to the nest.

This nest, about five feet off the ground in an elderberry bush, was about a mile from my home. It didn't take me long to cover that distance, and when I returned with my photographic equipment the handsome bird was still on the eggs. And there he stayed while I struggled to set up the tripod in a tangle of bushes. Even when I bent aside some leaves with a forked stick, he didn't jump from the nest but, to my delight, broke into song.

My joy was short-lived, however, for the leaves suddenly slipped from the fork and startled Mr. Grosbeak. He cut short his song and flew away. Never again have I had the chance to photograph a male rose-breasted grosbeak singing on the nest.

Goldfinches are late nesters among the fringillids, delaying their first broods until July when there are plenty of ripe seeds for their young. Then the males bound around the maples and the thorn apples and over the arrowwood bushes, giving good evidence where their mates are nesting. A female's *ba-by* call locates a nest exactly.

By mid-September other species such as the cardinals and song sparrows have raised second broods, and the young have flown. But one day, in making the rounds at Cornell's Sapsucker Woods, I found two goldfinch nests cradling babies swaddled in creamy white down. Another nest held freshly laid eggs. Not many birds nest here in September, not even goldfinches, so these broods probably were exceptions.

Paul Lemmons

COME AND GET IT! *Hungry goldfish crowd the edge of a backyard pool in North Carolina as a cardinal passes out tidbits of food. For days the bird followed this strange routine. Alighting on the pool fence, he chirped. As the seven goldfish gathered, he fluttered down and began to feed them. In their eagerness they almost leaped from the water. Food gone, the bird flew off for more. Perhaps this foster parent had lost his own brood.*

SAVORING SUET *at a California feeder, pine siskins flash the yellow in wings and tail that helps identify them. These finches are often playful with human friends.*

The bills of all the fringillids are adapted for cracking seeds. They range in size from the heavy, conical beaks of the cardinals and grosbeaks to the small, canary-like bills of the finches and sparrows. The unique "pruning-shear" mandibles of the crossbills are excellent tools for opening pine cones to expose the seeds.

The availability of this food largely determines the movements of the crossbills. They may not show up in a locality for years; then suddenly the woods are full of them. They may stay a month or the winter. Other irregular migrants are the redpolls. Some years they never venture south of British Columbia. However, most fringillids have definite winter ranges in the South, in Mexico, and in Central America. A few, such as the rose-breasted grosbeak, migrate to South America.

With winter's thaw we welcome them back. Their fresh, cheerful voices awaken thoughts of greening woods and fields, blue skies, and bright flowers. How delightful the full-voiced, robinlike songs of the rose-breasted and black-headed grosbeaks; how pleasing the loud warbles of the purple and house finches. But perhaps cheeriest of all are the piping whistles of my stay-at-home friends the cardinals.

Walter A. Weber

Cardinal
Richmondena cardinalis

A FLASH OF RED, vivid against the spring sky, flits across the meadow and comes to rest amid the white blossoms of a dogwood. *Whoit whoit whoit, cheer cheer cheer* sings the fiery bird, and the whistle echoes and re-echoes over the fresh green fields.

Such flamboyant good looks and proud voice distinguish the cardinal, or redbird, as he is often called. "In richness of plumage, elegance of motion, and strength of song, this species surpasses all its kindred in the United States," declared Audubon. Seven states—Illinois, Indiana, Kentucky, North Carolina, Ohio, Virginia, and West Virginia—agree. All have chosen this beauty as their state bird.

Only the summer tanager rivals the male in full red color, but the tanager lacks the proud crest which the cardinal raises and lowers at will. A black mask, a stout coral-red bill, and dark red feet also mark the cardinal. So vivid is his color that he was named cardinal for the red hat and robes of a prince of the church.

Much more subdued is the dress of the female. She has an olive-gray back, dull reddish wings and crest, and soft pink-brown underparts.

We rarely see a cardinal without seeing its mate. They apparently remain together throughout the year. In the early winter months the bond may be relaxed. Then, in late winter and early spring, they show renewed tenderness in singing and feeding together.

Unlike the female of most species, the female cardinal is as accomplished a vocalist as the male. They may sing in any month, but on spring mornings when paired birds perch and perform in the tops of high trees, the countryside fairly rings with their penetrating music.

"During the love-season," continues Audubon, "the song is emitted with increased emphasis by this proud musician, who, as if aware of his powers, swells his throat, spreads his rosy tail, droops his wings, and leans alternately to the right and left, as if on the eve of expiring with delight at the delicious sounds of his own voice." Yet some listeners prefer the female's softer music.

The male cardinal fiercely defends his territory. He warns off rivals with angry cries; if an intruder persists, the cardinal darts out to attack on short, rounded wings. He may even flail at his own image in a window, mirror, or automobile hubcap. One bird was seen pecking away at a piece of red cardboard.

Cardinals may build their nests in backyards, parks, and gardens, along roadsides, and on farms, but they seem to prefer open woodlands. In the Everglades they follow the canals and settle in bushes along the banks. In Arizona they have been seen in mesquite. In Mississippi they are found in canebrakes. Most often the nest is hidden in a thicket, a patch of shrubbery, or in a sapling no more than ten feet from the ground.

As the female weaves the deep cup of bark strips, rootlets, and grass and lines it with fine grass or hair, the male follows her about and voices his most melodious song. He feeds her during the two weeks that she incubates the three or four greenish- or bluish-white eggs spotted with brown. While she prepares for a second brood, he often assumes the care of the fledglings, feeding them grasshoppers, beetles, caterpillars, and other insects. One hungry nestling was observed swallowing with ease a grub two inches long and as thick as a pencil.

So strong is the male cardinal's instinct to feed young birds that he sometimes stuffs food down the throats of nestlings of other species. One hard-working individual in North Carolina even played foster parent to goldfish in a backyard pool (page 324)!

When out of the nest, the fledglings wear a plumage even browner and duller than their mother's garb. Their bills are blackish. But soon their underparts turn lighter and the crests of the young males become reddish. By fall the youngsters have molted, and in their first winter plumage they look like their parents.

Young cardinals have been noted singing at three and four weeks of age, their sound a soft warbling quite unlike the adult's. When they are about two months old, they begin to introduce adult phrases into their warbling.

The cardinal has more than his share of enemies. Snakes, owls, and cats raid the nest. House wrens puncture his eggs; catbirds and mockingbirds compete with him for nesting sites. In most of the cardinal's range cowbirds leave their eggs in his nest. And blue jays seem ever ready to attack the young.

The adult cardinal sometimes indulges in anting, a peculiar habit not yet fully understood by ornithologists (page 193). It will pick up the insects, crush them, and rub them through its plumage. Afterward the plumage looks wet, as if juices had been squeezed from the ants.

ONCE PRIMARILY a southern bird, the cardinal in recent years has steadily extended its range northward. The eastern race prevails from Florida and the Gulf Coast to the Dakotas. Some now live as far north as Maine, Nova Scotia, and southern Ontario. Other races range through the Southwest and into Mexico.

Though nonmigratory, cardinals often wander widely during the winter, sometimes in small flocks. At feeding stations they are prized visitors, cracking with strong bills the sunflower seeds they seem to relish above all else. Home-

FROM SPIKY CREST *to rounded tail, male cardinals sport red suits. Both sexes wear black masks.*
Males (upper) and female, 7½-8½"; Walter A. Weber, National Geographic staff artist

owners who wish to boast, "I have a pair of cardinals out back this year," put out a variety of seeds, raisins, scratch feed, millet, and bits of nuts, wheat bread, and corn bread.

Often cardinals can be coaxed onto back porch or steps and will feed unless frightened by a movement within the house. Even when they have retreated into the backyard shrubbery they reveal themselves by bright song and the characteristic call note, a sharp *tsip!*

Once the cardinal was eagerly sought as a cage bird. Hardy, beautiful, and a good singer, it lived well in captivity when properly cared for. But its rich, red plumage usually became somewhat dull and faded, and the song gradually lost variety.

Today in the United States the cardinal is deservedly protected. And thanks to its expansion northward, more and more people find the drab winter days brightened by the fiery beauty and vibrant song of the cardinal.

Range: S. E. South Dakota to S. Ontario and S. W. Connecticut, south to the Gulf Coast and S. Florida; also S. California to N. Texas, south to British Honduras. *Characteristics:* sharp red crest, coral-colored bill. Male is all red except for black mask. Female has olive-gray head and back, dull reddish wings, tail, and crest; soft pink-brown underparts. Young are browner, duller than female and have blackish bill.

Female pyrrhuloxia, Eliot Porter

Pyrrhuloxia
Pyrrhuloxia sinuata

A SLENDER, SOFT-GRAY BIRD, glowing with touches of red, perches among the prickly branches of a mesquite tree. With its back to the viewer it looks for the moment much like a female cardinal, although slightly grayer.

Then the bird turns, displaying a red breast, a heavy yellow bill, and a red crest. No doubt now: This aristocratic-looking bird is the male pyrrhuloxia, whose name stems from Greek words meaning "crooked-billed red bird."

A pale relative of the cardinal, he resides in southwestern deserts and plains. You may see him hopping on the ground as he searches for caterpillars, grasshoppers, and weevils. Or you may find him feeding on the fresh catkins of a cottonwood tree, the bright red fruit of the Christmas cactus, or in stands of elder, hackberry, and graythorn. He may alight on the seed spike of a grain sorghum, bite off the top, and eat the seeds downward until his bill is lower than his feet. Most often he feeds on mesquite.

In February the winter flocks break up and competition begins for territories. Often the brownish-gray female will join her mate in chasing off other claimants. By early May definite boundaries are established, and in the early morning you may hear the males proclaiming *quink quink quink quink quink*, all in one pitch, or a slurred, whistled *what-cheer, what-cheer*. After this wake-up serenade the male may make a complete circuit of his territory, pausing now and then to sing again.

The female selects the nest site in a thorny thicket, builds a compact cup of twigs, weed stems, and shreds of fine bark, then lines it with grasses. The three or four white eggs are dotted with purplish brown. The young resemble their mother but have lighter underparts.

A shy bird, quick to take flight when crowded, the pyrrhuloxia can be lured to feeding stations with kitchen scraps. Watch his crest—as it moves he seems to change expression. Ornithologist Florence Merriam Bailey observed that when the crest is flattened, "the short curved bill and round head suggest a bored parrot in a cage, but when the crest is raised to its full height and thrown forward, the beautiful bird is the picture of alert interest and vivacity."

As winter approaches, pyrrhuloxias congregate and wander in search of food but do not migrate.

Range: S. Arizona to S. E. Texas, south to central Mexico. *Characteristics:* slender body; heavy, parrotlike bill is yellow in summer, paler in winter. Male is grayish with red on crest, face, tail, wings, and breast. Female is brownish gray with reddish crest, buff breast, and touches of red in wings and tail. Young resemble the female.

Male pyrrhuloxia, length 7½-8½"; Lyman K. Stuart

Rose-breasted Grosbeak
Pheucticus ludovicianus
(Picture on following page)

"THE EVENING WAS CALM and beautiful, the sky sparkled with stars.... Suddenly there burst on my soul the serenade of the Rose-breasted bird, so rich, so mellow, so loud in the stillness of the night, that sleep fled from my eyelids. Never did I enjoy music more." Thus Audubon in 1834 described the song of a rose-breasted grosbeak in the Mohawk River solitudes in New York.

Today you may hear this handsome bird's melody in farmland, city park, or suburb. He sounds much like a robin, but his warble is sweeter and the rapid notes seem continuous. Rarely are two successive notes on the same pitch. His call note is a metallic *clink, clink*.

The rosebreast may arrive in the eastern United States and southern Canada in early May. For breeding he favors an area where a woodland meets a clearing grown up in shrubs, with water close at hand. Males often compete fiercely for mates. As the streaked brown female perches demurely, the males dive and wheel overhead, black wings flashing with white, breasts aglow with a large triangular patch of rosy red.

Combat over, the winner becomes quiet and

affectionate. You may see him touch bills with his mate. The male often helps her build the saucerlike nest of twigs and weeds. Usually they place it five to ten feet above the ground in the crotch of an elderberry or on a horizontal branch of an aspen or small oak. In the mountains of Georgia they favor thickets of rhododendron. So frail is the nest that you can look through the bottom and glimpse the three to five pale blue eggs spotted with brown.

In other species, rarely does a conspicuously colored male incubate. The male rose-breasted grosbeak, however, shares this task with the duller female. Despite the danger of attracting intruders, he even sings while on the eggs.

Young males resemble their mother, except for touches of rose on wing linings and breast. Even in their first breeding season they wear some brown on wings and tail.

Rosebreasts feed almost equally on animal and vegetable matter. They relish wild fruit and have been seen eating the seeds of elm and catalpa and the blossoms of hickory and beech. They earn the gratitude of farmers by devouring cucumber and potato beetles, hickory borers, cankerworms, and the Rocky Mountain locust. Leaf beetle larvae are often fed to nestlings.

In fall the rosebreasts head for wooded highlands south of the border. En route they hide in the leaves at the top of tall trees and voice only the sharp *clink* notes. By this time the male has lost much of his brilliance and only a trace of pink remains on his breast.

Range: N. E. British Columbia to Nova Scotia, south to Kansas and Georgia; winters from central Mexico to N. South America. *Characteristics:* large pale bill. Breeding male has black upperparts, red breast, white wing patches, belly, and rump. Female and young have buffy head stripes, brownish back, whitish wing bars, streaked whitish underparts. Fall male resembles female but retains black wings and tail.

Male rose-breasted grosbeak, length 7-8½"; Arthur A. Allen

Female rose-breasted grosbeak
Frederick Kent Truslow

Male (left) and female blackheads
length 6½-7¾", Allan Brooks

Black-headed Grosbeak

Pheucticus melanocephalus

A CLOSE RELATIVE of the rosebreast, the black-headed grosbeak ranges from eastern foothills of the Rocky Mountains to the Pacific. Habits of the two species are similar; where their ranges overlap, they may hybridize.

The blackhead usually builds its nest of twigs, weeds, and rootlets in open woodlands, orchards, or streamside thickets. Both parents incubate the three or four bluish eggs spotted with brown.

The birds feed on insects and fruit and visit campsites in western parks to forage for crumbs. Their loud and beautiful song contrasts sharply with their little call note, *eek*.

Range: S. British Columbia to Saskatchewan, south to S. Mexico; winters mainly in Mexico. *Characteristics;* large pale bill, tawny collar and breast, yellow belly. Male has black head, black-and-white wings and tail. Female and young have streaked brownish head and back, whitish face stripes and wing markings.

Female blue grosbeak, Thase Daniel (also right)

Blue Grosbeak

Guiraca caerulea

AT FIRST GLANCE the male blue grosbeak may deceive you. In poor light his purplish-blue plumage appears black and you may mistake him for a cowbird. But look again. The heavy beak and chestnut wing bars proclaim his identity.

He breeds mainly in the southern United States, in fields overgrown with brambles, in streamside thickets, orchards, and shrubbery around houses. His mate builds a flimsy nest in a small tree or bush. Often she includes a discarded snakeskin (below). She incubates the three or four bluish-white eggs, but the male helps feed insects to the nestlings.

The blue grosbeak sings diligently in early morning and late afternoon. It voices a rapid finchlike warble with short phrases rising and falling. The call note is an explosive *spink!*

In fall, when the birds feed in fields of grain before heading south of the border, the male's plumage is edged with brown.

Range: central California to South Dakota and S. New Jersey, south to Costa Rica; winters to Panama. *Characteristics:* heavy bill, chestnut wing bars. Male is deep blue. Female is brown with dusky wings and tail, sometimes touches of blue. Young males are mixed brown and blue.

Male blue grosbeak, length 6-7½"

Indigo Bunting
Passerina cyanea

THE SKY GLOWS RED above the treetops as dusk begins to settle over the abandoned farm. The summer air is warm and heavy and scented with clover hay. A mother skunk and her brood stroll through the underbrush, and a towhee calls from its brambled fortress.

High above, on the stub of an old hickory, a small bird pours out a high-pitched song: *sweet-sweet, where-where, here-here, see it-see it.* Each pair of notes is on a different pitch. Toward the end the song descends and weakens.

Seen against the sky, the ardent singer appears blackish. But when the sun's slanting rays strike his plumage, it flashes vivid blue, identifying the vocalist as the male indigo bunting.

It is usually the middle of May before he appears in his breeding range, which extends from Canada to the Gulf Coast. But he makes up for his late arrival by singing most of the summer, at any time from sunup to sundown. You may even hear him in late August, long after other birds have grown quiet.

Old pastures, brushy clearings, and burned-over fields are the best places to look for him. He favors areas that offer dense ground cover and an occasional tree or wire to sing from. If you happen on his nest, his mate — a brown bird faintly streaked — will fly before you in alarm. Perching nearby, she will twitch her tail from side to side and utter a sharp, brittle *tsick.*

She weaves the cup of grass, stems, and dead leaves and hides it in weeds, ferns, or shrubs. Twice a year she lays three or four bluish-white eggs. She builds a new nest for the second brood.

The male doesn't incubate the eggs, but he often brings food to the female on the nest and helps feed the young. In summer he searches for insects; in fall the family dines on weed seeds.

In his first breeding plumage the male glistens blue all over except for brown wing coverts. Were it not for his smaller size, sparrowlike bill, and lack of wing bars, you might confuse him with the blue grosbeak. The mature male in fall and winter looks like the female, but glints of blue remain in his wings and tail.

This handsome eastern finch may breed as far west as Arizona. Where its summer range overlaps that of the lazuli bunting in the Great Plains area, the two species often hybridize.

Range: S. Manitoba to S. New Brunswick, south to S. E. Texas and N. Florida; sporadically west to Colorado and Arizona. Winters from central Mexico and West Indies to Panama. *Characteristics:* small sharp bill. Male is blue with touches of black on wings. Female is brown with paler, streaked underparts. Fall and young male resemble female with blue on wings and tail.

Lazuli Bunting
Passerina amoena

A WESTERN COUNTERPART of the indigo bunting, the lazuli ranges from Canada to Baja California and east to Oklahoma. You may find him in moist coastal forests, or among the aspens, willows, and wild rose thickets along a rushing mountain stream, or in the brush of a burned-over field. In California he has been seen at 10,000 feet in Kings Canyon National Park and below sea level in Death Valley.

From conspicuous song perches he announces his arrival and territorial claims each spring in a series of shrill phrases of varying pitch. He often couples his notes, but not as consistently as the indigo bunting. You'll probably see him high on some sunny station, a jewel-like bird of azure, cinnamon, and white. Soon after he arrives a female joins him and helps defend the territory.

In courtship he spreads wide his wings, disclosing the full glory of his colors. The object of his affections is a plain brownish bird with a touch of blue on her wings and tail. She builds a deep cup-shaped nest of dried grass and plant stems and lines it with fine grass or animal hair. Audubon found lazuli bunting nests lined with buffalo hair. Seldom is the snug home more than a few feet above ground.

The four bluish-white eggs hatch in about 12 days. Soon the harried mother is scurrying about gathering small grasshoppers and other insects for her nestlings. Where the nest is open to the sun, a quarter of her time at home may be spent in shading the young with spread wings. After a nest life of 10 to 12 days the babies leave the nurs-

Male (left) and female indigos
length 5¼-5¾", Allan Brooks

ery. Then their father looks after them while his mate builds a nest for a second brood. The new nest is usually situated quite close to the old.

By late summer the young birds look like their mother but without the bluish traces. Then lazuli buntings wander widely in search of insects and weed seeds. By early October most of these birds have left the United States for the winter. Their abandoned nests are not wasted, however. Fam-

ilies of white-footed mice often move in, roof them over, and use them for winter shelter.

Range: S. British Columbia to N. E. South Dakota, south to Baja California and W. Oklahoma; winters from S. Arizona to S. Mexico. *Characteristics:* small sharp bill. Male has blue upperparts, cinnamon breast and sides, white wing bars and belly. Female is brownish with paler underparts and wing bars; blue on wings and tail. Young resemble the female.

Male (upper) and female lazulis, length 5-5½"; Eliot Porter

Varied Bunting
Passerina versicolor

JUST AS THE LAZULI BUNTING replaces the indigo in the west, so this beautiful species replaces the lazuli along our southwestern border.

Not a common bird, this variegated little finch lives mainly in Mexico. In the breeding season he crosses into Arizona and Texas. Here *versicolor* spends the summer in open country among brushy pastures, in mesquite chaparral, or in streamside thickets.

You'll find him on the ground most of the time. When an intruder approaches, the bird disappears into the dense shrubbery. When the danger passes, he perches atop a bush and pours out his bright, crisp finch song with great enthusiasm.

Although he wears some blue like the lazuli and the indigo, the male varied bunting is mainly garbed in dark reddish purple which looks black from a distance. The bright red nape patch provides the surest badge of identification. In fall his gorgeous "Joseph's coat" is somewhat dulled by brownish feather tips.

The gray-brown female fashions a nest of grass, weed stems, and bark strips. She usually hides it in a tangle of vegetation close to the ground. In it she lays three or four bluish-white eggs.

Range: central Arizona and S. Texas, south to Guatemala; migratory in the north. *Characteristics:* small sharp bill. Male has purplish-blue crown and rump, vermilion nape patch, reddish-purple back and throat, black on tail. Female is gray-brown with lighter underparts and touches of bluish gray on wings, tail, and rump. Young resemble the female.

Male varied, length 4½-5½"
Allan Brooks

333

Male and (inset) female painted buntings, length 5-5½"

Painted Bunting
Passerina ciris

ALL FOUR AMERICAN FINCHES of the genus *Passerina* are notable for their colors. But beside this beauty the others seem pale. Spanish colonists called him *mariposa pintada*—painted butterfly. The French labeled him *nonpareil*—without equal. Nonpareil remains his common name through the southern states he ranges.

Startle him while you're walking in the woodlands and he darts for cover, his blue head, green back, and vivid red rump and underparts a blur of color. Unlike the others in his genus, he keeps this handsome plumage throughout the year. The female has none of his brilliant colors but in her own way is just as distinctive. She is the only small finch dressed entirely in greenish and olive-yellowish hues.

The male arrives first in the spring, announcing his presence with a pleasant warble from atop a tree or even a house. He stakes out his territory in brushy areas near streams or swamps, at woodland edges, and in towns. When the fe-

Frederick Kent Truslow

males appear, he competes fiercely for a mate.

The female builds a compact nest of grass, leaves, and weed stalks, usually in a bush or sapling about three feet from the ground. In coastal regions she may hide it in a clump of Spanish moss. She lays three or four bluish-white eggs speckled with reddish brown.

Painted buntings feed principally on seeds, favoring those of foxtail grass. In cotton country they serve the farmer by eating boll weevils and cotton worms as well as other insects.

Range: S. New Mexico to E. Kansas and S. E. North Carolina, south to N. Mexico and central Florida; winters to the West Indies and Panama. *Characteristics:* male has purplish-blue head and nape, yellowish-green back, purplish-red rump, vermilion underparts. Female has greenish upperparts, olive-yellowish underparts. Young are grayish brown.

Dickcissel
Spiza americana

DICK-DICK-CISS-CISS-CISS. The staccato notes come across a midwestern alfalfa field in early May. You see the singer perched atop a swaying weed; with his yellowish breast and black bib he looks like a small meadowlark. But the curious chant, which gives him his name, and a chestnut shoulder patch identify him as a dickcissel.

Raising a family doesn't interfere with his singing, for the female does the work. She resembles a house sparrow but is paler and shows touches of yellow on her breast. She darts across the meadow gathering weed and grass stems for the nest. Placed in a clump of grass or in a low bush, the nursery contains three to five pale blue eggs. After they hatch, the nestlings are fed seeds and insects. Mowing machines destroy many nests in clover and alfalfa fields.

In August most dickcissel families gather into flocks of several hundred birds and wing south of the border. But individuals and small groups may winter in California, New England, or southern Canada. A wanderer, the dickcissel may not return to last year's nesting area. He may even change his range. Before 1880 he was common east of the Allegheny Mountains. Then he became rare there; now he appears to be returning.

Range: E. Montana to Massachusetts, south to Texas and South Carolina; winters from central Mexico to N. South America. *Characteristics:* yellowish breast and eye stripe, chestnut shoulder patch, whitish belly. Male has gray head, streaked brown back, black bib (obscured in fall). Female is paler with brownish head, less yellow on breast. Young resemble the female.

Male dickcissel, length 6-7"; Helen Cruickshank

Allan D. Cruickshank, National Audubon Society

Male evening grosbeak, length 7-8½"

Evening Grosbeak
Hesperiphona vespertina

IN THE WINTER of 1889-90 a great wave of evening grosbeaks invaded New England for the first time, enlivening the snowy landscape with their yellow bodies and black-and-white wings. No longer would *Hesperiphona* be true to his name.

Once, like the Hesperides of Greek mythology, he resided only in the west. You would find him from the Great Lakes to British Columbia, and southward through Mexico. But today he breeds as far east as Massachusetts, and vagabond winter flocks roam as far south as the Carolinas.

Look for him in box elder or maple trees, feasting on seeds, or in chokecherry or dogwood, crunching the pits with his heavy, ivory-colored bill. *Cleer* or *clee-ip* rings his call, and his smoky mate may alight beside him.

They build their loose, shallow nest on a horizontal branch, usually spruce, 20 to 60 feet from the ground. The female incubates the three or four pale bluish-green eggs speckled with gray, olive, and brown.

An early observer believed this bird dwelled only "in dark retreats, and leaves them at the approach of night." Thus it received its pleasing but misleading common name.

Range: N. British Columbia to New Brunswick, south to central California and S. Mexico, and to N. E. Minnesota and Massachusetts. Winters to S. California and South Carolina. *Characteristics:* large pale bill. Male is dull yellow with black crown and tail, black-and-white wings. Female (pages 36-7) is silver-gray with yellow-tinged neck and sides, black-and-white wings and tail. Young resemble the female.

335

House Finch
Carpodacus mexicanus

HE WANDERS through the streets of western towns, searching for scraps of food, and flocks to sunny fields to gobble weed seeds. Perched on a backyard limb, he glows with bright red on forehead

Male (left) and female Allan Brooks

and breast; his cheery warble brightens the dullest day. The house finch, or linnet, is a favorite of all but orchard owners, who watch uneasily as he descends en masse on ripening fruit trees.

In April the flocks break up as the males pair off with brownish females. The birds place their nest of slender dry stems almost anywhere near a water supply: in the eaves of a building, the fork of an upright limb, in a tin cup, stovepipe, or old hat. They even occupy old oriole nests. The male serenades and feeds his mate as she

incubates the four or five speckled bluish-white eggs. Not until the second year do males show their full red colors.

The house finch has been introduced to Hawaii and accidentally to the East Coast. In 1940 cage-bird dealers illegally trapped these birds and shipped them to New York as "Hollywood finches." When government agents stepped in, the dealers released the birds. Now house finches are seen from Connecticut to Virginia.

Two closely related species dwell on islands off Baja California: the orange-tinted McGregor's house finch (*Carpodacus mcgregori*) on San Benito and Cedros Islands, and the darker and much larger Guadalupe house finch (*Carpodacus amplus*) on Guadalupe Island.

Range: S. British Columbia to W. Nebraska, south to S. Mexico; also from Connecticut to Virginia and in Hawaii. *Characteristics:* conical bill, brown back, lighter underparts streaked with brown. Male has bright red wash extending back from forehead; red breast and rump. Female and young lack the red markings.

Male (left) and female Allan Brooks

Purple Finch
Carpodacus purpureus

A NATIVE OF EVERGREEN FORESTS, the purple finch has adapted readily to civilization. You may see him among the trees in a city park or a suburb or crowded around a feeding station well stocked with sunflower seeds.

Not purple at all, the male looks like a large-billed sparrow that has been dipped in red wine. The brownish female is boldly streaked and shows white facial stripes and a dark jaw stripe.

In winter these wanderers may show up as far south as Texas and Florida. But in spring they wing north to breeding areas in Canada and in the northern and Pacific states. Once they bred abundantly in southern New England. But with the coming of the aggressive house sparrow, these finches declined in many areas there.

As they fly along in their characteristic undulating pattern, purple finches sound a sharp *tick* call note. Their song is clear and liquid, usually delivered from atop a tall tree. During the

courtship ritual, the male dances about with wings extended and vibrating so swiftly they seem to blur. Sometimes he sings with such enthusiasm that he rises into the air, as if borne on his own swelling song. If the female responds, he alights and they may touch bills.

One observer saw a male pick up a straw, perform an ecstatic dance, then roll over as if dead. The female roused him with a peck and flew off with the straw to start a nest.

The male may help build the nest of roots and grasses, lined with hair, usually in an evergreen 5 to 60 feet from the ground. While the female incubates the three or four bluish eggs spotted with brown at the larger end, he sings to her and brings food. Both feed the nestlings, who sometimes softly chirp *pee-wee pee-wee*.

When the young can fly well, the family begins its wanderings in search of food. In summer the finches feast on berries and other fruit. In winter and early spring they eat weed and grass seeds.

A hardy bird, the purple finch has been observed bathing in streams in below-freezing temperatures and singing after a blizzard. He is New Hampshire's state bird.

Range: N. British Columbia to Newfoundland, south to Baja California, central Alberta, West Virginia, and S. E. New York; winters to S. Arizona, also to S. E. Texas and central Florida. *Characteristics:* conical bill. Male has rosy head, rump, and breast; streaked brownish-red back, whitish belly. Female has heavy streaks, whitish eye stripe and underparts, dark jaw stripe, brownish upperparts. Young resemble female.

Opposite upper: male house finch, length 5-6¼"; Allan D. Cruickshank
Lower: male purple finches, length 5½-6¼"; C. B. Johnson. Both National Audubon Society

Male (left) and female
whitecollars
length 4-4½"
Allan Brooks

Male (left) and female pine grosbeaks, length 8-10"; Patricia Bailey Witherspoon

Male Cassin's
length 6-6½"
Arthur A. Allen

Cassin's Finch
Carpodacus cassinii

HIGH in the Cascades, Sierras, and other western ranges dwells this close relative of the purple finch (page 336). The Cassin's may be distinguished by his slightly larger size and paler rose breast. Also note the contrast between red crown and brownish neck in *cassinii*.

In May these finches build nests of twigs and grass high in pines or spruces. The cup holds four or five spotted bluish eggs. Descending to the lowlands in winter, Cassin's finches travel in small flocks. They warble a loud, lively song.

Range: S. British Columbia and S. Alberta to N. Wyoming, south to N. Baja California and N. New Mexico; winters to central Mexico. *Characteristics:* heavy bill. Male has red crown, rose breast and rump, streaked brownish-pink back, whitish belly. Female is olive-gray with dusky streaks; young resemble the female.

White-collared Seedeater
Sporophila torqueola

IN THE LOWER VALLEY of the Rio Grande you may see this tiny bird feasting on weed and grass seeds in pastures and marshes and along roadsides. He sings a loud *sweet sweet sweet cheer cheer*. In a nearby bush his mate sits on a com-

pact nest containing four or five bluish-green eggs spotted with brown.

Also known as Sharpe's seedeater, he is the only form of *torqueola* that lives in the United States. Unlike the southern races, he usually lacks the collar that gave the species its name.

Range: W. Mexico to S. Texas, south to Costa Rica. *Characteristics:* blunt bill, white wing bars, buffy underparts. Male has blackish head and upperparts, whitish throat and sometimes a whitish collar; incomplete breastband. Female has brownish upperparts.

Pine Grosbeak
Pinicola enucleator

IT IS WINTER in central Canada; great snows bathe the conifers. Seeds and wild fruit are scarce, for the summer has been dry. Now flocks of pine grosbeaks – pink males and yellow-gray females – wing south in search of food. In the northern United States you may see them descend on beeches, red cedars, and other trees and bushes, gathering the last nuts and fruit.

Watch them, perhaps two dozen, work over a white ash on a New England street. The weight of their stocky, robin-size bodies shakes snow from the limbs. With stubby, black beaks these largest of our finches strip open the seed coverings and extract the seeds, demonstrating the reason for their species name *enucleator*. You may approach closely, for in their wilderness haunts they have not learned to fear man.

In spring their sweet and melodious *tee tee*

tew song rings through the northern evergreen forests. They build a flat, loose nest of twigs and moss lined with grass or hair, 6 to 30 feet above the ground. The three or four pale bluish-green eggs are spotted with purplish brown.

Not strictly a migrant, the pine grosbeak may spend the winter in or near his breeding area, roaming about in small flocks. He sometimes takes a snow bath, tossing the white spray over his plumage as another bird would toss water.

The pine grosbeak is a bird we share with the Old World; it dwells in the northern coniferous forests of Scandinavia, Russia, and Siberia.

Range: N. Alaska to Newfoundland, south in the western mountains to central California and central New Mexico, in the east to central Ontario and N. New Hampshire; winters to S. New Mexico and Virginia. *Characteristics:* dark tail and wings, white wing bars. Male has rose head, back, and breast. Female has yellow head and rump, gray back, underparts. Young male resembles female, with red tinges on head and rump.

Gray-crowned Rosy Finch
Leucosticte tephrocotis

HARDY ALPINISTS, rosy finches dwell among snowbanks and glaciers on many of our western ranges. In spring, if you hike well above timberline, you may see a flock of them walking about at the edge of the retreating snow, picking up seeds and benumbed insects. Their chirping may remind you of house sparrows.

They build their nest, a sturdy cup of grasses or moss, in a cliffside niche or under a boulder, often at altitudes of 10,000 to 12,000 feet. The four or five eggs are as white as the snow that clings all year to the mountaintops. The eggs hatch in about 14 days.

In winter the birds wander in flocks, sometimes far out on the Great Plains. There they may feed at doorsteps and pass the night in the eaves of homes and outbuildings.

Three species of rosy finches in North America have been described. Plumages of these are variable, and some ornithologists consider they all belong to a single, widespread species.

Best known and widest ranging is the gray-crowned, a sparrow-sized brown bird splashed with pink. In the race called Hepburn's rosy finch, the gray head patch crosses the cheek.

The related species are the black rosy finch and the brown-capped rosy finch. The black rosy breeds in the high mountains from Montana to Nevada and Utah. He resembles the gray-crowned except that his body is almost black rather than brown. When roosting on a cliff out of sight, he may reveal himself with a rapid series of *chew* notes, each on a different pitch.

Range: islands in the Bering Sea and N. E. Alaska, south in the mountains to central California and N. W. Montana; winters to N. New Mexico and W. Nebraska. *Characteristics:* black forehead, light gray head patch, chestnut-brown back and underparts; pink wash on rump, flanks, and wings. Female is duller, less rosy.

Brown-capped Rosy Finch
Leucosticte australis

VISITORS TO PIKES PEAK in Colorado may see this bird, which looks much like a gray-crowned rosy finch without the gray crown.

In a cliff crevice the browncap weaves a compact nest of grass, flower stems, and moss. The female lays her three white eggs on a cushion of finer grass and feathers.

In winter browncaps retire to the valleys to forage in flocks with other rosy finches.

Range: S. Wyoming to N. New Mexico. *Characteristics:* male has dusky head, brown body tinged with rose. Female is duller.

Male brown-capped rosy finch, length 5¾-6¼"; Alfred M. Bailey

Left: male (upper) and female gray-crowned rosy finches, length 5¾-6¾"; Allan Brooks

European, 4¾-5½"; Eric Hosking, Photo Researchers

European Goldfinch
Carduelis carduelis

A NATIVE of Europe, Asia, and North Africa, this harlequin bird was introduced in various New World localities during the 19th century. But except in Bermuda, the species failed to take hold.

The most successful mainland breeding colonies were in New York, in the Long Island communities of Garden City, Freeport, and Massapequa, where the birds found thickets for their grassy nests. They laid their four or five pale blue, brown-speckled eggs and raised families on seeds and insects. The building boom of the mid-1950's apparently removed the natural habitat for the species. European goldfinches seen since are believed to have escaped from cages.

There is no mistaking this finch, whose red, white, and black head resembles a clown's. The only gold is a chevron on his wings. His song is a clear warble, his call a sibilant tweet.

Range: now, in the New World, only in Bermuda. *Characteristics:* white head with red face, black crown; brown back, black wings and tail, yellow wing patches; buff-white underparts.

Common Redpoll
Acanthis flammea

LIKE WINDBLOWN LEAVES they sweep over a snowy field to an alder tree. Chirping and twittering, they flutter through its seed-laden branches and glean in the snow below, red-capped heads bobbing as they feed. Cold? Fine! For these are common redpolls, birds that breed where spruce forests end and Arctic tundra begins – in Eurasia as well as North America. They flock south seeking seeds in winter and sometimes range as far as California and the Carolinas.

On his northern breeding ground the male redpoll carols a liquid, trilling courtship song. The female weaves a firm cup of twigs, moss, fibers, and feathers in the fork of a spruce or willow. Fed insects by her mate, she incubates the five or six blue-green, brown-spotted eggs.

Range: Arctic regions, south to S. Alaska and Newfoundland; winters to N. California, Ohio, and South Carolina. *Characteristics:* streaked brown upperparts, grayish underparts; red forehead, black chin. Male has pink breast and rump.

Hoary Redpoll
Acanthis hornemanni

THIS NORTHERN relative of the common redpoll has whiter plumage and similar habits except that he nests on the ground. Forms of both species may cross the North Atlantic from Greenland or Iceland to the British Isles.

Range: Arctic regions; winters irregularly to E. Montana and Maryland. *Characteristics:* paler than common redpoll, clear white rump. Male has light pink on breast.

Common redpolls (males with rosy breasts) length 5-5½", Arthur A. Allen

Pine Siskin
Spinus pinus

THIS DARK LITTLE FINCH roams the evergreen forests of North America. He travels in large flocks which descend on a stand of pine or spruce and work through the branches with a buzzing, rising *shreeee*, like a hissing valve on a radiator.

The siskin's voice is usually the best clue to his identity. His streaked plumage lacks any sure field marks save gold patches on wings and tail, best seen when they are spread (page 325).

The bird's habits are more noteworthy. He has no fixed breeding grounds but wanders about his range. Even his breeding season varies. In summer he eats conifer seeds, insects, and spiders. He is strangely fond of salt. A flock of siskins may suddenly swoop down to cluster around a salt lick or raid a dock area where fish are cured.

The female siskin builds the nest of rootlets, bark fiber, grass, and moss and lines it with down and hair, if available. It is placed well out on the limb of a hemlock or other evergreen. Her mate brings her food while she sits on the three or four pale blue-green eggs. These are spotted with brown and black.

After the young leave the nest, the birds resume their gypsylike roving. During winter pine siskins often join redpolls, goldfinches, and crossbills in the search for seeds. Some drift southward in undulating flight, twittering and buzzing as they go. At feeding stations they are usually tame and even bold. They often respond to human kindness by perching on their benefactors. Some are even more daring.

A Massachusetts bird fancier reported how a flock of siskins changed his sleeping habits one

Pine siskins, length 4½-5¼"; Eliot Porter

winter. They became accustomed to the breakfast of seeds that he put out for them, and gathered for it at dawn each day. If their friend was not up, they would enter his bedroom and tug at his hair or tweak his ear.

He tried to catch a few extra winks by burying his head under the bedclothes, leaving a "tunnel" to breathe through. But the birds discovered the ruse. Gingerly, one explored the corridor, then nipped the napper on the nose!

Range: S. Alaska, S. Manitoba, and Newfoundland, south in western mountains to Guatemala, also to Kansas, S. Ontario, and Connecticut; winters to the Gulf Coast and S. Florida. *Characteristics:* heavily streaked brown body; yellow patches on wings and tail, often concealed.

Male hoary redpoll, length 5¼-5½"; Allan Brooks

341

American Goldfinch
Spinus tristis

BOUNDING through the air, his yellow-and-black plumage flashing in the summer sun, this little finch flies his wavelike course, climbing then dipping. At the crest of each wave he pipes his clear, sweet call: *per-chic-o-ree! per-chic-o-ree!* Some people fancy that he is saying "Just look at me! Just look at me!"

A patch of tall weeds lures the bird down. As he feeds, the brilliance of his body glows against the grass of the field like a splash of yellow paint. In contrast, his jet black tail and wings stand out, as does the jaunty black cap that he wears pulled down upon his bill like a cadet's kepi. When his olive-yellow mate joins him to share a feast of thistle seeds, she hardly seems the same species, so modestly garbed is she by comparison. The two fill their crops, then dart off.

One of the goldfinch's calls, repeated over and over again in the autumn from a tree limb, sounds like weeping. More typical are the ecstatic bursts of song and swooping flights — for this is a gay bird, a joyous symbol of summer, fittingly called wild canary or yellowbird. His eating habits explain the name thistlebird.

Widely known and well loved, the American or common goldfinch ranges from coast to coast and from southern Canada southward through most of the United States. Washington, on the Pacific Ocean, claims him as its state bird. So does New Jersey on the Atlantic. So does Iowa in the nation's heartland.

In the northern states goldfinches arrive in April for the summer. They fan out across their breeding grounds — but not to breed. That comes later. Instead, they sport through underbrush and across fields in seemingly carefree flocks.

In May the seeds of elm trees attract them. They swarm through stately shade trees, filling the fresh green branches with flashes of yellow, twittering busily as they feed.

June brings a harvest of seeds — from dandelions by the roadside, from bachelor buttons in the garden, from evening primroses in the fields. Along with these the goldfinches sample tender buds and nip the new leaves of lettuce and beets while they drink the dew.

Finally, in July and August, the thistles reach full bloom. This seems to signal the start of the yellowbird's breeding season. Thistledown will be available when mated pairs want it for nest building; seeds will be ripe when parent birds and their hatchlings need them most.

So in the fullness of summer goldfinches begin their courtship. Flocks disintegrate as birds pair off. They mate too late to raise more than one brood a year. One nest found in early October contained fledglings only a few days old.

Farm country with a scattering of trees is one favored nesting ground for goldfinches. Riverside groves, roadside hedges, and the borders of fields are other choice spots. The female selects the site for the nest — often in the fork of a maple some 10 to 30 feet up, but sometimes in a thistle or even a cornstalk. While she inspects a likely place, her ardent mate dips and swoops above her, singing a high-pitched, twittering, breathless song of courtship.

The nest is woven of plant fibers and lined with a mattress of thistledown and other silky strands. The walls of a nest are often so thick and tightly woven that they will hold water. Young birds have been known to drown when left unsheltered by their parents in a rainstorm.

The female goldfinch incubates the four to six pale blue eggs 12 to 14 days. Her mate remains in constant attendance. He guards her, sings to her, even feeds her while she flutters her wings and begs like a baby bird (page 186).

GOLDFINCHES raise their nestlings almost entirely on seeds. They shuck the hard shells, swallow the insides, and later regurgitate the "cereal" into each youngster's throat. Thistle and dandelion seeds are the favorites. Chicory, aster, mullein, and goldenrod also rate high with these birds. Two or three may be seen hanging on a weed stalk until it sags to the ground with their weight. Then they stand on it and finish plucking its crop of seeds.

The birds also eat a few insects, especially in the spring. They take aphids, caterpillars, beetles, small grasshoppers, and cankerworms.

As their young develop, goldfinches tend to stay away longer and longer from the nest. It becomes somewhat untidy. The fledglings leave home when 15 or 16 days old.

With the coming of October most goldfinches start to drift southward from their northern range. They usually migrate in flocks, moving a little each day. But when plenty of food is available, some of the birds stay near their breeding grounds the year round, often passing the winter with siskins, redpolls, and purple finches.

When snow flies, these hardy ones may flock to your feeder and cockily steal a handout from under the bills of larger birds. They find shelter in evergreen thickets and seem unperturbed by the cold. One was seen in New England settling down for the night in the sheltered side of a footprint in the snow!

Range: S. Canada south to N. Baja California, central Utah, N. Louisiana, and South Carolina; winters to S. Mexico and the Gulf Coast. *Characteristics:* summer male is bright yellow with black cap, black wings and tail with white markings. Body of female and winter male (page 23) is olive-yellow tinged with brown.

FLASHING YELLOW *against the green of summer, an American goldfinch attends his mate. Their well-knit nest is lined with thistledown.*

Male (upper) and female, length 4½-5½"; Woodrow Goodpaster, National Audubon Society

Lesser Goldfinch
Spinus psaltria

TEE YEE TEE YER comes the plaintive song from the sycamore. You see a small finch with a dark back and bright yellow breast. As he takes off in swooping flight, his black wings flash with white. You recognize him as the lesser goldfinch, abundant resident of the west.

Approach the tree and you may find the olive-yellow female incubating four or five pale blue eggs in a cup-shaped nest of grass and plant down. This handsome pair may remain together in winter, when they join flocks roaming in search of thistle and other weed seeds. With their stout, cone-shaped bills they crack open the thistle seeds to extract the starchy kernels. In dry country they have been known to take turns hanging upside down from a garden faucet while the water dripped into their open bills.

In one subspecies, which ranges through the southern Rockies, the male has a black back except in immature plumage, when his back is green. Discovered along the Arkansas River in Colorado, this form is known as the Arkansas goldfinch. The male of the more western race keeps the green back when adult; this subspecies is often called the green-backed goldfinch.

Range: S. W. Washington to N. E. California and N. W. Oklahoma, south to N. South America.

Male lesser goldfinch, length 3¾-4¼″
Eliot Porter

Characteristics: male has black crown, olive-green or black back, black wings with bold white markings; yellow underparts. Female has olive-green head and back, dark rump, blackish wings, olive-yellow underparts. Young resemble the female with buff tinges.

Lawrence's Goldfinch
Spinus lawrencei

YELLOW WING BARS and a black face distinguish this goldfinch from the others. You may see flocks in the hot, dry lowlands of California, feasting on fiddle-neck and other seeds or clustered around a water hole, bathing, preening, and singing a song similar to that of the American goldfinch. Their call sounds like *tink-oo.*

They breed on oak-clad hillsides. The female builds a nest of grass, hair, and lichens for her four or five white eggs. With winter, *lawrencei,* named for 19th century ornithologist George H. Lawrence, wings east to open country where he wanders widely in search of seeds. In spring he may ignore last year's nesting area for another.

Range: California west of the Sierra Nevada to N. Baja California; winters east to W. Texas. *Characteristics:* yellow wing bars. Male has black on face, wings, tail; gray head, greenish-gray back, yellow rump and breast, whitish belly. Female and young are duller, lack black face.

Male Lawrence's goldfinch, length 4-4½″
Allan D. Cruickshank, National Audubon Society

Red Crossbill
Loxia curvirostra

GREAT NORTHERN PINES stand frocked in snow. On the lower limbs stocky red and olive-gray birds climb about, sometimes using both bills and feet like parrots. Watch one as he snips off a cone with his crossed, pruning-shear bill (page 19). He hops to the ground, holds the cone upside down between his feet, and slips his open bill under a scale. He pries it apart with a lateral motion of those remarkably adapted mandibles and scoops out the seeds with his tongue.

He doesn't cut off the larger cones but hangs upside down from a limb as he pries them open. The sound of cracking scales sometimes reveals a hidden crossbill. If frightened, he may swing underneath a limb and hang motionless. You may mistake him for a cone.

The abundance of the cone crop largely determines the movement of red crossbills through coniferous forests of the northern hemisphere. When cones are scarce, the birds may wander in flocks far to the south. They often pause to feed in garden evergreens as they travel.

When cones are abundant in the northern forests, the crossbills do not migrate and they may even start nesting in January. In some areas, however, they do not breed until August. Placed in a conifer, the saucer-shaped nest of twigs and bark holds three to five greenish-white eggs spotted with brown and purple. Males do not acquire the red coat of adulthood until their third year.

These birds sing a mixture of trills, warbles, and chipping notes. Their call is *jip-jip*.

Range: S. E. Alaska to Newfoundland, south in the west to Nicaragua, in the east to N. Wisconsin, Tennessee, and North Carolina; wanders in winter to N. Florida and the Gulf Coast. *Characteristics:* crossed bill. Male is brick red (brightest on rump) with dusky wings and tail. Female has olive-gray head and back, yellowish rump and underparts. Young are streaked gray.

White-winged Crossbill
Loxia leucoptera

WHITE WING BARS and a brighter coat distinguish this bird from the red crossbill. Both dwell in boreal forests of the northern hemisphere, but *leucoptera* ranges farther north and not as far south. Their habits are similar.

Whitewings call to each other with a plaintive *peet* or a dry, unmusical *chif-chif*. Their song is a vigorous outburst of warbles and trills. A bird may dart out from a treetop perch to end its song on the wing. The two to four blue-green eggs are blotched with brown.

Range: N. Alaska to Labrador, south to N. Oregon and N. New Hampshire; wanders in winter to Colorado and North Carolina. *Characteristics:* crossed bill, white wing bars. Male is rose pink with black wings and tail. Female and young are streaked olive-gray with yellowish rump.

Male (upper) and female (left) red crossbills, length 5¼-6½" Lower: male whitewing length 6-6¾", Allan Brooks

345

MINSTRELS OF
PRAIRIE AND FOREST

Sparrows
and Buntings
Family Fringillidae, Part 2

By ARTHUR A. ALLEN

N O QUESTION ABOUT IT. A clay-colored sparrow had come to Ithaca, New York, and was singing his fool head off among scattered cedars in a field not far from the Cornell University campus. Surely he could not expect to find a mate here, for the closest part of his normal breeding range was nearly 500 miles away in central Michigan. Still he kept on singing as he moved from one tree to another, although he enjoyed little privacy because of all the bird watchers he had attracted. He stayed for more than a month, then left in July.

Next May he returned, however, singing with even more enthusiasm. Finally in early June he was seen with a worm in his bill winging toward a certain cedar. In the tree a female chipping sparrow sat on her nest brooding her young. Circumstantial evidence pointed to an unusual case of hybridism. But I could not find one feather on the fledglings, scan them as I might, that differed from a juvenile chippy's. The lonesome clay-colored sparrow had simply adopted these youngsters after chasing the real father out of the territory.

Interbreeding among separate sparrow species is very rare, for nature provides many ways to preserve the integrity of each kind. During the mating season their calls, courtship rituals, and color patterns attract only members of the same clan.

Typically, sparrows are inconspicuous brown-and-gray birds with plumage more or less streaked. Those not streaked, such as adult juncos and towhees, wear the family stripes on their breasts when they are juveniles, just as young robins and bluebirds have spotted breasts characteristic of the thrush family.

Hardy, adapting to every kind of habitat, the 51 species of sparrows breeding in the United States and Canada have evolved several times that number of subspecies. Adaptations may arise over a long period of time as a species becomes more abundant and expands into new territory. Some birds become isolated from the old home, adapt to their new surroundings, and gradually develop recognizable differences from the original stock.

So variable is the ubiquitous song sparrow that 31 races are recognized. They differ in size and shades of brown. A person familiar only with the small, pale desert birds of Arizona, or even the darker ones in New England, would scarcely recognize the large slaty-brown Alaskan race as the same species. If it were not for all the intermediate forms, these extremes probably would be considered separate species. Indeed, several of the little seaside sparrows of the Atlantic and Gulf coasts have changed sufficiently in different marshes so that they rate full species rank.

Many sparrows have songs that rival those of the thrushes. Ornithologist Frank Chapman compared the music of Bachman's sparrow of the South to the "capti-

THE WATER'S FINE! *White-crowned sparrows, wintering in Arizona, take a dip. They breed in the Far North, as does the white-throated sparrow (opposite).*

Arthur A. Allen. Opposite: G. Ronald Austing, National Audubon Society

vating song of the hermit thrush in the purity of tone and execution." In the north woods the white-throated sparrow wins praise with his melodious *pure sweet Canada Canada Canada*. On the other hand, the *che dick* of the Henslow's sparrow and the dry trill of the grasshopper sparrow lack any musical appeal.

Since the bird's song announces his presence to others of his kind, it's important that his voice carry as far as possible. So he usually sings from an exposed perch. Chipping sparrows fly to the tops of trees or perch on power lines. Henslow's and grasshopper sparrows balance on the tips of high weeds, while song and field sparrows favor the tops of bushes. Longspurs, which live on prairie and tundra where high perches are scarce, sing in flight.

Sparrows quickly recognize their own songs when played back to them through a loudspeaker. I recall a windy day on the tundra near Hudson Bay. I hadn't been able to approach a shy Lapland longspur closer than 75 feet. But when he heard a recording of his song pouring through the speaker he flew directly at it, and before I realized it he was singing within ten inches of my ear!

Another time I lured a song sparrow into camera range with a tape recorder and a mirror. About ten feet from my photographic blind I arranged a spray of blooming forsythia in a bottle of water and set this in front of the mirror. Then I plugged in the tape recorder and played song sparrow phrases. The result was miraculous. In no time at all a song sparrow flew down to the recorder and landed on the forsythia. Spying his reflection in the mirror, he challenged his "rival" with a beautiful song. Snap! I had my picture.

Through the years I have stumbled onto the nest of every kind of sparrow that breeds near my home. But for a long time the grasshopper sparrow's eluded me. Then my luck changed. I spied a four-leaf clover on the edge of a field I had been scouring for two weeks. Normally I'm not superstitious, but on a hunch I walked straight out into the field and stopped. A yard away a female grasshopper sparrow flushed from four eggs. Pure luck had led me to her nest.

I recall another nest that was hard to find. In the shinnery oak country of southern Oklahoma I once noticed a female lark sparrow sneaking off through the brush. But search as I might I could not find her nest. In disgust I kicked a battered aluminum basin that lay upside down on the sandy soil. There was the nest!

It had been covered by the basin, no doubt an effective fortress against predators and trampling cattle. When I replaced the old pan I noticed it had a hole in the bottom – the sparrow's doorway. What a prosaic home, I thought, for a lovely bird.

GRASSHOPPER SPARROW *sings like its supper. The tiny bird is named for its insectlike buzzing, not for the grasshoppers it catches. The orphaned song sparrow (right) will make charming music with* sweet sweet sweet *notes when it grows up. Here it opens wide to plead for a morsel.*

Eliot Porter. Right: Charles E. Mohr, National Audubon Society

349

Western male (left) and juvenile rufous-sided towhees, length 7-8¾"; Allan Brooks

Rufous-sided Towhee
Pipilo erythrophthalmus

A GREAT RATTLING and scuffling comes from the dry leaves by a country lane. It sounds like a whole family of squirrels or a covey of quail in the underbrush. But come closer. A single bird, black-headed with ruddy sides, is making all the fuss as he rummages for insects, seeds, and berries. Now with a flurry of wings he explodes from cover – a rufous-sided towhee. As he flies off he sounds his name loud and clear in a double note of alarm – *to-whee*. Many hear it as *che-wink* and call him that.

Ranging from southern Canada to Central America, this handsome bird inhabits patches of thick underbrush. There are 15 recognized subspecies. Western representatives were formerly considered a separate species called the spotted towhee (above). Unlike the eastern bird (opposite), the back in this form is heavily sprinkled with white spots. A race in the southeastern United States, the white-eyed towhee, has white irises instead of the usual red.

In the northeast the male towhee arrives at his breeding ground in late April and establishes his territory with a drawn-out song: *drink your teee!* When the female shows up, he courts her by opening and closing his wings and flirting his long tail to show the white markings. His mate may build two nests in a season to accommodate two broods. She prods stems, leaves, and bark into a loose structure lined with grass and hair.

The four to six white eggs are finely dotted with reddish brown. Brown head and back camouflage the incubating female so well that an observer may come within a few feet without seeing her. She will stay as long as she dares, then may play the part of a cripple to draw attention from the eggs. Or she may hover near, with tail fanned as though to shield the nest.

The male often brings food to his mate while she is incubating; occasionally he may take a turn on the eggs. Young towhees remain in the nest 10 to 12 days after they hatch, but if danger threatens they may leave their vulnerable home before they are able to fly. Though the parents try to protect them, many a nestling falls prey to an animal or snake.

The parasitic cowbird victimizes this species with great success. As many as eight cowbird eggs have been found in a towhee nest, and towhee parents often raise young cowbirds.

After taking wing, juvenile towhees stay in a family group for a while. But they soon disperse, for towhees are solitary birds. When frost nips hard in early fall, the northern chewinks form no migrating flocks but simply slip away southward in solitude in the night.

Towhees have sometimes been blamed (probably wrongly) for pulling up new corn. In North Carolina they were once denied protection and listed as game birds for 25 years.

Range: S. British Columbia to S.W. Maine, south to Guatemala; migratory in the north. *Characteristics:* male has black head and throat, black back with white spots; reddish-brown sides, white belly, long tail white near tip. Female has brown head, throat, and back. Young are brown with dark-streaked underparts.

Abert's Towhee

Pipilo aberti

Abert's, length 8-9"; Allan Brooks

LOOK SHARP if you want to catch a glimpse of this big cinnamon-brown towhee with a black patch across his face. He takes cover in dense thickets the moment anyone intrudes upon his remote and desolate territory. His call note, a single *peek*, may be all that identifies the shy hermit of the Southwest.

Abert's towhee lives in desert regions, generally along the basin of the Colorado River. He slips through tangled growths of willow, cottonwood, cane, chaparral, and mesquite that line the Gila River and other streams and washes. He feeds on insects, seeds, and fruit, scratching at leaves and flood debris, even clawing at the bark of trees to get at grubs.

In a thick clump of underbrush, usually a few feet above the ground, the towhee builds an untidy-looking nest with grass stems and weeds protruding at random around the outside. The deep cup within, however, is tightly fashioned and well lined with fine rootlets and hair.

The female towhee, resembling the male, sits on this nest in awkward pose, her bill cocked high in one direction, her tail pointing skyward in the other. She lays three or four pale blue-green eggs with a scrawl of hair lines and black spots near the big end. They look like the eggs of a red-winged blackbird.

Abert's towhee is named for the man who first collected one of the species, Lt. James William Abert of the U. S. Army. He shot his bird in 1846, according to his journal, at the settlement of Valverde on the Rio Grande near Socorro, New Mexico. The settlement has since vanished, and ornithologists are puzzled by Abert's records. For not another Abert's towhee has been discovered in this region.

Range: S. E. Nevada and S. W. Utah to S. W. New Mexico, south along the Colorado River basin to the Gulf of California. *Characteristics:* grayish brown with black mask, buffy brown underparts, reddish-brown tinge on throat.

Eastern male rufous-sided towhee, John H. Gerard, National Audubon Society

Brown Towhee

Pipilo fuscus

GARBED IN DRAB gray-brown plumage, this abundant western bird looks much like an over-grown sparrow. Suburbanites in California are used to the brown towhee, scratching for insects in the dry leaves beneath the garden shrubbery. Ranchers in Texas are accustomed to seeing him kick away the twigs beneath the chaparral as he diligently searches for seeds. He is too familiar to be especially noticed.

The brown towhee's voice is as undistinguished as his appearance. His song is a harsh monotone – a single metallic note long repeated, *chink-chink-ink-ink-ink-ink-ink-ink*, with sometimes a halfhearted trill added at the end.

In the breeding season the male gives a sharp squawk of anger when another male towhee intrudes on his courtship. This pallid bird attacks his rival with a fury of fluttering wings and hammering beak. Often other males join the fray and the duel degenerates into a donnybrook.

So aggressive is the male brown towhee at this season that the sight of his reflection in a windowpane may set him off for hours. One bird was reported to have fought his image until blood from his bruised bill smeared the glass. He paused only when utterly exhausted or when changing light erased the reflection. Next morning he renewed the battle; and so he continued hammering away, day after day, right through the breeding season!

In a cuplike nest a few feet off the ground and well protected by foliage the female towhee lays three or four bluish eggs with dark spots. She raises two broods a season.

Gardeners know the brown towhee best because of his eating habits. In spring he steals his fill of tender peas and lettuce; in late summer he falls to with zest as plums, apricots, peaches, and grapes ripen in California orchards and vineyards. Yet the damage done is slight compared to the service the bird renders by devouring harmful insects and weed seeds.

The brown towhee has 12 subspecies. Best known of these races are the California towhee, which ranges west of the Sierras, and the cañon towhee of the southwestern desert country. The latter wears a reddish crown and ranchers and hunters call him "camp bird," for he seems a fixture near cabins and bunkhouses, scavenging for crumbs and nesting in a brush pile.

Range: S. W. Oregon to Arizona and central Texas, south to S. Mexico. *Characteristics:* gray-brown with buffy throat, dark tail rusty beneath.

Brown towhee, length 8¼-10"; Allan D. Cruickshank, National Audubon Society

Greentail, length 6¼-7″; Eliot Porter

Olive sparrows, length 5½-6″

Green-tailed Towhee
Chlorura chlorura

WAIT FOR STRONG LIGHT if you want to see green in the tail of the green-tailed towhee. At times it may look yellowish or olive.

Some experts feel that "green-tailed" does not quite fit this bird. Nor does "towhee" seem right either, for the glimpse of yellow on the underside of the wings when the bird is in flight suggests a warbler, while his white throat and reddish crown could be a sparrow's. Perhaps, as has been suggested, he should be named the red-capped sparrow-warbler.

Yet the greentail's song is like a towhee's. It starts with clear notes and ends in raspy ones: *weet-chur-cheeeeeee—churrr.* When alarmed or excited, the bird mews plaintively.

This smallest of the towhees ranges through western mountain regions and in migration may appear in western Kansas and Oklahoma. He nests on or near the ground in the heart of a sage bush or a clump of greasewood. The nest is a nondescript structure, carelessly woven but lined with fine grasses, and perhaps horsehair, to take the four whitish eggs freckled with brown.

Scratching beneath the underbrush, the parents hunt for insects to feed their gaping young. The birds also eat weed seeds. Sometimes they scamper across a patch of open ground, tails upright and oddly spread.

Range: S. W. Oregon and S. E. Washington to S. E. Wyoming, south to S. California and S. New Mexico; winters to central Mexico. *Characteristics:* reddish crown, white throat, gray head and breast, olive back and tail, yellow under wings.

Olive Sparrow
Arremonops rufivirgata

THIS ATTRACTIVE little Mexican bird ranges north of the border into southern Texas. Some call him the Texas sparrow. He looks like a small edition of the green-tailed towhee – a long-tailed bird with olive-and-gray plumage. The difference lies in the brown stripes on his head and the buffy tinge of his breast. The young are brown above with olive on wings and tail.

The olive sparrow is too well camouflaged to be easily glimpsed, especially since he frequents dense thickets of reeds and underbrush, scuffing away leaves like a towhee to find insects and seed pods. He only forsakes cover to dash like a shadow to another bush.

Often this sparrow can be heard but not seen. He will flutter up to a low perch, well screened by foliage, and sing a song which is nothing but a series of chips, all on one pitch. They start deliberately, then pick up speed until they trail off into a rattle.

Where the feeding is good, several of the birds may gather, industriously poking through the chaparral, sometimes interrupting to chase each other playfully with chirps and squeals.

The olive sparrow builds a big, domed nest of twigs, grass, stems, and leaves, couching it usually a few feet off the ground in a thick bush or a cactus plant. Here the female lays three or four pure white eggs.

Range: S. Texas south to Costa Rica. *Characteristics:* brown stripes on gray crown; olive back and wings, grayish-buff underparts shading to white on the abdomen.

Henslow's Sparrow
Passerherbulus henslowii

CLINGING to a weed stalk in a damp eastern meadow, this little stump-tailed sparrow throws back his big, flattish head and sings *tsi-lick*. It lasts only two-fifths of a second and is not much of a song. Yet the bird may repeat his emphatic little hiccup all day and far into the night.

Henslow's sparrow is hard to find unless he sings. In his camouflaged plumage he scuttles through the grass like a mouse. He pokes his bill into clusters of moist grass roots and weeds to snap up insects and seeds. He flies rarely, and then in erratic undulations.

In breeding season Henslow's sparrow joins a loose colony. His partly domed nest rests on the ground, hidden by grass and weeds. The four or five dainty eggs have rusty spots.

Range: E. South Dakota to S. New Hampshire, south to E. Kansas and North Carolina; winters from S. E. Texas to Florida and north along the coast to South Carolina. *Characteristics:* dark-striped olive head, large pale bill, russet wings and back, streaked buffy sides, short tail.

Savannah Sparrow
Passerculus sandwichensis

TINY, SHARP EYES, each with a yellow line over it, peer from a weed patch in a meadow. The Savannah sparrow teeters a moment on flesh-colored legs, then with lowered head sprints off through the grass.

The many subspecies of this short-tailed sparrow cover most of North America. Alexander Wilson reported in 1811 his discovery of the species in Savannah, Georgia. The bird frequents low, moist, open areas: fields that border marshes, tidal flats, and the shores of lakes and streams.

Seeds and insects—especially beetles—comprise this sparrow's diet. He flies only occasionally—low, erratic flights, a few feet at a time. He may flutter up to a post or weed stalk to sing his feeble, lisping notes: *tsit-tsit-tsit, tseeeee-tsaaay.* You have to be very close to hear the first three chips.

In the courting season the males chase each other and display to the females by vibrating their wings, either on the ground or in flight. The sexes look alike. Mated birds build their nest in a hollow. In the cup of stems and moss the female lays four or five bluish, rust-specked eggs. Both parents incubate them.

Range: N. Alaska to N. Labrador, south to Guatemala, Missouri, and W. Maryland; winters to the West Indies. *Characteristics:* yellow eyebrow stripe, grayish crown stripe; brown head and back, whitish underparts, all streaked; stubby, notched tail.

Grasshopper Sparrow
Ammodramus savannarum

IN AN ABANDONED, weedy pasture the only signs of life are a small brown bird sunning on a rock and an occasional insectlike buzz.

There is no reason to connect the buzz with the bird—unless the bird has a striped outsize head, a buffy breast without bold stripes, and a stub tail. Then there is reason enough. These field marks identify the grasshopper sparrow, a bird whose song so closely matches the sound of a grasshopper that he bears the insect's name.

Dwelling in dry fields and meadows through most of the United States, the grasshopper sparrow probably devours more insects than other sparrows. If flushed, he makes a low, twisting, wrenlike flight, then drops to cover.

During nesting season these sparrows often gather in loose colonies. They build a grass cup, lined with rootlets and partially domed, set in a weed-hidden hollow. The four or five white eggs are spotted with red-brown about the larger end.

Range: S. E. British Columbia to Maine, south to S. California, central Colorado, and the Gulf Coast; winters from central California and North Carolina to El Salvador. *Characteristics:* streaked brown upperparts, clear buffy breast and white belly; large head, short tail. Young have streaked breasts.

Sharp-tailed Sparrow
Ammospiza caudacuta

DEVOURING seeds and snails and sand fleas, a half-dozen small, streaked sparrows scamper like tiny rodents through the rank grass of a salt marsh. They stop, stretch their necks to look around, and now you can see distinctive markings on their faces—ocher lines and gray ear patches. When they run off again, they flirt the short, pointed tails that give them their name.

Sharp-tailed sparrows inhabit both tidal and freshwater marshes. Most of the races range along the Atlantic Coast. These are terrestrial birds, generally loath to fly except for short flights. The birds gather in flocks and swarm through the grass. Their song is little more than a hiss—like dipping a hot pan in water.

The sharptail builds a loose grass nest amid seaweed or driftwood or sometimes sets it in a tussock of marsh grass. Here are laid four or five pale bluish eggs with brown speckles.

Range: N. E. British Columbia to N. Quebec, south to North Dakota and along Atlantic Coast to North Carolina; winters along coast from New York to S. Texas. *Characteristics:* ocher face stripes, gray ear patch, brown back with white streaks; streaked buffy breast, ocher in some races; sharp tail.

Henslow's
length 4¾-5¼"

Grasshopper
length 4½-5⅓"

Savannah
length 4½-6"

Ipswich
length 6-6¼"

Sharptail
length 5-6"

WALTER A. WEBER

Walter A. Weber, National Geographic staff artist

Ipswich Sparrow
Passerculus princeps

SABLE ISLAND, a bleak strip of sand dunes about 100 miles off Nova Scotia, is the only breeding place of the Ipswich sparrow. In summer the bird picks insects from the island's shoreline refuse and gleans beach-grass seeds from the edge of the dunes. In winter most of the colony scatters southward along the Atlantic Coast. The first specimen of this brown-and-whitish bird was collected at Ipswich, Massachusetts, in 1868.

The Ipswich sparrow, an insular form of the Savannah sparrow, is shy when approached during winter on an East Coast beach. He is quick to fly yet reluctant to leave the dunes. But on his island breeding grounds he seems almost tame, for he is unused to the sight of humans there. His call is a dry little *tsip*.

In a sheltered hollow the Ipswich weaves a cup of beach grass for the four or five eggs – white, bluish, or olive and splashed with brown.

Range: Sable Island, Nova Scotia; winters from Massachusetts to S. Georgia. *Characteristics:* similar to Savannah sparrow but larger, lighter in hue with paler markings.

Male (upper) and female lark buntings, length 5½-7½"
Walter A. Weber
National Geographic staff artist

Baird's, length 5-5½"; Allan Brooks

Baird's Sparrow
Ammodramus bairdii

AUDUBON, journeying across the northern Great Plains in 1843, discovered a little sparrow with an ocher stripe on its crown. He named the bird for Spencer F. Baird, a young naturalist friend. Baird's sparrow was the last bird that Audubon described and named. Its portrait completed the octavo edition of his famed *The Birds of America*, providing plate number 500.

Strangely, Audubon's description remained all that was known of the bird until 1873. Then, when Baird was a noted ornithologist, soon to become Secretary of the Smithsonian Institution, his sparrow was rediscovered.

The bird can still be found where Audubon first saw him, in the grasslands between the Mississippi and the Rockies. His voice identifies him best — a few chips followed by a trill that is lower and more musical than the toneless whispers of the Savannah and grasshopper sparrows.

Baird's sparrow searches dead, matted vegetation for insects and seeds. If frightened, he runs through the grass or makes a zigzag flight.

On northern breeding grounds the bird builds a cuplike nest of stems and grass in the shade of a plant or in a clump of rank growth. The nest shelters three to five white eggs, darkly lined and splotched with brown at the large end.

Range: S. Alberta to S. Manitoba, south to N. W. Montana and W. Minnesota; winters from S. E. Arizona and S. New Mexico to central Mexico. *Characteristics:* ocher crown stripe, necklace of black streaks; streaked yellow-brown upperparts, pale underparts.

Lark Bunting
Calamospiza melanocorys

THEY COME to the Great Plains from Mexico and Louisiana, and their coming is a lovely thing to see. They fly in by the hundreds, the females in striped brown plumage, the breeding males in gleaming black. Greening fields give them rest and food but do not stay the forward motion of the flock as a whole. The rear ranks of birds flutter continually to the fore, and the entire assembly rolls over the fresh land like some marvelous living wheel.

Then they are off again, the whole flock taking wing in unison, belling a chorus of sweet, clear warbles. Thus the lark buntings race the spring season north.

They breed on the grasslands that stretch down the center of the continent, east of the Rockies. Whether dry plain or moist prairie, the lark bunting's breeding ground offers seeds and insects, particularly grasshoppers.

The splendid male often sings in flight, rocketing upward like a lark. The drab female incubates the four or five pale blue eggs. These are cradled in a loose grass cup set in a hollow overhung by vegetation. The gregarious birds may nest in loose colonies.

In winter the male's finery gives way to the same plumage as his mate's. But conspicuous light shoulder patches generally remain.

Range: S. Alberta and S. W. Manitoba, south to S. Montana and east of the Rockies to S. E. New Mexico and N. Texas; winters from S. California to S. Louisiana, south to central Mexico. *Characteristics:* breeding male is black except for white wing patches; female, winter male, and young have streaked brown upperparts, streaked white underparts. Some of the fall flock show white or buffy wing patches.

Le Conte's Sparrow
Passerherbulus caudacutus

PRAIRIE MARSHES in Canada and the north central United States are the breeding grounds of this sharp-tailed moppet, named for a physician-naturalist. But he wanders even to New York.

Le Conte's sparrow hunts for seeds and insects in wet, matted vegetation. He runs more than he flies and shows himself best when he mounts a stalk to utter a thin buzz, beak agape.

In a sheltered clump of old growth the birds build a grass cup for the four or five white or greenish eggs marked with brown.

Range: N. Alberta to N. Ontario, south to N. Montana and N. Michigan; winters from W. Kansas to South Carolina, south to S. Texas and N. W. Florida. *Characteristics:* whitish crown stripe, buff-ocher eye stripe, breast, and sides; pinkish-brown nape, streaked brown upperparts.

Le Conte's, length 4½-5¼"; Allan Brooks

Seaside Sparrow
Ammospiza maritima

ON A SUMMERTIME HIKE along a marshy mid-Atlantic shore you are almost sure to pass near a seaside sparrow. Yet you may never see one.

Every one of the bird's seven races inhabits salt marshes, favoring the wetter parts where the tides slide in through muddy channels lined with coarse grasses and reeds. If you wade into the mud, hide in a stand of marsh grass, and make squeaking noises on the back of your hand to imitate the bird's distress call, a seaside sparrow may climb a nearby reed stalk to look you over. That way you can glimpse him.

He is large for a sparrow and dresses conservatively in dark gray plumage relieved only by the white stripe on his jaw and a streak of yellow between bill and eye. He eats insects and spiders, also small crabs and other marine creatures. When undisturbed, he often wades along the mudbanks like a rail or sandpiper.

Sometimes the bird perches on a stalk to sing a few short weak notes followed by a buzz and a long, lower-pitched trill. Occasionally he performs during a short upward flight. His alarm call is a single sharp squeak.

These sparrows weave a nest of coarse stems lined with fine grasses and set it just beyond the reach of normal high tide. Sometimes the nest is in a hump of dried seaweed; once in a while the birds affix it to several stout grass stems above the high-water mark. It holds three or four white eggs heavily spotted with brown.

Range: salt marshes along Atlantic Coast from Massachusetts to N. Florida, and Gulf Coast from S. Texas to central Florida; northern subspecies winter from Virginia southward. *Characteristics:* dark gray upperparts, dingy underparts; yellow line before eye, white streak on jaw.

Seaside sparrows, length 5½-6½"; Eliot Porter

Vesper Sparrow
Pooecetes gramineus

IN THE HUSH of evening, as shadows lengthen over meadows and woods, a sweet, clear bird song echoes—two long, low notes, two higher ones, then a rippling trill. From a distant fence post or telephone wire the vesper sparrow sings, and his music seems to complement the peacefulness of the sunset.

The little caroler, garbed in sober, striped browns, shows a flash of white in his tail when he flies off. He ranges upland fields and pastures throughout much of the continent. He shies away from buildings, yet often takes a dust bath in the middle of a gravel road.

The male conducts his courtship mostly on the ground, scampering before or after the female with wings raised and tail spread. Occasionally he flies high to sing a mating song. Rival males may compete fiercely for the female.

The pair build their nest in a grassy hollow, sometimes in the shelter of a leafy bush or surrounding tussocks. It is a neat cup of grass and rootlets. The young hatch from four or five white eggs thickly marked with brown. Their parents eat the broken egg shells and keep the nest scrupulously clean as they take turns brooding and feeding the nestlings.

Vesper sparrows feed mainly on insects during spring and summer, though their diet includes seeds. In the autumn the birds begin to flock. A score or two at a time may be seen winging their way southward.

The vesper sparrow was once called the grass finch and sometimes the bay-winged bunting. He sings off and on all day, sometimes even in the middle of the night. But his vesper song earned him his present name.

Range: British Columbia to Nova Scotia, south to central California and central North Carolina; winters to S. Baja California and the Gulf Coast. *Characteristics:* striped brown upperparts, streaked whitish belly, chestnut wing patch; white outer tail feathers show in flight.

Dusky Seaside Sparrow
Ammospiza nigrescens

CAPE KENNEDY juts from a long outer sandbank that lines much of the east coast of Florida. Here on launching pads stand giant "birds" poised for blast-off. The partly dry salt marshes near the space center are home to another bird, tiny but very much alive. This is the dusky seaside sparrow, a black-streaked relative of *Ammospiza maritima* (page 357).

The dusky is hard to see as he walks and flits about in the tall reeds. But he is not shy and will climb a stalk to eye you if you make a few birdlike squeaks with your lips against the back of your hand. He feeds largely on crickets, grasshoppers, spiders, and seeds.

This sparrow's song, like the seaside's, is made up of buzzes and trills. He sings frequently during nesting season, sometimes on the wing. The birds place their grass nest a foot off the ground in a cluster of rushes. The three or four white eggs are blotched with brown.

Range: salt marshes of E. Florida near Cape Kennedy. *Characteristics:* similar to seaside sparrow but darker; black streaks on underparts.

358

Vesper sparrow, length 5-6½"; Eliot Porter

Dusky seaside, length 5½-6½"; Allan Brooks

Cape Sable Sparrow
Ammospiza mirabilis

THE TOTAL POPULATION of this species lives in a small stretch of marsh near the southern tip of the Florida peninsula. The Cape Sable sparrow, like the dusky seaside sparrow, is an isolated form of the seaside sparrow, cut off from his nearest cousins by about 200 miles.

The bird lived on Cape Sable until 1935, when a tremendous hurricane sent a wall of water over the region, inundating his breeding grounds. The sparrow then moved inland, venturing even into freshwater marshes. Despite floods and the fires that sometimes rage through the matted vegetation beneath the live marsh grass, the species has survived.

This shy and secretive bird spends most of his time on or near the ground. He searches for insects and spiders and sometimes picks up a few sand fleas and mollusks. Only rarely does he eat seeds or vegetable food of any kind. His song is like the dusky seaside sparrow's. He usually sings while on the ground.

During breeding season the Cape Sable sparrow is quick to fly, rising out of the tall grass and winging off for a couple of hundred yards before landing. Approached then, he runs through the grass as though trying to avoid a second flight.

This sparrow builds a grass nest and weaves it into the marsh grass on or near the ground. The four or five blue eggs are evenly and heavily marked with browns and grays.

Range: near Cape Sable in S. W. Florida. *Characteristics:* yellow eye stripe, light olive-green upperparts, whitish underparts.

Lark Sparrow
Chondestes grammacus

THIS HANDSOME BIRD with gaily striped head ranks among the finest sparrow vocalists. His song is a sweet mingling of rich notes and varied trills and buzzes. He sings from a low perch and sometimes while hovering.

The lark sparrow is a bird of the grasslands and ranges across the United States except for the Atlantic Coast. He seems to thrive best in open pastures dotted with trees and bushes. Farmers see him in the orchard and along the edge of a field. Strollers along a country lane come upon him frolicking in the dust ahead of them. Sometimes he leaps up to snatch a passing insect, then continues to skip and scamper along the road, playful and unafraid.

Courting, the male spreads his white-rimmed tail and dances and flutters before the female. The pair nest on the ground or as high as ten feet up in a low tree. The three to five white eggs are spotted and scrawled with black and brown. The young birds resemble adults except for the fine streaks on their breasts.

Lark sparrows rummage along the ground for insects and weed seeds. In autumn they may flock together. Sometimes a score of the birds perch on a fence and suddenly burst into song.

Range: W. Oregon and S. British Columbia to central Pennsylvania, south to N. Mexico and central North Carolina; winters to El Salvador and S. Florida. *Characteristics:* chestnut crown and ear patch, black-and-white striped head; streaked brown back, dark tail with white corners, white breast with single dark spot.

359

Lark sparrow, length 5½-6¾"; Eliot Porter

Cape Sable, length 6"; Allan Brooks

Rufous-crowned Sparrow
Aimophila ruficeps

"WHY FLY?" the rufous-crowned sparrow seems to ask. This bird of southwestern mountain and canyon slopes prefers to walk.

Leisurely, he moves from brush clump to grass tuft gathering seeds. If threatened, he may mew in alarm before creeping away. His song is a gurgling warble. The grassy nest with four white or pale blue eggs rests on the ground.

Range: central California to central Oklahoma, south to S. Mexico. *Characteristics:* rusty crown, black "whiskers," chestnut-streaked grayish back, buffy-brown underparts.

Rufous-crown, length 5-6"; Helen Cruickshank

Rufous-winged sparrow, length 5-5½"; Eliot Porter

Rufous-winged Sparrow
Aimophila carpalis

THESE SPARROWS were first seen in the United States in 1872. They were plentiful in southern Arizona amid the tall desert grass and brush. But fires and overgrazing destroyed their habitat, and they vanished into Mexico for half a century. Now some are back in the Tucson area, breeding where patches of the wild grass grow again.

The rufous-winged sparrow is a tame bird, easily seen as he feeds along the ground. His song is a series of fast chips. He waits for the rains before nesting in a hackberry bush. The well-woven grass home holds four pale blue eggs.

Range: S. Arizona and N. W. Mexico. *Characteristics:* rufous crown stripes and shoulder patches, black "whiskers," streaked brown upperparts, grayish underparts.

Cassin's Sparrow
Aimophila cassinii

EVEN THE CACTUS seems to sag in the noon heat. Yet during his breeding season this sparrow, colored like his arid surroundings, often flutters up like a skylark to sing his high, clear trill. He drops back to a desert shrub as his song ends, then rises again for a fresh outpouring.

Cassin's sparrow may sing all night on the plains and in canyons. His nest, a deep cup of bark and grass, is set in a low bush or on the ground in a grass clump or at the base of a cactus. It holds three or four white or bluish eggs.

Range: S. E. Arizona to W. Kansas, south to N. Mexico; winters to central Mexico. *Characteristics:* grayish upperparts marked with brown; buffy-white underparts, often broadly marked with brown on the sides.

Bachman's Sparrow
Aimophila aestivalis

THIS SHY SOUTHERN BIRD was discovered by the Rev. John Bachman near Charleston, South Carolina, in 1832. Audubon named the sparrow for his good friend, but it is also known as the pinewoods sparrow.

Neglected fields and open woodlands of oak or pine with an undergrowth of scrub palmetto are among the favorite haunts of Bachman's sparrow. A fleeting glimpse of him in such surroundings is about all most bird watchers can hope for. When disturbed, the bird sounds a snakelike hiss and runs off through the tall wire grass. He does not flush easily. If finally stirred to flight, he flutters but a short distance before dropping to cover.

Bachman's sparrow lacks prominent field marks, but his song gives him away. It is a clear, liquid whistle followed by a trill or warble that may drop in pitch and vary its tempo from a leisurely series of notes to an accelerating rivulet of sound. Of all the sparrow songs this is ranked as one of the finest.

Early morning and late afternoon are the best times to hear this minstrel of the southern uplands. He may perform from a pine stump, a low bough, or a perch on a brush pile. Occasionally, he sings as he flutters aloft in erratic flight. He may have many variations in one performance. An observer in Louisiana heard this bird sing 52 times from the same perch in 15 minutes.

The bird feeds mainly on the ground. With his rather large bill he picks up beetles, spiders, grasshoppers, crickets, caterpillars, and moths. Though insects comprise most of his diet, he also eats the seeds of grasses, pines, and sedges.

In a clump of grass or a tangle of vines the female weaves a nest of grass tops domed like the nest of a meadowlark, with an entrance at the side. In this well-concealed home on the ground she lays four eggs. They are pure white, unlike the eggs of most sparrows.

The female, who looks like her mate, incubates the eggs without help from him. But when the young emerge after about 12 days, their father assists in the feeding.

Range: S. Missouri to W. Pennsylvania, south to S. E. Texas and central Florida. *Characteristics:* chestnut-streaked gray back, unstreaked buffy breast, wings edged in yellow. Young have streaked underparts.

Bachman's, length 5¾″

Botteri's, length 5¼-6¼″

Cassin's, length 5¼-5¾″
Allan Brooks

Botteri's Sparrow
Aimophila botterii

LIKE A FEATHERED FIELD MOUSE, this little brown bird scurries through the waving grass of the southwestern plains. Here, in the ancient home of the Apache, Botteri's sparrow forages for weed seeds and insects and sings a sweet song, much like the tinkling of a canary. The female lays her three to five white eggs in a grass nest set on the ground.

Range: S. E. Arizona and S. Texas, south to S. Mexico; migratory in northern part of range. *Characteristics:* streaked brown upperparts, unstreaked buffy-gray underparts, dark brown tail.

Black-throated Sparrow
Amphispiza bilineata

As SUNRISE spreads a copper glow across the Mojave Desert in California, grayish sparrows begin to tune up. They sing from creosote bushes or spears of yucca on the rocky hillsides.

Heads thrown back, black throats swelling, they sound clear, sweet notes and varied trills: *cheet cheet cheeeeeeee*. Soon they're in full voice, and the morning chorus seems to rise with the gathering heat waves. When a bird has sung his fill he flies to the ground to scratch and feed under the bushes.

Also called the desert sparrow, the handsome blackthroat inhabits the Great Basin and adjacent areas of the Southwest and Mexico. You may find him on juniper-dotted slopes up to 7,000 feet. He leaves the colder uplands to winter in the desert regions or south of the border.

During March and April blackthroats seek nest sites in sagebrush, mesquite, cactus, and other low growth. In the heart of a clump they build a cup of bark shreds and grass for three or four white eggs. Where sheep range the eggs may rest on a lining of wool. These energetic birds usually raise a second brood in late spring.

When danger approaches the nest, the parents show intense excitement. They call to each other with tinkling *weet* notes and fly from bush to bush. Sometimes the male bursts into song.

Range: N. E. California to S. W. Wyoming, south to central Mexico; migratory in the north. *Characteristics:* brownish-gray head and back, white face stripes and breast, black throat; blackish tail with white edges. Young have white throat and gray-streaked breast.

Sage sparrow, length 5-6"
Walter A. Weber, National Geographic staff artist

Sage Sparrow
Amphispiza belli

JERKING his tail nervously, this gray bird of the Great Basin hugs the shadows of the sagebrush. He scuttles between the bushes like a mouse. When flushed, he makes short, low flights. If you see him head on, the dark "button" on his white breast quickly identifies him.

In spring he rises to the bush tops to sing a simple *tsit-tsoo-tsee-tsay*. The three or four speckled white, bluish, or greenish eggs are laid in a twiggy cup in a bush.

Bell's sparrow, a darker race in California, was once considered a separate species.

Range: central Washington to N. W. Colorado, south to central Baja California, N. Arizona, and N. W. New Mexico; winters to mainland N. Mexico and W. Texas. *Characteristics:* grayish upperparts, white head markings, eye rings, and underparts; streaks on back, throat, and sides; dusky breast spot. Flicks tail.

Black-throated sparrow, length 4¾-5¼"; Lyman K. Stuart

Slate-colored Junco
Junco hyemalis

"LEADEN SKIES ABOVE, snow below." A winter's day, a junco's plumage—the two go together. On dark wings these jaunty snowbirds swoop down on a field to rummage for seeds among the brown weeds that poke up through the snow. White tail sides flashing, they swarm to a feeder, chattering softly as they move about. Over most of the United States, wherever there's promise of some dried berries or small seeds, these juncos enliven the bleak months.

You'll have no trouble identifying them. That sudden change of colors on the lower breast—from slate-gray to pure white—is a clincher.

With the advent of spring some juncos travel as far as the forests of northern Alaska to breed. Others, in the east, head for the conifers in the nearest mountains. Frequently they nest by the roadside or on the edge of a clearing.

They build a deep cup of bark shreds, moss, and grass on the ground or among upturned roots and low growth. While the female incubates the four or five brown-spotted greenish eggs, her mate sings sweet trills from a treetop perch.

Young males may keep a touch of brown in their plumage until their third year. Adult females, somewhat paler than the males, may also show a hint of brown in their sides.

Range: N. W. Alaska to Labrador, south to N. British Columbia, central Minnesota, Connecticut, and in the mountains to N. Georgia; winters to N. W. Mexico and N. Florida. *Characteristics:* gray upperparts and breast, white belly and tail edges. Young have brownish back and buffy underparts, heavily streaked.

White-winged Junco
Junco aikeni

SUNSET RAYS cast a warm haze over the still forest of yellow pines in the Black Hills of South Dakota and Wyoming. A musical little junco trill breaks the hush. More than likely the singer is a whitewing. You may find this large gray junco hereabouts the year round; in summer you will find him nowhere else.

As he forages for seeds and insects in brushy clearings, you notice more white in his wings and tail than in others of his genus.

For nesting, whitewings seem to prefer a hillside site above a stream. They raise two broods a year under logs, in tree roots, or on rock ledges. They may settle around lumber camps or tuck a cozy nest of grass and hair in a tin can at a refuse heap. The four or five greenish eggs are dotted with brown.

Range: S. E. Montana, W. South Dakota, N. E. Wyoming, and N. W. Nebraska; winters to N. Arizona and W. Kansas. *Characteristics:* gray upperparts and breast, white wing bars and belly, prominent white tail sides.

363

Slate-colored junco, length 5½-6½"; Allan D. Cruickshank, National Audubon Society

Oregon Junco
Junco oreganus

SHELTERED by a young redwood, Oregon juncos hop about a California garden, gathering the spill from a feeding tray. They utter little smacking notes as they feed, and with each hop the outer tail feathers blink white. When the seeds are gone, the flock moves off amid a flurry of soft twittering.

In the western mountains these juncos sometimes range up to timberline near the haunts of rosy finches. They breed on cliffs, on fern-clad hillsides, and in openings in coniferous forests where sunlight encourages brushy growth. Usually built on the ground, the nest of grass and weeds holds four or five bluish eggs spotted with brown and lavender.

Oregon juncos occasionally hybridize with gray-headed and slate-colored juncos. One race of *oreganus*, the pink-sided junco, was formerly regarded as a separate species. In this form the sides are bright pink, and the male's head is gray rather than black.

In winter flocks of Oregon juncos roam western foothills, canyons, and suburbs where brushy growth and garden plantings offer a supply of seeds and berries. Some wander far to the east.

Range: S. E. Alaska to S. W. Saskatchewan, south to N. Baja California and N. W. Wyoming; winters to mainland N. Mexico and central Texas. *Characteristics:* pinkish bill, rusty back, pinkish-brown sides, white belly and tail edges. Male has black head, female gray.

Male (left) and female Oregon juncos, length 5-6"
Walter A. Weber, National Geographic staff artist

Mexican junco, length 5½-6½"; Eliot Porter

Mexican Junco
Junco phaeonotus

AMONG THE mountain conifers of his southwestern home this natty bird delights campers with his boldness. He forages about campsites and even brings his offspring to the picnic table for a handout. Many call him the Arizona junco.

Two traits distinguish him. He is the only junco in the United States with yellow eyes. And he doesn't hop; he shuffles about as he feeds on seeds and insects. His sweet, rather elaborate song consists of three parts, and his nest, hidden under a log or trailing branch, holds three or four bluish-white eggs, plain or lightly spotted.

Two related species are Baird's junco (*Junco bairdi*) of Baja California and the Guadalupe junco (*Junco insularis*) of Guadalupe Island.

Range: S. E. Arizona and S. W. New Mexico, south to S. Mexico. *Characteristics:* bright yellow eyes, gray head and sides, rufous back, whitish underparts, white tail edges.

Gray-headed junco, length 5½-6"; Eliot Porter

Chipping Sparrow
Spizella passerina

OVER MUCH OF THE EAST the familiar chippy has forsaken the wilds for the abodes of men. He hops about gardens and orchards seeking insect larvae and seeds. In the west he inhabits open glades in evergreen forests. From low tree limbs he sings his dry chipping trill hour upon hour.

The three to five speckled bluish eggs are laid in a grassy nest built in a shrub, young conifer, or porch vine. Chipping sparrows winter as far north as central California and Maryland.

Range: central Yukon to Newfoundland, south to Nicaragua and N. Florida; migratory in the north. *Characteristics:* dark bill, rufous cap, black eye stripe, white eyebrow stripe, grayish underparts. Young in summer have streaked breast (page 35); in winter crown is striped.

Tree sparrows, 5½-6½"; Richard Hooke National Audubon Society; Allan Brooks

Chipping sparrow, 5-5¾"; Allan D. Cruickshank National Audubon Society

Gray-headed Junco
Junco caniceps

WHEN THE SLOPES bloom with wildflowers, flocks of grayheads spread through the southern and central Rockies. The rolling trills of these juncos are among the most familiar bird sounds in the dry coniferous forests above 6,000 feet.

When summer is at hand and insect food abounds, grayheads build a grassy nest on the ground to hold the four or five speckled white eggs. When snow comes, the birds flock to the foothills or head south; many visit wilderness camps in quest of food.

Grayheads that breed in the central Rockies have a pale bill. Those that nest in the southwestern mountains have a dark upper mandible.

Range: N. Nevada to S. Wyoming, south to central Arizona and W. Texas; winters to S. California and central Mexico. *Characteristics:* gray head, chest, and sides; rufous back, white belly and tail edges, dark eyes.

Tree Sparrow
Spizella arborea

WITH THE FIRST hard chills of autumn come the tree sparrows. From Arctic breeding grounds they wing into southern Canada and the United States in vast numbers, often in company with juncos. In the west they gather in willow thickets along creeks; in the east they congregate in weedy fields near swamps.

Foraging in midwinter, they pick fallen seeds from the snow, leaving countless little tracks. Some peck open the pods on swaying weed stalks; others swarm to rural dooryards for handouts, their *teelwit* feeding notes sounding like a symphony of tiny bells. As spring nears, these chestnut-capped birds with the dusky breast "button" begin singing their sweet, canarylike notes and trills. These bursts of melody increase in volume and frequency until the birds depart.

In the Far North tree sparrows tuck a feather-lined nest of grass and stems under a tussock among dwarf willows or shrubs of the tundra. It holds three to five spotted greenish eggs.

These birds resemble chipping sparrows, which in some areas arrive from the south in spring when tree sparrows head north. Hence *arborea* is also known as the winter chippy.

Range: N. Alaska to Labrador, south to N. British Columbia and central Quebec; winters from S. British Columbia to Nova Scotia, south to N. California, central Arizona, and North Carolina. *Characteristics:* reddish-brown cap and eye stripe, grayish face, neck, and breast; streaked brownish back, white wing bars and belly, dark breast spot. The bill is dark above, yellow below.

Field Sparrow
Spizella pusilla

A PINK BILL and timid manner distinguish this rustic from the relatives it resembles most – the tree and the chipping sparrows.

The field sparrow shuns human habitation as carefully as it avoids cultivated fields. The fields this sparrow favors are brushy pastures and abandoned farmland. There and at woodland edges it skulks in undergrowth or moves along the ground searching for small insects.

The bird does not collect in large flocks and is often found alone. From a low tree limb or bush the male sings a sweet song, *che-wee che-wee*, beginning slowly, then increasing the tempo to a breathless trill. The clear, plaintive opening notes lend an air of melancholy to the countryside.

Sometimes called the bush sparrow or huckleberry bird, *pusilla* weaves a hair-lined, grassy nest in a brier or berry bush. The four or five white or greenish eggs are spotted with brown and lilac. Ordinarily the young remain in the nest nine or ten days. But if danger threatens, they may tumble out on the fifth or sixth day and hop away to hide in the grass. Two broods are raised each year.

Field sparrows may winter as far north as Massachusetts. Joining other sparrows, they comb roadsides and brown fields for seeds.

Range: N. W. Montana to S. Maine, south to central Texas and S. Georgia; winters to N. E. Mexico and central Florida. *Characteristics:* pink bill, rusty cap, gray face; streaked rusty back, brown tail, white wing bars, buffy eye rings and breast. Young are duller with brown cap.

Clay-colored sparrow, length 5-5½"

Clay-colored Sparrow
Spizella pallida

PALE, inconspicuous, secretive, *pallida* is hard to see even when he is abundant. In the central and northern grasslands he breeds in dense streamside shrubbery. In the Great Lakes area he summers in the new growth of forest clearings.

From a low perch that enables him to see out over the thickets, he sings a slow song of three or four buzzing notes. You may think you're listening to a cicada. The *chip* call note may not impress you either, but it serves at least to advertise

366

Field sparrow, length 5¼-6"
Eliot Porter

the sparrow's presence. During nesting the male sings through the day. Occasionally he helps his mate incubate the four blue-green eggs spotted with black and brown.

When they hatch after 10 or 11 days, their mother feeds the nestlings small insects and caterpillars. The nursery of grass and twigs may be hidden in a clump of grass or placed up to six feet high in a bush or small tree.

This sparrow with the distinctly outlined ear patch may sometimes be confused with two look-alikes, the Brewer's and the chipping sparrows. The former lacks the broad central crown stripe, and the latter has a rufous cap.

Like many other birds, the clay-colored sparrow wanders far from his usual haunts. He may be found as far east as Massachusetts or Florida.

Range: N. E. British Columbia to central Manitoba, south to S. E. Colorado and S. Ontario, and sparsely to N. Texas; winters from S. Texas to S. Mexico. *Characteristics:* brown cap, grayish eyebrow and crown stripe, dark-bordered brown ear patch; streaked brown back, whitish underparts. Young have buffy rump and chest.

Worthen's Sparrow
Spizella wortheni

A SPECIMEN of this Mexican sparrow was collected during the breeding season near Silver City in southwestern New Mexico in 1884. Despite intensive searching, ornithologists have never recorded the bird north of the border since then.

It is easily mistaken for a chipping or a field sparrow; indeed some authorities suggest the Worthen's may be a race of the field sparrow.

In Mexico *wortheni* breeds in scrubby land and weedy fields. The nest of rootlets and grass holds three or four speckled bluish eggs. Males sing their slurred notes and trills from bushes.

Range: N. Mexico, possibly to S. New Mexico. *Characteristics:* paler than field sparrow, with shorter tail, more conspicuous white eye rings.

Black-chinned Sparrow
Spizella atrogularis

QUICK TO FLEE when approached, the blackchin lurks in the chaparral on southwestern hillsides. His distinctive plumage combines a sparrow's streaked back and a gray junco hood. The best time to see him is in early summer when he mounts a tall shrub or yucca spear to sing. Then the canyons ring with his lively refrain: *sweet, sweet, sweet, weet-trrrrrrr.*

Blackchins breed in small colonies, each pair occupying a territory of four to ten acres. Set in a bush, the grassy nest cups three or four bluish-white eggs. These may be plain or spotted.

Range: central California to W. Texas, south to S. Mexico; migratory in the north. *Characteristics:* pinkish bill, gray head and underparts, streaked brown back. Male has black chin patch.

Brewer's Sparrow
Spizella breweri

AT DAWN AND DUSK a chorus of buzzy trills rises from the sea of blue-green sagebrush. Even in the midday heat of the desert, a few Brewer's sparrows persist with their canarylike song.

They sing from sagebrush, hide in it, nest in it, and hunt insects among its branches and leaves. In some parts of the sagebrush flats these pale sparrows outnumber all other birds. Where the aromatic shrub grows in the mountains, you may find Brewer's sparrows breeding as high as 9,000 feet. The three or four spotted greenish-blue eggs are cradled in a hair-lined, twiggy nest.

This sparrow was named in 1856 for Thomas M. Brewer, an authority on birds' eggs.

Range: S. Yukon to S. W. South Dakota, south to S. California and N. W. New Mexico; winters to central Mexico and S. Texas. *Characteristics:* finely streaked brown crown, brown ear patches, streaked back, buffy wing bars, gray eyebrow stripe and underparts. Young have streaked chest.

Worthen's sparrow, 5-5½″

Black-chinned sparrow, 5-5½″
Allan Brooks

Brewer's sparrow, length 5-5¼″
Thase Daniel

Goldencrown
length 6-7"

Whitethroats
*adult (lower) and young
length 6-7"*

Whitecrown
length 5½-7½"

Juvenile whitecrown

Fox sparrow
length 6¼-7½"

WALTER A. WEBER

Walter A. Weber, National Geographic staff artist

Golden-crowned Sparrow
Zonotrichia atricapilla

OH DEAR ME. The sad, sweet melody is heard in far western canyons, on chaparral-covered hillsides, and along fence rows – the winter haunts of the goldencrown. Country people nicknamed the singer "rainbird," for they often heard him just before or after a drizzle. Some translate his whistled, descending notes as *three blind mice*.

In spring this large handsome sparrow heads north along the coast to breed among spruces, stunted firs, or streamside alders. The nest of twigs and moss, built in a low fork or on the ground, holds four or five spotted greenish-blue eggs. Goldencrowns dine mainly on seeds.

Range: W. Alaska to N. Washington and S. W. Alberta; winters to N. Baja California. *Characteristics:* black-bordered yellow crown stripe; streaked brown back, white wing bars, grayish throat and breast, brownish flanks. Young lack the well-defined crown pattern.

Fox Sparrow
Passerella iliaca

THROUGH the cold months small flocks of fox sparrows scratch along brushy woodland borders. Kicking with both feet at the same time, they clear away leaf litter and dig for seeds and insects. You may hear snatches of their rich caroling, which ranks high among sparrow songs.

They sing best in their northern summer home. There, on the ground or in a bush, they build a grassy cup for four spotted greenish eggs.

The rusty tail that suggests the color of a red fox and the thickly marked breast identify this sparrow. The 18 races vary considerably in the color of the head and back and in bill size.

Range: N. Alaska to N. Labrador, south to N. W. Washington, in the mountains to S. California and central Colorado, and to central Alberta and Newfoundland; winters to Baja California, S. Arizona, and central Florida. *Characteristics:* rusty, brownish, or grayish upperparts; rusty tail, heavily streaked underparts.

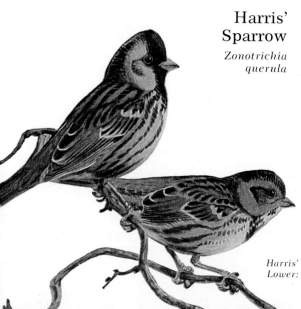

White-crowned Sparrow
Zonotrichia leucophrys

A GOOD DEAL had been known about the remarkable homing ability of birds, but the performance of a western subspecies of this sparrow astonished ornithologists. Caught in their winter home in the region around San Jose, California, 574 Gambel's whitecrowns were banded, shipped to the Patuxent Wildlife Research Center in Maryland, and released in October, 1962.

This was thousands of miles from their normal north-south migration route, but a year later eight of these mites that weigh about an ounce were found back in San Jose. What fantastic navigation system guided them back to their homestead? The secret remains locked in nature.

In Gambel's and two Pacific Coast forms the white eyebrow stripe begins at the bill. In the eastern race, breeding as far east as Labrador, and in one that frequents the Rockies and Sierra Nevada, the stripe begins at the eye.

Whitecrowns often display their striking head feathers by puffing out the crown to form a low crest. They feed and nest in brushy thickets; the nursery holds four spotted greenish eggs. The pleasing song begins with plaintive whistled notes and ends with a husky trill.

Range: N. Alaska to Labrador, south to S. California, N. New Mexico, central Manitoba, and S. E. Quebec; winters from S. British Columbia to Missouri and W. North Carolina, south to S. Mexico and the Gulf Coast. *Characteristics:* black-and-white striped crown, streaked brown back, white wing bars, gray underparts. Young have brownish head stripes, pinkish or yellowish bill.

White-throated Sparrow
Zonotrichia albicollis

POOR SAM PEABODY PEABODY PEABODY. You may hear the whitethroat sing a brief version of this sweet, melancholy song in winter as he scratches in thickets over much of the United States.

But the Peabody bird is in best voice in his summer home, punctuating the wilderness hush with his pensive notes. In burned-over clearings or among evergreens the female builds a nest of grass and moss on the ground or in a bush. In it she lays four or five spotted greenish eggs.

Range: S. Yukon to Newfoundland, south to central British Columbia, West Virginia, and Connecticut; winters from N. California, S. Arizona, and Connecticut to S. Texas and N. Florida. *Characteristics:* yellow spot in front of eye; black-and-white striped crown, white throat patch, wing bars; streaked brown back, grayish underparts. Young have brownish head pattern.

Harris' Sparrow
Zonotrichia querula

GEORGE MIKSCH SUTTON discovered the eggs of Harris' sparrow near Churchill, Manitoba, in 1931, 97 years after the first specimen of the bird was collected. Placed on the ground and concealed by a shrub, the grass-lined, mossy cup held four greenish-blue eggs blotched with brown.

While breeding, these birds whistle a quavering song. In winter they add chuckling notes and often sing in chorus at sundown. They feed on seeds among thickets and hedgerows.

Range: N. Canada, from Mackenzie delta to Hudson Bay, south to N. E. Saskatchewan and N. Manitoba; winters from S. British Columbia to N. Utah and Iowa, south to S. California, S. Texas, and Tennessee. *Characteristics:* black crown, face, and bib; streaked body. Crown is grayish in winter. Young have buffy head, whitish throat.

Harris' sparrow, length 7-7¾"
Lower: juvenile, Allan Brooks

Eastern song sparrows, length 5¼-6½"; Arthur A. Allen

 ## Song Sparrow
Melospiza melodia

WHAT BIRD LIVES up to his name more faithfully than *melodia*? Day or night, in any season, you may hear his delightful little jingle – a few long bright notes, then short notes and trills. Thoreau rendered the ditty as *Maids! Maids! Maids! hang up your teakettle-ettle-ettle.* When winter has scarcely relaxed its icy grip, this heavily streaked little bird with a dark breast spot may repeat his cheerful melody as many as 300 times an hour, for this is the time to warn off territorial intruders and attract a mate.

Migrant song sparrows, arriving to stake a claim, may find the grounds taken by year-round residents. Then the claimants battle fiercely. Sometimes an attack serves to reveal the intruder's sex, since plumages of both sexes are alike.

If the stranger flees, it's a male. If it simply sits and calls *eee eee eee*, it's a female!

Song sparrows breed over much of the United States in gardens, bushy fields, stream borders, swamps, and coastal marshes. They do not nest in the Deep South, in forests, or barren land.

The female usually conceals her first nest of the season in a clump of grass. Later she weaves her grassy cup in a bush. She alone incubates the three to five brown-spotted greenish eggs, which hatch in 12 days. Should her brood fall victim to cats, rats, snakes, or storms, she quickly builds another nest. She may weave as many as four to rear the usual two broods per season.

She frequently acts as foster mother for cowbirds. One song sparrow was seen feeding no fewer than five young cowbirds!

Song sparrows dine mostly on weed seeds picked from the ground. In summer they also

370

look for beetles, caterpillars, and grasshoppers.

Thirty-one forms of this adaptable species breed north of Mexico. Those of the arid regions are generally paler and smaller than the species in humid areas, while races of the Alaskan islands are the largest and darkest (below). Voice, the breast spot, and the pumping action of the tail in flight are usually helpful in identifying a song sparrow in its many guises.

As the cold months approach, many song sparrows leave their northern haunts. But others remain, braving the harsh winter and cheering us with an occasional burst of song.

Range: Aleutian Islands to Newfoundland, south to S. Mexico, N. New Mexico, N. Kansas, and N. W. South Carolina; migratory races winter to S. Texas and S. Florida. *Characteristics:* streaked brown head and back, dark eyeline, streaked whitish underparts, central breast spot.

Aleutian song sparrow, length 6³⁄₄-8″
Desert song sparrow (upper)
length 5¹⁄₄-6″, Allan Brooks

Swamp Sparrow
Melospiza georgiana

IF YOUR GARDEN grows weedy, this dark little sparrow may visit it in fall to reap the seeds. This is the best time to make his acquaintance, but don't crowd him, else he quickly darts for cover.

In spring and summer you may need hip boots, for then the swamp sparrow frequents bogs and sluggish streams bordered by thickets. He creeps in and out of the marsh bushes and nimbly climbs rushes and cattails. He feeds on aquatic insects and frequently mounts a swaying stalk to sing a simple trill, somewhat like the chipping sparrow's but more musical.

A pair of swamp sparrows build their grassy nest among reeds or in a dense tussock of grass. Often the nursery is arched with grasses and must be entered from the side. The four or five blue-green eggs are spotted with brown. Young birds trying their wings sometimes fall into the water and are seized by fish or large frogs.

In winter swamp sparrows leave the wetlands to roam brushy uplands with other sparrows.

Range: Mackenzie River region and N. E. British Columbia to Newfoundland, south to E. Nebraska and Delaware; winters to central Mexico and S. Florida. *Characteristics:* rusty crown, grayish face and breast, dark eyeline; grayish-white throat, streaked brown back. Young have streaked brownish crown and streaked breast.

Lincoln's Sparrow
Melospiza lincolnii

AUDUBON heard the wild, liquid music of this sparrow one summer morning in 1833 near the Natashquan River in Quebec. One of his companions, young Thomas Lincoln of Maine, added the bird to their scientific collections, and Audubon named the species for him.

Along the borders of streams and swamps *lincolnii* builds a grassy nest cup on the ground or in a tussock for the four or five spotted greenish eggs. The family feeds on seeds and insects.

While nesting, Lincoln's sparrow sings a fine song, bubbling like a house wren's, sweet and clear like a purple finch's. In habits and actions the Lincoln's resembles a song sparrow.

Exceedingly shy, this bird is seldom seen in migration. Painstaking bird watchers occasionally glimpse him skulking in a brushy field. Squeaking may lure him from cover.

Range: N. W. Alaska to Labrador, south in the mountains to S. California and N. New Mexico, and to S. Manitoba, N. Wisconsin, and Nova Scotia; winters from N. California, Missouri, and N. Georgia south to El Salvador. *Characteristics:* striped brownish crown, streaked buffy-olive back, finely streaked buffy breast, whitish belly.

Upper: swamp sparrow, length 5-5¾"; Eliot Porter
Lower: Lincoln's sparrow, length 5-6"; Arthur A. Allen

Lapland Longspur
Calcarius lapponicus

IN THE NORTH POLAR REGION, where continents end in scattered islands and frozen seas, the land seems almost too bleak to support life. Yet creatures prosper here, among them this small bird with long rear claws that project behind like a dragoon's spurs. His range is circumpolar: He breeds in Siberia, northern Russia, and Lapland, for which he was named in the 18th century. He is also called the Alaska longspur, for in summer he is familiar there as well as across Canada.

He favors wet, hummocky areas with dwarf plants. Here he runs about searching grass tufts for insects and seeds. The male bird perches on tussocks and weed stalks, the black and brown of his breeding plumage contrasting crisply with the white. He utters a rattling, whistling call— *ticky-tick tew*—often on the wing. Courting, he may fly up 30 feet or so, set his wings at an angle, and float down singing a liquid serenade.

In a loose nest of moss, grass, feathers, and hair, concealed under a shrub or in a clump of grass, the female lays four to seven eggs, olive-hued and well splotched with purples and browns.

With the approach of winter in Arctic North America longspur families join great flocks that often include horned larks and snow buntings. Most flights head south by way of the open prairies. Some enter New England.

After the fall molt the male's new feathers are tipped with brown or buff, obscuring his striking pattern. As spring brings the birds north again, the male's feather tips wear away, revealing the markings of his breeding plumage.

Sometimes mass migrations of birds end in tragedy. In 1904 a multitude of Lapland longspurs flew northward over Minnesota on a dark night filled with heavy, wet snow. Next morning their bodies littered village streets and roofs, and some 750,000 carpeted the ice of two lakes. Skulls were crushed, necks broken as the longspurs flew into obstructions or simply into the ground or frozen lakes. Weakness resulting from hunger may have played a part, for examination of 100 stomachs revealed that all were empty.

Range: N. Alaska to central Greenland, south to S. W. Alaska, N. Ontario, and Labrador; winters from S. British Columbia, South Dakota, and New Brunswick to N. E. California, S. Louisiana, and N. Virginia. *Characteristics:* streaked brown upperparts, long dark legs, dark tail with white edges. Breeding male has black head and throat, chestnut nape, whitish underparts. Female and winter male have brownish head.

Male (right) and female Lapland longspurs, length 6-7"; Arthur A. Allen

Chestnut-collared longspurs
male (left) and female, length 5½-6½"

McCown's longspurs
male (right) and female
length 5¾-6"

Allan Brooks

Chestnut-collared Longspur
Calcarius ornatus

THIS LONGSPUR frequents the dry grasslands of the North American prairies. A dark little bundle easily mistaken at a distance for a bobolink, he sways on a weed stalk, then flutters high to sing his sweet, faint flight song.

Holding his quivering wings high, spreading his tail, and throwing his head back, he sinks like a slowly falling leaf toward the ground, warbling and twittering all the while.

On the open ground the chestnut-collared long-spur places a grass-lined nest in a hollow. The three to five speckled, greenish eggs lie exposed to rain and sun if the drab mother bird is not there to shield them.

After the eggs hatch, the black-breasted male helps feed the nestlings grasshoppers and larvae. By fall the juvenile birds join their parents in searching for seeds.

Range: S. Alberta to S. Manitoba, south to N. E. Colorado and S. W. Minnesota; winters from N. Arizona and central Kansas south to N. Mexico and N. Louisiana. *Characteristics:* white tail with dark triangle at tip. Breeding male has black crown, black-and-white cheeks, chestnut nape, whitish throat; streaked brownish upperparts, black underparts. Female and winter male are streaked brownish.

McCown's Longspur
Rhynchophanes mccownii

AN ARMY CAPTAIN, John P. McCown, discovered this bird in the 1850's in west Texas, far from the prairie breeding ground it shares with the chestnut-collared longspur. McCown's has the same habits as its cousin, but its nape is gray instead of chestnut, and its tail patch is T-shaped.

Range: S. Alberta to S. W. Manitoba, south to N. E. Colorado and N. W. Nebraska; winters from central Arizona, W. Kansas, and central Oklahoma south to N. Mexico and S. Texas. *Characteristics:* breeding male has black crown, gray nape, streaked brown upperparts, grayish underparts, black breast patch; black T on tail. Markings faint in winter. Female is brownish.

Snow Bunting
Plectrophenax nivalis

HIS NICKNAME is "snowflake," and when he migrates south in late fall, the reason is clear. For he travels in flocks, every bird swooping and veering in unison, and as they pass overhead only the white undersides of the wings and the white bellies can be seen. They look like giant snowflakes blown before an autumn gust and are indeed harbingers of the winter to come.

They may land while real snow is falling and

throng to haystacks, barnyards, or lakeshores lined with forest debris. Snow is their element as long as it does not bury the seed supply. What is a New England winter to circumpolar land birds that breed farther north than any other species?

By late March they are starting north, filling the air with their calls – a tremulous purring, or a chorus of whistles and trills that John Burroughs likened to "the laughter of children."

Under a rock or in a cavity they build their nest of moss and sedges, lined with feathers and fur. The spotted eggs number four to seven, and the tiny nestlings are fed moths, crane flies, and mosquitoes by their handsome parents.

Range: N. Ellesmere Island to N. Greenland, south to S. W. Alaska and N. Labrador; winters to N. W. California, N. Utah, N. New Mexico, and Virginia. *Characteristics:* plumage mostly white. Breeding male has black on back, wings, and tail. Female and winter male have rusty splotches.

McKay's Bunting
Plectrophenax hyperboreus

Now ISOLATED on two islands off western Alaska, this bird evolved into a separate species of snow bunting with more white and less rusty brown in his plumage. He breeds on tundra and along rocky shores. The three or four spotted eggs are cupped in a rock crevice or hollow log.

Winter finds the birds visiting Eskimo villages on the mainland coast to feed beside huts and on sod roofs. The male's song resembles that of the American goldfinch.

Range: St. Matthew and Hall Islands; winters to Nunivak Island and W. coastal Alaska. *Characteristics:* breeding male almost pure white; female and winter male have touches of brown.

Smith's Longspur
Calcarius pictus

THIS BUFFY BIRD breeds on the tundra from the shores of the Bering Sea to Hudson Bay. Circling above high ridges with his fellows, the male calls with a series of dry clicks that sound like the winding of a cheap watch. His song is sweeter and usually given from the ground.

The female warms her four to six clay-colored, dark-spotted eggs in a ground cavity lined with grass. In fall the families flock south, often in company with Lapland longspurs. They can be seen in the prairie states, thronging roadsides, swarming across airfields in search of weed seeds. It was during a spring migration in 1827 that the species was discovered beside the Saskatchewan River. Later Audubon named it for his friend, Dr. Gideon B. Smith.

Range: N. Alaska to N. Ontario; winters from Kansas and central Iowa to central Texas and N. W. Louisiana. *Characteristics:* buffy with black-streaked upperparts, white-edged tail. Breeding male has black-and-white face. Female and winter male are paler, less strongly marked.

Male Smith's longspur in breeding plumage length 5³⁄₄-6¹⁄₂"

Walter A. Weber
National Geographic
staff artist

Male McKay's in breeding plumage length 7"

Male snow buntings (in breeding plumage, right) length 6-7¹⁄₄

IN THE FIELD WITH A MODERN AUDUBON

What Bird Is That?

By ROGER TORY PETERSON

QUICK ON THE DRAW *with binoculars and notebook, students and teachers from the University of Michigan Biological Station near Pellston "look at the birdie" before the author's camera.*

D URING MY TEENS I saw some strange birds around my home in Jamestown, nestled among the green hills of western New York. I have never seen them there since — nor anywhere else in the Northeast for that matter. The truth is, the little pocket guide that I carried in those days was misleading. It led me to mistake the indigo bunting for the blue grosbeak; it made me certain that I had seen such improbable strays as the scissor-tailed flycatcher of Texas.

I acquired more basic handbooks, but they proved too technical. One described the familiar robin in unnecessary detail: "Eye incompletely ringed with three broken white spots; chin white, streaked narrowly with black...." Such bird-in-hand descriptions were of little help in identifying birds at a distance. But this was the era prior to 1925, when few professional ornithologists trusted their eyes — to identify a bird with certainty they had to shoot it.

Ludlow Griscom, who was to become the dean of northeastern bird watchers, put an end to this "shotgun school" of ornithology. As a boy in New York City he had spent his free mornings in the Ramble, a wooded area in Central Park near the American Museum of Natural History. Since no one could shoot in the park, he learned to name bird migrants at a glance.

Later, one of Griscom's elders, a member of the renowned Linnaean Society, went hat in hand to ring a doorbell in Connecticut and ask permission to shoot a warbling vireo out of an elm tree. The lady of the house granted the request; this was proper field ornithology in those days. But Griscom had the impertinence to

tell the gentleman that he need not shoot a bird to determine what it is. To prove his point Griscom aimed his glass at a small bird in the treetops and pronounced it to be a female Cape May warbler.

Doubting, the oldtimer raised his fowling piece and fired. Down tumbled the bird — and it *was* a female Cape May warbler! Griscom then pointed out other obscure warblers and turned out to be right each time.

To make these snap identifications Griscom relied on the birds' field characters, the markings that are readily visible at a distance. A museum man with a cedar waxwing in his hand looks for tiny red tips on the secondary wing feathers. But a field man like Griscom, sighting what he thinks is a cedar waxwing, looks for its flash mark — the broad yellow band at the tip of the bird's tail.

Perhaps Griscom's most faithful followers were a handful of young men who called themselves the Bronx County Bird Club. These sons of sidewalk and pavement learned their birds in the parks, vacant lots, and along the waterfront of the sprawling metropolis. They religiously attended meetings of the Linnaean Society at the American Museum, and they revered Griscom as a deity. They hung on his every word and could quote his book, *Birds of the New York City Region*, chapter and verse. When describing the rare birds they had seen, they used his terminology and even his speech inflections.

It was with this group that I tagged along when I first went to New York as a young man to study at the National Academy of Design. I was so persistent that the members finally admitted me — the first non-Bronx applicant — to the clan. Competing with them sharpened my skill at identification.

An inspiration struck me one day as I was reading Ernest Thompson Seton's novel, *Two Little Savages*. The young hero, Yan, noticed that various kinds of mounted ducks had special patterns — spots, stripes, blotches, and bars. He put these patterns on paper so that when he saw live ducks at a distance he would know them.

It seemed to me that all birds could be interpreted in some such fashion, and during the next several years while attending art school I devised my first field guide. It compared the birds' patterns and pointed out distinctions between similar species with little arrows. Thus was born the "Peterson system."

C OLOR IS THE FIRST THING most people note about a flower. But you can't sort out birds successfully by color alone. The efficient way to identify most species is to place them in their obvious categories — sparrows, jays, woodpeckers, or whatever — then run them down by their patterns and field marks. Thus to identify a bird you should weigh the answers to these eight important questions:

1. How large is it?   Is it the size of a crow, a pigeon, a robin, a sparrow, or a wren? Is it a bit larger or smaller than one of these? A well-known bird is a more reliable unit of measure than length in inches. Often you can compare a new bird directly with a familiar species — a rare gull in a flock of ordinary herring gulls, a strange duck among a flight of mallards.

2. What is its silhouette?   Is it compact like a starling, slim like a grackle, or of average proportions like a robin? Does it have a crest like a blue jay? Is it long-necked or long-legged like a heron? Are its wings long and pointed like a swallow's, or short, wide, and rounded like a quail's? Is its tail long like a cuckoo's, short like a starling's, rounded like a jay's, forked like a barn swallow's, notched like a sparrow's, or pointed like a mourning dove's? Is its bill as stubby as a sparrow's, as thick as a cardinal's, as thin and sharp as a warbler's?

3. What are its field marks or flash marks? Look for conspicuous patches like the shoulder patch on a red-winged blackbird or the black bib of a chickadee. Notice bands or stripes like the white band on the end of an eastern kingbird's tail. Check for spots like the one centered on the breast of the song sparrow.

Some birds such as the flicker have conspicuous rump patches. Others such as the meadowlark or junco show white flashes on the sides of their tails. Note whether the wings are unmarked or have one or two whitish bars across them, or a patch.

4. How does the bird behave? Does it hop or walk? Does it flit about nervously, or does it sit quite still, then sally forth after passing insects? If it chases insects it may be a flycatcher, though some warblers and other species share the habit. Woodpeckers are master tree climbers. Nuthatches are good at climbing too, but usually go headfirst down the tree trunk.

Water birds also have distinctive actions. Some ducks dive; others just tip up, exposing their sterns while they feed on the bottom. Diving ducks taxi across the water like heavily laden sea-

UP TO HIS BIRD BLIND *climbs John H. Gerard for the vigil that resulted in the blue jay portrait on page 139. Spotting the nest in his Illinois backyard, the photographer built the high platform bit by bit so as not to panic the birds.*

Tentlike blinds with portholes for lenses may be sweatboxes in summer, iceboxes in winter. But birders will suffer in them hour after hour, day after day, for the sake of a close-up.

SILHOUETTES *identify these telephone-line sitters. From left: cliff swallow, barn swallow, purple martin, kingfisher, grackle, starling, bluebird, red-winged blackbird, cowbird, mourning dove, and at far right, house sparrow.*

planes; marsh ducks spring up directly. Some birds that swim or wade probe the mud; others just pick at the surface. The spotted sandpiper teeters up and down nervously as if too delicately balanced on its matchstick legs, while its relative the yellowlegs merely makes a sedate bob or curtsy.

5. How does the bird fly?   Goldfinches dip and climb, nighthawks lurch this way and that, doves and starlings fly swift and true as an arrow. Swallows skim; so do terns. Gulls and hawks soar. Herons flap slowly and steadily. Meadowlarks have almost the same shape as starlings but fly with several quick flaps and a sail.

Though some species prefer to travel alone, birds of a feather often flock together. You can tell some geese by the military precision of their long wedge formations and lines; others travel in shifting mobs. Starlings and sandpipers maneuver marvelously in their tight flocks. Swallows migrate in loose companies.

In flight style birds may be likened to aircraft. Gulls, albatrosses, and vultures are the sailplanes. Hummingbirds, hovering before flowers, are helicopters. Falcons are pursuit planes or dive bombers. Grouse take off with a burst of speed but have no great endurance. Ducks are durable fliers, built for long distances.

6. How does the bird sound?   No two species of birds make exactly the same sounds. Voice, like plumage and behavior, is one of the isolating factors which guard the integrity of the species. The novice birder may confess that to him all bird songs sound alike. But if he has a good ear, he soon changes his mind and before long may depend more on his ear than his eye. During the spring migration season I actually do more than 90 percent of my fieldwork by ear alone.

In earlier days when we heard an unfamiliar song we simply tried to learn it and ferret out the singer. The tape recorder was unknown then. Thanks to this modern

OUTLINED IN FLIGHT, *these birds give themselves away by characteristic shapes of wings and tails. From left: starling (upper), kingfisher (lower), bobwhite, grackle, barn swallow, mourning dove, and chimney swift.*

WHAT BIRDS *are those in the treetops? To charm them into the open, this member of the field-glass fraternity gives a birdlike cheep by kissing the back of her thumb. High-pitched squeaks and bright chirps produced by mechanical bird calls also pique the curiosity of many species. Soon a feathered audience gathers, enabling human admirers to observe the birds at close range.*

tool, the voices of most North American birds are filed in that great clearinghouse of avian acoustics, the Laboratory of Ornithology at Cornell University.

Before the days of sound recordings writers tried to interpret bird voices on the printed page in three different ways. One was by musical notation. This was the least satisfactory method, since few bird songs can be translated into notes. A second way was to adapt the song to some catchy phrase. Canadians insisted that the white-throated sparrow sang "Pure sweet Canada Canada Canada," while Bostonians thought it sounded more like "Poor Sam Peabody Peabody Peabody."

Quite a few birds say their own names so distinctly that they leave no doubt about their identity. Among these are the chickadee, phoebe, bobwhite, and whip-poor-will. In England a little leaf warbler is called the chiffchaff because it seems to say *chiff, chaff, chiff, chiff, chaff* in endless metronomic cadence. But on the Continent people seem to hear this same bird quite differently. In Finland it says *til, tal, til, til, tal;* in Germany, *zilp, zalp, zilp, zilp, zalp;* in France, *tyip, tyap, tyip, tyip, tyap;* and in Spain, *sib, sab, sib, sib, sab.* Despite the differences in ears, words and phrases are valuable aids in remembering songs.

A clever way of analyzing songs, a sort of musical shorthand, was devised some

ACTIONS *reveal identity. From left: Wrens cock their tails; flycatchers perch upright. Woodpeckers use the tail as a prop when climbing trees; nuthatches descend headfirst; sparrows hop along the ground.*

years ago by Aretas Saunders, who used symbols to represent quality, tempo, and changes in pitch. This idea was most ingenious, but the advent of the tape recorder sent the Saunders system into eclipse.

Modern technicians run a tape through an oscillograph and get a series of blurs and squiggles called an audiospectrogram—a visual interpretation of a bird's song. Such precise analysis is useful to science. But to most bird watchers there is no substitute for simply learning the songs. The best way to learn them at home is to listen, again and again, to recordings such as those included with this book.

When you try to identify a bird by sound, listen carefully to the rhythm of the song —the number of notes, their length, the way they are grouped or accented. Then notice the quality: Does the bird whistle, warble, buzz, trill, or somehow combine all these? Finally, make note of the pitch and volume of the song.

7. Where did you see the bird?   Ludlow Griscom could look at a bit of woodland or swamp in New England and predict with complete accuracy just what birds he would find there. For birds generally stay within their special habitats except when they are migrating. You would not expect to find a meadowlark in the woods, for example, nor a wood thrush in a meadow.

Birds seldom venture beyond their geographical ranges. A Baltimore oriole would be a startling sight in California, as would a Canada jay in New Jersey. But birds have wings; they fly, and the occasional wind-driven stray or a bird with a pioneering spirit may turn up far from home. To many people it is the hope of finding one of these waifs that gives field birding its special glamour.

FLASH PATTERNS *help identify many birds at a glimpse. White-tipped tail distinguishes the eastern kingbird (left); white-sided tail marks the meadowlark (center). Wing bars aid in sorting out look-alike warblers.*

382

A few birds, such as the osprey, the barn owl, the peregrine falcon, the barn swallow, and some shorebirds, appear throughout so much of the world that they can almost be called cosmopolitan. Others like the familiar robin range from coast to coast in North America but only accidentally show up in the Old World.

A few birds are extremely local. Kirtland's warbler summers only in certain counties of Michigan, where its total population does not exceed 1,000. I once had the honor of unveiling a large statue to this tiny bird before the courthouse at Mio, Michigan, in the heart of the pine barrens where the *rara avis* breeds.

8. When did you see it? At my Connecticut home two red-capped sparrows use a feeding tray near the patio. One, a tree sparrow, shows up only during winter.

LOOK FOR SPECIAL MARKINGS *such as a stripe over the eye, eye rings, a striped crown, or a crown patch. The orange crown patch, the eye rings, and the black-striped breast of the bird in the hand (below) identify it as an ovenbird.*
Emory Kristof. Sketches by Roger Tory Peterson

Bird habitats

Ocean

Garden and glade

Beach and dune   *Deciduous forest*

After mid-April he is replaced by the chipping sparrow. I need only look at the calendar to tell which bird I am seeing. Similarly, I know that a spotted thrush on my property in summer is a wood thrush. In winter it's a hermit thrush. In May, September, and October I must make sure it isn't a migrant—a gray-cheeked thrush, a Swainson's thrush, or a veery. It helps to know when to expect certain birds. Many clubs and natural history societies publish timetables for the birds in their areas.

T HE BIRD WATCHER needs one tool—a good pair of binoculars. This is the badge of the brotherhood, as essential to the hobby as a knowledge of the eight factors of identification. Any stranger displaying a pair in the woods can be approached in confidence by another of the clan. It is like the twig of heather which, displayed in ancient Scotland, was a symbol of friendship and trust when Pict met Pict on the moor.

Evergreen forest

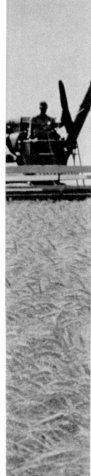

Farmland

Salt flats

Desert

I am frequently asked about the best magnification. As a boy, I first used a little pair of four-power glasses that I bought in response to an ad in *Bird-Lore*, the predecessor to *Audubon Magazine*. These cherished binoculars made each bird look four times as big and four times as handsome. But four magnifications isn't really enough. On the other hand, 12-power glasses are so sensitive that few people can hold them steady enough to use effectively. Veteran bird watchers seem to prefer glasses of seven, eight, or nine power.

Most binoculars display two figures such as 7×35, 8×40, or 9×40. The first number represents the magnification, the second the width in millimeters of the large lenses. Divide the first into the second, square the result, and you have the light-gathering index. Thus, for an 8×40 glass, the index would be five squared, or 25. A light-gathering index of 25 is ideal. A 7×30 glass has an index of only 18, a bit dark. A 7×50 glass, with an index of about 51, would be a help in dark woodlands, or on rainy days, or at dusk.

Marsh

BIRD MIGRATION

BARN SWALLOW

JUNC

GOLDEN PLOVER

ROBIN

James P. Blair, National Geographic photographer

Exploring nature is fun with an Audubon Junior Club

TINY TRAVELER, *a white-throated sparrow, takes a bow before young Audubon Explorers in the Audubon Center at Greenwich, Connecticut. Today's lesson: bird banding and its importance in tracing migration routes like those shown on the chart.*

Centers and summer camps such as this teach young and old the ways of birds and mammals and the need to protect them.

Starting in 1886 in New York City, Audubon groups sprang up in an attempt to stop the slaughter of birds. These were days when a lady would rather die than wear a hat without flowing egret plumes; when a gentleman sighed with delight to see bobolinks served at Delmonico's. Shotguns blasted away to fill the demand,

and Audubon members hired wardens to protect the egret rookeries. Two wardens were slain before the sale of plumage was outlawed. In 1905 the National Audubon Society, as it is now called, was founded.

Today its wardens patrol nearly 1,000,000 acres of land and water. Its educational programs foster conservation, open people's eyes and minds to nature's wonders, and answer some of the inevitable questions curious children ask.

Why doesn't a bird fall off its perch when it goes to sleep? When a bird falls asleep, it relaxes and slumps until its body rests against the perch. This pulls a tendon in its leg, causing its toes to clamp around the perch. The bird must straighten its legs to release this clamp.

Binoculars should have a wide field of vision so you do not waste time trying to spot the bird before studying it. Most glasses of seven or eight power have a field of vision of between 130 and 150 yards at a 1,000-yard range. A telescope has high magnification but a small field of vision. It gives a good look at waterfowl that are too far away for binoculars to sort out. Use the scope on a support, and if it has a zoom lens you can find your bird at low magnification and a large field of vision, then zoom right in to 50 or 60 magnifications.

When you purchase binoculars, ask for coated lenses; they can increase light transmission 20 percent or more. Don't accept glasses with chromatic aberration, showing rainbows at the edges of bright objects. And make sure they are aligned.

I am hardly the person to give advice about the care of binoculars, since I have often been called a destroyer of equipment. But let me say, piously, that they should have tender treatment. A sharp bump may knock them out of alignment. Don't clean the lenses with your sleeve; use a chamois or a lens tissue. Keep the binoculars in a case when you are not using them. And little leather caps that fit over the eyepieces will protect them from dust and rain while you are carrying the glasses.

JOHN JAMES AUDUBON found bird watching a lonely occupation, generally considered the hobby of an eccentric. When he chanced to meet Alexander Wilson, an itinerant scholar who also painted birds, the two men regarded each other with mutual suspicion. Today birders are legion. One statistician, Roger Barton, estimates the number of binocular toters and housewives who watch birds at the window feeders at no fewer than ten million. Since World War II the number of birders has "exploded" far faster than the general population. Indeed, many more people watch birds nowadays than shoot them.

Birding can be a placid occupation for maiden aunts, a rough-and-tumble sport, or a hair-raising adventure. One of my more sedentary friends describes himself as the "white-breasted nuthatch type of a bird watcher." On the other hand consider the late Robert Porter Allen. Tough as nails, Bob pursued whooping cranes through almost impassable muskeg to their Alberta nesting grounds. When he returned to civilization, he had the look of a man who had visited hell.

Ornithologist friends of mine have fallen from cliffs and trees. They have broken arms, legs, and ribs. They have been chased by tribesmen, robbed by bandits, charged by bulls. They have cracked up in airplanes. They have nearly frozen to death. They have almost drowned – as Philip Humphrey and I can attest after having been caught in a rowboat three miles off the coast of Patagonia by a rising gale. And they have been wounded by the birds themselves. Eric Hosking, Britain's ace bird photographer, lost an eye to a tawny owl that he was documenting.

As my friend James Fisher, the eminent British ornithologist, once put it: "The observation of birds may be a superstition, a tradition, an art, a science, a pleasure, a hobby, or a bore. This depends entirely on the nature of the observer."

Today many people think of birding as a sport – the game of recognition. Not even experts always agree on the identity of the birds they see. For example, I recall a day in Baja California with Carl Buchheister, President of the National Audubon Society. We had hired a taxi in the town of La Paz for a tour of the area. On the shore we spotted a small plover which we couldn't agree on. Was it a Wilson's plover or just a semipalmated? After we had argued about it for a bit, our Mexican driver turned to us and interrupted: "Pardon señores, but I, Lalo, will settle the point. I have a book." And lo and behold, he showed that our plover was a Wilson's – by producing a battered copy of my own *Field Guide to Western Birds!*

As he sees a bird in the field, the bird watcher generally ticks it off on his little checklist, much as a golfer keeps score. In fact, one ornithologist refers to this practice as "ornithogolfing." Checklists are available for most of the United States and for many other parts of the world.

Sightings for a single day may easily exceed 100 during the peak period of bird migration. My own record is 162, seen in a day in Massachusetts, but some bird watchers in California and Texas have topped 200.

When experts vie in a sort of tournament of bird spotting, the event is usually called "the Big Day." Contestants start before dawn and continue until after dark —their lists begin and end with owls. The idea is to keep on the move, with a fast car and good brakes. You plan your strategy so that you can be at the best spots at the best time of day. A variation on this event is the Audubon Christmas Bird Count — a cold-weather "Big Day" with somewhat different ground rules. Any number can play the game. They do not have to stick together but must stay within a 15-mile circle. At the end of the day their totals are pooled.

Each December 15,000 or more bird watchers in the United States and Canada take part in this mass exercise. Southern groups, of course, compile the largest lists —a recent winner listed 200 species seen in the Cape Kennedy region of Florida.

When you see a certain bird for the first time, it goes on your life list. Of course, new birds or "lifers" become fewer as the years pass. To compensate, many enthusiasts travel extensively. Guy Emerson, former president of the Audubon Society and a banker, always engineered his business trips so he would be in Texas when the waves of migrating warblers came through, in San Francisco when the shorebirds were at their best, and in Salt Lake City when the waterfowl were nesting. For a number of years Emerson held the record for the most species seen in

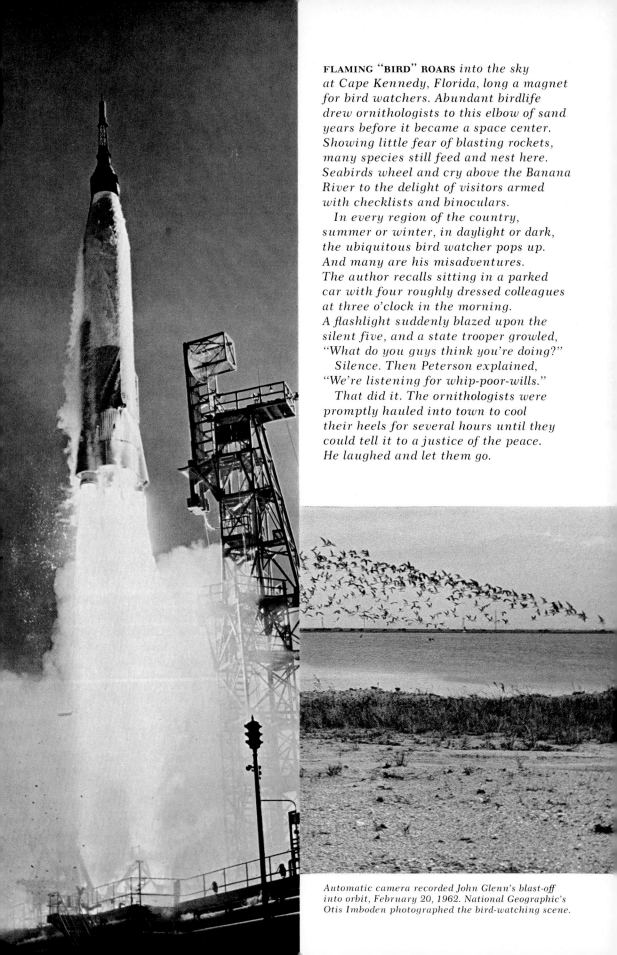

FLAMING "BIRD" ROARS *into the sky at Cape Kennedy, Florida, long a magnet for bird watchers. Abundant birdlife drew ornithologists to this elbow of sand years before it became a space center. Showing little fear of blasting rockets, many species still feed and nest here. Seabirds wheel and cry above the Banana River to the delight of visitors armed with checklists and binoculars.*

In every region of the country, summer or winter, in daylight or dark, the ubiquitous bird watcher pops up. And many are his misadventures. The author recalls sitting in a parked car with four roughly dressed colleagues at three o'clock in the morning. A flashlight suddenly blazed upon the silent five, and a state trooper growled, "What do you guys think you're doing?"

Silence. Then Peterson explained, "We're listening for whip-poor-wills."

That did it. The ornithologists were promptly hauled into town to cool their heels for several hours until they could tell it to a justice of the peace. He laughed and let them go.

Automatic camera recorded John Glenn's blast-off into orbit, February 20, 1962. National Geographic's Otis Imboden photographed the bird-watching scene.

Clay-colored sparrow, Donald R. Gunn

TO RECORD A SPARROW'S SONG, *Dr. Arthur A. Allen (opposite) aims a reflector which amplifies the sound into a microphone 900 times. Dr. Peter Paul Kellogg, in charge of sound recording at Cornell, analyzes the song with an oscilloscope (above).*

North America in a single year — 497 in 1939. In 1953, I beat him with a tally of 572. Then three years later my record was eclipsed by that of a young Englishman, Stuart Keith, who logged 594, a large percentage of all 675 species of birds that normally occur in North America.

Stuart Keith, ever restless, has gone on to explore birdlife systematically throughout the rest of the world. So have many other aficionados of the sport. Edward Chalif, a famous teacher of dancing, conducts his classes six months of the year, then roams the world with his binoculars for the other six. American travel agencies nowadays arrange birding tours to Europe, Africa, and Iceland.

G ENERALS, admirals, governors, senators, prime ministers, kings, and presidents fill the ranks of those who thrill to the flush of a wing. Prince Philip of Great Britain is an enthusiast specializing in bird photography. Lord Alanbrooke, Chief of the Imperial General Staff during World War II, was an inveterate birder who enjoyed squatting in a blind for hours, patiently filming rare species. The echoes of gunfire had barely died out at the end of the war when Alanbrooke was off to investigate a falcon's aerie from a lofty blind in England. We once worked together for a week filming redshanks and oystercatchers on the Hilbre Islands, at the edge of the Irish Sea near Liverpool.

Birding offers a tranquillity that eases the strain of heavy responsibilities. But there is more to it than just ticking off species on a checklist. You may grow interested in bird banding. You may study migration, ecology, bird populations, or conservation. You may become as technical as you like without losing your amateur status, as Crawford H. Greenewalt, Chairman of Du Pont's Finance Committee and a Trustee of the National Geographic Society, has done with his scholarly studies of hummingbirds. Or you may join the ranks of the professionals.

Long hours at a drafting table, drawing birds under fluorescent lights, once compelled me to visit an oculist. My name obviously did not ring a bell with him, so I merely explained that I was an artist in need of a new pair of glasses for close, detailed work. He examined my eyes and told me that I had astigmatism.

"What do I do about that?" I asked.

"Why don't you take up bird watching?" he replied.

I had taken it up when I was 11, when my seventh grade teacher sparked my interest by starting a Junior Audubon Club. Since then, I have found in birds the finest expression of the natural world. They are quick, incisive, and beautiful. They respond sensitively to the laws of nature. They demonstrate clearly the subtle forces of natural selection and adaptation.

Bird watching has been called an escape. Perhaps. But in a world that often perturbs us with its synthetic quality, a world that seems sometimes to be getting out of hand, this is an escape from the artificial—a return to reality.

Robert B. Goodman. Opposite: David G. Allen

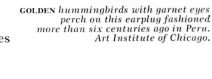

AGE AFTER AGE *records man's delight in birds. Feathered fancies adorn his legends, his buildings, his costume— even this tiny spoon used by ancient Incas. From the Dumbarton Oaks Collection, Washington, D. C.*

Index

GOLDEN *hummingbirds with garnet eyes perch on this earplug fashioned more than six centuries ago in Peru. Art Institute of Chicago.*

Page listings for illustrated biographies are in **boldface**, other illustrations in *italics;* text references in roman. Songs on the records are indexed under the species' common names. (The symbol ♪ in a biography means that bird's song is in the album.)

BIRDS BRIGHTEN *a Senate wing corridor
at the U. S. Capitol in Washington, D. C.
Design by Constantino Brumidi.*

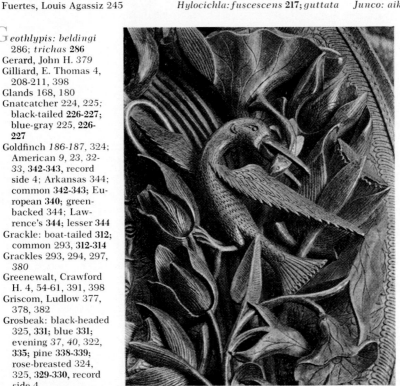

KINGFISHER, *carved in high relief, clutches its prey amid flowers on a box. Kashmiri craftsman polished the traditional figures with agate. Brian Brake, Magnum.*

RAVEN, *mythical creator of the world and clan symbol among Northwest Coast Indians, forms this Haida chief's rattle in the Museum of the American Indian, New York. Ravens peer from the 83-foot totem pole at Tacoma, Washington, topped by an eagle clan figure (right).*

KING OF THE CROWS *hears advice from his councillors on how to combat owls in an illuminated manuscript probably written in Syria about 1200. This book of fables followed an ancient tradition of using animal characters. Bibliothèque Nationale, Paris.*

DRINKING *the waters of everlasting life, white doves symbolize good Christians in this fifth century mosaic in a chapel at Ravenna, Italy.*

Acknowledgments and Reference Guide

THE EDITORS are indebted to many scholars and scientific organizations whose work contributed information to this book—for example, the Cornell Laboratory of Ornithology at Ithaca, New York, where researchers have thrown new light on bird behavior. Scientists at the Smithsonian Institution in Washington, D. C., gave generously of their special knowledge. Color engravings for this book were minutely checked against bird skins in the Smithsonian's vast collection. The array of published bird studies there and at the Library of Congress provided a matchless resource.

Books of general scope frequently consulted include The Life of Birds by Joel C. Welty; Birds of the World by Oliver L. Austin, Jr., and Arthur Singer; Living Birds of the World by E. Thomas Gilliard; and Fundamentals of Ornithology by Josselyn Van Tyne and Andrew J. Berger.

In preparing the bird biographies, constant resort was made to Arthur Cleveland Bent's life histories of North American birds, an unprecedented work compiled by this determined New Englander over a period of 44 years. Field marks and plumage descriptions were checked against Robert Ridgway's classic volumes on The Birds of North and Middle America, Richard H. Pough's Audubon Land Bird Guide and Audubon Western Bird Guide, and Roger Tory Peterson's A Field Guide to the Birds and A Field Guide to Western Birds. Peterson's guides were particularly helpful in transliterating bird songs.

Bird names and ranges follow the fifth edition of the Check-list of North American Birds, prepared by a committee of the American Ornithologists' Union headed by Alexander Wetmore. Elliott Coues's Key to North American Birds proved helpful in determining the derivation of certain bird names. Periodicals such as The Condor, The Auk, and The Wilson Bulletin were useful for field studies on individual species.

Many regional works were consulted, including the following: Alabama Birds by Thomas A. Imhof; Alaska Bird Trails by Herbert Brandt; The Birds of Alaska by Ira N. Gabrielson and Frederick C. Lincoln; Arizona and Its Bird Life by Herbert Brandt; The Birds of California by William Leon Dawson; Birds of Canada by P. A. Taverner; Arctic Birds of Canada by L. L. Snyder; Birds of the Connecticut Valley in Massachusetts by Aaron Clark Bagg and Samuel Atkins Eliot, Jr.; Florida Bird Life by Arthur H. Howell; Georgia Birds by Thomas D. Burleigh; Birds of the Labrador Peninsula by W. E. Clyde Todd; Louisiana Birds by George H. Lowery, Jr.; The Birds of Minnesota by Thomas S. Roberts; A Natural History of American Birds of Eastern and Central North America by Edward Howe Forbush and John Bichard May; New Mexico Birds by J. Stokley Ligon; The Birds of Nova Scotia by Robie W. Tufts; Birds of Oregon by Ira N. Gabrielson and Stanley G. Jewett; Birds of the Pacific States by Ralph Hoffmann; Birds of Western Pennsylvania by W. E. Clyde Todd; South Carolina Bird Life by Alexander Sprunt, Jr., and E. Burnham Chamberlain; and Birds of Washington State by Stanley G. Jewett, Walter P. Taylor, William T. Shaw, and John W. Aldrich.

Excerpts from Hummingbirds by Crawford H.

LOVE-STRUCK *Pennsylvania Dutch potter united distelfinks— stylized birds—to form a heart shape. Index of American Design.*